I0887550

THEATER
IN THE
AMERICAS

A Series from
Southern
Illinois
University
Press
Robert A.
Schanke
Series Editor

Richard Barr | The Playwright's Producer

David A. Crespy

With a Foreword by Edward Albee

Southern Illinois University Press

Carbondale and Edwardsville

Printed in the United States of America

16 15 14 13 4 3 2 1

Library of Congress Cataloging-in-Publication Data
Crespy, David Allison.
Richard Barr : the playwright's producer / David A. Crespy ; with a foreword by Edward Albee.
p. cm. — (Theater in the Americas)
Includes bibliographical references and index.
ISBN 978-0-8093-3140-6 (pbk. : alk. paper)
ISBN 0-8093-3140-3 (pbk. : alk. paper)
ISBN 978-0-8093-3141-3 (ebook)
ISBN 0-8093-3141-1 (ebook)
1. Barr, Richard. 2. Theatrical producers and directors—United States—Biography. I. Title.
PN2287.B22C84 2013
792.02'32092—dc23
[B] 2012034893

Printed on recycled paper. ♻
The paper used in this publication meets the minimum requirements of American National Standard for Information Sciences—Permanence of Paper for Printed Library Materials, ANSI Z39.48-1992.∞

In loving memory of my brother, Jonathan Brooks Crespy

CONTENTS

FOREWORD

You have, ahead of you, a record of the life and accomplishments of one of the most important figures in American theatre in the 1960s and 1970s—a man whose audacity, combined with intelligence and courage, did much to bring maturity to an important arena of our culture, one largely beset by the destructive forces of commercialism but not yet engulfed by them.

It is an exciting and educating journey, led by a man who understood that in the battle for the life of the serious arts in our country, caution and compromise are the twin handmaidens of disaster.

I was privileged to accompany Richard Barr on much of this adventure, and I learned so much—about how the arts are run (often into the ground) in our society and how integrity, joined to talent, can often win in the face of terrible odds.

Learn and enjoy!

New York City, 2011 *Edward Albee*

ACKNOWLEDGMENTS

I could not have written this book without the guidance and inspiration of the following artists, scholars, and historians, whose contribution I acknowledge here. I am very grateful also for the support of my colleagues at the University of Missouri Department of Theatre, including my department chairs, Dr. Weldon Durham, Patrick Atkinson, and Clyde Ruffin. I am particularly grateful for the research leave provided by the University of Missouri Research Board, which gave me time to complete a first draft of my book.

I acknowledge, first of all, the kind assistance of Edward Albee, who provided me with several interviews, encouragement, editorial advice, and access to Richard Barr's unpublished autobiography, "You Have to Hock Your House," from his own private collection. I am grateful for Mr. Albee's insights into the support and production of new work, which he has done throughout his career. I add to that a special thank you to Mr. Albee's assistant, Jakob Holder, for his assistance as well. I thank my agent at Curtis Brown, Ltd., Mitchell Waters, for supporting this book and the initial research I did in the Albee-Barr-Wilder Playwrights Unit. I thank the staff at Southern Illinois University Press, and in particular my editors Robert Schanke, Kristine Priddy, Wayne Larsen, and Julie Bush, for their special guidance, mentorship, and support during the writing of this book.

My original research into the world of Richard Barr began at the City University of New York under the guidance of Dr. Judith Milhous, and I thank her for teaching me about the nature of historiography and the writing of theatre history. I thank, too, Dr. Marvin Carlson for his seemingly inexhaustible knowledge of the theatre in general. I thank Dr. David Willinger, who first sponsored my research on the Albee-Barr-Wilder Playwrights Unit as an independent study and who augmented my knowledge of off-off-Broadway theatre with his own experiences as a professional playwright and director at Theatre for the New City. I would also like to specially acknowledge the assistance of Dr. Edwin Wilson, who offered his support of my study by mentoring my externship at Curtis Brown, Ltd. and arranging "A Tribute to Edward Albee," a theatre conference held at the CUNY Graduate Center in November 1997 where I presented my initial research. I thank brilliant theatre critic, director, and playwright Michael Smith for the idea to move beyond my original work on the Albee-Barr-Wilder Playwrights Unit and shift the focus to Richard Barr himself.

I gratefully acknowledge the assistance of Rod Bladell, Christine Karatnytsky, Kevin Winkler, and Robert Taylor of the Billy Rose Theatre Division of the New York Public Library for the Performing Arts for their assistance in the research and use of archival materials regarding the Albee-Barr-Wilder producing partnership and the Playwrights Unit. I acknowledge the assistance of Alan Woods and Nena Couch of the Jerome Lawrence and Robert E. Lee Theatre Research Institute of The Ohio State University for allowing me to use the Michael Kasdan Collection and for granting me permission to use photos from that collection for this work. I also acknowledge and thank Frederic Wilson of the Harvard Theatre Collection at the Houghton Library of Harvard University for his assistance in my use of the Alix Jeffry Photographic Archive and for permission to use photos from that archive for this book.

I acknowledge and thank the many playwrights, actors, directors, designers, stage managers, house managers, and other theatre professionals who worked within the Albee-Barr-Wilder producing partnership and who generously provided interviews regarding their experiences for the purpose of this book. These interviewees include Maureen Anderman, Arthur Anderson, Howard Atlee, Clark Bason, Tobias Beckwith, David Bixler, Joseph Cali, Irving Cheskin, Jerome Cline, Edward M. Cohen, Mart Crowley, Alice Drummond, James Duff, Gene Feist, Carol Fischer, Richard Foltz, Frank Gagliano, Judith Granite, John Guare, A. R. Gurney, Mary Hamill, Libby Hellman, Shirley Herz, Bruce Hoover, Stephen Jacobsen, Page Johnson, Michael Kahn, Lee Kalcheim, Milton Katselas, Charles Kindl, Perry Knowlton, Richard Lipsett, Barbara Luchs, Laurence Luckinbill, Linda Magyar Feinfeld, Vivian Matalon, Elizabeth Ireland McCann, Ursule Molinaro, Bob Moss, Tony Musante, Rod and Marcia Merrill Nash, Glyn O'Malley, Edward Parone, Robert Patrick, Emanuel Peluso, Harvey Perr, Barry Plaxen, Kenneth Pressman, James Prideaux, Harvey Sabinson, Gerald Schoenfeld, Russ Thacker, Jean-Claude van Itallie, Peter White, Lanford Wilson, Mark Wright, and Paul Zindel.

In particular, I would like to acknowledge the late playwright, director, and activist Doric Wilson, that wonderful and occasionally outrageous raconteur, for bringing New York's off-off-Broadway scene of the 1960s to life for me as a researcher. His recent passing has left the New York theatre with an enormous gap of knowledge, talent, and experience it will not soon replace.

Finally, I would like to thank my beautiful wife, Shari Weinman Crespy, for her wonderful editorial eye and loving support, and my three sons, Jules, Emmett, and Jonathan, for their love and constant encouragement.

RICHARD BARR

INTRODUCTION

"You Have to Hock Your House: The Story of a Producer"

Richard Barr wrote in the frontispiece to his unpublished autobiography, "You Have to Hock Your House: The Story of a Producer," that "when Shakespeare walks in, I wish to be the producer who presents him."[1] What follows here is the story of that producer, his lifelong commitment to American playwrights and playwriting, and his devotion to one playwright in particular, Edward Albee. While not a biography per se, what you have before you is the adventure of a producer's career, and perhaps a hands-on training manual for young, idealistic producers who care about plays and playwrights. Using some sixty interviews with the actors, directors, designers, stage managers, and fellow producers who worked with Barr, as well as fifty-two boxes of Barr's papers at the New York Public Library for the Performing Arts at Lincoln Center and Barr's own memoirs, I have tried to make sense of a fifty-year career that began with Barr's years at Princeton's Theatre Intime and ended with his important contribution as the president of the League of American Theatres and Producers, now known as the Broadway League.

For the average theatregoer in America, Richard Barr is not a household name. Perhaps even among current working Broadway professionals he is not well known, but he was the last of the great independent producers. Barr was a practical producer of new work in the American theatre, living on the edge of both enormous artistic success and utter financial ruin. More than once he had to "hock his house" in order to fund his riskier projects. He produced the plays that other producers passed on; many were controversial and considered shocking, especially the plays of Edward Albee. He produced the first or early plays of many of the major playwrights of the American theatre, including those by Terrence McNally, Mart Crowley, Megan Terry, Jean-Claude van Itallie, Doric Wilson, Sam Shepard, Adrienne Kennedy, Lanford Wilson, John Guare, A. R. Gurney, Ron Tavel, and Ursule Molinaro, as well as shows by performance artists and dancers like Ruth Draper, Robert Wilson, Valerie Bettis, Paul Draper, Paul Taylor, and Twyla Tharp. To fit his career into a single sentence: he began it with Orson Welles, continued by producing nearly all of Edward Albee's plays, and finished by producing Stephen Sondheim's *Sweeney Todd: The Demon Barber of Fleet Street.*

An important aspect of Richard Barr's life was his sexual orientation; he was openly gay, never making it secret, but at the same time, he was intensely private about his relationships. There is little mention of anything but friendships in his unpublished memoirs, and he points this out himself in its introduction: "What it [the memoirs] is not about is my life in bed. I have had several mistresses in my life, and quite a few misters, but no emotional crises developed from these encounters. My emotional curves relate only to the theatre, and there has been no real purpose other than that of the theatre."[2] Though Barr refrains from a frank exploration of the gay relationships he had in his life, his homosexuality had an important bearing on the choice of work he produced, the connections he made with fellow artists, and the impact of the original productions he brought to Broadway and elsewhere. It would be impossible and unwise to exclude Barr's own gay identity from his biography. This was, after all, the producer who brought *The Boys in the Band* to the American theatre. At the same time, while it is important to acknowledge that Barr was a gay producer who produced a major gay drama, as well as several plays that raise questions about sexual orientation, Richard was also a producer who broke many other barriers in drama in terms of African American theatre, experimental absurdist theater, modern dance, and even the performance art of Robert Wilson. Like many gay men of his generation, he would have insisted that his sexual orientation should be considered a personal issue that was irrelevant. Nonetheless, it remains part of Barr's legacy, an aspect that I believe was used against him but a facet that should be celebrated because of Barr's willingness to produce theatre that was openly gay. It is also important that with Edward Albee, Clinton Wilder, and later Charles Woodward, all of whom were gay, Barr ran an operation that gave professional opportunities for many gay theatre professionals, a point that was not lost on others who were working then in the theatre. It was, ostensibly, a gay theatre, and yet because of the times, this was an unspoken aspect of the Albee-Barr-Wilder operation.

Richard Barr was one of America's great theatre visionaries, and his framework for new play production was always the play and the playwright. Moreover, he believed Broadway was vibrant and resourceful enough to produce some of the most important plays and playwrights in America. When others abandoned Broadway as a venue for producing new work for regional or off- or off-off-Broadway theatre, he remained one of its strongest advocates. What follows, then, is the story of how Richard Barr made his journey, nearly losing his house in the process, from a theatre unknown to a producer whose career changed the course of playwriting in America.

1

PRIVILEGE WITH A PRICE

Washington, Princeton, and Early Theatre Efforts

The early-twentieth-century Washington, D.C., Jewish community that produced Richard Barr (born Richard Alphonse Baer) was one that followed traditions of southern Reform Jewry. Unlike its brash cousin in New York, the Washington Jewish community was assimilationist, finding ways to fit in with the majority Christian culture. Yet, still there were clear lines drawn between the gentile and Jewish communities, between the world of the debutante in the gentile community and the world of the bar mitzvahs and confirmations at Washington Hebrew Congregation, the reform synagogue attended by the Baer family. Like many of the more established Washington Jewish families, Barr's family had come from the Alsace area in France.[1] By the time of the 1871 annexation to Germany of most of Alsace and parts of Lorraine in the Franco-Prussian War, these Germanic Jews sought the promise of real economic opportunity in the United States.[2] Barr's family made this move in the early part of the nineteenth century, and by the time of Richard's birth, they had been living in America for several generations.[3]

Though he insists in his unpublished autobiography, "You Have to Hock Your House," that Judaism "has never been an important part of my life, although I have neither hidden nor denied it," Richard and both of his sisters attended the Sunday religious school.[4] He opted not to have a bar mitzvah, instead choosing the easier confirmation route. And though his father served as the Washington Hebrew Congregation's president and occasionally attended the synagogue on the Sabbath, he was not a traditional synagogue-going Jew. Richard's father, David Alphonse Baer, a prominent Washington, D.C., builder, was born in Georgetown. His mother, Ruth Nanette (Israel) Barr, was raised in Waterloo, Iowa, and made a living as a reporter for a local paper in Reading, Pennsylvania, where she met Baer. The bright and progressive couple were married in Reading on 6 December 1916, and Richard was born on 6 September 1917. David Baer was a young lawyer moving toward success, having been admitted to practice before the Supreme Court early in his career, but he decided to become a builder in Washington because of the unlimited opportunities for construction in the 1920s. Ruth remained a society columnist for the Underwood & Underwood agency, which sent releases to the *Washington Post*, and during World War II, she was a civil defense volunteer.

Richard was raised in the "Victorian manner" with a governess, "Miss Middlemiss," whom he despised. He wondered how his middle-class Jewish family could afford her and a black cook, Ida Watkins, who worked with them for nearly thirty years, leaving only to become a practical nurse. The Baers also employed a laundress named Curlew and a butler, Ulysses S. Roebuck, a "gigantic black man" who sometimes drove Barr to school in a Model T Ford. This embarrassed Richard, because his classmates arrived in Cadillacs and Packards.[5] In 1922, David Baer built his home on Wyoming Avenue, and though vacant at the time, it became one of Washington's most exclusive neighborhoods. The Baers had several distinguished neighbors, including Warren Harding and William Howard Taft, with his "famous white moustache," both of whom Richard would occasionally meet with his nanny. Herbert Hoover lived a block away, and Woodrow Wilson lived two blocks down the street. Barr often saw Wilson sitting at the window toward the end of his life, "staring into space."[6]

Richard's home on Wyoming Avenue represented his parents' attempt to move beyond the confines of the old Jewish neighborhood. Though neither of his sisters, Carol Fischer and Barbara Luchs, remembered any overt anti-Semitism in the Washington of the 1920s, there were clear lines drawn between Jewish and gentile neighborhoods. Since they did not live in a Jewish neighborhood, Barr grew up with non-Jewish friends. One was Narcissa Sullivan, the daughter of Mark Sullivan, a muckraking political columnist for the *New York Herald Tribune* and a member of Hoover's "Medicine Ball Cabinet."[7] As he grew older, Narcie Sullivan became "very important" in Barr's life, particularly as an entrée into the debutante community. Narcie and her friends invited Richard to monthly private dances, which was something of a scandal. Though his mother approved of his going to these dances, Ruth's friends in the Jewish community did not.

While living on Wyoming Avenue, Richard gathered his early childhood friends and staged plays; the family's chauffeur, Roebuck, would take the "enormous Austrian curtain" covering a window at the head of the stairs and hang it across the marble pillars leading into the Baers' living room to create a stage. The performances were improvised affairs that "the various families suffered through with laughter and applause." Eight-year-old Richard, always theatrically minded, was also "enticed" at one point to "tight-wire walk" the clothesline that crossed the high brick walls on either side of their driveway. As a result, Barr fell, dangling over a fifteen-foot drop to the cement driveway by his knees. He managed to rescue himself by inching across the line, hanging upside down by his knees. He saw this childhood experience as a metaphor for his life in the theatre.[8]

Richard attended the Sidwell Friends School in Washington, a Quaker institution and one of the most exclusive private schools in the District. He was an energetic and enthusiastic student; "I was the perennial president of my class," he remembers in his memoirs, making his stage debut in the third grade as a robin in a children's operetta titled *The Golden Whistle*. His mother provided the costuming expertise. Barr attended his first major professional theatre experience at this time, the vaudeville comedy team of Weber and Fields at Keith's Theatre. Sitting with his grandmother, he burst out in high, piercing laughter and was so boisterous that the ushers threatened to remove him if he didn't stop "performing."[9] His other early theatregoing experiences included a minstrel show on the Steel Pier in Atlantic City and a performance by John Philip Sousa conducting his famous band. At Washington's Ruth's Theatre, Barr was delighted by the performances of Sir Harry Lauder, a songwriter and English music hall comedian known for his folksy renditions of Scottish songs and comedy routines. Affected by these childhood experiences, he would later present similar solo performers on Broadway, including Ethel Waters and Ruth Draper.

Shortly after the family moved into their Wyoming Avenue home, Barr's maternal grandmother suffered a stroke. She and his aunt Bertha moved in, living with the Baers until Richard left for Princeton some eleven years later. Not long after, his father lost much of his wealth during the Depression. The newly expanded Baer family moved out of their Wyoming Avenue home and into the Alban Towers apartment building, occupying two apartments for many years. David Baer, along with his business partner, architect Robert O. Scholtz, had built the stylish and very fashionable apartments, and since he controlled a major portion of its real estate, the family could live there at no cost.

Because of the change in their fortunes, however, Richard was pulled out of private school and sent to his father's alma mater, the public Western High School. Western High had been founded in 1890 and was one of the more prestigious secondary schools in D.C. David wanted his children to be exposed to the "people," though the students were actually the same ones Richard had gone to school with at Sidwell. The young male students had a choice between cadet corps or athletics as an extracurricular activity. Though Barr was a fairly strong athlete, he chose to join the cadet corps because of family tradition. As a young cadet, he was invited to perform drills at Franklin D. Roosevelt's first inauguration and marched up Pennsylvania Avenue past Roosevelt himself. Barr's sisters both recalled Western High School, which had an excellent reputation in dramatic productions, as the place where Richard really caught the acting bug. He skipped his first year of high school because of his excellent training at Sidwell and performed in Western's senior production of *Charley's Aunt*. When asked which role he wanted, young Barr replied, "Why, Charley, of course," assuming it was the starring role. Ironically, his teacher gave the starring role of Jack to his archrival, and this led to Barr's first real lesson in the theatre: "Read the play before you decide which role you wish to act!"[10]

Richard's father insisted he join the local social club for Jewish boys, as Baer had been a member himself. But Barr was bored by the various initiations, meetings, and planned outings and resented being forced to join. The vast majority of his friends were gentile; he knew many of them from his days at the Sidwell Friends School. The only outing he enjoyed with the club was a trip that he planned himself, to see *Richard of Bordeaux*, which opened 2 February 1934 on Broadway. Dennis King played the role originated by John Gielgud in London. Barr was enormously affected by the play, which one *New York Times* critic called a "glowing pageant." His friends, however, "all hated it."[11]

Though he was very close to his former Sidwell friends, having made some inroads into the non-Jewish "sub-deb" world of Narcissa Sullivan, he was uncomfortable with the Washington clubs. According to Barr, the lines between Jew and gentile were "rarely crossed in the 1920s and 1930s." Outside of David Baer's business partner, Robert O. Scholtz, the Baers did not know many other gentiles and "never socialized with them." Ironically, his parents were opposed to Zionism because they felt they were Americans first, Jews afterward. Richard himself felt that being in the theatre made it easier for him to "continue moving in society primarily as an American, and not as a Jew." But though he felt no attachment to any organized religion, and his decision to be an agnostic was not on his "conscience," his Jewish background remained on his mind.[12]

At the age of sixteen, Barr made his way to Princeton University, noting the very strict "Jewish quota" at the time. Though he had been an excellent student and had passed his "college boards" with flying colors, he "sneaked by the quota" because of the recommendations of Milton King, a prominent Washington lawyer, and Mark Sullivan. His parents accompanied him on his drive to Princeton, nervous about his traveling alone, but Barr recalled his sudden independence after they left as "one of the most vivid memories I have of Princeton and, indeed, of my early youth." He was finally alone, able to do what he wanted when he wanted to do it, already thinking like the independent producer he was to become.[13]

His infatuation with theatre as a profession began his freshman year at Princeton. While the university did not have a theatre training program, it had a remarkable number of important theatre alumni: Joshua Logan, Norris Houghton, Bretaigne Windust, Margaret Sullivan, José Ferrer, Lemuel Ayers, and Mel Ferrer. These professionals owed the beginnings of their careers to the extracurricular theatre activities of the school's famous Triangle Club and, more important for Barr, its Theatre Intime. Princeton's Theatre Intime was founded in 1919, when "an intrepid cast of five" performed "a parody of Nijinsky and the Ballet Russe" in a "Witherspoon Hall dormitory room" with "their curtain a blanket hung over a string." It was meant to be a small, avant-garde theatre similar to Strindberg's Intimate Theatre in Stockholm, and the troupe produced more adventurous work than its more famous sister organization, the Triangle Club. By the fall of 1921, Theatre Intime obtained the use of Murray-Dodge Hall, which had previously been used as a chapel, and this remained its home. It was and is an entirely student-run organization without any financial support from the university. Producing everything from dramas to musicals, magic shows to folk music, Theatre Intime was known for producing lesser known plays as well as student-written dramas. A number of original plays received their American premieres at Theatre Intime, including John Milton's *Samson Agonistes*, Jules Romains's *Give the Earth a Little Longer*, Jean Cocteau's *The Typewriter*, John O'Hara's *Searching Sun*, and W. H. Auden's *Age of Anxiety*.[14]

The group had periods of growth and creativity followed by years of inactivity and low membership. By the 1930s, not long before Barr became involved, the group shifted from student writing to professional plays. It was during this time, from about 1929 to 1933, that some of its most famous stars, including James Stewart, Joshua Logan, and Norris Houghton, became student members. As the years went by, the private club became an open theatrical organization with an ongoing relationship with Princeton's Triangle Club. By the time of Barr's arrival at Princeton in 1934, even though

Theatre Intime was not as famous as the Triangle Club, its work was "serious, and most important of all, not faculty supervised." Theatre Intime was producing four to five plays a year, and its theatre space held ninety seats. It also sponsored an original play contest, though "no work from the Intime was ever moved to Broadway, or anywhere else, for that matter." Despite the "questionable" quality of the scripts, the experience was "invaluable," providing Richard with important directing and producing experience.[15]

Soon after Barr's arrival at Princeton, there were advertisements for Theatre Intime auditions in the *Daily Princetonian* for Patrick Hamilton's famous play *Rope's End*, later adapted by Alfred Hitchcock into the film thriller *Rope*. Barr was chagrined to discover that freshmen were not eligible for acting roles. Being "fairly persistent," Richard managed to insert himself as a general assistant to the production and secured an understudy role, serving as the stand-in for the lead character, Rupert Cadell. He learned the lines quickly and perfectly, a talent he used in several occasions with great success. About two weeks into the rehearsals, the actor playing the lead, Herbert (Ottie) Swope Jr., was experiencing personal issues and had to return to New York for several days. The Theatre Intime producers were "miffed" at Ottie's decision. Worried about the progress of the rehearsals, they allowed Barr to serve as Ottie's stand-in, despite the fact that he was a freshman. He knew the lines perfectly, so "they had no choice." As rehearsals progressed, it became clear that Barr was a far better performer than Ottie, so Theatre Intime "fired" Ottie and gave Richard the role. He opened on 14 March 1934 with a positive review in the *Daily Princetonian*: "R. A. Baer '38, who played the part (of Rupert) was easily the star of the evening. In him, the Intime has a real find which we may hope they will value and employ in more significant roles. His portrayal of the dilettante, post-war cynical poet and man about town was admirable. He lived his part, never dropping out of it as the amateur is so apt to do, and he was equally good as he shows off this role to play the double part of detective and judge."[16]

Barr was stunned by the response: "Well, with a notice like that how could one resist taking the theatre seriously as a career? I certainly couldn't." He immediately called his parents to let them know about his decision, which they accepted with "amused tolerance." Richard's next major break came when Theatre Intime decided to produce *Peer Gynt* at the McCarter Theatre during its 1935–1936 season. McCarter was a "first-class" roadhouse with large facilities. It was not unusual to see stars at McCarter, such as Eva Le Gallienne in *L'Aiglon*, or even a world premiere, such as Thornton Wilder's *Our Town* (at which, Barr notes, some of the audience walked out).[17] Because of the venue, director Lemuel Ayers (later a major designer on Broadway) decided to produce *Peer Gynt* with three different Peers, featuring a new one for each act. Barr helped Ayers pull together a translation that satisfied their "undergraduate opinion," and, using actresses from the Finch School for Girls in New York City (Princeton didn't admit women until 1967), the production was successful enough to bring it to the "tiny" Finch School theatre in New York City for a few performances.

In the fall of 1937, when Barr was a junior, Theatre Intime produced his adaptation of Jonson's *Volpone* with him playing Mosca. The students built an extension to the tiny Intime stage consisting of "a forestage with two adjoining side stages." This created four different playing areas, which made the stage "extremely flexible" and eliminated the proscenium, giving Barr "freedom" as an actor and director.[18] The Intime's production attracted the attention of major theatre professionals. One was director and actor José Ferrer, who had just graduated from Princeton himself in 1933. Another was Albert McCleery, who later went on to establish himself as a *Theatre Arts Magazine* writer and a producer of the highbrow NBC Matinee Theatre and later Maurice Evans's *Hamlet* on television.[19] Both Ferrer and McCleery later figured importantly in Richard's life.

Barr received a call from Ferrer in the spring of 1937, encouraging him to serve as an intern at the Suffern County Theatre, where other famous Princeton alumni such as Bretaigne Windust and Joshua Logan had worked. He received a summer of acting, diction, and fencing training, and though his parents willingly paid the three hundred dollar fee, it was at some sacrifice, since Barr's father was still struggling through the Depression. Barr was "determined to be a great actor," and after his busy schedule of rehearsals and classes, he disappeared in the fields and shouted Shakespeare to the wind. After a "glorious summer" in the theatre cleaning paint cans and building scenery, Barr returned to his last year at Princeton as a seasoned "semi-professional—or, so I thought."[20]

Having conquered the role of Mosca in *Volpone*, Barr was ready for a greater challenge at the age of twenty: Falstaff. He adapted the various incarnations of Shakespeare's character Falstaff into a single evening of theatre. It was a performance of which Richard remained very proud, feeling it to be "a viable evening in the theatre" that he could have produced professionally.

Adding to his growing résumé as an actor and adapter, Barr now took on the financial responsibilities of the student-funded Theatre Intime as its new president. He was responsible for paying for every aspect of production, including all royalties, production expenses, travel and lodging for the guest artists (usually women), scenery, props, and costumes. The Intime was usually "broke," and occasionally the theatre borrowed money from the university to help cover expenses. But through Richard's clever and prudent management, Theatre Intime paid back its $2,000 loan, which was a substantial debt for Depression years. To celebrate this achievement, Theatre Intime planned a "big bash" after the last performance of *Falstaff* and brought "beer, a piano, food," and "some of our Lawrenceville School neighbors" in for the fun.[21] In their euphoria of having freed Theatre Intime from its university debt, the students grabbed Barr, still fully dressed in his costume for Falstaff, and tossed him into a filled bathtub in one of the nearby dorms. A young Lawrenceville prep student came over to shake his hand and complimented him on the performance. This was none other than Clinton Wilder, who was to be Barr's coproducer on many Albee productions.

José Ferrer, who had seen Barr in both his *Volpone* and *Falstaff* roles at Princeton, was invited to direct the next Princeton Triangle show and decided to cast Barr as the Countess of Sessex in the 1937 Triangle production of *Fol-De-Rol*. This madcap Triangle show was set in Restoration England with a "vaporous Charles II" sending his minions—the Duke of Clarendon, "a villain who has designs on his throne," and the Countess of Sessex, "a villainess with designs on the King's person"—to purchase the "Isle of Blight." A series of mishaps ensue, with the plot "coagulating" to the happy ending with the cast singing Princeton's alma mater, "Old Nassau."[22] Barr auditioned for the cross-gender role of the Countess of Sessex by performing a Lady Bracknell monologue from *The Importance of Being Ernest*. The *Time* magazine reporter noted that the "delighted" audience responded with hearty laughter: "It guffawed whenever possible at Alexander Hays Lehmann's well-horsed lines, admired the direction of Graduate Jose Ferrer, applauded the trouper hardihood of Actors Richard Cowdery and Richard Baer."[23] Typical of Triangle shows, which gave undergraduates the opportunity to showcase their enthusiasm for theatre while having fun on tour, *Fol-De-Rol* also gave Barr the opportunity to show off his wares as an archvillainess: "So, wearing Lucy Monroe gowns rented from Brooks Costume Company, sporting black lipstick and black fingernail polish, imitating Lynn Fontanne, I slinked onto the stage to minor triumph—except to my mother, who thought I was just fine as an actor, but disapproved of the role."[24]

At Princeton, Barr had an extraordinary career as an undergraduate performer and producer. He ended his Theatre Intime connection with roles such as Prospero, Falstaff, and Peer Gynt under his belt. He also adapted these classics to the modern stage. Finally, he managed Theatre Intime and brought it into the black. He used all these skills and then some when he took on his next challenge, as assistant to Orson Welles on Broadway and in Hollywood.

2

PLAYING WITH MARTIANS

Stage and Screen with Orson Welles and the Mercury Theatre

Richard Barr was twenty years old when he graduated from Princeton in 1938. Because he was without a job or a source of income, he decided to apply to four different institutional theatres, hoping for some form of employment or internship. He first sought out the Cornell-McClintic organization, which was founded by Katharine Cornell. Barr met with her husband, the imaginative director Guthrie McClintic, who, Barr notes, was "polite, questioned me in depth, and wished me luck."[1] Later, McClintic became his mentor, and he refers to McClintic's directing and casting techniques frequently throughout his unpublished memoirs. Nothing, however, came through after this initial interview. The Cornell-McClintic organization was a traditional Broadway operation working with seasoned professionals. Barr was better suited for an organization geared toward neophytes and visionaries.

Richard continued his search with the Playwrights Producing Company and interviewed with playwright Elmer Rice, who was managing this new operation. Rice, a well-known American expressionist, was an interesting choice for Barr, who later made his career presenting experimental playwrights. But Rice was "equally polite and non-committal."[2] Barr waited many more years before becoming associated with a playwrights' theatre.

He then auditioned for Maurice Evans's company. Evans was already a major star, having brought his production of *Richard II* to Broadway. Barr auditioned as Shakespeare's Falstaff at the National Theatre (now the Nederlander) for Margaret Webster, the company director: "Since . . . I was an expert in all the classics, I chose the most likely for a twenty-one-year old." After he performed Falstaff's "sack" speech from *Henry IV, Part II*, Webster merely thanked him "and did not, to my knowledge, laugh aloud."[3] Again, nothing came of the audition, and certainly no promise of a job.

By this time, Barr had reached the end of his possibilities and the summer itself, so his final audition was with the Mercury Theatre, the hot new company on Broadway in 1938 under the brilliant enfant terrible Orson Welles and Welles's equally gifted coproducer John Houseman. It was a smart choice for the young Barr. Welles was very similar to him in temperament and style and not much older. And it was a fortuitous moment to join the Mercury family. The theatre's first year had brought innovative productions of *Julius Caesar* and *Doctor Faustus* (which Richard had seen). It was also on the radio with its first successful season of *Mercury Theatre on the Air*, starting with its radio adaptation of *Dracula* in July 1938.

Richard had already written to Houseman while still a Princeton student about his great success as Falstaff. Houseman, perhaps genuinely intrigued by the production (since Welles mentioned that he had heard of it), agreed to an interview. Barr felt that Houseman was the organizational backbone of the Mercury operation, though Welles's creative force spilled into every decision. When Houseman finally left, after the failure of Welles's 1939 film project, *Heart of Darkness*, the Mercury Theatre "fell apart."[4] Houseman confirms in his memoir that a Richard "Baer" and Howard Teichmann from Wisconsin were brought in as apprentices to replace female apprentices returning to college and later assumed "positions of importance in the Mercury hierarchy."[5]

For his interview, Richard was ushered into a makeshift space in the back of the theatre, where under "a small light" he met with Houseman in a small chaotic office, "scarcely large enough for a desk, and even in those days, Jack was a big man."[6] Barr's actual interview with John Houseman was perfunctory. Houseman "posed the conventional questions" and "was his most polite self." Richard explained that he wanted to be like Welles, an auteur director who reinterpreted and reassembled scripts to fit his own acting abilities. At this rather outrageous declaration, Houseman then suggested "that a bit of experience and training would be helpful." To this, Barr, realizing that perhaps he had gone too far, noted to Houseman that he "wasn't too concerned about salary."[7] This lack of concern was key to his securing a position with the Mercury.

The Mercury Theatre was already beginning the steep financial decline that would end with the disastrous production of *Five Kings*. Having been heralded the "boy wonder of Broadway," Welles had seriously overreached with the production of William Gillette's *Too Much Johnson*, in which he tried to interweave film footage in a theatrical setting. Barr had arrived as the Mercury attempted a summer stock tryout of *Too Much Johnson* at the Stony Creek Summer Theater.[8] Houseman was leaving New York for a week in order to check the progress on this summer stock tryout and told Richard to come back in ten days. Though not a heartening response, it was far more positive then his other job-hunting experiences, and so he decided to take Houseman at his word, hoping that in ten days, there would be a formal job offer.

As he waited for an answer, Richard was not without resources, having negotiated a kind of internship of his own in the theatre with the help of his parents. Barr's parents were both "inveterate theatre-goers," and though somewhat suspicious, they adopted a "wait and see" attitude regarding their son's interest in the theatre. David Baer understood the risks of a career in the arts, having worked with the creative talents of a major architect, Robert O. Scholtz, to build several landmark hotels and office buildings in Washington, D.C. Though Richard was the first in his family to embark on a career in the theatre, his mother had worked for some time as a writer and had always advised her children, and later her grandchildren, that the theatre was not an extravagance but a necessity. Barr gave his father assurances that he felt confident he could survive the "vicissitudes of a theatre life." Though his father had only just dug himself out of the Depression's financial crisis, he agreed to support Richard's theatrical endeavor for five years, giving him seventy-five dollars a month and covering his medical bills. Richard quickly managed to find an apartment boardinghouse at 495 West End Avenue, owned by an elderly Scottish couple, the Mairs, who were fascinated by an actor rooming with them. They happily provided a "*very* small" room and two meals a day, breakfast in his room and dinner with the other boarders, for fifty dollars a month. Barr ate a fifteen-cent lunch, which consisted of "a cream cheese and jelly sandwich on date-nut bread for a dime and a grape soda for a nickel," at the local Chock Full o' Nuts near the Mercury's building.[9]

Barr waited exactly ten days and returned to Houseman's office only to discover that Houseman was still out of town and unavailable. However, by lingering at the office with Augusta Weissberger, the Mercury's business manager, he was able to convince her that he had arrived to start working for the theatre. With that, Weissberger immediately sent Barr to cash a check for her at the bank for $325, and thus began his career with the Mercury Theatre.[10] Since Welles was disastrous with handling money and Barr instinctively knew how to dole it out to him, Richard would become the trusted cash distributor as the two worked together on Broadway and in Hollywood.

Barr's position at the Mercury was somewhat nebulous, as were the positions of the other "slaves" who followed Orson Welles in endless numbers. Barr worked closely with Weissberger and Houseman in the administrative offices, and this included taking Orson his allowance, performing the odd supernumerary role, and even, on occasion, taking Welles's wife's furs to summer storage. Because the Mercury Theatre was poor with few full-time staff, Barr was kept very busy. For his first meeting with Welles, Barr was given fifty dollars by Gustie Weissberger to take to the actor at the St. Regis Hotel. Barr made his way to the hotel at noon and called up to his room; Welles's deep basso voice invited him up. Barr went to the room, buzzed the door, and waited and waited until the door was suddenly "flung open, and there, six feet four inches, was Orson Welles stark-naked."[11] Welles kindly thanked Barr for the money, and that was that. It wasn't until many weeks later that he encountered Welles again.

Barr watched Ruth Ford and Paula Laurence rehearse for the doomed *Too Much Johnson* sitting outside the Mercury's tiny balcony office. Welles was never present for these rehearsals because he was too busy racing from one radio acting job to another (most famously playing the Shadow), using a rented ambulance, siren blaring, to circumvent traffic. By the summer of 1938, the Mercury Theatre itself was busy producing its own radio shows for CBS, including *First Person Singular*, which dramatized such stories as *Dracula*, *Treasure Island*, and *A Tale of Two Cities*, along with other classic "action" stories.[12] Barr was impressed by Welles's "uncanny" first-person singular format of telling stories through the eyes of a protagonist. Welles selected his favorite scenes from novels, and then John Houseman (and sometimes Welles or another writer) adapted the stories using the viewpoint of either a major or a minor character. The process allowed many stories to be adapted to the radio format, an achievement that had not been previously possible.[13] Barr was in charge of making a temporary recording of each of the shows in "acetate" format for Welles's use so that he could edit the program for its final airing.

One of the first radio shows Barr performed in, ironically enough, was H. G. Wells's *The War of the Worlds*, the famous Mercury show that paralyzed the nation with fear and mass hysteria in 1938. As was normal, an acetate was made of the show in the afternoon, and when Orson Welles arrived, it was clear that he was not pleased with the script, thinking that it was very "corny" and said as much "loudly and clearly at the first rehearsal in the studio at Madison Avenue."[14] The script by Houseman and Howard Koch had not impressed anyone on Welles's staff, least of all Koch himself, who, "after three days of slaving" on Welles's fantasy, "was ready to give up."[15] But though it nearly brought Koch to a nervous breakdown, the script's device for the telling of the story was innovative: an ongoing news report of the attack, interrupted by the typical commercial and technical interruptions for any radio show.[16] It was clear to Barr that "there was at no time the slightest intention of terrifying anyone." On 30 October 1938, no one in the station thought very much of the script, including Orson Welles, who considered it "the worst, silliest thing he had ever done; just a Halloween prank."[17]

Working with Paul Stewart, a Broadway and radio actor who became the show's associate producer, the cast rehearsed without Welles, as was their custom, and when Welles called in from rehearsals for the Mercury's next offering, *Danton's Death*, he was told by one of the CBS sound men that the show "just didn't come off." Houseman ironically quipped, "Twenty-seven hours later, quite a few of his employers would have found themselves a good deal happier if he had turned out to be right."[18] Barr played a "voice in the crowd," earning fifteen dollars for his role in the *War of the Worlds* broadcast, and after Welles finally arrived, they began rehearsing the show in earnest. "All during rehearsals," Barr recalls in his memoirs, "Welles railed at the text, cursing the writers, and at the whole idea of his presenting so silly a show."[19]

Not anticipating the reaction of the radio audience, the cast followed the format of the developing news story, flowing around the performance of Bernard Hermann and the CBS Orchestra in CBS Studio One, playing the role of "Ramon Raquello and His Orchestra."[20] The story of an alien object landing in Grovers Mill, New Jersey, with Martians rising out of the vessel and killing people with death rays was believable only to listeners who tuned in later in the program, missing the introduction (most had been listening to Edgar Bergen and his puppet Charlie McCarthy at the time). However, the show was so realistic to the latecomers that, famously, phone calls started lighting up the CBS switchboards, which were "swamped into uselessness." The studio was filled with "vague rumors" of "deaths and suicides, and panic injuries by the thousands."[21] Thousands more in the immediate outlying areas in New York and New Jersey fled their homes and attempted to contact the authorities.[22] The panic effect of the *War of the Worlds* broadcast was so powerful that CBS later agreed to never again simulate a real broadcast without some kind of intermittent spoiler.[23]

Virginia Welles, Orson's wife, called in to tell the cast that the show was "absolutely marvelous, and hair-raising," and yet the Mercury players responded only with laughter, not believing that the dull show they believed they had written had any shock value at all. At the break, a CBS pageboy came into the studio to report that "Flint, Michigan, is on the phone." A group of vigilantes hiding in their basement there, attempting to prepare for the invasion, "were damned angry" and ready to use their shotguns on Welles himself.[24] This was followed by a mayor in a "mid-western city" demanding to talk to Welles, yelling, "There are mobs in my streets! Women and children crowding my churches! Violence, looting, rioting! If this is just some crummy joke, then I'm coming right to New York and beat you up!"[25] And that was just the beginning.

After the playing of the *Mercury Theatre on the Air*'s final theme, the studio phone began to ring, and "all the hysterics were in the streets with towels around their heads."[26] At that point, Barr recalled a bomb threat occurring; the police were called, and the entire cast hid in the ladies' room on the third floor of the CBS building. Richard was then sent to tell the cast rehearsing *Danton's Death* at the Mercury Theatre that Welles wasn't coming because of controversy over the broadcast. There he found Joseph Cotten, Martin Gabel, Arlene Francis, and the others waiting for Welles to rehearse, and when Barr "burst in with the news that a Halloween program about the invasion from Mars had frightened the hell out of citizenry," not one of the actors believed him, knowing Welles's elaborate tricks to avoid rehearsing. Barr dragged the actors outside to prove to them it was no joke, pointing to the "moving news sign on the Times building" where they saw the headlines "Orson Welles frightens the nation." The rehearsals for *Danton's Death* were held up for three days while, according to Barr, "Orson hid."[27]

Following the broadcast, it was Richard's job to scan the mail that the Mercury received in its tiny office. Many of the letters were "amusing," but the most famous among them was Alexander Woolcott's barb referring to the more popular Charlie McCarthy: "This only goes to prove, my beamish boy, that all the intelligent people were listening to the dummy . . . and all the dummies were listening to you."[28] Despite the panic that arose from the Mercury Theatre's *War of the Worlds*, Barr felt it only proved that Welles was the master of his craft of radio storytelling: "Orson did not direct his shows; he conducted them. Standing on a podium in front of a dynamic microphone . . . he waved his arms, cued every music, sound and speech cue."[29] Houseman notes that Welles's "sense of tempo, that night, was infallible," especially his use of radio silence. The most famous moment came near the end when a shortwave radio operator attempted to determine who was still alive in Manhattan. According to Houseman, there was a five-minute silence before the cast acknowledged it was a show and not an actual newscast.[30]

Despite the furor over the panic, Welles and the Mercury Theatre escaped unscathed because of Arnold Weissberger's fancy legal footwork that absolved the Mercury from "all legal liability resulting from the content of our show."[31] The show's success led to Welles's broadcasts moving to a new space, Liederkrantz Hall, which was specially outfitted to be "the most advanced radio studio in the country." Bernard Hermann and his orchestra were now able to see Welles through "soundproof glass," and Hermann could "hear through his earphones" with much improved acoustics. And in December 1938, the *Mercury Theatre on the Air* became the *Campbell Playhouse*, with new sponsorship from the Campbell Soup Company.[32]

With these improvements, Welles became obsessed with the quality of the show, in particular its music and sound effects. During the 1939 *Campbell Playhouse* radio production of *The Count of Monte Cristo*, two actors, Ray Collins and Everett Sloane, "got down as close to the mike and urinal as possible" in order to recreate the "right subterranean reverberation" of the dungeon. Despite the chaos and hysteria that accompanied each *Campbell Playhouse* production, there was always Welles's masterful control, creating the wonderful *First Person Singular* style. But without the deft adaptation and scriptwriting abilities of Houseman and Howard Koch, Welles's radio theatre would have never survived. It was here that Richard Barr developed his ear for great writers. Welles felt that playwriting for radio shouldn't attempt to be traditional playwriting, since "radio was the best story-teller there is."[33] Welles wanted a new kind of writing for radio that swept the listener into the narrative of the speaker, connecting the listener emotionally to the speaker's particular plight. Richard's radio days with the Mercury taught him, ironically enough, how "not to run things" and yet how to control this chaos to best effect, bringing about the collaboration of artists and writers with a maximum of productivity and a minimum of cost.

The two major Welles theatre productions in which Richard was directly involved were the final Mercury production of *Danton's Death*, by Georg Büchner, and Welles's collaborative effort with the Theatre Guild, *Five Kings*, a compilation of scenes from Shakespeare's history plays. In *Danton's Death*, Richard made his Broadway acting debut as a "convention attendant," and though the play had a "distinguished cast," it was doomed to failure because Welles manhandled the adaptation: he rearranged the scenes, which damaged the play's structure.[34] Barr wrote a note to himself at that time, "Don't necessarily trust a playwright's judgment in his sequence of scenes, but do not destroy his intention." By moving Saint-Just's important speech to the end of the play, because he was playing the role, Welles had "destroyed the drama of the close of Büchner's play."[35]

In his role of convention attendant, Richard wore "a wig which Orson said made me look like Theophile Gautier [the French writer]." While impressed by Marc Blitzstein's score, Barr was even more impressed by Jean Rosenthal's lighting and the set by Jan Tichacek, which consisted of "an elevator and a cyclorama."[36] As one of Welles's "slaves," Barr was responsible for helping paste hundreds of masks, purchased in Halloween shops all across Manhattan, on the cyclorama.[37] The effect of the masks was to create a "hydra-headed mob" at times and "a huge canopy of staring faces which gave the strange ominous effect of a rigid dance of death" at other times. This was all lit by Jean Rosenthal, a "genius of lighting" whose voice Barr could hear, counting on the light bridge as the great mask effect took place, and, according to Barr, "the audience could also hear her—loud and clear."[38]

The far more impressive technique, however, was Welles's use of voices. Like his orchestration of voices in his radio shows, Welles was obsessed with finding the right vocal quality in his theatrical productions. In his rehearsal notes, Richard wrote that "a surprising amount of time and patience was taken by Orson in directing the inflection and intensity of various speeches in the mob interjections." Barr was fascinated by the depth to which Welles explored the "interpretation, voice and quality" for each line and the "effect of many voices from all parts of the theatre," noting that Welles had the actors in "the wings, the bridge, the grid, and even various holes in the wall."[39] However, despite his attention to some details, Welles was not as engaged with *Danton's Death* as he had been with earlier Mercury productions, and the rehearsals were derailed with Welles's strange absences and invented delays.

Barr found Welles's professional behavior "singularly unsuccessful," though his feelings were colored by some of his other more "obnoxious" duties for the director. One of his more humiliating tasks during the rehearsals for *Danton's Death* was bringing Welles his "regular" lunch every day on a tray, "without spilling," from the local Longchamps, a popular 1930s restaurant chain, which consisted of "a large rare steak, salad, and a double portion of pistachio ice cream." Horrified that he, a former Ivy League student, was being used in this way, Richard worried that this was not "advancing his acting career." Still, this function seemed to endear him to Welles, and it was the beginning of an intimacy that carried Barr to Hollywood.[40]

More important, Barr's lifestyle, during his Mercury Theatre days, was changing. He left the room-and-board arrangement with the Mairs and shared an apartment with Otis Bigelow, an actor and playwright, and Gordon Merrick, another actor (who later penned *The Lord Won't Mind*, a gay novel published in the 1970s). They shared an apartment on East Fifty-Fourth

Street, "sandwiched between the nightclub El Morocco and a store selling artificial limbs."[41] By choosing to live with Bigelow, who remained Barr's lifelong friend and who was "among gay men in New York" known as "a legend" because of his good looks, Barr was affirming his decision to live as a gay man within a gay community.[42] This corner of the Upper East Side of Manhattan on Third Avenue, one of the more important gay neighborhoods in New York City in the late 1930s and 1940s, was notorious because of its elevated train; the "nooks and shadows" in the areas beneath the tracks provided ample privacy for cruising.[43] Barr later thrived in a similar community of gifted, supportive, and like-minded young gay theatre professionals in Greenwich Village, though he was rarely involved in any long-term gay relationship. He had short-term intimacies with many lovers (which may account for his death later from an AIDS-related illness) and boasted as much in his memoirs.[44] Barr found a safe haven in his gay partners and friends. It was something that fed his creativity and his sense of identity. His sexual orientation also led him to produce risky, controversial new plays; he believed that "theatre should have a higher calling than just profits."[45] Still, he kept this part of his life private and certainly did not share it with his fellow Mercury "slaves."

The last theatrical production under the Welles-Houseman management, *Five Kings*, negotiated by Houseman as a collaboration with the Theatre Guild, was so enormous that the Mercury could not possibly accommodate it in its tiny Comedy Theatre. From the beginning, the sheer size of the production was clearly beyond the reach of the fledgling Mercury players and fraught with disaster. As Houseman mourns in his biography, "To tell the story of *Five Kings* is like trying to record the terminal stages of a complicated and fatal disease."[46] However, *Five Kings* provided an important acting opportunity for Richard, and in his mind, it represented "the most ambitious" stage production of the Mercury's brief existence. Rehearsals began in "various empty stages that the Guild was able to procure" in New York, and eventually the plan was to tour the production out of town to Boston, Washington, and Philadelphia before returning to open in New York. As he did for his other productions, Welles sought "a viable theatrical solution to the problem of moving an historical play" through the various settings created by welding together six different Shakespearean worlds.[47] The production focused on the character of Falstaff, played by Welles and later reprised in Welles's film *The Chimes at Midnight*. At the heart of this "burlap and wood" production was a "large revolving platform" that cinematically moved from interior castle scenes to exterior war scenes almost seamlessly.[48]

Richard thought the rehearsal space too small for the large company of twenty, but the cast was "doubled and tripled in smaller roles," with some roles given to "a bevy of extras" to be hired in each regional location.[49] Burgess Meredith played Prince Hal, and John Emery played Hotspur. Barr was used as a stand-in for Welles, who was "absent a good deal of the time." Orson was busy with the now far-more-lucrative *Campbell Playhouse* and missed many of the early rehearsals of *Five Kings*, leaving Barr "playing Falstaff opposite Burgess Meredith, much to Meredith's annoyance." Richard learned all the lines for all the actors in the production as "sole male understudy for the entire company" and was eventually assigned the role of the assistant stage manager and prompter. A supremely efficient understudy, Barr knew the show so well that he could prompt without a script. Nevertheless, he missed one cue entirely, being too busy counting the house, and left Welles "stranded" onstage. "Falstaff" caught Barr in the wings in his prompter's position and questioned, "Where the hell is the book? If I ever catch you without the book, you're fired." It was a fair criticism, and Richard "began to learn some theatre manners." Finally, the rehearsals were moved to the National, the same stage where Barr had auditioned as Falstaff for Margaret Webster of Maurice Evans's company. He was now "playing" Falstaff once again.[50]

Houseman and Welles's relationship with the Theatre Guild's administrative directors, Lawrence Langner and Theresa Helburn, was tenuous at best. Unfortunately, it was Langner and Helburn's habit to drop in, unannounced, on productions sponsored by the guild. Not wanting either at his "undisciplined and desultory" rehearsals, Welles worked out an ingenious plan to avoid their influence.[51] When it was suspected that these two luminaries from the guild were expected, "the plan went into action." A chair and a bottle of scotch was brought out for Welles, and he regaled the company with "a long description of the movies then currently playing on Broadway."[52] This lasted until Langner and Helburn left, and then rehearsals resumed as normal. Welles was a "prolific raconteur," and these conversation breaks gave Welles's imagination "fancy free rein," sending him off on stories of "sagas of adventure in distant places" or "fantasies that were invented on the spot" to cover up his own egregiously bad behavior. Aside from visits from Langner and Helburn, Welles often required that Richard and fellow "slave" Howard Teichmann act out his elaborate ruses. On one occasion, Welles "burst" into rehearsal in a beautiful dinner jacket over two hours later than scheduled, pretending that he was being chased by the mob because of a dangerous romantic fling with a mob boss's doll. "Baer and Teichmann were sent to mount guard before the building," Houseman recalls, "while rehearsals got under way."[53]

But Barr learned something from Welles's insistence on total control of rehearsals: "No one, but no one, speaks to the actors about the play except the director." This became the rule for the later Albee-Barr-Wilder producing process, with director Alan Schneider at the heart of the operation. Even Edward Albee was not permitted to interfere in the actors' process involving his own plays. Richard was impressed by Welles's ability to craft the adaptation of *Five Kings* and the physicality of its setting into a seamless whole, using an "enormous revolve" that moved the action of the play from an interior setting such as a tavern to an exterior setting such as a battlefield, "without a curtain."[54] The seemingly effortless filmic technique actually required a herculean effort on the part of the actors. According to Barr, the cast "put in ungodly hours, sixteen to eighteen hours a day on occasion," and performed these labors before the notion of overtime existed, with the extras being rehearsed separately from the principals in the production. The battle scenes were particularly effective, "with actual arrows flying across the stage" and hand-to-hand combat with broadswords taking place "simultaneously."[55] Such stunts were dangerous in early performances as the revolve "had an alarming way of jumping into reverse, whirling at twice its forward speed and hurling masses of scenery into the orchestra pit."[56]

Despite these problems, and though the entire second act had yet to be staged, it was imperative that *Five Kings* open and honor the Theatre Guild's many theatre bookings. On Monday, 27 February 1940, the show opened half-staged and without ever having a full dress rehearsal. It played into the wee morning hours of the next day, closing the second of three acts at one o'clock in the morning. While the show was incomplete, the exhausted critics saw there were signs of genius through its unrehearsed wildness.[57] But all-night rehearsals and performances racked up large amounts of "golden hours" on crew bills that the guild balked at paying. Once again, Barr attended to Welles's personal needs until the end of these brutal rehearsals, getting him a taxi or walking him to his rooms at the Copley Hotel and ordering him breakfast and coffee in the morning. During the difficult trials of *Five Kings*, their friendship deepened and contributed to Welles's decision to take Barr with him to Hollywood.

Plunging ahead with the production in Boston required sacrifices on all fronts, including those made by Richard himself. Though the forty-five-dollar weekly salary that Barr was now receiving as a supernumerary and production assistant on *Five Kings* was three times the amount he had made on *Danton's Death*, he was forced to room with other members of the cast in order to make ends meet. However, despite these privations, Barr was also privy to luminaries of the American stage and music scene. At one point he dined with Aaron Copland, who wrote incidental music for *Five Kings*. During the dinner, Richard was "giving forth on modern composers" when Copland stopped him and inquired about how many composers Barr actually knew. "Well," Barr retorted, "I know you!" To Copland's great credit, he overlooked Barr's "Princeton pomposity" and continued the friendship, an important one, as it was a relationship Richard shared with Edward Albee, who had been mentored by Copland as well.[58]

By the time *Five Kings* reached Washington, it had been cut forty minutes; according to Houseman, "the show was finding itself." Welles continued to "grapple with the seemingly impenetrable mountain of material," even as he slipped back to New York to continue his appearances with the *Campbell Playhouse*.[59] During the D.C. tryout, Welles fell sick, and Richard had his first serious opportunity to take on the understudy role of Falstaff. But because the costume didn't fit Barr and there was no time to actually rehearse, Welles forced himself to go on, even though "he was a very ill fellow." Later during the D.C. run, another actor, an alcoholic, came down "with the D.T.'s" and could not go on, so Richard took on five characters, but he couldn't contact his family in time for them to see him in his first professional roles.[60]

In Philadelphia, the turntable "went bad," and "so did the Theatre Guild." The electronic system at the Chestnut Theatre could not accommodate the revolving stage motor, and the actors were forced to revolve the stage by hand. As the "lazy Susan ground its uneven, agonizingly slow way around the stage," the actors did their transitions in slow motion, trying to time their movements to allow the scenery to "catch up with them while the play died under their feet."[61] After receiving mediocre reviews in Philadelphia and despite the "frenzy" that suddenly seized "Wonder Boy" Welles in his attempt to save his show from its inevitable collapse, *Five Kings* finally closed when the funding from the Theatre Guild had dried up. Because the closing left the Theatre Guild's subscribers without a show, it also brought the guild's "vintage years" to a close and caused the collapse of the Mercury Theatre.[62] The *Campbell Playhouse* continued its life on radio, with the Mercury players maintaining their roles. But supernumeraries and production assistants like Richard "were out of jobs," and he went back to surviving on his father's stipend. It wasn't the last time he would fall back upon his family to help him survive the vicissitudes of the theatre.[63]

In the summer of 1939, Barr left to try his luck at the Bucks County Playhouse, a new summer stock company forming in New Hope, Pennsylvania, under the direction of Edward Everett Horton.[64] Elizabeth North cast him in the second production ever staged there, James Barrie's *What Every Woman Knows*, directed by St. John Terrell, later known for his tent-show musicals at the Lambertville Music Circus.[65] Though there was to be no salary, at least Barr had the opportunity to act, even if it was disappointing to go from the hysteria of *Five Kings* to the mundane world of summer stock, staging old chestnuts like Barrie's play. Barr was serious about pursuing acting, however, and stock was to be the mainstay of his directing career. He borrowed Virginia Welles's car while she was visiting with family in Chicago and went off to New Hope, literally and figuratively.

But shortly after Barr's arrival at the playhouse, "a familiar voice" rang him on the phone. It was Welles requesting that he drive back to New York for another project. Barr was reluctant, protesting he had a job for the summer, but Welles bellowed into the phone, "If it were not worth your while, I would not be calling you. Come at once." Barr did not have much choice. He had to return the Welles family car at any rate, and "it was always more exciting to be with him [Orson] than anyone." Barr drove back immediately and arrived later that evening at Welles's duplex on West Fifty-Seventh Street, welcomed by the butler, Charles, a new addition to the Welles household. The meeting included John Houseman, Welles, and Barr but no other member of the Mercury group, which suggested that Barr's participation in the next move was a significant one. Welles had just been offered "the most glorious deal ever given up to that time," to direct four films at $100,000 a picture. The offer came from George Schaefer, head of RKO Pictures, who had worked his way up from a sales position.[66] Barr was hired to be, in Houseman's own words, Welles's "secretary, valet, and major domo." His pay was higher than anything he'd been paid thus far, sixty-five dollars a week, and for Barr, "the Hollywood safari was on."[67]

Richard was enthralled being a captive audience with Houseman and Welles on the Twentieth Century Limited headed to Chicago. Particularly mesmerizing for Richard was the conversation between Welles and Houseman, which he described as "the most entertaining, enlightened and instructive verbal display I have ever heard between two people." He was impressed not only by their impeccable use of language but also by the infinite range of subjects they covered. He thought of Welles as a "modern Samuel Johnson," with Houseman as his Boswell. Though Richard felt he was "not in their league," they treated him with "considerable courtesy." In contrast, Welles treated most of his associates miserably. "One could be furious with Orson," writes Barr, "only to end the day licking his hand."[68]

Welles decided to make a splash in the Hollywood scene by arriving "in style" at the Trocadero nightclub for dinner. Unfortunately, at 6:30 P.M., no one was there to impress, since most of the stars didn't arrive for dinner until 9:30 P.M. Despite the protestations of an icy maître d', Welles and his staff were accommodated, "leaving before one other soul arrived for dinner."[69] The cold reception was just the beginning of Hollywood's resentment of Welles's presence. His contract with RKO gave him sole control of his films, allowing him to serve as director and producer with minimal control exerted by studio head George Schaefer. Hollywood was infuriated that this brash young theatre director and actor, with no experience in film, was being given the kind of control that had been given only to producers like David O. Selznick. Worse was Welles's own habit of flaunting his presence in the face of what Simon Callow terms the "concentrated malice" of Hollywood. Welles's extravagance was kept in check only by the constant monitoring of Barr and Arnold Weissberger, who were but two in the "army of minders" for Welles, who had no self-control over the flow of his expenditures.[70]

After a few months at the Chateau Marmont, Welles settled into a mansion in Brentwood and began work on the films in earnest. By August 1939, he brokered a deal with George Schaefer on the first film under the RKO contract, a re-visioning of Joseph Conrad's *Heart of Darkness*. The show, which had already been produced in November 1938 as an original *Mercury Theatre on the Air* broadcast, had been "a great success," and Welles was trying to capitalize on it. Though Houseman was lukewarm about the project, the question of the central character, Kurtz, and his "ambiguity of greatness," as Callow points out, was a reflection of Welles's own extraordinary burst on the Hollywood scene. Welles took a strong anti-Nazi, anti-fascist approach to the film. This became the heart of his artistic credo in the 1930s and early 1940s, much to the chagrin of RKO Pictures, which had a large distributorship in Germany.[71] Barr describes the story as a "tale of a white man who is captured by a black tribe, but becomes a god," and in the end that white man, Kurtz, is a "Nazi in disguise" intent on converting the natives to fascism. The eyes of the camera were to be Kurtz's own, a direct extension of Welles's own "first person singular approach." There were to be "no cuts in the picture; only a few dissolves, and the action was to be continuous." This effect was created by the miniaturization of the entire world of the story and Welles's somewhat mysterious notion of the "subjective camera."[72]

Though asked by Welles to write the script, Houseman was not thrilled with the *Heart of Darkness* project and gave up after a short time, departing for New York to keep their lucrative *Campbell Playhouse* radio broadcasts running.[73] Other major problems with Welles's vision of *Heart of Darkness* included the miniaturization of the entire jungle in order to get the proper photography of the location. The cost of the camera itself was prohibitive, and RKO was not particularly wild about the "subjective camera" anyway, since it meant that Welles was only to be heard, not seen. Since he had been hired as an actor, director, writer, and producer, RKO "could not understand why one-fourth of their investment would never materialize on the screen." Also, Welles wanted to cast "the most beautiful woman in the world" in the role of Elsa.[74] At first it was clear that Dolores del Rio, the sultry Mexican movie star with whom Welles was having an extramarital affair, was his first choice. But she became unavailable, so other actresses were considered, including Dita Parlo, a major European star, who turned out to be a Nazi sympathizer. Ingrid Bergman was a possibility but wanted too much money, and Carole Lombard turned down the role.[75] Finally selected was Dolly Haas, the future wife of theatre cartoonist Al Hirschfeld. She was a German-Jewish film star who had immigrated to the United States to escape the rise of Adolf Hitler.[76] The rest of the actors were cast from the Mercury company, since Welles had essentially written the script for them. These included Ray Collins, Everett Sloane, George Coulouris, Joseph Cotten, Agnes Moorehead, and Paul Stewart. Welles arranged for them to be put on the RKO payroll, which proved to be the financial straw that broke the *Heart of Darkness* film project's back.[77]

Because Welles wanted absolute fidelity to the real lives of the indigenous people in the film, Barr was to create "a cross section of all the primitive tribes who had ever existed in recorded history." Working with the RKO assigned secretary, Barr ground out three thousand pages of a "history of anthropology," and on Welles's return from a trip to New York to record for the *Campbell Playhouse*, Barr "rushed up to the plane with the overweight package." Welles seemed to have forgotten it entirely, and Barr was certain that Welles never read it. When the production budget came in at over $1 million, double what had been negotiated by Welles and Schaefer, *Heart of Darkness* was canceled. Welles ended up with a much smaller budget film, *The Smiler with a Knife*, based on the novel by Nicholas Blake.[78]

Welles rarely came to the office during the *Heart of Darkness* debacle, and Barr, who was in complete control of the operation, struggled to keep his expenses in line using income produced by his CBS and RKO contracts. Barr constantly coaxed funds out of Weissberger; he and Houseman were the sole Mercury company members who knew how desperate things were becoming. Since he had to deal with Welles's "extra-curricular activities" as well, Weissberger arranged to set up an account in Barr's name. Thereafter, Richard dispensed small amounts to Welles and paid the household bills, which included supporting a beautiful Brentwood mansion with a pool, a French butler, a chauffeur, and a nurse for his daughter, Christopher, as well as a second household for his tumultuous romance with Dolores del Rio.[79]

Richard Barr thought the elaborate parties at the Brentwood mansion, which included innumerable Hollywood celebrities, were "a lot of fun." The largest party occurred when Welles announced that *Heart of Darkness* had been "postponed" and that *The Smiler with a Knife* was to be the next picture. The partygoers featured the Mercury performers Ray Collins, Everett Sloane, Agnes Moorehead, Paul Stewart, George Coulouris, and Joseph Cotten, who had recently arrived in Hollywood.[80] But hiding behind the celebration lurked financial disaster, because there were no RKO funds to hold the Mercury actors for *The Smiler with a Knife* until actual production. Adding to the oncoming financial maelstrom, Welles wanted to purchase a plane to facilitate his endless trips back and forth to New York.[81]

Though Barr enjoyed the "vicarious thrill" of being the "major domo" of Welles's affairs—running his household, working with the staff, and keeping track of his finances—it was clear that tension was mounting. One letter from Weissberger to Barr makes it clear that Welles did "not think of his income in concrete terms in relationship to his expenditures," and Weissberger warned Barr from trying to secure local loans. The only way to secure further funding from Schaefer was to start work soon for RKO.[82] Though Richard managed to wrangle funds from CBS to keep the wolves from the door, he had not told Weissberger that he was making payments on several hideaway homes for Welles's dalliances.[83] The homes could be leased only as long as Welles could maintain his privacy and anonymity, neither of which lasted very long.[84] The constant scramble to pay these monthly expenses reinforced the reluctance of CBS to foot Welles's bills, despite Barr's "frantic letters and telegrams."[85] Barr rented three homes for Welles, and when Welles was forced to leave, Barr and Welles's press agent, Herbert Drake, took up residence in one of them. Since Barr was living off of a weekly salary of sixty-five dollars, he didn't feel much remorse.

The Mercury Theatre actors continued their radio broadcasts, now in Hollywood, and performed them from the Max Reinhardt Workshop for Stage, Screen and Radio on Sunset Boulevard. Barr met Reinhardt, who was often in his studio, and describes him in his memoirs as having "sadness in his eyes." Barr notes that the German director was struggling financially at the time, though he was considered one of the finest European directors of his generation, having made his famous 1935 film adaptation of *A Midsummer Night's Dream*. But Hollywood was not making him any deals.[86] Welles continued producing radio shows, despite his now legendary inability to put forward a project to the liking of RKO executive George Schaefer. Now RKO wasn't buying Welles's latest lower-cost offering of *The Smiler with a Knife* because of *Smiler*'s relentlessly anti-fascist message.[87]

The growing tensions exploded at a dinner at Chasen's, which included Barr, Herbert Drake, Richard Wilson, William Alland, and Albert Schneider.[88] The dinner had been arranged to dream up a project that RKO would support, since both *Heart of Darkness* and *The Smiler with a Knife* had been rejected. Welles had now been in Hollywood for six months and had nothing to show for it. The Hollywood press was positively gleeful in its attacks on the "boy genius." At the dinner, John Houseman, as the producer of the Mercury Theatre productions, challenged Welles to be honest about the Mercury actors' salaries. Houseman knew that RKO wasn't providing any further funding and that no more money was coming from CBS. Welles reversed the challenge to Houseman—"What would you do?" To which Houseman returned in kind, "Tell them the truth!" Welles exploded at him with cries of "I never lie to actors!," "Crook!," and "Thief!" With that, Houseman made a quick exit with Welles hurling flaming cans of jellied alcohol at him.[89] Houseman drove across the country back to the East Coast, leaving Welles with a rather civil but clear letter of separation. Throughout their partnership, Welles had been shockingly "rude" to Houseman; Houseman, to his credit, had suffered it because of the great art they had created. But now their partnership seemed to be at an end, and Barr struggled to fill the gaping administrative hole in the Mercury operation, a near impossibility since Welles and Houseman complemented each other's artistic sensibilities so perfectly.

Yet despite the explosive end to their partnership, Welles, with his back against the wall, was soon forced, once again, to collaborate with Houseman on his next film project, *Citizen Kane*. The script they would develop together with Herman Mankiewicz would prove to be a defining moment in both of their careers. Still, in Richard's view, the work that Houseman did as a writing assistant on *Citizen Kane* effectively sealed his fate as Welles's employee, and the brilliant partnership between the two as equals was "dissolved." And it was in the initial discussions between Houseman and Welles to bring in Mankiewicz as a scriptwriter that the success and the controversy of *Citizen Kane* began. Richard Barr, a fly-on-the-wall observer to all these discussions and decisions, thus became the star witness in the later debate over who *Citizen Kane*'s true "author" was.

At the time of the film's consideration for the 1941 Academy Awards, Welles had already attempted to gain sole credit for its writing, something he had also done with Howard Koch's radio scripts.[90] But Welles and Mankiewicz shared the credit for the writing of *Citizen Kane* and won its only Academy Award together. Later, Pauline Kael argued for Mankiewicz's sole credit for the screenplay, which was answered in kind by Peter Bogdanovich's *This Is Orson Welles*. Bogdanovich suggests that Welles deserved more credit for the screenplay—and perhaps sole credit as the film's auteur—based in part on an affidavit made by Barr. Houseman proposed that Welles and Mankiewicz had had a traditional relationship of film director and screenwriter: Mankiewicz provided the substance and structure of the film, and Welles provided the directing that carried it into full cinematic expression. Welles revised the script several times into its final shooting version, and, as Houseman points out, it was "no denigration of Welles' talent to observe that, throughout his career, he functioned most effectively and created most freely when he was supported by a strong text."[91] Mankiewicz was hired as an uncredited "screenplay doctor extraordinaire" and signed an agreement created by Arnold Weissberger that the script was the property of the Mercury Theatre.[92] But the controversy goes even deeper than the writing of *Citizen Kane*. The question was—who had conceived of the original film? Here again, Barr's affidavit is at the heart of the issue.

Ironically, as Barr himself makes clear in his memoirs, he had no idea whose original idea it was to make *Citizen Kane*, despite what is stated in his personal affidavit. The affidavit implies that Welles had outlined the entire *Citizen Kane* project to John Houseman at the Twenty-One Club in New York City. But Barr denies even knowing that this affidavit even existed. As far as he knew, before he had left Welles's employ, the affidavit had been dictated by Herbert Drake, Welles's press agent, in order for Welles to apply for sole authorship with the Writers Guild of America.[93] This was something Welles had been forced to do since Mankiewicz had gone to the Writers Guild to dispute Welles's authorship of the script.[94] But there was no way for Barr to have attended the Twenty-One Club lunch to confirm Welles's claim, since he was managing Welles's affairs in Hollywood.[95] Houseman argues in his autobiography that Welles approached him at the Twenty-One Club stating that he had gotten the idea about the project from Mankiewicz and wanted Houseman to help convince Mankiewicz to write the script.[96] Welles and Mankiewicz had collaborated on the idea after a discussion at Mankiewicz's bedside, where he was convalescing with a broken leg after an auto accident.[97] Houseman was unclear why Welles didn't want to write the script himself, because, at the time, Mankiewicz was "notoriously unreliable." However, Welles insisted that it was Mankiewicz he wanted, and it was Houseman who managed to get Mankiewicz to agree. Houseman was the one who had the relationship with Mankiewicz, having had him write several *Campbell Playhouse* scripts, and Mankiewicz preferred to deal with Houseman instead of Welles too.[98]

Houseman visited with Mankiewicz at his home in Beverly Hills and discussed Welles's idea with him.[99] According to Barr's affidavit, Welles was a part of these initial meetings with Mankiewicz, and "the idea was suggested and elaborated upon by Welles," which seems to contradict Houseman's version.[100] Shortly after this initial meeting, according to the affidavit, Mankiewicz was retained by Mercury Productions to write the script, and "it was determined" that Houseman and Mankiewicz would move to a dude ranch at Victorville. This decision, according to Welles biographer Simon Callow, was based upon the condition that Mankiewicz stop drinking for the duration of the writing.[101]

Houseman and Mankiewicz set to work writing the screenplay in Victorville, with Mankiewicz receiving editorial comments from Houseman and then dictating the script to a secretary. But Richard noted in his affidavit: "As portions of the script were finished, the finished portions were sent in relays to Mercury Productions at RKO where they were revised by Welles. . . . The revisions made by Welles were not limited to mere general suggestions, but included the actual rewriting of words, dialogue, change of sequences, ideas and characterizations, and also the addition or elimination of certain scenes."[102] Barr emphasizes in his memoirs that "Orson wrote a considerable portion of the script, because I watched him do it, and, further, I discussed the scenes with him."[103] Welles actually provided Mankiewicz with an early draft of the screenplay titled "John Citizen, U.S.A.," which included "three hundred pages of dialogue with occasional stage directions." But Kael and Bogdanovich have debated about what happened after Houseman and Mankiewicz moved to Victorville to complete the script, focusing on how the script had been revised. In Barr's affidavit, he stated, "During the time that Mankiewicz and Houseman were in Victorville, Welles made at least two trips to Victorville for the purpose of discussing the script with Houseman and Mankiewicz."[104] He noted that he and Orson were driven by "Alfalfa" to Victorville on at least two occasions, with him reading the freshly completed script installment to Welles, who was often "cursing the results" and making "terrible noises" at anything he disliked. Welles then went to work on Mankiewicz's "dull" script back at the office, doing any rewriting he thought it needed, sometimes even revising it as he and Barr were driving back from Victorville.[105] He then turned his pages over to his secretary, Katherine Trosper, who knew well what she had typed for Welles.[106] Though Kael notes that Mankiewicz's secretary, Mrs. Alexander, insisted that Mankiewicz did all the work himself without a single page of the shooting script being written by Welles, Bogdanovich asserts that Barr and Trosper felt there was no way for Alexander to have known that, since she was not involved with that aspect of the production.[107]

Once the script was completed in Victorville, Houseman and Mankiewicz returned to Hollywood and revised the entire script per Welles's suggestions.

As this was being done, Welles, now in supervision of the process, added more changes "with respect to sequences, ideas, characterizations and making suggestions with respect to the elimination or addition of new scenes." Houseman continued in his editorial fashion, not actually writing the screenplay itself but acting as a critic and "making suggestions as the script was developed." Barr was at a loss at the time of the affidavit as to how many changes occurred but avowed that Houseman, Welles, and Mankiewicz were drawing upon many different biographies, including those of Joseph Pulitzer, William Randolph Hearst, and Samuel Insull to create the newspaper mogul who became Charles Foster Kane, mitigating the accusation that the film was based solely upon the life of Hearst.[108] Controversies of authorship aside, at this point the RKO production team was starting to invest itself in the material as it was unfolding, page by page, from Welles, Mankiewicz, and Houseman.

The RKO team began "gathering" as soon as the script neared completion, including meetings between Welles and his cameraman, Gregg Toland, one of the most innovative film artists of his time.[109] An immediate energy filled the Welles team as they moved forward on the project, and Welles and Toland went into conference on each page of the script as it was completed, discussing camera positioning and angles.[110] The famous scene in the film when the camera was to take Susan Kane's point of view, staring directly from backstage into "the glare of the lights" downstage, was considered an impossible shot, and yet, according to Barr, "Gregg knew how to do it."[111]

The creative team of Toland, Welles, and Perry Ferguson, the art director assigned by Van Nest Polglase, the RKO chief designer, worked together, with Ferguson carefully drawing out "cartoons" of each scene. These storyboards were placed on the walls of the office that Barr was managing so that all of *Citizen Kane* could be seen in sequence. Once done, according to Barr, there were constant shifts and changes demanded by the script and camera angle choices. Another important member of the team was Robert Wise, the film editor, a young "whiz kid" not much older than Welles. Wise also brought along his talented assistant, Mark Robson, who created one of the most innovative aspects of the film by crushing the "newsreel footage" underfoot to simulate its timeworn aspect.[112]

Once the cameraman, art director, and film editors were in place, Welles brought in the Mercury players, who were all novices to film. Welles had to teach them how to act on film, but because he himself had so little film experience—and following the suggestion of Perry Ferguson—he pretended to do a series of "tests" with the actors in their roles, in costume and on the set, which were later used as actual footage.[113] Barr was impressed by the special gifts of makeup artist Maurice Seiderman, who had invented "a plastic which applied to the skin would seem to wither and age it." This plastic also had the ability to make it through a day's filming without replacement and not only helped Welles as Kane "age" but gave Kane's youthful look a more dashing appearance.[114]

Because of the makeup techniques Seiderman needed to use, Welles was forced to come to the studio in the wee morning hours to give the artist enough time to create his effects. Barr joined Welles, since "Orson liked company," and went over the business for the day. At nine in the morning, "promptly," Welles arrived fully made-up on the set, and filming lasted until six in the evening.[115] This was followed by dinner and a nine o'clock viewing of the daily "rushes" of the shooting from the day before. By its ten o'clock completion, Barr joined Welles for the ride home—and much of the film followed this strict schedule. As Welles's executive assistant and associate producer, Barr was impressed by Welles's utter discipline during the shooting of *Citizen Kane*, a far cry from what he had experienced with Welles with the Mercury Theatre. Welles as a film director engendered a collaborative freedom that few others permitted, and this allowed him to make extraordinary demands of his production team.

While most of the roles had been precast with members of Welles's Mercury players, Barr was involved with several minor aspects of the casting. The casting of Susan Alexander, who was to be Kane's mistress and second wife, was proving problematic for Welles until the discovery of "a young lady with the stage name of Linda Winters." Welles had auditioned "about ten" strippers before he discovered her, selecting her because of her "cheapness." Her real name was Dorothy Comingore, an actress first discovered by Charlie Chaplin, who had something of a reputation as a leftist troublemaker at Warner Brothers. Welles took several tests of her and, though she didn't have much experience, hired her on the spot. Comingore was brilliant in the role of Susan Alexander, and Barr notes specifically the power of the scene she plays with Welles when she attacks him for the terrible reviews she receives as an opera star. That particular scene took fifty takes and finally succeeded only when Welles was able to really provoke Comingore's anger. Welles's direction of Comingore in that scene, Richard thought, "was cruel, but it was worth it." Ironically, because of her success as Susan Alexander in *Citizen Kane*, Comingore later turned down a number of roles until the studios were no longer interested and was later blacklisted because of her left-leaning views, succumbing to paranoia and mental illness.[116]

Barr also assisted in the casting of Fortunio Bonanova, who played the role of Signor Matiste, Susan Kane's Italian voice teacher, one of the comic high points of the film. Welles had seen Bonanova playing opposite Katharine Cornell in *The Green Hat* (Welles thought that he looked like "a leading man in a dirty movie") and came to Welles's attention because he had tripped while stepping into the Brentwood mansion at one of Welles's parties and had fallen on his face. When the "very small, but gem-like part" of Signor Matiste was being cast, Barr reminded Welles of Bonanova's ability to turn his pratfall into one of the major events of the party, and Welles cast him.[117]

Barr also helped cast Alan Ladd, who was a favorite client of Barr's friend Sue Carroll, a Hollywood agent known for her "tasteful" casting and for the fact that she "fought intelligently for her clients." Ladd, who played one of the reporters in *Citizen Kane*, eventually married Carroll; her casting talents led to his future stardom. Barr also assisted in the casting of the offscreen vocalist for Susan Alexander, since Dorothy Comingore did not have a strong singing voice. Barr was required to attend the regular RKO auditions, which were held periodically to screen new talent. At one of these auditions, Barr selected Jean Forward, a sixteen-year-old, because her voice was just bad enough to suggest Alexander's mediocre talent. In the signing of the contract with the young woman as an uncredited performer, RKO sought assurances that the girl and her family would not sue, because the girl was actually cast as a "bad singer."[118]

The other bit of casting Richard was involved with was his own. As associate producer on the film, Barr had wanted to play Billings, but because of an admittedly poor screen test, this role was later cut. He did play a number of other roles in the film, including the role of "first man," and as such he has the first line of *Citizen Kane*. Welles had promised Barr that he would give him this particular honor on one of their Victorville trips. The scene takes place at the end of the "March of Time" newsreel sequence, and just after the newsreel comes to an abrupt end, Barr's voice is heard saying, "That's it. Stand by. I'll tell you if we want to run it again."[119] An actual appearance by Barr occurs after Kane's political speech at Madison Square Garden about midway through the film. As Kane triumphantly steps from the podium and is about to get into a car with his wife, Richard can be seen to Welles's left side, beaming, and with and without his top hat—an apparent continuity problem. He notes that "since I was running back and forth to the office between takes, I could never remember whether the hat was on or off." After seeing the rushes, Barr realized he had "goofed," but since they couldn't match the shots, they were not done over. He glibly points out that this scene is "imperfect but unnoticeable" unless one is looking.[120]

Despite this minor glitch, Richard felt that *Citizen Kane* was the peak achievement of Welles's collaborative filmmaking technique. It was "shot within a reasonable amount of time," and the negative cost of the film "was not over $700,000," which was a remarkable figure considering the film's "complexity."[121] The cinematographer was engaged very early in the process, allowing a great deal of planning and consideration on the part of the various RKO departments involved with the film, who "vied with each other for excellence."[122] Much of this drive for excellence was brought on by Welles's own enthusiasm and his "incredible personality," which pushed these RKO professionals to do their utmost for him.[123]

After postproduction, there was a clamor for the film to be shown, especially since much of the filming had been done in secret. Welles had wanted privacy not only from the press but from the RKO executives themselves, including studio head George Schaefer.[124] But the news about the film had started to leak, and the most disturbing rumors were about the film's closeness to the biography of William Randolph Hearst. Soon after a private screening for Louella Parsons, the gossip columnist at the *Los Angeles Examiner*, a Hearst publication, in January 1941, the Hearst organization went on a campaign to prevent *Citizen Kane* from opening. It threatened to release a major story on Hollywood's hiring of illegal immigrants that was patently anti-Semitic, hoping that other studio heads (many of whom were Jewish) would pressure the RKO board not to release the film.[125] Despite this, George Schaefer, who was struggling to survive in his own job, gave the green light for the opening, even though a number of theatres had been intimidated by the Hearst organization and wouldn't show the film, including Radio City Music Hall. Schaefer brought Welles to a private screening for the New York distributors of the film and their lawyers. And after an agreed-upon cutting of the film, it finally opened in New York at the Palace on 1 May 1941 to jubilant criticism and a fanfare of positive press, though later theatres that showed the film across America sustained losses, due to the Hearst campaign to destroy Welles and *Citizen Kane*.[126]

Richard Barr describes the opening night performance of *Citizen Kane* at the El Capitan Theatre in Hollywood as being "not particularly eventful," though Welles biographer Charles Higham paints it as "sensational; all Hollywood was there." Barr notes that while the "house was packed," the audience wasn't impressed by the film; there was "no cheering," but on the other hand, "no one walked out."[127] It was a star-studded event, with Welles bringing the glamorous Dolores del Rio, though Richard, an associate producer, found it difficult to be noticed at all, pulling up at the same moment as Welles did—with his own starlet in tow.

The ongoing strife with the Hearst organization cost the film any profitability. Hearst had threatened to sue Welles also but backed off because he was unwilling to be cross-examined in court. And Welles and Barr, at the advice of attorney Arnold Weissberger, continued to deny that the film had anything to do with Hearst. Welles's publicist, Herbert Drake, continued to point out that tycoons such as Harold Fowler McCormick and Samuel Insull were just as pertinent in the creation of Charles Foster Kane.[128] It wasn't until forty years later, when Barr was being interviewed by the *Buffalo Courier News*, that the full impact of what Welles had done with the film seemed to have finally been acknowledged by the film community, and by Barr himself, as an extraordinary work of art critical of Hearst and, perhaps, the greatest American film ever made.[129]

Barr continued with Welles, who had turned to another film project, tentatively titled *Mexican Melodrama*, a film adaptation of Arthur Calder-Marshall's anti-Nazi novel, *The Way to Santiago*.[130] The central character of Lionel Transit, a "diabolical but beautiful" charismatic charlatan, was based partly upon Anthony Chilton, the handsome villain of *The Smiler with a Knife*.[131] The film was to be made in Mexico and was to feature Welles with his current paramour, Dolores del Rio. Richard was to explore Mexican jungles and find an appropriate shooting location. Welles had intended to do this himself but was too busy with the Broadway production of *Native Son*.[132] Barr traveled to New York, where he met with Welles and del Rio. The actress used her connections to help him not only find suitable jungles but also hire "an entire motion picture studio and an entire laboratory," all at RKO's expense. Richard, having done similar research for *Heart of Darkness*, should have known this was another of Welles's wild goose chases, but ever the loyal Mercury player, he made the appropriate connections through del Rio and got to work.

One of the most helpful people to Barr on the *Way to Santiago* project was del Rio's friend Carmen Figueroa, who knew everyone in the Mexican film industry in the 1940s.[133] Upon Barr's arrival in Mexico City, Figueroa set up all Barr's visits to potential film studios and laboratories. She also arranged for Richard to attend a party to which he was "invited on certain very strict conditions." As it turned out, William Randolph Hearst was vacationing in Mexico at the time with "his entire retinue," including Marion Davies, whom Welles had cruelly parodied as Susan Alexander in *Citizen Kane*. Figueroa's party was being held specifically for Hearst, his sons, and their families. By that point, Hearst's sons had already threatened to "shoot on sight any of the Mercury gang." Barr, however, was a complete unknown, young and "not that conspicuous." For Figueroa it was a game, "the kind of situation she adored," and Barr was titillated by the possibilities as well. Richard went to the party, keeping his "mouth shut," and met Davies herself, who was "absolutely charming" to him, though the precarious situation became even more nerve-wracking when Richard and Hearst ended up sitting on either end of the same couch. It turns out that Figueroa didn't keep her part of the bargain, and the Hearst family discovered that Barr was a "Welles spy." Though Richard was totally unknown to them, he made a quick exit but later noted that he didn't take the situation "seriously enough to wear a bullet-proof vest."[134]

Richard Barr still had the Mexican jungles to explore, and he made his journeys with the famous ethnographer and caricaturist José Miguel Covarrubias to the Isthmus of Tehuantepec. Diego Rivera, whose studio Barr had visited several times with Figueroa, also assisted by organizing the trip. Barr quickly flew to Minatitlán and from there traveled by train, by bus, and finally by horseback to a "very tiny, primitive village" in the deep interior of the isthmus. He met the tribal chief of the village, who, oddly enough, had a large picture of Hollywood starlet Nancy Kelly from *Photoplay* magazine pasted on his wall. Barr gained the chief's good graces by intimating that he knew Kelly from Hollywood, and that sealed the deal. After a week of his jungle investigation, Barr took photos of locations, some by canoe. He then returned to Hollywood, just in time to discover that Welles and del Rio had fought and the film project was canceled.[135]

Though *Citizen Kane* was not a commercial success, its critical acclaim and the notoriety associated with the Hearst imbroglio made Welles and his Mercury Productions very famous. During this time between projects, Barr was visited by a number of eccentric celebrities, curious about Welles's interest in various artistic projects. A "voluble" Harold Clurman came to seek work for his Group Theatre performers, who were struggling financially. Another visitor was the controversial surrealist author Henry Miller, who had come to see Welles, but unfortunately, Welles had no idea who Miller was. Barr, the Princeton sophisticate, knew only too well and invited Miller and his girlfriend at the time to listen to his "rare wax jazz discs."[136] Sadly, Miller was not a fan of jazz, though forgiving enough to maintain a cordial friendship for some years. But this steady parade of celebrities and guests was to come to an abrupt end, just before Richard was to serve, albeit briefly, as an executive assistant on *The Magnificent Ambersons*, Welles's last major project for RKO.

Richard still ran business matters for Welles and Mercury Productions, but he was frustrated with the position. Though grateful to be employed, he was an assistant to someone who was already where he wanted to be—in control of his own career, busy with the kind of artistic projects that he could only dream about. He wasn't without resources. Barr had convinced

Welles to raise his salary to $150 a week, writing his promotion letter himself to studio head George Schaefer. However, more important than financial security, Barr wanted a sense of direction and the kind of connections that would lead him to success. He was lonely in Hollywood, which was unlike New York, where one could meet people on the street and "for a nickel you could go practically anywhere." In the transient Los Angeles world of automobiles and highways, he felt isolated. Forlorn, he jumped into his "Plymouth convertible with its flashy white-wall tires" and drowned his woes at a Hollywood Boulevard bar, where he sat "staring at the bottles" and wondering, "Has the growth process ceased?"[137]

Richard had developed an intimacy with Welles that few others had achieved—Welles told Barr stories about his father's drinking and the inventions he claimed his father had patented, including the headlamps for bicycles that had become popular during World War I.[138] While a close bond existed between the two, there was suspicion on Welles's part that Barr was too ambitious to keep as an assistant. Having been an associate producer on *Citizen Kane*, he was ready to move on in his career. Then a fateful change occurred—the break that Barr had hoped for. He suddenly found himself faced with an opportunity to produce independent of Mercury Productions, and it sealed his fate with Welles.

Barr was approached, in the spring of 1941, by a young MCA representative who made him an offer to produce a new project. MCA was famous at the time for stealing talent, and Barr was fair game. At the time, he admits that he was "arrogant" and "ambitious" and, "having made one film, naturally I knew everything," so he felt he was ready to strike out on his own as a producer. The young MCA executive assured Richard that he had direct connections with Schaefer and that with Barr's own "direct channel" to Schaefer through Welles, the project would be given the green light. Naively, Richard approached Welles about the project, and Welles immediately fired and replaced him. Even though Barr was only two years younger, Welles suddenly decided Richard was "too young to run the administration of the Mercury," which he had plans to expand. With Welles unexpectedly behind him and the project looming ahead, Barr was abruptly on a trajectory of his own, guided by his new MCA agent, who later turned out to be none other than Lew Wasserman, the future head of MCA and Universal Pictures. Barr was set to produce an adaptation of Theodore Dreiser's *Sister Carrie* but was suddenly fired from the project, just as Schaefer himself had been fired because of the controversy over *Citizen Kane*, the disastrous *Pan American* (which later became *It's All True*), and the failure of *The Magnificent Ambersons*. Barr briefly managed to secure a position through the help of screenwriter Leonard Spigelgass with the "B" picture unit at MGM, headed by Dore Schary, but Richard found himself looking again for a job after Schary's sudden departure.[139]

Despite the shoddy dismissal from Welles's employ, Barr was grateful for his Mercury Theatre experience, since it had afforded him years of connections that would serve him well as a producer. He had received an education in theatre, radio, and film that couldn't be bought anywhere at that time—and he had received a salary while doing it. Barr felt an enormous debt to Welles, despite having seen the worst of Welles's excesses. Through Welles, he learned how to deal with "geniuses," those artists whose enormous talent and drive deserved special ministrations. Later, when dealing with Edward Albee's needs, Barr applied this knowledge of how to both nurture and promote talent within fiscal constraints. Under Welles, Richard had experienced an internship as a journeyman producer, learning how to connect acting, directing, and design talent for a project and recognizing the centrality of the writer to that equation. And it was this apprenticeship that lingered with Barr in all his future endeavors. Though he, like many young men of his generation, was to be waylaid for several years by military service during World War II, true to his ability to make the best out of a challenging situation, his talent at organizing production and working with film and theatre artists was to be engaged—but this time by Uncle Sam.

3

A THEATRICAL WARRIOR

Lieutenant Richard Barr

Barr's involvement in World War II began with a Sunday morning brunch at his home on 7 December 1941. He had invited an eclectic circle of friends, including actors Forrest Tucker, Alexis Smith, and even Marina Koshetz Schubert, the actress daughter of the celebrated Russian opera singer Nina Koshetz, to celebrate his freedom after having served Orson Welles for three years. When the radio blared news of the bombing of Pearl Harbor, Koshetz rushed to the phone to contact her mother, who was visiting La Jolla, just south of Los Angeles, stating, "Mother! Mother! Come home at once! You're directly in the line of fire!" Barr sought to enlist immediately but was rejected because of poor eyesight, having applied to the US Army Air Corps. His 20/200 vision made him legally blind, but as US involvement in the war expanded, as Barr notes in his memoir, "they were not so particular."[1]

Despite his rather conservative upbringing, Richard believed the United States should have been engaged in the war from the beginning. He was close to both Leonard Spigelgass and Dore Schary, who were involved with the prewar interventionist group called Fight for Freedom, an organization with few members in the conservative entertainment industry. In fact, during this time, there was a series of Senate hearings exploring whether Hollywood was guilty of disseminating "war propaganda" even as Europe was falling under the sway of Hitler and Nazi Germany. The hearings fell apart after the bombing of Pearl Harbor, and support that had been clandestine before the war became immediately energized and active.[2] Barr's desire to enlist, however, was a way to defend his liberal credentials. He felt it important to contrast his beliefs with those of his colleagues in Hollywood who would later stand accused of communism. He had serious doubts about communism, a political system that many in 1930s Hollywood took seriously as a possibility for American government. Barr had given the matter some thought, having studied history and communism in particular at Princeton, and his greatest fear was any limitation of free speech, especially in terms of theatre and film.[3]

Hollywood united quickly and effectively against the war. The rollout of various operations included the newly formed Office of War Information (OWI), which came to involve itself in every aspect of film production. OWI's functions included the promotion of certain types of films and later filmmaking itself with the Army Air Corps First Motion Picture Unit (AACFMPU), to which Barr was assigned.[4] Despite the sixty-five-mile drive from Los Angeles, he enlisted at March Field, a relatively little used facility, expanded in the decade before World War II to provide operational facilities for the Army Air Corps. Undaunted by basic training, which was not dissimilar to the kind of "close-order drills" he had experienced as a cadet at Western High School, Barr did well and was quickly moved to administrative duties. During his three months of basic training, he was under the benevolent dictatorship of a certain sergeant whose daily "gravelly" muster orders included: "Fall in! Quickly, quietly, and with a minimum of confusion!" These words became a personal mantra, and Barr put up with the regimen of drills, orders, and training in order to apply for Officers' Candidate School, after which he might secure a possible specialty assignment within his field. Richard successfully passed his qualifying exams and was flown to OCS in Miami, where he continued his training, now as a young officer candidate. He was miserable about the heat, the tedious classes he was forced to take, and "the foolishness that tried to train a potential Air Force administrative officer into a miniature version of a West Point cadet." A. E. Hotchner, who later worked with Barr at the AACFMPU, was also in OCS training in Miami that summer, noting that it was the hottest summer ever thus recorded.[5]

Both Barr and Hotchner were quartered in local Miami hotels, which had been stripped of comfort and turned into barracks for the officer candidates, with "army cots, bare rooms, and mess halls."[6] The training was only made worse when his "friend," the sergeant from March Field, arrived and began his mustering techniques once again. After the grueling experience of OCS, Barr was able to procure a West Coast assignment. Through Leonard Spigelgass,

Richard was sent to the AACFMPU, founded by Warner Brothers producer Jack Warner and his writer Owen Crump. The unit included some of the most talented film artists in Hollywood, all of whom received commissions as officers, including Robert Sterling, George Montgomery, William Holden, and Ronald Reagan.[7] It was to report directly to Washington as part of the Army Air Corps—and for Barr, its independence was key to its success.

After his OCS training, Barr was commissioned a second lieutenant and moved back to his old haunt on Larabee Street in Los Angeles, where he had lived while he was in Hollywood with Orson Welles. The first unit was actually on the Warner lot, the "old Monogram Studio" in East Hollywood, and had no equipment. It consisted of empty soundstages and a headquarters, and, at least initially, there were no crews or technicians to make any of the films. That changed quickly as Owen Crump sent word via trade papers about the need for studio talent to enlist. The response was overwhelming and included everyone from major stars who were hoping to avoid combat duty to middle-aged film technicians desperate to serve their country. Richard and other unit officers went from studio to studio recruiting the best talent they could find, and most were commissioned directly or drafted immediately without basic training—the first time in US military service history such a thing was allowed. Many had no filmmaking skills whatsoever, and these Barr drilled relentlessly, having just graduated "with gold bars on my shoulders." Though he wasn't entirely sure why he was drilling them, he paraded them for unit commanders Warner and Crump, who probably wondered "just what all this pomp and circumstance had to do with making films."[8]

Soon thereafter, the entire operation was moved to the old Hal Roach studios, which had recently been shuttered, in Culver City, California. These studios were handsomely equipped with "working stages, cutting rooms, projection rooms, sound mixing equipment—the works."[9] The first feature was a six-reel training film, *Live and Learn*, about the hazards, sometimes fatal, made by young cadets in their basic flight training. Within two months, the unit proposed over two hundred films, and shortly thereafter at least three hundred short films "were in some process of planning, writing, research, shooting, cutting, dubbing or scoring."[10] The unit was "bursting with activity," and Barr was particularly important in the writers' department, serving second in command under First Lieutenant H. Clark Ramsey.[11] One of the unit's top writers was George Oppenheimer, a major screenwriter who was later the drama critic for *Newsday*. Oppenheimer was over the age limit to get a commission but "enlisted anyway as a sergeant" and eventually became a major because of his service. He and such writers as Norman Krasna, Jerome Chodorov, and Robert Carson served as the core group of writers in the unit.

The actors that Richard recruited for the First Motion Picture Unit included Alan Ladd, Arthur Kennedy, John Beal, Robert Sterling, George Montgomery, William Holden, Craig Stevens, and Ronald Reagan. While there was a lot of filmmaking done at the unit (a total of four hundred films were made), there was also a fair amount of servicemen's hijinks and hilarity. The need to appear "military" was at odds with the artistic license necessary to filmmaking.[12] The assignments that each of these experienced studio professionals took did not always correspond to their talents, especially the actors. For instance, Arthur Kennedy evinced a talent for gardening, so he was assigned to that duty in addition to performing in films. And all the unit employees lived off-post for the most part, arriving daily in an "assortment of expensive cars," which Richard Barr found "formidable," parked in the studio lot. He was in charge of keeping the enlisted men within limits, and his fellow servicemen appreciated "benevolent despotism."[13]

Richard grew close with Reagan, a personnel officer of the unit, as well as with his wife, Jane Wyman. The future president's conduct as a military officer was exemplary; Reagan performed his duties so well that he was later promoted from lieutenant to captain and later to chief administrative officer. His position at "Fort Roach," as the unit came to be known, was to recruit talent. He narrated several films for the unit but primarily served as an administrator, presiding over weekly staff meetings with Barr, some of which were "very funny" but for the most part were "dull." Reagan had a serious respect for military decorum, such as saluting, and was unhappy that his fellow servicemen at the First Motion Picture Unit were not as serious about their military bearing.[14] Still, Reagan had a great sense of humor and was "a good sport." When Reagan was elected governor of California, Barr was contacted by a reporter who wanted some gossip, but Barr refused, stating only that Reagan had served his country honorably as "an extremely conscientious adjutant" who had performed all his duties "with proper military bearing."[15]

One of the first films that Richard worked on was titled *Recognition of the Japanese Zero* and featured Reagan. The film was made to help pilots distinguish between the P-40, which was an American plane, and the Zero, which was their target. Because of their similarity, American pilots were shooting down their own planes, so the film had to be made quickly. Written by George Oppenheimer, it was shot and edited with haste. The only task to be done before the film was viewed by Warner and Crump was the composite print mixing of the film and sound. This is where an act of "deviltry" occurred that became part of the norm at "Fort Roach." Barr's art director, Bertram Tuttle, had discovered an old stag reel in the vaults of the

Hal Roach studio while taking an inventory for stock footage. Tuttle, who shared Barr's sense of humor, switched the films and sent the pornographic stag film to be mixed with Reagan's narration. When they ran the film, without supervising the mixing of film and soundtrack in any way, it matched up perfectly with a hilarious result. The fact that Barr and Tuttle were not court-martialed was a sign of Crump and Warner's sense of humor and of the fun and camaraderie at "Fort Roach." Another "Hollywood moment" occurred when Barr brought the real Mae West to narrate a film about the proper use of life preservers nicknamed "Mae Wests" in honor of the actress's buxom hourglass figure. West was able, through her fame and sense of humor, to convince these young pilots to make use of the vests to save their own lives. She arrived for two evenings at midnight in a chauffeured limousine, completing the task with professionalism and grace.

One of the Army Air Corps' most important projects was to destroy the launching pads of the new and deadly V-2 rockets, which the Germans were planning to use against Allied forces during the D-Day invasion. The concrete bunkers that housed the V-2s were recreated in Florida, where it was discovered that they were penetrable only by specially designed "bunker-busting" bombs dropped from directly overhead at two hundred feet. A film crew was sent to Florida to shoot the bombing missions. Once it was made, the film was rushed back to California to be edited, mixed with a soundtrack, and narrated by Owen Crump. For this to work efficiently, every studio in Hollywood had to be shuttered so that absolute attention could be given to the V-2 bombing film. Twenty-four hours after receiving the footage, the film was completed and on its way to Churchill's British forces within ten days of the original order.[16]

One particularly impressive filmed model was a detailed mock-up of the city of Tokyo, based upon actual combat photography.[17] An entire soundstage was used, with a camera mounted on a movable derrick to simulate what pilots and their flight crews saw over Tokyo. The model was "complete with thousands of buildings and its nearby coastline" and was constantly updated to be as accurate as possible and to show damage done by previous American aircraft bombing.[18] This same flight path was also simulated as a radar image, so that flight crews could learn what they saw on their radar, making a similar run up the Japanese coast into Tokyo. The footage was sent to the B-29 airbase in Guam and was considered one of the most important projects of the First Motion Picture Unit.

By September 1945, with VE Day and the war's end in Europe, Barr began "cancelling certain directives" for various film projects. As he curtailed these expenses, the normal work of an executive assistant at any studio, he was nearly "court-martialled." Washington insisted that the films be made, "war or no war," and this he did, though he had little desire to make films no one would see. Luckily, Albert McCleery contacted him. McCleery had seen Richard's work at Princeton and had stayed in touch with him. McCleery, a former paratrooper, had been given the opportunity to head the drama department of a new university founded in Biarritz for the purpose of educating GIs and preparing them for civilian life, and he was desperate for experienced staff to help him mount professional-level theatre productions on a shoestring. He had written a book on community theatre, *Curtains Going Up*, and later was the head of the theatre department at Fordham University.[19] McCleery's project helped to transition the ambitious Barr into his postwar future in the professional theatre.

At the order of General Dwight D. Eisenhower, the Biarritz American University (BAU) was created in a small resort town in the Basque region of France that had never housed a university before. In a period of approximately six weeks, over 270 professors were selected to teach a student body of nearly 4,000 students, with 900 additional personnel.[20] The university had two major objectives: to provide education opportunities for soldiers awaiting US redeployment, and to ease the transition from army to civilian life.[21] Initially, senior faculty were invited from major institutions, but later the faculty came through personal invitations extended to civilians and military officers with significant training in their fields.

The Theatre and Radio Arts Branch included an integrated range of studies in these fields, with courses in acting, directing, design, and training in speech, radio, and motion pictures. Hubert C. Heffner was one of the earliest participants, along with David S. Haws, a captain who had been trained in the theatre at Cornell University. Albert McCleery joined them and went back to the States to secure more faculty, which included some of the great names of the theatre at that time, including Guthrie McClintic, Richard Whorf, and Mordecai Gorelik, and stars such as Marlene Dietrich. The department produced film and radio productions in addition to theatre. The students lived in rented villas, some of which were luxury accommodations, donated by their owners for use by faculty, students, and other personnel. Barr was hired to lecture but primarily served as an assistant director to McCleery, who proposed a season including William Saroyan's *The Time of Your Life*; Ben Hecht's *The Front Page*; Jules Romains's *Dr. Knock*, a Molière-esque comedy; and *Richard III*, as conceived and designed by Richard Whorf. Barr later moved it to Broadway.[22]

McCleery directed an enormously successful production of *The Time of Your Life*. When the cultural attaché of the American embassy got wind of this premiere, he contemplated taking it to Paris between terms so that it could be played to French audiences. Barr was in charge of the ambassador's gala viewing at Biarritz to confirm its quality. A sumptuous banquet of black market foods was prepared at Biarritz's Palace Hotel as the Theatre and Radio Arts Branch planned to "entertain him royally." Barr left early to hold the show in order to make sure that the banqueting guests had ample time make it to the curtain. In a hurry to get to the theatre, Richard decided to jump the embankments of the various German entrenchments dug in front of the theatre. Acknowledging he was "somewhat euphoric" over the ambassador's presence and a possible Paris production and having had "several glasses of wine by this time," Barr misjudged the width of the trench, hit his chin on the other side, fell to the bottom, and passed out. He lay unconscious for a portion of the performance but managed to pull himself up. Dazed and in shock, he managed to make it back to his villa. He was on his way up the stairs when Mordecai Gorelik noticed to his horror that his chin "was hanging out" and gently suggested that he go to the infirmary. The medics there sent him to the hospital, where it was discovered that he had lacerated his chin and broken five of his teeth. The surgeon pulled several of his teeth (perhaps one too many), but Barr later had his jaw and teeth more expertly set by a Los Angeles dental surgeon.

The show was trucked from Biarritz to Paris, where it was performed on a small stage at the Cercle Militaire, Place St. Augustin.[23] The Paris production was very well received, despite the fact that it was performed entirely by GIs. It was attended by many of the city's greatest artists and writers, including Gertrude Stein and her partner, Alice B. Toklas. Subsequently, Stein invited McCleery, Whorf, and other members of the production to her home for a reading of her play *Yes Is for a Very Young Man*. Barr, who had heard Stein speak at Princeton, did not care much for her work, and did not go to the reading, much to his later embarrassment. He considered it one of his "stupidest decisions," but the worst was yet to come.

Stein had lectured at the BAU and was interested in her work being put on by the Theatre Branch. Though the younger audience members were impressed by Stein's work, McCleery and Whorf were not, and the script did not win over the staff, including Richard Barr.[24] The script was subsequently buried in papers on a desk in the Theatre Branch office, and neither Barr nor his colleagues "dared" to call Stein with a rejection. The script remained unnoticed until the office cat "peed all over it," leaving everyone in the office "hysterical, embarrassed and traumatized."[25] McCleery wrote to Stein that her script had, "in some inexplicable fashion," been lost, and this ended the incident. While Barr swears to the accuracy of this story, other sources imply that Stein withdrew the script because she did not want a workshop performance of the play presented in front of a "handpicked audience."[26] She also had concerns about the GIs taking liberties with the text.[27] Years later, Richard became "an ardent fan" of Stein's writing and felt guilty over this missed opportunity. One statement from her lecture at Princeton stayed with him regarding new plays and new work in general: "The characteristic quality of a classic is that it is beautiful. . . . If everyone were not so indolent they would realise that beauty is beauty even when it is irritating and stimulating not only when it is accepted and classic."[28] Stein's statement eerily presaged the reaction to Edward Albee's plays, which, though now classics, when first produced by Barr, were considered to be more than a little "irritating."

The most significant production Richard Barr worked on at Biarritz was *Richard III*, serving as an assistant to Richard Whorf. Whorf had been drafted by McCleery because of his versatility as a principal performer and designer for the brilliant actors Alfred Lunt and Lynn Fontanne. Whorf began in the 1920s as a child star, with a natural gift for design and known for being a "sullen" character actor.[29] Whorf and Barr cut Shakespeare's play to help it move quickly, and it became at their hands "a rapidly moving melodrama" more suitable to their GI audiences, capturing the rise and fall of a fascist dictator.[30] Having contemplated a production of *Richard III* for many years, Whorf adapted and codirected the production and designing all the settings and costumes with very limited resources. Barr and Whorf struggled to cast the show from the Biarritz GIs and, after casting the Civilian Actress Technicians, or CATs, for the female roles, searched high and low for an actor to play the title role. As luck would have it, a talented young paratrooper named William Windom auditioned and was cast as Richard. Windom went on to have an important career on Broadway, in film, and on television, playing James Thurber in *My World and Welcome to It* among many other roles. Alvin Epstein, later a seminal performer of Samuel Beckett's work, was cast as Lord Rivers. Another key figure was Marshall Migatz, the late producer and founder of several summer stock theatres in the Chicago area, who later gave Barr work as a director.[31] Migatz handled the publicity for the Biarritz production of *Richard III* and years later received acclaim for producing Colleen Dewhurst, Jason Robards, and José Quintero in a seminal production of O'Neill's *A Moon for the Misbegotten*.[32]

The Biarritz American University production of *Richard III* was scenically stunning, despite the fact that it was a daily ordeal to acquire any materials in war-ravaged Europe. To find materials for this visually powerful production, the students were sent out to "scour" the European Theater of Operations "for costume materials and props." Aluminum sheets from sides of Nazi planes were shaped into shields for the soldiers in the play. German officers' uniforms were used to create the jerseys and satin dresses, and parachute silk was used for the banners.[33] Barr created a simple, expressionistic lighting design using single spotlights, including one in "deep red" to accentuate the melodramatic elements of the plot. His extensive record collection was put to work as the production sound design.[34] Because of the strong resonance for its recently liberated audiences, the play was wildly received by over 4,000 Biarritz students and local audiences.[35]

All Biarritz students were expected to attend and write critiques, enhancing the educational value of the production.[36] Since the show was such a success, Brigadier General Samuel L. McCroskey, the commanding officer of the school, decided that it should tour throughout Europe. Though many members of the company were scheduled for redeployment, all volunteered to continue for a three-month tour.[37] Whorf himself had to return to Hollywood, but Captain Barr continued with the company and kept Whorf informed of the various venues and performances of the show.[38] The tour was a ragtag theatrical caravan of "trucks, jeeps, or whatever transportation was at hand," and its stops included Berlin, Nuremberg, Salzburg, Antwerp, Le Havre, Vienna, Mannheim, and Frankfurt.[39] In Antwerp, the company performed in the enormous Festspielhaus, home to Max Reinhardt's company. The Festspielhaus technician was so overwhelmed by Richard Barr's complicated light plot of over 120 cues that he asked Barr to help run the board, using an improvised sign language. When the *Richard III* company arrived in Nuremberg, the trials were still taking place, and all the judges attended the production. Barr personally contacted Robert Jackson, the chief American judge, requesting tickets to the trials themselves. Jackson offered passes to the entire company, and the troupe members watched the trials for two days.[40]

After the tour, Barr joined a friend and took a jeep trip across Europe "in easy stages," enjoying what was left of his USAAF service in style. When he arrived in Biarritz, his discharge papers had come through, and he made his way back to Hollywood. Once there, Barr contacted a friend, David Lewis, producer of the film classic *Camille* and lifelong partner of James Whale, the director of *Frankenstein*, for advice on his future in Hollywood. The war had taken its toll on Barr's career, and Lewis thought that he had "zero" bargaining power as a former Welles employee. Fortunately, David Baer was selling one of his Washington properties. The proceeds provided $20,000 to Barr and his sisters, so at least financially, Barr was solvent. But his professional life had been wrenched by the "strange interlude" of war after four and a half years, and the return to civilian life was a terrible "jolt." Though still in love with the theatre, he found himself left with a West Coast career mostly in film. The years with Welles and with the Army Air Corps had given him a "false sense of security." At the age of twenty-eight, Richard was starting all over again, and he worried that his parents' admonitions had been right. He was not a talented enough actor to make a career of it professionally. His experience and expertise had led him to directing and producing. As he contemplated these choices and his options, he found himself once again relying upon his growing list of contacts to help him sort out the possibilities, and even though he wanted out of the film industry, he had to dive back in to find his own voice as a director.

4

LEARNING THE DIRECTOR'S CRAFT

Stock, Broadway, and City Center

Through Irving Rapper, a Welles connection, Richard Barr secured a position in 1947 as dialogue director for the film *The Voice of the Turtle* while he decided what to do with his career. Rapper had directed several of Bette Davis's finest films, including the classics *Now, Voyager* (1942) and *The Corn Is Green* (1945), and was one of a dying breed of Hollywood directors who had begun their careers on the Broadway stage. *Voice of the Turtle* was an unlikely romance starring Ronald Reagan, Eleanor Parker, and Eve Arden. Based on the popular play by John Van Druten, it paired a worldly young New Yorker, Sally Middleton, with a young GI, Sergeant Bill Page, over the course of a forbidden weekend. A big hit on the New York stage, the show had a risqué reputation since it focused on its heroine's libido. Jack Warner had wanted Reagan to star in it when he was done with his Fort Roach duties.[1] Barr's job was to go over the script with the actors in advance of a take, ensuring that lines had been memorized correctly and that any regional or foreign dialect was pronounced properly.[2] He became a valued member of the *Voice of the Turtle* team—he got along well with Rapper and was a convivial socializer. Though Barr found Reagan to be "his usual uninteresting self," he enjoyed Eve Arden, who "was a ball."[3] After filming was done for the day, Barr became the film's social director, utilizing his skills of organization and socializing to great effect, talents he later used as a theatre producer. The producer for the film, Charles Hoffman, thanked him for making the task of producing much more pleasant than it otherwise would have been.[4]

The Voice of the Turtle was not a hit because the original play had been "blue-penciled" by Warner Brothers to please film industry censors. The film script was as coy about the couple never sleeping with each other as the play was charming about the couple doing quite the opposite.[5] Because of this hack job, Rapper tried to pull out of the assignment but was persuaded by Jack Warner stay on the job. The seeds of Barr's beliefs about the sanctity of playwrights' writing were sowed by this incident.

It was during this time that Richard changed his name to Richard David Barr because there was already another Richard Baer in the professional theatre and film business in Hollywood. This other Richard Baer was a former lieutenant who had served with Barr in the air force in the same unit in which Barr served as a captain, and at that time there was enough of a difference between a Captain Baer and a Lieutenant Baer to prevent confusion. However, after the war, both Richard Baers were employees in the Warner Brothers studio. Lieutenant Baer was a major director and producer, whereas Captain Baer, Richard Barr, was a dialogue director, and "that was not so fine." According to Barr, it was when he started receiving phone calls intended for the other Baer that things became dicey, particularly when he received a message from the other Richard Baer's girlfriend to the effect of, "Darling, let's not go to the movies tonight. Why don't you come to my house and spend the night with me?" Barr decided he must act, and thus he did, taking his father's first name as his middle name.[6]

After finishing *The Voice of the Turtle*, Richard was out of a job, but he caught a lucky break. Sophie Rosenstein, the acting coach for the young starlets at Warner Brothers and former teacher of actress Frances Farmer, decided to take a leave of absence from her job to marry Gig Young, and Barr became a temporary replacement while Rosenstein was on leave. Frustrated that the studios had never allowed him to be anything more than an assistant on any project, Richard decided to translate "large sections of Maeterlinck's *Pelleas and Melisande*" for the training of Warner Brothers' ingenues and "put the poor things to work." The Warner "brass" attended some of the students' presentations and were left "mystified" by their starlets' achievements.[7]

Barr's luck was to change again when an opportunity to direct came through his close relationship with young actress Jehanne Monteagle Miller, whom he had met while stationed at Fort Roach. Before Barr had left for Biarritz, he and Miller had become close and even discussed marriage, but he was struggling with his sexual identity and was still in the Army Air

Corps. The two "tabled the idea" of marriage, and Miller subsequently wed actor Lionel Stander.[8] Returning from France after the war, Richard moved into the Standers' guesthouse along with painter Robert Skiles, a GI with whom Barr had developed a relationship in Biarritz. Barr became close friends with Lionel Stander, a Hollywood character actor best known for his run-in with the House Un-American Activities Committee who later played the loyal butler Max on television's *Hart to Hart*. After hearing about the brilliant GI production of *Richard III* from Skiles, Stander encouraged Richard to direct a modern production of Shakespeare's *Macbeth*. Stander, Sol Cornberg, and Everett Wile were dedicated to bringing "fine theatre" to the West Coast and produced Barr's "modernized" Shakespeare production.[9]

Drawing upon Orson Welles's own modernist approach to Shakespeare, Richard developed a "twentieth century version of *Macbeth*" and edited the play into lightning-quick melodrama similar to Richard Whorf's *Richard III*. Barr also explored Wellesian special effects and came up with the notion for the witches to wear fluorescent masks that seemed to "hang in space." He experimented with the expressionist spotlight effect that he had used in Biarritz on *Richard III* and with yet another Welles effect—the cinematic use of lighting to force the audience's eye to move at rapid pace with the story. To provide the sound design for the evening, Barr used his wax record collection once again, selecting recordings of Shostakovich. His talented roommate, Robert Skiles, designed the costumes, masks, and setting.[10]

The production was advertised as a "twentieth century version" of *Macbeth*. Richard Barr was finally directing his own professional stage production. His *Macbeth* was staged at El Patio Theatre in Los Angeles, one of the city's few legitimate theatres in the 1950s. The play featured Herbert Rudley in the title role, a respected Broadway performer famous for his Macduff in Maurice Evans's production of *Macbeth*. Barr scored a second directorial coup by casting Frances Chaney, a talented character actress married to Ring Lardner Jr. Barr added to this cast Richard Irving as Banquo, Betty Buckner as Lady Macduff, and Stanley Prager as the Porter.[11] Barr also cast Robert Skiles as Ross in the production, and Barr's father provided a substantial share of backing with Stander and his partners.[12] Unfortunately, stymied by an appalling dress rehearsal and terribly embarrassed by thinking he had wasted his father's financial support, Barr froze and could not continue rehearsing. Stander, an old hand in the theatre, gently coaxed Richard from directorial rigor mortis, noting that awful dress rehearsals were usually followed by successful openings. Barr's reaction is surprising, since he had been used to working in Welles's chaos, but by the next dress rehearsal the show had righted itself, and his modernized *Macbeth* opened successfully.

In the early preview article about the show, titled "War-Tried 'Macbeth' to Open at El Patio," special note is made of Barr's modern techniques of staging and of adapting Shakespeare, borrowed from his Biarritz *Richard III*. The "murder story" of *Macbeth* was to be staged with costumed performers "speaking the standard lines, but in the manner of everyday Americans." In the article, Barr discusses his use of contemporary sound and lighting design and points out that the show would be the first of a series of modernized Shakespearean productions originating in Hollywood. He felt his current adaptation of *Macbeth* was a "natural" to transfer to television, film, or radio.[13] The *Los Angeles Times* called the production "streamlined Shakespeare" and noted that its "modern manner" played in a "new spirit," though it took the production to task for staging the show on Thanksgiving night. Also mentioned was the lighting, which used a "motion-picture technique" that provided a "phrasing" that gave "speed to the action" of the play. Herbert Rudley was cited for his "dominating presence," and Barr's direction of the play was also called out.[14] The review in the *Hollywood Citizen-News* was mixed, questioning the "Americanese" interpretation, staged in a modern spin that "might give Shakespeare or Bacon a restless grave."[15] But despite the cautious acceptance of the *Hollywood Citizen-News*, Barr was singularly pleased with the response he received, including a letter of praise from noted screenwriter Malvin Wald at Universal Pictures.[16]

Shortly after *Macbeth*, Richard returned to New York. It was a felicitous moment to leave Los Angeles. By the end of 1947, the McCarthy era was in full swing. Many of Barr's closest friends were blacklisted, including Lionel Stander, one of his most loyal supporters. Barr's decision to leave the West Coast may have been precipitated by the expanding *Red Channels* list, which was rapidly engulfing many of the top names in Hollywood.[17] Oddly, by maintaining his friendship with Ronald Reagan, Barr believed he bought some insulation from accusations of communism. But he was also leaving because Hollywood was becoming rapidly less friendly to gays; during the days of the Red Scare, homosexuality was viewed along with communism as a threat to national security.[18] Worse, as a former employee of the Mercury Theatre, which was considered Welles's leftist offshoot of the Federal Theatre Project, he could have been easily targeted by Joseph McCarthy and his operatives in Hollywood. Perhaps more important, he was leaving Hollywood to become involved in the next big project in the American theatre. Like the Mercury Theatre that preceded it, Fiorello LaGuardia's newly minted City Center, with performances of opera, music, and dance discounted for working-class audiences, was the next best thing in the American theatre.

Barr received word that his friend José Ferrer was teaming up with Richard Whorf at City Center in New York City to create a dynamic new theatre company to complement the music and dance already being presented in the upstart New York City–owned institution.

City Center had already produced a string of successful musicals, operas, and symphonic and dance performances but had had no luck establishing a non-musical theatre company. The first dramatic company had been a failure. Called the "Company of Twelve" and led by Haila Stoddard, Harold Bromley, and Bryon McGrath, this first attempt also included actors Montgomery Clift, Mildred Natwick, Philip Bourneuf, and Herbert Berghof. Their revival of the Joseph Jefferson production of *Rip Van Winkle* was a critical success but a financial failure.[19] Jean Dalrymple, the prodigious producer, publicist, and gadfly for the City Center, had contacted José Ferrer at the behest of her board, and after several attempts, Ferrer was finally convinced to establish City Center's theatre company.[20] Already a great success onstage and in film, by 1947 Ferrer had recently been seen in *Cyrano de Bergerac* and, at City Center, in *Othello*, starring opposite Paul Robeson and Ferrer's wife, Uta Hagen. Unfortunately, Ferrer was going through a divorce with Hagen and felt she interfered negatively on any productions in which he was involved. But, in an odd combination of postmarital peace offering and aesthetics, Dalrymple negotiated a deal in which Ferrer would direct his ex-wife in a production of *Angel Street*.[21] Ironically, Ferrer also cast Phyllis Hill, the "other woman" who had ended his marriage.[22]

In the midst of all this was Richard Barr. He was still very close to Ferrer, and Ferrer's support was crucial to his career as a young director. Ferrer had been impressed by Barr's adaptation of the Stefan Zweig translation of *Volpone* at Theatre Intime and wanted to use it at City Center. The adaptation tightened the play and gave the roles more substance.[23] The cast, which included John Carradine, Leonard Cimino, Paula Laurence, and Earl Jones, was "delighted" with the meatier roles and the agreeable pace of the comedy.[24] In the end, Ferrer arranged for City Center to pay $100 for Richard's work as a translator, hiring him as an actor as well.

Barr encouraged Ferrer to use Richard Whorf as his artistic codirector. Whorf was multitalented as a performer and designer and thus a benefit to the new dramatic company at City Center, which was on a strict budget. Whorf was a perfect foil to Ferrer, playing Mosca to Ferrer's Volpone. Barr was also able to stay with Hagen and Ferrer at their home in Ossining, New York, living in "luxury" while he was working on the City Center productions. *Volpone* was to be staged for as little as possible, since the newly created New York City Theatre Company was to be a low-ticket price venture.[25]

Ferrer turned out to be an excellent administrator, and rehearsals got underway very quickly. The company accepted the Actors' Equity stock company contract instead of Broadway minimum wage, a difference of ten dollars a week per actor. Ferrer hired Herbert Brodkin, an experienced scenic designer, and Emeline C. Roche, a tasteful and economic costume designer, and rehearsals began under director Martin Ritt, a former Group Theatre director who had worked under Elia Kazan. After a few days, however, Ritt didn't agree with Ferrer and Whorf on the general concept of the show, and rehearsals came to a stop. Ritt agreed to step down, and Barr was hired by Harry Friedgut, the director of City Center, to take over direction of the play, Barr's first Broadway production.

Volpone opened on 18 January 1948 with "continual laughter and bursts of applause"; the audience was "enchanted" as Ferrer, Whorf, and Carradine played it in the commedia dell'arte spirit. From her "last-row-on-the-center-aisle-seat," Jean Dalrymple was pleased to see the critics exit the theatre with smiles on their faces and hoped that the New York City Theatre Company would succeed where others had failed. The only naysayer was *New York Times* critic Brooks Atkinson, who was unhappy with this lean, slapstick production of *Volpone* and called it a "broad and noisy stage circus, which scholars might describe as commedia dell'arte and theatre-goers would call burlesque."[26] George Jean Nathan was less concerned with the liberties taken by Ferrer, Barr, and Whorf, noting that the show "was as free from scholastic reverence as a subsidized college football player and even more athletic."[27] Barr was undaunted by the mix of reviews, and the eight other New York newspapers gave the show "money notices," which heartened the company members. With that in mind, they leapt into rehearsals for the next production, Patrick Hamilton's *Angel Street*, a hit thriller that had a starring role for Uta Hagen as Mrs. Manningham with Ferrer playing her evil husband.[28]

Because Hagen had played the role of Mrs. Manningham in stock and knew the play much better than Richard did, Ferrer made it clear that Barr was to stay to one side of the actors, particularly Hagen, whom he was about to divorce. The production was made more complicated by the fact that Ferrer's lover, Phyllis Hill, was playing Nancy. Because Barr was so close to Ferrer, the situation left a permanent personal wedge between him and Hagen, despite his later casting of her in the award-winning production of *Who's Afraid of Virginia Woolf?* nearly sixteen years later.[29] Dalrymple noted that with four experienced actors playing the *Angel Street* roles, it appeared to her that Barr spent the better part of his job "sitting in a chair enjoying their work." Still, Hagen received wonderful notices, and audiences poured into City Center to see the production.[30] Brooks Atkinson, who enjoyed the "creep-show," was even impressed with Barr's "sapient" direction, noting that the company wasn't above "laying it on sufficiently thick" and rose to the melodrama inherent in the production.[31] George Jean Nathan was less thrilled about it, lamenting with "considerable critical regret that any such ambitious enterprise should have followed Jonson with a purely commercial showshop offering."[32]

The final production Richard Barr directed for City Center, *A Tragedian in Spite of Himself*, was an evening of Anton Chekhov's one-act plays in early February 1948, including *The Bear*, *On the Harmfulness of Tobacco*, and *The Wedding*, and also a compilation of material from Chekhov's short stories. Though Barr shared credit with Ferrer for directing the pieces, he doesn't mention his direction of the show in his memoirs, suggesting that he mostly kept out of the actors' way. Neither Brooks Atkinson nor George Jean Nathan were wild about the Chekhov comedies, but Atkinson noted they were well served by the City Center company's virile acting: "Being livelier actors than most, Jose Ferrer, Richard Whorf and their associates play the sketches broadly in picturesque costumes."[33] The production cemented the fact that Ferrer's company had become "accepted as a permanent component of the City Center family," and Ferrer was asked to create a new spring season.[34] Unfortunately, far more lucrative offers were coming to his actors from commercial interests, and he couldn't keep the company intact. And with his newly found fame as a Broadway director, Barr himself was finding work in summer stock and landing professional opportunities on Broadway.

That summer, he began directing stock at the John Drew Theater in East Hampton, and in fact continued to direct stock throughout his career. The John Drew Theater, built in 1931 at Guild Hall in East Hampton, was a "charming four-hundred-seat" house that, in Barr's opinion, was an ideal venue for summer stock of the 1940s. He had mixed feelings about being a Jewish resident director working in the "notoriously anti-Semitic" East Hampton community and was actually warned away from certain places. But to Barr's relief, he experienced no such bigotry and notes that he was "a model Jewish boy" that summer.[35] His move was fairly typical for the time—most theatre artists, whether young and new or seasoned and famous, were a part of the profitable summer stock theatre in the 1940s.[36] This was the heyday of stock, when great stars from Broadway, television, and film considered it de rigueur to go on the road. Stock was particularly important, before the advent of television, as a steady living for performers. The Council of Stock Theatres negotiated cheaper rates with the Actors' Equity Association, and the actors enjoyed the limited runs, usually a week of eight performances, and major roles not usually available to them on Broadway.

At the John Drew Theater that summer, Barr directed *Romeo and Juliet*, with Ferrer as Romeo—a role Ferrer doubted he would be cast in anywhere else. Mary Anderson played Juliet; she had debuted as Maybelle Merriwether in *Gone with the Wind* but ended her film career in the 1950s. Ray Walston, famous later for creating the role of Uncle Martin in the television series *My Favorite Martian*, was cast as Friar Lawrence. Ferrer assisted with the direction of the show, taking Anderson aside to rehearse privately in the theatre while Barr rehearsed the rest of the company on the lawn of Guild Hall.[37] With a growing list of Hollywood and Broadway contacts, Richard Barr combined star casting with his simple, modernist directing approach that became his signature style. He asked Walston to play Friar Lawrence as a young "baseball-playing priest" with the result that "the play fairly skipped along."[38] He used a balcony window in the theatre for the famous balcony scene, having Anderson enter from outside and climb a ladder, covered by an umbrella in inclement weather. The production was put together, in Barr's opinion, "quickly, quietly, and with a minimum of confusion."[39] That summer at the John Drew, he also directed productions of *Meet the Wife* by Lynn Starling with Mary Boland, followed by Ilka Chase in Noël Coward's *Design for Living.*

A defining moment came with his production of *The Beaux' Stratagem* featuring Brian Aherne, the Oscar-nominated British star.[40] Aherne was at the end of a long career in theatre and film but was still busy with *The Beaux' Stratagem*, a "package show," which he had been touring since the 1930s. Barr's company of actors, including seasoned performers like Walston and a young, unknown Maureen Stapleton (recommended to Barr by Guthrie McClintic), played the smaller parts, while Aherne's company took on the meatier roles.[41] Barr's actors were taken aside by Aherne after the final rehearsal for the show and admonished to "just learn your lines and stay out of the way of the professional actors." Richard soothed their ruffled feathers and advised them to take "a deep breath" and carry on, horrified though they were by Aherne's behavior.[42] He garnered genuine loyalty from actors that continued over the course of his career.

One particular trait endeared him to actors: he refused to use auditions or have actors do cold readings, a directorial choice learned from his mentor Guthrie McClintic. Barr had worked closely with McClintic at Biarritz, where McClintic had served as a lecturer and worked with Albert McCleery on Maxwell Anderson's *Winterset.*[43] Traditional auditions typically gave the actor only a few minutes to go off and learn the material and then perform it cold with an offstage stage manager. McClintic found this totally "insensitive" and refused to do it.[44] Instead, McClintic simply interviewed the actors with a range of questions, and even if he had never seen them perform, he "managed to grasp the range of their possibility."[45] McClintic's interviews were psychological, and his record was impressive. He cast countless actors this way, giving some their first professional Broadway appearances, including Marlon Brando, Montgomery Clift, Orson Welles, Tyrone Power, Burgess Meredith, and Maureen Stapleton—all stars Barr worked with in his career.

Likewise, Richard Barr's own casting process was based on interviews and on his habit of voraciously attending the theatre and taking notes on "interesting performances." He had an easy repartee with all his actors, regardless of their fame or experience, and developed a long "magic list" of performers that he "thumbed through" over many years. Barr felt that auditions were frantic and useless: "They hold a lot of auditions and then end up frantically hiring anyone." Instead, he built his magic list from the performances he attended and from readings in his production office held three times a year. Though years later, as a producer, he gave the director and playwright final say in casting, his list was an important resource. With it, he boasted that Albee's *The Death of Bessie Smith* was cast over the telephone in a single afternoon.[46]

At the John Drew Theater, Richard directed his first original script, *Honest John* by Buddy Ebsen, the talented character actor and dancer of stage and screen. *Honest John* was a comedy, originally planned for production on Broadway by the Bonfils and Somnes producing team. Ebsen was to star and direct, but the deal fell through.[47] Francis I. Curtis bought the rights and planned to direct it himself at the John Drew, but since Curtis needed to continue his administrative duties, Barr assumed direction of the show.[48] It opened on 2 September 1948 and did well enough that he was asked to bring it to Reading, Pennsylvania, to play for another week. In the meantime, he lost an actress playing a comic "gun moll" in the production and was forced to recast.[49] Barr gave the role to a young Lee Grant, whose audition he had seen at a backers' audition for Mervyn Nelson's *The Ivy Green*, an original play he later directed. Grant became one of his favorite actresses, and he cast her in his next show, *Arms and the Man*.

After the summer ended, Barr was invited by the Equity Library Theatre (ELT) to try something new in its workshop productions. The ELT had been founded in 1943 to provide employment for journeymen performers and an opportunity to develop their stage skills.[50] The work was unpaid, and there was no charge to the audiences. The ELT wanted Barr to direct Shaw's *Arms and the Man* "in the round," a new approach in the late 1940s that involved the audience sitting onstage, surrounding the performance area. Barr had experimented with this technique with McCleery in Biarritz and was eager to try it on his own. He chose Lee Grant for the leading role of Raina Petkoff and staged it using "boxlike cubes," which were easily rearranged into tables, desks, chairs, sofas, or whatever scenery was needed. The ELT workshop production opened on 29 November 1948 in a small auditorium at the offices for the Lighthouse for the Blind. *New York Journal-American* reviewer Robert Garland praised Barr's direction, calling the show "a revival of one of its best revivals."[51]

After *Arms and the Man*, Richard Whorf contacted Richard Barr regarding the possible restaging of their Biarritz *Richard III* at the Copley Theatre in Boston. Whorf had made his start with the Copley Players, and the idea of a revival of the production had struck a chord with the Boston Repertory Theatre Association (BRTA). The BRTA had been founded by Michael Linenthal and Gerald Savory in 1947 to build upon the repertory theatre movement led by the American National Theatre and Academy (ANTA) in the late 1940s. The Shubert Organization loaned the BRTA its Copley Theatre, which was mostly dark at the time.[52] Barr believed that Whorf's proposal, because of his Hollywood star status, was bound to succeed, so Richard immediately planned to produce the show at the Copley. Whorf was to star and design sets and costumes, and Barr was to adapt the text, direct the show, and design the lighting. Their intent was to recreate their Biarritz production, including an enforced poverty of production. However, since the original production had relied upon the ingenuity of GIs procuring materials from the spoils of war, and there were no ready supplies for the current show, the poverty was real. Despite the lack of German plunder, they were able to secure a donation of "leftovers" from the Brooks Brothers pageant at the 1948 New York World's Fair. These costumes consisted of tunics made of burlap, which took "light perfectly on the stage." Whorf went to Brooks Brothers himself to cut out "dozens of coats of arms in the shape of shields" from the donated fabric. These were then applied to the fronts of the costumes at "chest-level." Whorf created shoes by using dancers' tights and inserting a leather sole. The sets were a series of banners, similar to those of the original Biarritz production, and once again, Barr used his wax records for the sound design. Even the actresses were involved in the battle scenes, wearing "felt head coverings" and "black tights." Barr choreographed the battles himself to the sound of Gustav Holst's *The Planets*, imitating Welles's own battle scenes from *Five Kings*. Barr used his "simple and melodramatic" spotlight system with "single red spotlights for soliloquies and other pertinent moments."[53]

The Boston critics were genuinely pleased with the production, which opened on 17 January 1949. Elliot Norton of the *Boston Post* roundly praised its design, calling it "ingenious and handsome" and "richly decked in primary colors."[54] Whorf identified opposing factions in the play by dressing all of the characters on one side in black and white and the other in red. Using those colors out of necessity in Biarritz, based upon the parachute silk used in Nazi rallies, the result was so successful that he repeated the color scheme in his Boston and New York productions.[55] Norton also noted that the production was lighted well to "allow for the swift and fluent change of moment" and that the production was "acted loudly and broadly."[56] Elinor Hughes of the *Boston Herald*, who wrote her review entirely in verse, proclaimed that it was "one of the best Shakespeare revivals in several years" and was acted and directed "with intelligence and fire."[57] The review that secured *Richard III*'s Broadway transfer appeared in *Variety* and called the play "one of the most striking Shakespeare revivals ever staged" and "a masterpiece of stagecraft that culminates in a pantomimic battle scene of astounding effectiveness." The *Variety* review chirped that the production "seems almost certain to achieve the same on Broadway."[58]

Several New York producers came to the show in Boston, but "the only serious one" was Herman Levin, a relative newcomer to Broadway but who later produced major new productions including *The Great White Hope* and *My Fair Lady*. He and Howard Stix Cullman provided the necessary $15,000 backing, and *Richard III* was quickly remounted on Broadway at the Booth Theatre a month later on 8 February 1949.[59] The swiftness of the transfer was facilitated by Whorf, a favorite son of the Boston theatre, who negotiated with the local unions to put the local New York union stamp on all the stage settings after midnight of the closing, allowing the entire set to move to New York without having to be rebuilt. Barr recast several of the roles, adding Ray Walston in the role of Sir Richard Ratcliffe, Douglass Watson in the role of the Marquis of Dorset, and William Windom as an understudy for Whorf.

Richard Barr had plucked Windom, the original Biarritz Richard III, from the insurance business, as Windom had abandoned the theatre three years earlier. Barr enrolled him in the Actors' Equity Association, and Windom went on to a lengthy Broadway, film, and television career thereafter. Barr also hired a "splendid sound technician" from Masque Sound named Saki, who learned how to "play the waxes," using six different records from Barr's collection. Saki became so proficient in this "wax record technique" that he was able to create a "mechanical effect" between needle drops simulating a "full symphony orchestra."[60] Unfortunately, the musicians' union got word of this. An anonymous letter was written to the *New York Times* by one of the stagehands, and the use of records without proper rights or musicians was never again permitted.[61] Barr, ever practical and parsimonious, bristled at this decision, which brought about "excessive union penalties."[62]

The New York reviews were decidedly mixed, with excess of both praise and criticism. One of the major talking points of the play had been its reduced production costs; it came in for under $16,000, and that included bonds for the actors' salaries. Richard Watts of the *New York Post* wrote that the show was "rigorously and rousingly brought to the stage of the Booth theatre" and noted that Barr's "staging is proudly and unashamedly melodramatic, even going so far as to play a red spotlight on Richard's malignant features, and it never fails in vitality, excitement and resource."[63] The director himself was particularly pleased by this review, which was one of several to celebrate his directing choices. Ward Morehouse of the *Sun* offered that the production is "capably staged by Richard Barr, and one in which the dauntless Whorf gives a performance of distinction."[64] Barr's experience with Welles's Mercury Theatre had been realized in his staging of Whorf's *Richard III*, and his cinematic modernism gave the play a forceful energy, typical of his directing style for years to come.

Brooks Atkinson of the *New York Times* was more circumspect on both Barr's cutting and staging of the play. And while Atkinson was not entirely disappointed in the production, he questioned the heaviness of Barr's melodramatic direction, noting "speed and drive do not solve all the problems of Shakespeare. There must be a little art in it, too."[65] The show was caustically received by academic Kappo Phelan of *The Commonweal*, who belittled the design, calling it "merely painted imitations of the usual architectural arrangements—arches and alleys—together with the trite and overdone pit-entrance plan." Phelan was particularly incensed over Barr's lighting design, stating that it "declines into nonsense." He was even more pointed regarding Barr's direction of the battle scene, complaining, "Mr. Barr's abysmal direction of the battle scene loses him entirely in a mess of silhouettes plus a hoarse voice reiterating the 'horse' entreaty."[66] The production played for twenty-three performances, closing on 26 February 1949, and while not one of the most auspicious productions on Broadway at the time, it made its splash.

Continuing in his "basic training" as a director, Richard Barr spent the summer of 1949 directing stock at the Chevy Chase Country Club, just outside Chicago. His connection was Marshall Migatz, who had served as the Biarritz publicist. Migatz was the boy wonder of the Chicago theatre scene, nicknamed "the Shubert of summer stock."[67] Migatz was also the first to bring the star system of summer stock to the Chicago area.[68] He was helped by Barr, who brought New York actors like Paula Laurence, Signe Hasso, Dennis King, and Buddy Ebsen to the Chicago area to try their luck with midwestern audiences.[69] Though Migatz had a ballroom space available, the stage space was "the size of a postage stamp." Working with designer Paul S. Haney, it was possible, however, to create a "thrust"-type stage in the space by raising an adjacent hydraulic bandstand and adding chairs to either side of the stage. Tyrone Guthrie first used the "thrust" stage at the Edinburgh Festival in his production of *Ane Satyre of the Thrie Estaits* by David Lindsay.[70] But Richard Barr believed his Chevy Chase summer theatre thrust stage arrangement predated Guthrie's by four years, and though it was unusual for the time, he had built up a stable of actors who knew how to work with this new format.[71] For Otis Bigelow, his roommate from his Mercury Theatre days who joined the Chevy Chase summer theatre, Barr's seven-hundred-seat thrust stage "formed entirely new problems in acting and staging because of the unusual sightlines." He felt as though the audience "all seem to be sitting in your lap while you're working." Despite this, Bigelow thought the thrust staging was successful because Barr cast actors who had worked together frequently "under normal theatrical circumstances," and "we rather welcomed the challenge."[72]

That summer, Richard Barr staged a record number of shows at Chevy Chase with "name performers," including Buster Keaton in *Three Men on a Horse*, Peggy Ann Garner in *Peg o' My Heart*, Nina Foch in *Light Up the Sky*, Signe Hasso in *Love from a Stranger*, Mady Christians in *The Vinegar Tree*, Buddy Ebsen in *The Man from Home*, Haila Stoddard and Tom Drake in *Her Cardboard Lover*, Dennis King in *The Second Man*, and Charles Ruggles in *Nothing but the Truth*. The shows were staged in advance with star performers, leaving only one run-through with the local stock company. Barr struggled somewhat with Keaton, who was "not much fun, but affable enough." Keaton changed all his moves from the Stockbridge, Massachusetts, performance Richard had taken notes on, and so "opening night was a shambles."[73] Peggy Ann Garner, who had triumphed as Francie in the film *A Tree Grows in Brooklyn*, toured in *Peg o' My Heart* as a prelude to her debut on Broadway in Mel Dinelli's drama *The Man* at the Fulton Theatre.[74] Barr's experience with Nina Foch, the star of such films as *My Name Is Julia Ross* and *Johnny Allegro*, was particularly memorable, as he performed with Foch in Moss Hart's satire of the Broadway theatre, *Light Up the Sky*, playing Carleton Fitzgerald, the director. Barr modeled his performance on his personal idol Guthrie McClintic and even performed his imitation for McClintic himself, who "managed to force a smile."[75] Though Orson Welles had a tremendous impact on Richard, it was McClintic's style of directing and casting that most influenced Barr's producing and directing choices. McClintic, one of America's most famously closeted gay directors, along with his equally closeted wife, Katharine Cornell, made a large impression on Barr socially as well. Like McClintic, he never advertised the fact he was gay, and though many theatre professionals knew, just as many were tacitly excluded. Barr would live his gay life in and out of the closet, never one to hide his sexual orientation in his Greenwich Village life downtown, but not one to share it with his League of New York Theatres colleagues uptown.

After *Light Up the Sky*, Barr directed Signe Hasso in Frank Vosper's *Love from a Stranger*, adapted from the short story "Philomel Cottage" by Agatha Christie. The Swedish-born actress, though still a popular, exotic performer, was not satisfied with the mediocre fare offered to her in American film.[76] She traveled cross-country performing in many companies, most notably in Tyrone Guthrie's production of Friedrich Schiller's *Mary Stuart*.[77] Mady Christians, the star of the original Broadway production *I Remember Mama*, performed for Barr in Paul Osborn's romantic comedy of the 1930s, *The Vinegar Tree*. The season ended in September, after many stars and many traveling productions, when Richard directed the comic genius Charles Ruggles in James Montgomery's 1918 comedy, *Nothing but the Truth*. Barr's Chicago season of directing summer stock was the second of four years of serving as a resident stock director, and he continued to direct stock throughout his life. However, his career with the Chevy Chase summer theatre ended after only one season.

Shortly after Barr's work in Chicago, his agent, Miriam Howell, contacted him to take over the Roy Hargrave production of *The Ivy Green*, a dark exploration of the life of Charles Dickens that Barr had first seen in a backers' audition. Richard was to hop aboard this sinking ship on the road in Hamilton, Ontario, and then hope for a miracle in Toronto, Boston, and New York. Barr recalled advice given him by McClintic on how to save a production. Lee Shubert had asked McClintic to take over the 1945 production of *Dark of the Moon*, which was stumbling. Shubert offered him $1,000 dollars a day, a case of scotch, and a suite at the Ritz. McClintic found a production that was "discouraged by divided authority on top" and simply took charge. He changed the script minimally and tried to bring out the "great possibilities" he saw in the play.[78]

Though Barr was "scared to death," he followed McClintic's model and, after watching the show in rehearsal, focused on editing the script. Because his changes were minimal, he quickly found that he had the support of "the producers, the author, and finally, the cast." But, despite a supporting cast of stalwart experienced professionals, including Hurd Hatfield, Judith Evelyn, Barnard Hughes, and Ruth White, the production stumbled and closed after seven performances on 9 April 1949. Brooks Atkinson, who called the stage adaptation of Dickens's life "about as untheatrical as possible," noted, however, that the production was "a worthy piece of work without being a continuously stimulating drama."[79] The play was not "fixable," and so it "folded" at the Hudson Theatre, where Richard had had his New York debut in the Princeton Triangle performance of *Fol-De-Rol*.[80]

In December 1949, Barr received kudos from the New York critics for directing a workshop production of John Millington Synge's *Deirdre of the Sorrows* at the Abbe Practical Workshop on Riverside Drive. Atkinson extolled Barr's direction of *Deirdre,* noting that he had directed it "reverently and lovingly" and had "mastered the poetic turmoil that flares through the play." Richard's direction struck a particular chord with the *New York Times* reviewer, who recognized that the play was helmed by "a man who appreciates it."[81] Richard Watts also commended the direction: "Richard Barr's direction indicates an understanding of the drama's quality, and the actors, while not nearly up to the demands of a difficult work, are at least direct and modest."[82]

Though Richard received praise for his sensitive direction of a rarely performed classic, these were not the "money" reviews of a young star director. His directorial wheels were spinning, and he wasn't going anywhere. With the sudden death of his father in 1950 and frustrated with his directing career, Barr took his grieving mother on a whirlwind tour of European theatre. He saw Marivaux at the Comédie-Française and a French production of *Un Tram Nommé Désir* at the Théâtre Édouard VII in Paris and attended the Moscow Art Theatre in the Soviet Union.[83] He was charmed by Noël Coward's *Fallen Angels* with comediennes Hermione Gingold and Hermione Baddeley, the famous two Hermiones, who turned their renowned competitive blend of humor into a wild frenzy of comedy.[84] The production would stay with him as he continued his journeyman directing work that summer in Marblehead, Massachusetts.

Struggling to jump-start his directing career, Barr picked up a gig as a summer stock resident director at the Marblehead Playhouse, working out of a local high school. He struggled with the local town fathers, who already had turned down his "scandalous" production of *The Fourposter* with Hume Cronyn and Jessica Tandy. Instead, Barr opened the season with the packaged production of Nancy Walker in the Leonard Bernstein musical *On the Town* with Portia Nelson and Nita Naldi, the former silent film star. He followed this with a production of *The Barretts of Wimpole Street* with Susan Peters on 10 July 1950. The former MGM star performed from a wheelchair because an accident had paralyzed her in 1945. It was during the summer in Marblehead that Richard encountered Estelle Parsons, "a very nice girl," who entertained the stock company in her home with her singing and piano playing. She remained on Barr's mind and on his "magic list." Years later, he cast her in his Cherry Lane Theatre production of William Hanley's *Mrs. Dally Has a Lover* as well as in Edward Albee's *Malcolm*, in the role of Laureen.

At Marblehead, Barr set aside ambition and worked hard on particular "directing problems," such as how to handle stars or "staging instinctively" rather than by elaborate blocking patterns planned in advance. By engaging the talents of actors such as Franchot Tone in *The Second Man*, Kay Francis in *The Web and the Rock*, and Joan Blondell in *Happy Birthday*, Barr was "learning something about my profession."[85] While he never returned to Marblehead, he had paid his dues as a director, learning skills that he used later when he finally moved to his first Broadway show as a producer. But before that would happen, Barr had one more opportunity to establish a name for himself as a director.

In October 1950, Richard Barr was invited to join the newly created Arena Stage at the Edison Hotel to remount his production of *Arms and the Man*, two years after he had staged it for the Equity Library Theatre. Arena staging was new to Broadway, and the critics were mixed in their assessment of its aesthetic appeal and its appropriateness.[86] Barr persuaded Francis Lederer to play the role of Captain Bluntschli and wanted Maureen Stapleton as Louka, but the producers, David Heilweil and Derrick Lynn-Thomas, were unimpressed with Stapleton, whom they decided "couldn't act" and was "too fat." Instead, they asked Barr to cast Anne Jackson, Stapleton's closest friend. Lee Grant came back as Raina and played the role "to perfection." The production ran for 108 performances, but Brooks Atkinson was not impressed with Lederer's Bluntschli and felt that Lee Grant was not experienced enough to play the role of Raina. Nevertheless, he was enthusiastic about the arena staging and thought that there was "still some fun it" with the actors relishing the slapstick.[87] Barr's direction was called "fuzzy and vacuous" by Otis Guernsey of the *New York Herald Tribune*, with the theater-in-the-round staging appearing to "contain more of foolishness than of satire."[88] Robert Coleman of the *Daily Mirror* was kinder, writing, "Richard Barr's direction is first-rate, on the whole," but he wished that the entire play had been "keyed throughout at a more robust pitch."[89] The reviews of Barr's direction were not particularly heartening, and though he continued to focus on his directing for a short while thereafter, his directing career had reached its zenith, at least on Broadway.

Still, in 1951, Richard Barr picked up a number of projects as a director, including a production of Noël Coward's *Design for Living* that he directed at the Hilltop Theatre in the Round in Baltimore, Maryland, with Marsha Hunt and Morton DaCosta.[90] He directed an out-of-town tryout at the Trenton Civic Theatre of *The Woman with Red Hair*, a melodrama written by radio writer Sam Locke (with Paul Roberts) and featuring John Emery and Frances Reid. It received a mixed notice in *Variety*, which commented that the show had a strong plot but needed "plenty of doctoring" and gave strong reviews to both Emery and Reid.[91] Then in February 1951, Barr put his years with Welles's Mercury Theatre to good use as he crafted a beautifully produced recording of Shakespeare's *The Tempest*, which he directed and narrated, featuring Raymond Massey as Prospero, Margaret Phillips as Miranda, Hurd Hatfield as Ferdinand, Lee Grant as Ariel, and Lionel Stander as Caliban. The recording was a resounding success in a period notable for several major recordings of classics, with Claudia Cassidy of the *Chicago Tribune* calling it "a literate blueprint for study" and observing that the "stage directions and the play are clearly spoken, sometimes brought to life."[92] Another review called it "an interesting production that successfully recreates the poetry and appeal of the Bard's fair tale" with a "warm dramatic quality that lifts the play off the library-shelf category and makes it good theatre, even on disks."[93]

Though the trajectory of Barr's directing career had been a brief and downward spiral and was not as important as his later producing career, it was invaluable. As a producer, he later drew upon his directing training to help cast shows, work with other directors and actors, and develop economical approaches to production and design and nuanced relationships with writers. Barr realized that he wasn't the next Joshua Logan or Elia Kazan, and certainly not the next Orson Welles. Still, he "wanted to continue working in the theatre" and had a deep desire to make a name for himself. In order to do that, however, he realized he had to become his "own boss."[94] Barr continued to direct throughout his career. He worked with favorite actors and directed revivals of plays to which he felt he could bring a special approach. He also directed when he needed the money or had to replace a director for a show he was producing. More important, Barr was about to channel his directorial talents into his career as a producer, with his first Broadway productions.

5

BROADWAY BEGINNINGS

Ethel Waters, Ruth Draper, and Theatrical Collage

Richard Barr faced his career disruption with his usual ebullience and a practical sense of what he could do to improve his luck. It changed quickly. The opportunity to produce came through his friend actress Paula Laurence, who had married the Lunts' stage manager and technical director of many years, Charles Bowden. Laurence "decided" that Barr and Bowden should be producing partners. Neither had made a dent as a director, and it was time to take matters into their own hands.

Four years older than Barr, Bowden was the director of the Westport Country Playhouse for the Theatre Guild. He had an ambition to break free of his role in stage management and had recently produced his first show on Broadway, Hugh Hastings's *Seagulls over Sorrento.* Though the show was a twelve-performance flop, it had received a favorable critical response. Richard was impressed. A friend of Bowden and Barr's suggested that they contact the distinguished blues singer Ethel Waters, who in 1953 was enjoying some recent success as a writer and an actress. Her autobiography, *His Eye Is on the Sparrow,* had come out in 1951, and she had recently starred in Carson McCullers's *Member of the Wedding,* playing Berenice Sadie Brown, a maid, opposite the young and rising Julie Harris. The play was made into a film in 1952, and, at age fifty-seven, Waters hoped to build upon its success to rehabilitate her singing career on Broadway, which had not seen her since *Blue Holiday* in 1945. With Bowden busy as managing director at the Westport Country Playhouse, Richard directed Waters's solo performance, *At Home with Ethel Waters*, which was tried out successfully at the Sea Cliff Long Island Playhouse on 29 June 1951 in a specially designed living room setting. Reginald Beane, who had debuted as an actor and musician with Waters in *Mamba's Daughters* in 1939, accompanied her on the piano.

The production moved to Broadway for a six-week limited run on 23 September 1953 and featured twenty-two songs of Waters's hits, such as "Stormy Weather," "Cabin in the Sky," "Lady Be Good," "Happiness Is Jes' a Thing Called Joe," and "Somethin' Told Me Not to Trust That Man." Waters was clearly nervous about the performance, since it had been twenty-six years since she had made her New York debut.[1] Though critics were pleased with her return to Broadway, the show closed just after its first three weeks.[2] Brooks Atkinson made pointed remarks about Waters's weight and faulted the set, with its "elegant living-room with books, glass doors, and an easy chair," for sucking the warmth and friendliness from Waters's singing, which he described as being performed as "an afterthought." Even Robert Mackintosh's formal evening gown was a drag on Waters's normally natural and heartfelt style, which would usually cause her to "light up like a Christmas tree" and warm a theatre "like a tropical heat wave."[3] Walter Kerr also expressed concerns about the quality of Waters's performance, noting that her voice "still soars up an octave without any sort of warning, but it scrapes a bit when it gets there," and worse, "there are, truth to tell, a few pallid moments in the entertainment."[4] Directorially, Barr faulted himself for taking the "rough and tumble" out of Waters's performance but felt she was past her prime for that type of presentation. He couldn't give her the direction she needed, as he was a hands-off director who set up a suitable ground plan and then kept out of the actors' way until particular moments needed to be cleaned up. Still, of the eight major reviewers in the New York newspapers, six of them gave the production strong notices. Despite the short run, Bowden and Barr were given credit for providing Waters a tasteful venue to perform for New York audiences. The quality of the production did not go unnoticed by another solo performer, Ruth Draper, the famous actress and monologist, who immediately contacted Barr and Bowden to schedule her own return to Broadway.

Bowden had served as manager to Ruth Draper's performances in the late 1940s at the Empire Theatre, and she was actually "annoyed with Chuck" for not contacting her, now that he was producing solo performances.[5] The eccentric monologist had not been on Broadway in nearly seven years and was impatient to take the stage once again. Having performed since the early 1920s, Draper had not actively promoted her work after World War II and believed she had lost her place in the performing community of New York and London, where she was a known entity. By the early 1950s, she was ready for a comeback, and Barr and Bowden were eager to be the producers to resurrect her career.[6] But after the failure of their first venture and without deep-pocketed investors, neither Barr nor Bowden had the $15,000 to produce the show, let alone funds for a strong publicity campaign to promote a forgotten Broadway monologist.[7] Draper agreed to back the show, noting that she did not allow anyone but herself to "put up money" for her appearances.

Her new show opened in January 1954 for a four-week limited run at the Vanderbilt Theatre with strong reviews and praise for her producers, Bowden and Barr. Observing what her program touted as a "farewell New York engagement," Brooks Atkinson of the *New York Times* wrote, "The simple people Miss Draper endows with a certain divinity. . . . She recognizes, not only their fortitude, but the intelligence that keeps them balanced and stable amid the squalor of the world."[8] Draper's $15,000 investment was earned back within three weeks.[9] She continued to invest in her own shows during the next three years, and Barr and Bowden used the funding to send a promotional man in advance of her performances. Her audiences now included a new generation of young admirers, and major stars like Katharine Hepburn, who knew Draper's reputation, brought others to see her.[10] This was an important break for the producers financially, and the experience of producing Draper was particularly gratifying in terms of critical acclaim.

After Draper's show, Richard Barr accepted various directing projects in order to support himself, since the shows he produced hadn't yet created an adequate income stream. Displaying the same esoteric tastes that led him to direct Synge's *Deirdre of the Sorrows*, he directed Christopher Fry's *The Boy with the Cart*, a religious drama, at the Broadway Chapel Players at the Broadway Tabernacle Church. It featured Bill Penn as Cuthman, the boy with the cart, and a positive review in the *New York Times* complimented Barr's "intelligent" direction and the "professional" acting of the group of amateurs putting on the show.[11] The play proved to be immensely popular with parishioners and quickly sold out, despite the fact that it was staged in a very minimal production with no use of props.[12] Barr subsequently directed Ethel Waters as Hagar in *Mamba's Daughters* at the Salt Creek Summer Theatre under the producing aegis of Marshall Migatz. The production received fairly strong reviews, with Sydney Harris of the *Chicago Daily News* calling it "sometimes moving and sometimes merely maudlin," with Waters in the fierce yet tender role of Hagar that she had created on Broadway fifteen years earlier.[13]

Trying to find their next project, Barr and Bowden held a backers' audition in July 1954 for a new comedy, *Angelica*, with Paula Laurence and Neil Laurence, which was featured on the cover of the 18 July 1954 *New York Herald Tribune*. Bowden then directed a new production at the Bucks County Playhouse of *The Shoemaker's Children* by Phoebe and Henry Ephron, who were screenwriters with Broadway ambitions (and the parents of Nora Ephron, later a major screenwriter in her own right). Bowden and Barr hoped to bring the show to Broadway but never did.[14] Oddly enough, they also made plans, which never materialized, for setting up a "musical tent" at the Laurel Park Racecourse in Maryland, midway between Washington and Baltimore, with a twelve-week season after the last race of the spring.[15]

In the meantime, audiences refused to accept Ruth Draper's farewell, insisting that she continue to perform. To satisfy her fans, and to help her nephew Paul Draper's career, she agreed to appear with Paul, a dancer who had been blacklisted in Hollywood, in December 1954. Barr and Bowden agreed to produce Ruth again, this time with her nephew. It was a fortuitous pairing. Paul Draper's considerable and unconventional talents in both tap dancing and ballet were a perfect prelude to Ruth's monologues. He performed with Larry Adler, a harmonica virtuoso (who had also been blacklisted), doing interpretive tap dances to the music of Bach, Handel, and Debussy in the first act of the evening and then to Youmans, Lecuona, and Porter in the second act. Paul's "very funny dances" received special mention in the *New York Times* review, including "A Sharp Character," "In a Dance Hall," and "Satire on a Political Speech." While all of Ruth Draper's monologues garnered strong praise from the reviewer, "Opening a Bazaar" showed off her skills as a monologist at her "versatile best." The evening was a tremendous success and played the entirety of its three-week run.[16]

Richard Barr felt that Ruth Draper's work should be recorded for posterity, and with his recording background with the Mercury Theatre and *The Tempest*, he had the skills to make this historic event happen. Draper's work until that time had rarely been recorded; she had even destroyed earlier recordings by Decca because of their poor quality.[17] She relented when Barr and Bowden promised to hire Richard Mohr, Arturo Toscanini's record producer, to produce her recordings. Arthur Rubenstein, a good friend of Draper's, assisted them in their efforts, and Toscanini himself persuaded Draper, now approaching her seventies, to make the recordings lest her material be lost forever.[18] RCA "jumped" at the opportunity, and between 1954 and 1955, she scheduled a total of nine recording sessions, making daily visits to the RCA studios on West Twenty-Fourth Street. Barr and Bowden, as well as Ruth's former stage manager Barnet Owens, were present at each.[19]

Draper recorded every monologue she had ever performed, including several that she had decided never to play onstage. These were routines performed entirely in a fake language of her own creation. No matter what the language, she made her routines "hilarious, often intelligible, and occasionally moving."[20] Though she made other recordings toward the end of her life, none were as effective as these earlier ones, carefully engineered by RCA.[21]

Barr and Bowden then produced what turned out to be Draper's final performances of her career, at the Playhouse Theatre opening on 25 December 1956. Though scheduled for a four-week run, she closed after only four performances on Saturday, 29 December 1956, and passed away in her sleep the following day.[22] Barr discovered that because of Draper's "thoroughness and good business sense," the Playhouse Theatre was fully paid for its scheduled run from her estate. He was particularly grateful to have had the opportunity to help Draper perform in the context and manner and at the moment she needed to perform. The ability to give theatrical artists the freedom to succeed or fail was key to Barr's producing style and was particularly important when he began his work with Edward Albee.[23]

After the passing of Ruth Draper, Barr and Bowden were on to new challenges, having decided that "two one-woman shows do not Broadway producers make." They pulled together an evening of short pieces of opera, drama, and dance, replicating their recent success that had included the combination of Draper's monologues and her nephew's dancing. They titled it *All in One*, attempting on Broadway the kind of short works Barr produced much later off-Broadway. Starting with the dramatic piece, Barr and Bowden quickly arranged to fly to New Orleans, where Maureen Stapleton was performing in a one-act play, Tennessee Williams's *27 Wagons Full of Cotton*, at Tulane University. Williams himself had directed the production, changing the set to incorporate a swing, on which the entire play took place.[24] After "corralling" Williams and Stapleton on a bed in a New Orleans hotel, the two young producers convinced Williams to involve his business partner and lover, Frank Merlo, who thought their idea of an evening of opera, dance, and theatre "theatre magic."[25] After procuring the rights to the play, they secured the talents of director Vincent J. Donehue and cast the show with Myron McCormick as Jake and Felice Orlandi as Silva, to play opposite a young Maureen Stapleton as Flora. A favorite of Williams's, Stapleton would later star in a number of his plays.

The second act of the evening was to be *Trouble in Tahiti*, an opera by a rising young talent, Leonard Bernstein. At that time the assistant conductor of the New York Philharmonic, Bernstein had already enjoyed considerable success with his musicals *On the Town* and *Wonderful Town* on Broadway.

To be able to bring Bernstein's troubling but musically fascinating *Trouble in Tahiti* to Broadway was a triumph. The one-act opera that had premiered at Brandeis University in June 1952 was a dark exploration of a troubled young couple, Sam and Dinah, that satirized their typical 1950s marriage, complete with a kitschy yet hip Andrews Sisters–type chorus.[26] Bernstein's libretto explored themes not unlike those of Albee's *The American Dream*, which Barr was to produce six years later. The characters Sam and Dinah were based on Bernstein's parents. Bernstein gave Barr permission to present the opera, with David Brooke staging the production. *All in One* began to take shape. Bernstein's opera started the evening. Once again, Barr and Bowden were to rely upon the remarkable talents of Paul Draper performing his tap dances as the midway note of the show. And the finale was the remarkable young Maureen Stapleton in Tennessee Williams's *27 Wagons Full of Cotton*. Bowden and Barr selected Eldon Elder as the set and lighting designer for the evening.

John Chapman of the *Daily News* acclaimed *All in One* to be a "stimulating little evening of music, drama, [and] dance," and both Walter Kerr and Brooks Atkinson offered strong if not glowing reviews of the evening as well.[27] Atkinson began his review on a grateful note—"Thanks for an evening of superb theatre art"—and while Kerr was somewhat more circumspect, he was supportive: "These diversified entertainments—handsomely and inexpensively backed up by some Eldon Elder set-pieces—do not necessarily constitute a breathtaking evening. But 'All in One' is consistently interesting and it provides a comfortable home for some wandering miniatures."[28] Richard Watts at the *New York Post*, who remained one of Barr's strongest supporters throughout his Albee years, noted, "You wouldn't be far wrong if you called 'All in One' a crazy, mixed-up evening in the theater," considering it "oddly assorted."[29] He did, however, find much to commend in Maureen Stapleton's performance in Williams's *27 Wagons Full of Cotton*, calling her portrayal of Flora, the "blowzy, half-idiotic child-woman," as "astonishingly brilliant" and "strangely touching" despite the fact that he found the play to be "rather studiously distasteful."[30]

Though both Kerr and Atkinson found *Trouble in Tahiti* a sober, intelligent work, they struggled with it stylistically. Both were taken with Alice Ghostley's performance in the role of Dinah. Atkinson called Ghostley "tender, rueful, pensive and lovely," while Kerr was just as enchanted, stating that she "flashes from one mood to another with both the grace and force of lightning."[31] But while reviews were strong, audiences didn't materialize, and Barr theorized that Atkinson's pronouncement of the evening as being "art" was box office death and that the one-act pieces caused audiences to "stay away." Though their collection of "miniatures" was not a commercial success, Barr and Bowden attempted to pull together a second evening of one-acts, including a performance of Shaw's *Man of Destiny* with Julie Harris and Marlon Brando to be directed by Lynn Fontanne; a one-act version of *Bus Stop* that William Inge had written expressly to be performed by Ina Claire; and the 1933 one-act opera by Kurt Weill, *The Seven Deadly Sins*, written for and starring Lotte Lenya.[32] Though this project fell through and *All in One* closed after only forty-seven performances, Barr's ability to make short plays as important and satisfying as longer works was key to how he successfully launched the career of Edward Albee and many other challenging playwrights. *All in One* was an important step in that formula.

Barr's next project with Bowden involved a reconnection with Nancy Walker, who approached the two producers the morning after *All in One* closed with a notion that she had for a production of Noël Coward's *Fallen Angels*. It was an idea that Barr himself had planted in her mind back in Marblehead, Massachusetts, in 1950. The diminutive star was a regular on television and had been involved with a number of Broadway hits, including original productions of Bernstein's *On the Town*, Jerome Lawrence and Robert E. Lee's *Look, Ma, I'm Dancin'!*, and Richard Rodgers and Lorenz Hart's *Pal Joey*. She had just finished a star turn in the Phoenix Theatre's *Phoenix 55*, a revue and series of sketches by Ira Wallach. The show was amiably received and had a strong run, and as Lewis Funke of the *New York Times* noted, Walker was "a low comedienne of the highest grade."[33] Still, Walker wanted to be considered an *actress* of the highest grade, and she appealed to Barr and Bowden to give her the vehicle to accommodate her desire. But they were uncertain if Noël Coward would give them rights to an Americanized *Fallen Angels*, retooled to show off Walker's comedic talents. Though Bowden had worked closely with Coward as stage manager for the Lunts, neither he nor Barr were sure the playwright would agree. Using their meager funds, Bowden immediately booked a flight for Jamaica, where Coward kept a home. While he was away, Barr made inquiries about a director, checking in with Tallulah Bankhead to see if she would consider directing, as Bankhead had originated the role of Julia Sterroll in *Fallen Angels*, but she passed on the project. Coward tentatively gave Bowden and Barr the rights to produce, but with some stipulations: that Chuck Bowden would direct it himself and that Coward would reserve the right to close it immediately if, when he attended the production after the opening, he was not pleased with what he saw. The producers leaped at this opportunity.

Neither of them had the capital to produce the show, however, and so they drew in a new partner, H. Ridgely Bullock Jr., a wealthy owner of a small successful summer playhouse, the Camden Hills Theatre in Maine.[34] Though Bullock was just beginning a three-year stint as a captain in the air force, he longed to stay in the theatrical business and be a Broadway producer. For his investment, Barr and Bowden gave him a full partnership, adding his name to their moniker, even though he was stationed in Japan. They remained Bowden, Barr, and Bullock throughout the latter's military service.[35]

Fallen Angels, an early Coward piece, is about the drunken revelry of two bored housewives. They discover they've had a premarital affair with the same young Frenchman, who just happens to be coming to town. They invite him to their home for a dalliance now that they are respectable married women and get rip-roaring drunk in the process. The second act is a wildly improvised drunk scene, and disaster ensues in the third act when the husbands return. Bowden and his wife adapted the play for American audiences, adding the character of Jasmine Spears, the maid, who was played by Alice Pearce. The setting was moved to Manhattan, the husbands were off to Westport to play golf, and the names were Americanized. Nancy Walker played Julia Starbuck with her golf-playing spouse played by William Windom. The Banburys became Jane and William Danbury, with Maurice Duclos, the long-lost French lover, played by Efrem Zimbalist Jr. Rehearsals began, but not without some flare-ups of confusion between Bowden and the fiery comic Walker. Barr stepped in as codirector and worked with Walker on one side of the stage, while Bowden directed the rest of the cast on the other. Despite the chaos, the directors and actors were of one mind regarding the result. The production was once again designed by Eldon Elder, who, according to critic Walter Kerr, created a set that was "faintly period" with a "blue foyer and a chandelier to remind you of a bygone and unlamented décor." Kerr pronounced it "fine."[36]

Thus, the two directors translated high British comedy into low vaudevillian farce in order to feature the comic ingenuity of Nancy Walker. The audiences greeted the show with gales of laughter. Brooks Atkinson wrote, "Nancy Walker is the funniest woman in the theatre." He pointed out Walker's ability to send up Coward's sophisticated confections of characterization: "Miss Walker's general lack of interest in everything that is clever and sophisticated is uproarious."[37] Walter Kerr noted that Walker "has discovered for herself how to make every curl of her lip, every lift of her eyebrow, every tipsy sashay into hostile space a triumph of laughter. . . . It should go into the record: Nancy Walker is now a great performer."[38] The audiences "screamed with laughter and approval" on opening night, but the second test of the production was about to occur, the visit from the author. Noël Coward arrived, as he agreed, on the second night of the run, bringing

Marlene Dietrich with him. Barr and Bowden held the cast onstage after the final curtain and waited for Coward to appear, praying for his approval. Coward's comments were terse, but he was pleased: "Ladies and Gentlemen, you are all geniuses, of course. I wrote this comedy thirty-two years ago. Tonight I recognized only seven minutes of it and I wasn't upset. So you really must all be geniuses!"[39] The triumph for the young producers was complete, and while not a hit, the show ran for a respectable 239 performances and closed on 11 August 1956. Bowden, Barr, and Bullock had established their producing credentials.

Their next offering, an Americanized French farce, *Hotel Paradiso*, had been translated from the original 1894 play, Georges Feydeau's *L'Hôtel du libre échange*, by British director Peter Glenville. For the opportunity to produce a French farce (ostensibly, a classical work) and move beyond comedy star vehicles, they hired Glenville to direct the production. This seemed an obvious choice; Glenville was eager to direct *Hotel Paradiso* on Broadway. He had adapted and directed it in London, starring Alec Guinness, and had just won a Tony Award for his direction of Terence Rattigan's *Separate Tables*. While Guinness was unavailable, Glenville desperately wanted to work with the vaudevillian comedian Bert Lahr. Lahr was himself interested in pursuing more classical work, having just completed his career-changing performance in *Waiting for Godot*.[40] Glenville was also determined to use actress Angela Lansbury, who had never worked onstage before and who wanted to escape film, which had pigeonholed her in older, motherly, and eccentric roles. She had just finished a film with Danny Kaye, *The Court Jester*, which had given her a rare opportunity to display her comedic skills, working with a company of "ace farceurs."[41] Lansbury was convinced by Glenville to make the trip to New York from California to audition. They worked together for nearly a month in order for him to ascertain that she was ready for Broadway. Rehearsals began shortly thereafter.[42] Lansbury noted that if she had not made the jump to theatre, her career as an actress would have "fizzled out."[43]

Needing to adapt his talents as a vaudevillian comedian to farce, Lahr struggled with Glenville, who wanted to tone down his comic "bits" as Monsieur Boniface.[44] Lansbury was utterly charmed by Lahr, who, she claimed, taught her everything she knew about comedy.[45] Lahr took Glenville's direction with a certain amount of resistance, but he always made it work "brilliantly." The actor graciously agreed to take a salary cut so that the show could run longer, playing for weeks at "a token salary."[46] The cast included James Coco, making his Broadway debut as "Tabu, a Professor," and originally starred Arthur Treacher as "Cot, an Architect." Unfortunately, Barr had the unenviable task of firing Treacher, since he was not as comically adaptable as Lahr. After a Washington, D.C., tryout in March 1957 at the National Theatre, it opened in New York on 11 April 1957 to strong reviews.

Walter Kerr pronounced it a "papier-mâché farce" and a comic "jungle gym" and extolled his readers to "take a chance" on the show, lavishing particularly strong praise on Bert Lahr. All the reviewers noted the moment in the play when an eager bellhop tries to open up a peephole, drilling through a wall into Lahr's behind. Kerr described Lahr's rapid montage of facial expressions: "Every shade of terror, mortification, ecstasy, and refined paralysis is exhaustively limned on the grave Lahr puss. Rembrandt never did a better job."[47] Lansbury also received strong reviews, with Tom Donnelly of the New York World-Telegram lauding her efforts: "Miss Lansbury contorts her body into a superb approximation of the letter 'S,' and moves this unlikely silhouette across the stage with marvelous dexterity . . . latching onto nefarious schemes with such electric vehemence that one can fairly hear her brain click."[48] Atkinson was the most reserved in his response, noting there was "not so much life as there may have been originally" in Hotel Paradiso but that "this rumpus is riotous, and the execution by the actor is bold, reckless and funny. Mr. Lahr is in very rare form."[49]

New York audiences did not race to see the farce, Barr surmised, because it *was* farce. Despite "impeccable" direction by Glenville and a very strong response from the press (including a *Life* magazine cover featuring Lahr), the show ultimately fizzled, closing before the summer's end on 13 July 1957 after only 108 performances.[50] Lahr himself was bitter about the audience response: "Farce has nothing to say, no special significance. . . . They've tried other farces since *Paradiso*; none of them have succeeded."[51] Bowden and Barr received strong commendations by the critics, but to survive as a producing team, they had to find a vehicle that actually produced a profit, and this they hoped to do with a bus-and-truck tour of a tried-and-true Broadway hit—*Auntie Mame.*

Barr and Bowden created three road companies for *Auntie Mame*, which turned out to be the last show produced by this team. The two believed road shows could be lucrative, since the major costs of the original Broadway production had already been paid, leaving the profits for the road producers to reap. But in 1954, there were very few shows on the road, so Barr and Bowden had joined a group of eleven producers to help rebuild the road industry. In the process, the group created the Producers League in February 1954 to address the situation. At least six touring attractions in 1955 were created to supplement productions touring under the aegis of the American Theater Society–Theatre Guild. Richard Barr served as secretary of the organization, and the goal was to sponsor "simple productions headed by stars."[52] Testing the viability of this plan was his and Bowden's three touring productions of *Auntie Mame*.

Auntie Mame was a runaway best-selling 1955 novel by Patrick Dennis, adapted by Jerome Lawrence and Robert E. Lee into a hit stage play and produced on Broadway in October 1956, starring Rosalind Russell in the title role. With other producers lining up to acquire rights, the road tour was a coup for Barr, Bowden, and Bullock. Most producers thought no one but Russell could play Mame, though many actresses were already begging to try the part on the road.[53] Barr and Bowden first had to acquire the rights to the show from its original producers, Robert Fryer and Lawrence Carr. In doing so, they gave up too large a percentage of the gross. This error was the beginning of a roller coaster of spiraling costs that doomed the production. Fryer and Carr demanded that the production had to bring in "big actresses," meaning stars. Barr was well suited to do this. He had directed Constance Bennett in a stock production of *Skylark* in Miami and felt that she was right for the role, though Bowden had reservations.[54] He then sought Sylvia Sidney for the second tour and, after a struggle, managed to secure her as well, though Barr thought she behaved unprofessionally during the tour itself. Lawrence was impressed with Sidney's performance, calling it one of the finest in terms of "sheer acting ability." Each of the performers who played Mame were on the phone constantly with the producers, with Constance Bennett calling at 2 A.M., Sylvia Sidney checking in at 4 A.M., and Shirl Conway, heading up the third company, mercifully calling in at 9 A.M.[55]

Despite the headaches, the productions received strong notices with Constance Bennett getting some rave reviews, including those from Josef Mossman of the *Detroit News*, who called the production "wild and wonderful." Harlow R. Hoyt of the *Cleveland Plain Dealer* noted that *Auntie Mame* fit Bennett well, and *Detroit Free Press* theatre critic J. Dorsey Callagan said the production "sparkled" and was performed at a "rolling drum fire of laughter."[56] The *Mame* road companies created great interest because of the fierce competition among the stars. However, the critical acclaim and obvious audience approval were not generating enough cash to support the venture, and eventually all three road companies closed at a loss. In Barr's opinion, they were "over-produced, underpriced on the road, and weighed down with royalties to the authors, stars, director and original producers." He and Bowden drew but a meager weekly salary. The failure of the *Auntie Mame* road companies, in Barr's opinion, resulted from their own inexperience, "desultory booking arrangements," and the technically demanding and difficult shows.[57]

One of the last productions that Barr was involved in with this partnership was *Season of Choice*, a southern melodrama in the manner of Tennessee Williams, written by Nathaniel Banks, a recent graduate of Yale. The play was presented in the Barbizon-Plaza Theatre on Central Park South and inspired Barr's concept of producing new work off-Broadway. The melodrama focused on the misadventures of Jason Redwine, a young man of the moneyed class who falls in love with his cousin Cassandra, but because of an inadvertent coupling, he is forced to marry the coarse, lower-class Dolly Lumpkin. The play featured Douglass Watson, a Broadway star; Betsy von Furstenberg, a rising young talent; and a young Keir Dullea as Jimmie Redwine. Brooks Atkinson's lackluster review did praise the performances of Watson and Colin Willcox as the high-spirited daughter, Harriet, and had kind words for the set design by Will Steven Armstrong. Though directed by Charles Bowden, Barr was involved with the casting. He was to work later with Keir Dullea (best known for his role as astronaut David Bowman in the 1968 film *2001: A Space Odyssey*) in *P.S. Your Cat Is Dead.*

The relationship between Bowden and Barr was deteriorating rapidly. Bowden and his wife, Paula Laurence, were using astrology for producing decisions. Ridgely Bullock had returned to the partnership after serving his time in the military and was eager to play a more active role. One evening in 1959, as Barr recalls, he "let it go" at both Bowden and Laurence while they were "alone at Jean Dalrymple's country house." Barr expressed his frustration at running a producing operation by committee and making decisions that would "depend on the stars—the *real* ones, not the earthly ones." Bowden then requested that they dissolve the partnership the next day at Barr's Eleventh Street attic apartment, and this the partners did, "quickly, quietly, and with a minimum of confusion." Barr considered his decision to produce independently "the best decision of my life." He was finally able to "really" begin his professional career in the theatre. And with the dissolution of the partnership, Barr did what he had done in the past when a chapter of his life had come to its close: he went on a European trip and saw the theatre there that he wanted to produce in America.[58]

6

THE ZOO STORY

Discovering Edward Albee

In 1959, after his trip to Europe, a deeply dissatisfied Richard Barr left his "pleasant" though undistinguished producing partnership with Charles Bowden without having achieved his goal: "to try and bring the theater up to the point in which the other arts had arrived in this country. . . . It seemed to me it was time to do something about the theater."[1] Broadway had overlooked major changes happening in Europe, all but ignoring the new absurdist movement that had taken hold there. Writers such as Samuel Beckett, Harold Pinter, Eugène Ionesco, Jean Genet, and Fernando Arrabal had transformed the European stage with theatrical experiments and by the early 1960s were rapidly approaching the acme of their writing careers. The excitement around their work was palpable, and New York producers were beginning to bring their plays to the United States.

Richard Barr wanted to be the first to produce this new theatre off-Broadway, where he believed a self-imposed poverty of production would allow it to succeed. He was disgusted with producing star vehicles that had little to do with art and everything to do with egos and profitability. This, combined with a lingering desire to continue directing, led Barr to consider four ways to become a "name" director like Orson Welles or Guthrie McClintic: (1) conceive of a production and raise the money himself; (2) use a summer stock tryout; (3) connect with a star through summer theatre who possessed rights to a strong vehicle; or (4) form his own company with a long-term plan. He chose the last option, which was the most precarious but also the most prestigious, and became an independent producer.[2]

Tired of appeasing the vanity of star actors and directors, Barr decided to shift his producing focus to the playwright. This was precipitated by his encounters with playwright William Inge, whom Barr knew socially and who would "drop by the house occasionally." On one particular evening, Inge launched into a tirade about his wildly successful Broadway play *Picnic*, which had been savaged by director Joshua Logan's demands.[3] In the original version, there was no fairy-tale ending. Madge doesn't leave to find her true love and no longer has the security of Alan's love to take her through life. It was an ending that Barr found "frightening, serious and sad," but it had been diluted to make the play "more palatable" to commercial Broadway audiences. Inge was tortured by this revision and told Barr, "I have just won the Pulitzer Prize; I have a major hit on Broadway; I am going to be very rich; and I am miserably unhappy."[4]

Disturbed by Inge's revelation and by the crass commercialism that had driven the decision, Richard vowed to change the system. Inge's experience was not new to him. He knew that playwrights were often forcibly locked into hotel rooms during out-of-town tryouts in order to change scripts to appease the tastes of producers, directors, stars, or "the wife of the biggest investor."[5] If this kind of manipulation was brought to bear on a major playwright, what chance did a lesser-known writer have to bring his or her own play intact to Broadway audiences? This deterioration of artistic values was why Richard had left Bowden, Barr, and Bullock: "That's when I got fed up with it all and went Off Broadway. . . . I wanted to do that which was and is not possible to do on Broadway. Give authority to the playwright. Turn the theatre back to the playwright."[6] His "Diaghilev complex was given a twinge," and his notion of the producer as a "catalytic agent" was clarified. Richard knew it was his job to create an off-Broadway theatre with the playwrights' work as its focus, so he "began to explore the possibilities of doing something about it."[7] He sought a family of theatre artists, including directors, designers, managers, and publicists, to serve the interests of the play and the playwright. Barr wanted artists who were willing to "sublimate their own egos to the artistic purpose at hand."[8]

By 1959, off-Broadway had already enjoyed several successes, including the defining 1952 production of Tennessee Williams's *Summer and Smoke* featuring Geraldine Page. Brooks Atkinson's transcendent review of that production essentially created the off-Broadway phenomenon.[9] In addition, there was the success of Julian Beck and Judith Malina's Living Theatre, an off-Broadway poets' theatre that had grown into a Greenwich Village arts institution. In particular, it was their production of Jack Gelber's *The Connection*, which opened in 1959, that galvanized the Greenwich Village theatre community into a new movement.[10] And while initially disparaged by the critics, *The Connection* quickly fused jazz, poetry, and theatre into a single artistic arena. Although the success of *The Connection* was giving off-Broadway new life and even stimulated the creation of the off-off-Broadway theatre, the off-Broadway theatre of the late 1950s was struggling with the same lowbrow tastes, high budgets, and reliance on frothy material that Broadway itself was.[11] The economic and aesthetic paralysis of off-Broadway was brought on by commercial success. It became glutted with weak, though profitable, productions.[12] Worse, new plays were the most expensive and therefore the least logical to produce.[13] Ironically, Barr was facing the same kinds of challenges off-Broadway that he had experienced on Broadway—but change was in the air.[14] He saw the opportunity to use his unique talents to reinvigorate off-Broadway, using the off-off-Broadway theatre as a creative impetus.

But Barr was hard-pressed to find a playwright and a play exciting enough to spark New York audiences and to create the theatre he envisioned. In 1959, he was reading through a stack of scripts that had been given to him by a talented young literary agent, Edward Parone, a frequent guest to his Eleventh Street Greenwich Village "attic," the townhouse apartment he shared with Oliver Thorndike.[15] Parone mentioned to Barr that he had a script currently being produced in Berlin at the Schiller Theater that could be an off-Broadway possibility. Richard read it right away. At first, he treated it as he had countless other first efforts by journeyman playwrights, with "the usual cynicism."[16] But this time, his experience was different. After the third page, he "guessed he was on to something"; by the tenth page, he "hoped he was on to something"; and finally, after reading the entire play, he "knew he was on to something."[17] Richard contacted Parone and immediately purchased the rights to the play for a mere $125.[18]

The play was Edward Albee's *The Zoo Story*, and it had been offered to several other producers who had turned it down, including Clinton Wilder (who later became Barr's partner) and David Merrick.[19] *The Zoo Story* had been performed at the Actors Studio, where it had been subject to the studio's usual savage criticism. But it had also received the embrace of studio member Norman Mailer, who announced it as "the best fucking one-act play" he had ever seen.[20] But none of the Actors Studio members had any idea what to do with a one-act script and had no plays with which to pair it; one-acts were so rarely produced. Having produced one-act variety evenings on Broadway, Richard felt *The Zoo Story* presented the perfect opportunity for an off-Broadway production. But before he could produce the play, Barr had to finalize all arrangements with Albee when he returned from Germany.[21] In Germany, the Schiller Theater had produced *The Zoo Story* with Samuel Beckett's *Krapp's Last Tape*, and Barr decided to do the same. This began the absurdist connection that Barr exploited as an aesthetic marketing tool to help audiences connect to Albee's plays.

Having worked with Orson Welles and possessing a keen appreciation for American theatre history, Barr was fascinated by Albee's experimental style. He associated Albee's *The Zoo Story* with Eugene O'Neill's early one-act seafaring plays. He believed Albee's play was a mix of traditional formal dramatic structure with a radical "metaphysical" subject matter. *The Zoo Story* was the "progenitor" of a new form Barr called "abstract realism." While not understanding "the full implications of the play" or "its mysteriously hidden humor" in his first readings of the script, Barr could tell the play was of "outstanding quality." It was written by a new American writer who had "great potential."[22]

But he was immediately faced with roadblocks in presenting *The Zoo Story* with *Krapp's Last Tape*. The producing director of the Cherry Lane Theatre, Noel Behn, owned the rights to *Krapp's Last Tape*. Behn was a talented writer and producer in his own right who later appeared in several Woody Allen films and worked as a creative consultant on the NBC television series *Homicide: Life on the Street*. But he was not interested in Albee's work and refused to sell the rights to Beckett's play to Barr.[23] Behn recommended Barnet Rosset, the editor of Grove Press, for other Beckett plays to produce. Barr contacted Rosset, who had enormous influence with other European absurdists and radical American writers such as Henry Miller. But after reading these authors' plays, Barr thought that none of them were as "interesting or prestigious" as the Beckett play. Beckett had already achieved some notoriety with his *Waiting for Godot*, successfully produced on Broadway in 1956, and it "seemed wiser" for Barr to connect a "new American writer with the older European."[24]

Beckett also insisted that only Alan Schneider could direct his work. And though Barr knew and liked Schneider's directing, Schneider was a rising young star much in demand. He used the Arena Stage in Washington, D.C., as his base but also directed Broadway, off-Broadway, regional, and academic productions. While waiting to resolve these issues, Parone let Barr know in September 1959 that Albee was ready to meet with him. Albee, for his part, had "instantly joined the William Morris Agency, and the Dramatists Guild at the same time," since he knew he had to protect himself.[25] The meeting took place over "cocktails" in Barr's attic apartment. Neither Albee nor

Barr knew what to expect from each other. The producer's first impression of Albee was of "a remarkably shy young man with extraordinarily expressive eyes." Though their conversation was formal, he was given hope by the occasional "glimpse of humor" in Albee's eyes. Richard Barr explained his yet-untested concept of featuring new playwrights off-Broadway, which "naturally appealed" to Albee.[26]

The playwright, having never met a producer before, found Barr to be "an intelligent human being"—a rarity in Albee's opinion. He had no other professional theatrical experience other than the German production of his play, but he was intrigued by Barr's "bizarre theory that playwrights were the most important people in the theatre." Albee was also impressed by the fact that Barr seemed to be listening to him.[27] Richard suggested that he wanted to pair Albee's work with Beckett's *Krapp's Last Tape*, as had been done at the Schiller Theater, and Albee was quite pleased with this possibility. Albee then suggested that Barr consider Milton Katselas as a director for the piece. He had met Katselas through Sanford Friedman, a novelist friend. Katselas was a young Greek-American director who was a protégé of Elia Kazan's and had studied with Lee Strasberg.[28] While he had no objections to Katselas, Richard made it clear to Albee that he was struggling on the project in three areas: raising the money for the production, acquiring the rights to produce *Krapp's Last Tape*, and securing Alan Schneider, per Beckett's desire. Albee understood and was supportive—though Katselas would prove to be a problem later. Barr realized that Albee was very capable of partnering in decisions about his own plays regardless of his lack of professional theatre experience.

In these early days of their relationship, Albee felt that Barr "didn't let me make very serious mistakes; he let me have the illusion of making my own mistakes and maybe making my own decisions."[29] Initially, Richard was a teacher and a mentor to Albee, making most of the decisions and explaining them to Albee as he made them. Later there was more equality to the partnership, as Albee felt surer of himself in the theatre and as he learned to direct his own plays (with Barr's encouragement). Eventually, the dynamics of the Albee-Barr partnership reversed over the years, with Albee taking on a more parental role.[30] Regardless of this changing dynamic, there was a deep mutual affection and respect between them, and their first meeting heralded a major new partnership that was particularly fruitful for the art of playwriting.

Barr's production of *The Zoo Story* and *Krapp's Last Tape* was facing a near total absence of funding. Richard attempted to "take a long shot" by writing a letter to David Merrick on 20 November 1959. Barr suggested to

Merrick that a new playwright's work might not merit a "$100,000 production" but perhaps a $10,000 production, "providing it is produced professionally with economic sense." In the letter, Richard also crystallized for Merrick, in writing, his signature producing style, experimenting with new work within the confines of a tight budget. He noted that a small investment in a gifted playwright off-Broadway might later result in "an Inge or a Williams and a money maker." Barr appealed to Merrick's shared distrust of the not-for-profit world, slamming the Ford Foundation for funding "second rate community theatres." Instead, he put forward an off-Broadway plan, which would utilize a stable of "painters, composers, and playwrights." Oddly enough, Barr stated that his ultimate goal was to "seriously influence, if not run, Lincoln Center." He was obsessed with gaining a toehold in the new Lincoln Center project and wanted to produce new plays in its Forum Theatre (later the Mitzi E. Newhouse Theater).[31] Despite Barr's grand plans, Merrick passed on the Albee and Beckett project. Barr had to find another "deep pocket" to realize his dreams of an off-Broadway playwrights theatre.

Through his former roommate Oliver Thorndike (who had passed away shortly after inviting Barr to share his apartment), Barr became close with his Greenwich Village neighbors Evelyn ("Evie") Lilly Lutz and her husband, Herbert Barr ("Whitey") Lutz. Evie was an heiress to the Lilly pharmaceutical fortune and was interested in ceramics. Whitey was something of a firebrand, buying stakes in the *Village Voice*, and had an interest in sculpture and painting.[32] He had penned several columns in the *Voice* criticizing Broadway and championing avant-garde theatre, including an article on the Living Theatre and *The Connection*.[33] Richard Barr wrote him a letter, complimenting his articles and agreeing that Broadway was in need of an invigorating burst. He explained that though he was keeping a foot in Broadway production, he didn't "wish to cater to the system with my blood and guts" any longer. Though he made it clear he owned the rights and was looking to fund *The Zoo Story*, he didn't ask for money but instead requested a *Voice* editorial article supporting his new venture. Referring to his recent European trip, Barr explained that "we're far behind them in trying new things" and that "there's a whole crop of new American writers waiting to be heard and I feel it's about time to do something about it." He ended the letter with both an embrace and criticism of the Living Theatre: "We need a daring theatre, though not so far out and quite so internal."[34] Richard received an immediate telephone call from Lutz, asking to be invited for cocktails at Barr's "attic." Here, he made the young producer an offer of $9,000 to help him mount the play. Barr was flabbergasted. Still, his instincts told him that the project was coming together too easily; something had to go wrong, and it did. He immediately went back to Noel Behn at the Cherry Lane to secure the space for the plays and, perhaps, rights to the Beckett play only to discover from Behn that Barney Rosset had sold the rights to *Krapp's Last Tape* to a neophyte producer, Harry Joe Brown Jr.

Brown was the son of film director/producer Harry Joe Brown, who had produced the Hollywood films *Knickerbocker Holiday* and *Billion Dollar Scandal*. Barr was forced to negotiate a deal with Brown to pull the two plays together. Brown insisted upon raising half the funds himself and holding half the control of the show. Barr was aggravated that though "the entire venture" was his, he had to share control and teach the ropes to a newcomer. Still, the plays were "perfectly matched," so Richard decided to "swallow his ego" and make the deal. Brown struggled to raise his $4,500 share, nearly causing the project to fail. Despite this, Barr gave Lutz back $4,500 as a good-faith gesture and patiently waited for Brown to raise money. Finally, "after a few more false promises," Brown raised his share, and the production was full speed ahead.[35]

The selection of a production staff for *The Zoo Story* and *Krapp's Last Tape* was crucial since the staff had to agree to Barr's idea of playwright as star. The staff would become the backbone of the Albee-Barr operation for nearly twenty years. Barr decided to call his operation Theater 1960, though it was still 1959. This was his way of "pushing the year ahead" to seem more avant-garde.[36] He continued this "numerical legerdemain," changing his theatre's name on 30 June of every year, for the next fourteen years until Barr and his partners, Wilder and Albee, dropped the idea "after years of annoying and confusing critics and patrons alike."[37] The new operation included Lutz's ambitious plans to establish a "drama school" to teach the "burgeoning talent" and to market productions to college audiences.[38] Also included were plans to produce other plays, including Ionesco's *The Killer* (with electronic music score by "Happenings" creator Allan Kaprow), Megan Terry's *Hothouse*, and *The Sudden Death of Anne Cinquefoil*, written by Katharine Hepburn's brother Richard. Barr readied his team of theatre artists with his declaration that "when Shakespeare walks in, I want to be ready!" He issued a manifesto through a *Voice of America* radio broadcast stating that he would "bring the theatre art up to the level of the other creative arts in this country," feeling that American theatre was nearly twenty-five years behind the times.[39]

Richard Barr was committed to changing the standard Broadway paradigm that with each show, you bring in a new cast, a new set of designers, a new director, and a new set of staff and management. Instead of these "ephemeral relationships," he wanted an organization that was "conducive to a continuity of effort."[40] This gave him the ability to produce new experimental work efficiently and quickly and to close it equally fast if it didn't work. He wanted to avoid the constant skirmishing that took place when theatre artists met for the first time. He selected a design team he thought would be able to work within the tight economics of off-Broadway, including Fred Voelpel, a young designer he knew from the John Drew Theater. Voelpel couldn't commit to the project but suggested another young designer, William Ritman, that he felt was right for the opportunity.

Ritman designed the performance space itself, and the individual plays worked within that unit setting. Ritman's concept for *The Zoo Story* and *Krapp's Last Tape* fit well within Barr's own design experiments, Barr having redesigned theatres himself with unit sets to accommodate several shows. Ritman was key to the Albee-Barr-Wilder team, and he designed every set for Albee's plays until his untimely death in 1984.

Barr's next astute administrative choice was that of Mark Wright as his production stage manager. He had met Wright during the trying times of the *Auntie Mame* road shows; Wright had gotten the job as the second assistant stage manager with the Constance Bennett company after a friend had dropped out. When Barr interviewed Wright, he felt as if he were interviewing himself. Wright was twelve years younger and a composer, having already written a children's musical.[41] In the interview, Barr asked Wright, "Well, young man, what do you want to do in the theatre?" Wright replied, "Well, Mr. Barr, I want to be sitting where you're sitting one day."[42] Barr liked Wright's unapologetic ambition, and he became the heart of the Albee-Barr-Wilder operation, serving as production stage manager on all the Albee shows. Later, Wright became an original play producer in his own right, producing Pinter's *The Birthday Party* with Haila Stoddard, Gretchen Cryer's musical *The Last Sweet Days of Isaac*, and Lanford Wilson's *The Gingham Dog* and *Lemon Sky*. Wright moved upstairs from Barr at his Eighth Street apartment and remained one of his closest friends.

Though Richard didn't have any money to pay him, Wright's first job was to retype the *Krapp's Last Tape* and *The Zoo Story* manuscripts, double-spaced, to make the scripts more readable for the actors. The new production stage manager was struck by Barr's generosity and adaptability: "Barr was so intelligent and so warm and so trusting." During the production of the two one-act plays, Wright ran the lights, the wardrobe, and the props for the show. It was an unheard-of combination of duties for a stage manager, especially for no pay.[43] Wright's greatest asset, however, was his ability to work with Alan Schneider, who, Barr noted, could be "irascible at times." Schneider had "quit or been replaced on other productions, but never on one of ours" because Wright was "always one step ahead of him in the exasperating details" of theatre production. Barr deeply admired Wright's "blessed combination of authority, diplomacy, professional know-how and total loyalty to the production" and believed that without Wright, his operation would have ceased to function.[44]

Michael Kasdan was Barr's other managerial coup. Kasdan had been an assistant manager on Cy Feuer and Ernest H. Martin's *Whoop Up!* on Broadway and was a replacement for Joan Kaiser, Barr's secretary at the time. He served as general manager for all the Albee-Barr productions, both off-Broadway and on. Like Wright, Kasdan also produced on his own or coproduced with either Barr or Barr's future partner Charles Woodward on such original shows and revivals as *Drat!*, *What the Butler Saw*, and Lanford Wilson's *The Rimers of Eldritch*. Kasdan (as a former Oberlin College dance major) also produced dance on Broadway, including the Paul Taylor and Martha Graham companies. It was Kasdan who encouraged Barr to produce modern dance, including the companies of Valerie Bettis, Paul Draper, and Twyla Tharp, on Broadway and off.

According to Bruce Hoover, a Broadway stage manager who worked closely with Kasdan on Barr's dance projects, the producer was reliant on Kasdan to execute his major producing decisions. After his Sardi's lunches, Barr was often less than sober.[45] Though he struggled with drink throughout his later career, he was wise enough to make sure others carried out his plans. Because of this, Kasdan became Barr's right hand in his operations, along with Mark Wright. Barr enjoyed this company of rivals, mentoring his junior colleagues in the transfer of shows he originated at his Playwrights Unit, the off-off-Broadway playwrights laboratory he later established with Clinton Wilder and Edward Albee.

His most important coup in his production team was the legendary director Alan Schneider. By the mid-1950s, Schneider was already a rising star on Broadway with such original play productions as the ANTA production of Randolph Goodman and Walter Carroll's *A Long Way from Home*, Marcelle Maurette's *Anastasia*, and Robert Whitehead's production of Liam O'Brien's *The Remarkable Mr. Pennypacker*. Barr was impressed by Schneider's résumé, noting, "Alan had already reached a prominence as a director that I never touched."[46] Schneider's Broadway productions were generally critically praised, though commercially unsuccessful, transfers from Zelda Fichandler's Arena Stage in Washington, D.C. Schneider wanted to work with Barr and Albee, primarily to direct absurdist authors and to move beyond some of the more commercial choices he had made, feeling himself becoming "the poor man's Josh Logan."[47]

By 1959, Schneider had established an important relationship with Samuel Beckett, having directed, though with disastrous results, the first American production of *Waiting for Godot* at the Coconut Grove Playhouse in Miami. Happily, Schneider subsequently directed the definitive first American production of Beckett's *Endgame*. His eclectic career moved from university productions to those at his home base at the Arena Stage, with forays on Broadway and off. Schneider's own tastes leaned toward off-Broadway productions of plays that were "foreign and literary and avant-garde." He struggled with his agent, Lucy Kroll, to let him work off-Broadway, even though the pay was abysmal, because the material was "better quality" than the Broadway shows he was being offered.[48] From a business standpoint, Schneider was relieved to connect with Barr, a professional producer, since his friend Harry Joe Brown Jr., who had no producing experience, controlled *Krapp's Last Tape* and hadn't raised the money to produce it.

Schneider initially thought Barr to be of the generation of "gentlemen producers looking for what was basically conventional, and hopefully, commercial material."[49] He was curious about why Barr had acquired the rights for *The Zoo Story*, which was written by a "mysterious and reclusive" playwright. The producer immediately liked Schneider because they shared a similar attitude toward new work: "The director's job is to dramatize the author's intention, not to superimpose an interpretation of his on the play." For both men, off-Broadway offered them an opportunity to work on material they respected. Barr was "delighted to offer him Albee's next play, and many more after that."[50] Though initially ambivalent, Schneider grew to like Barr, writing that he was "good-natured and agreeable even under difficult circumstances." Barr did not offer *The Zoo Story* to him, however, which caused Schneider a good deal of anxiety. Knowing that John Stix had directed *The Zoo Story* in an Actors Studio workshop, Schneider worried that Stix would direct that show and be offered *Krapp's Last Tape* as well. Edward Parone, the agent at William Morris who had discovered *The Zoo Story*, was also interested in directing it.[51] In the end, *The Zoo Story* was offered to Milton Katselas, and Schneider directed *Krapp's Last Tape*.

However, the larger issue became Schneider's prior commitment to direct *The Cherry Orchard* at the Arena Stage. While Schneider was waiting for Barr and Brown to rent a theatre for *Krapp's Last Tape* and *The Zoo Story*, Zelda Fichandler hired him to direct *The Cherry Orchard*. Barr and Brown then managed to secure the perfect venue, Washington Square's Provincetown Theater, the same theater where Eugene O'Neill had premiered his early work. Unfortunately, the Provincetown Theater opening of *Krapp and Zoo* (as nicknamed by Schneider) on 14 January 1960 was to occur two days after *The Cherry Orchard* was to open at the Arena Stage. Since Schneider had previously pulled out of other Arena contracts, he couldn't withdraw, nor was he able to change the date of the production, which was "as fixed and immutable as Zelda herself."[52] Richard Barr, however, wasn't deterred; there was only one actor in *Krapp's Last Tape*, Donald Davis, and he was a particularly amiable performer. Barr, "with his usual practicality," determined that Schneider could rehearse both *The Cherry Orchard* and Donald Davis in *Krapp's Last Tape* simultaneously.[53] Schneider and Davis could work at his mother's spacious apartment in Washington, D.C., and then complete rehearsals of *Krapp's Last Tape* in New York while *The Cherry Orchard* cast was on its winter break. For Schneider, Barr's flexibility was an example of his "vision and statesmanship" as a producer—qualities he saw "many times" thereafter.[54]

Schneider was also thrilled with Donald Davis as Krapp. Both he and Barr knew Davis well, and casting him was an easy decision after Eli Wallach and Martin Balsam turned down the role. Schneider had directed Davis as Tiresias in a successful television screening of *Oedipus the King*, presented on *Omnibus* in January 1957. Conveniently, Davis was on sabbatical from running his Crest Theatre in Toronto; in order to "share expenses," Barr invited Davis to share his Eleventh Street "attic."[55] During the Washington rehearsals, Barr's mother, Ruth, enjoyed having Davis stay with her. She was even "playing bridge in the living room" when Schneider and Davis were in the bedroom rehearsing.[56] Though Fichandler was "not entirely happy" about rehearsing *The Cherry Orchard* cast in the afternoons so that Schneider could rehearse with Davis in the evenings, she relented because Schneider was desperate for a New York hit.

Though the casting and rehearsal process was smooth sailing for Schneider and Davis on *Krapp's Last Tape*, the situation with *The Zoo Story* was exactly the opposite. Barr had hired Milton Katselas at Albee's suggestion, feeling that if Albee was happy with him, Katselas would be fine. While Barr's policy was to allow the playwright to be in the driver's seat, he actually wanted to direct the play himself and began to cast the production. He wanted to use Peter Falk to play the thirty-something Jerry, but Albee wanted the young, handsome George Maharis. He had seen Maharis play the role of Green Eyes in the Theater East production of Genet's *Deathwatch*.[57] Though disappointed, Barr conceded the choice of Maharis as Jerry and convinced a somewhat reluctant William Daniels to play the role of Peter. Daniels was concerned that "one guy had all the lines and the other guy just sat there."[58] Richard Barr paid the actors only fifty dollars a week and rented Tony Lo Bianco's inexpensive studio, where they could rehearse "for a pittance." He exhorted his little company to keep their focus on the playwright and on the fact that they were going to "take over Lincoln Center."[59]

By the second week of rehearsal, a problem was brewing with Milton Katselas and his directing approach. Mark Wright was the first to notice. The actors hadn't been blocked yet, and feeling that something was wrong, Wright slipped into a nearby pay phone and immediately contacted Barr. The producer, for his part, had already alerted Wright about Katselas, letting him know that "I don't know anything about this guy."[60] He was disturbed by what he observed in the rehearsals, and Albee too was becoming "very unhappy" with Katselas's "subjective approach." The director, though, believed he was doing typical "table work" for a new play. He felt a special connection with *The Zoo Story* because he lived on the Upper West Side of Manhattan and knew all the characters Albee had created. Having studied privately with Lee Strasberg, Katselas worked "very patiently and very slowly" to allow the actors to feel things out. Though rehearsals may have seemed to Barr to be "a bit in a muddle for awhile" and "perhaps went on longer than it needed to go on," Katselas confessed he was "nervous as hell" in his first directing role. George Maharis became very nervous with Albee in rehearsals, so Katselas asked Albee to give him a few days alone with the actors. After Mark Wright's phone call and Maharis's continued concerns about Katselas, Barr stepped in. According to Katselas, "There was a meeting or two about it, and then Richard came in and said to me, 'You have a choice, you could let me come in for a day or two and straighten a few things out, or you could take off.'"[61] Barr phrased it a bit differently: Katselas "could resign, he could be fired, or he could sit and watch me direct the play."[62] Albee encouraged him to stay.

Katselas watched as Barr worked with actors ("as painful as that was for a director"). After about two days, Katselas approached him and said, "I've got the picture," and Barr took off. According to Katselas, Barr was "minimizing the behavior," getting the play to be more "didactic" and more "let's get down to the argument," and was "simplifying the moves." What Barr did was "clarify things for the actors," though both Daniels and Maharis were somewhat mystified by his approach. Still, he offered a more seasoned, if traditional, directorial approach, and it seems from today's perspective that Barr and Katselas's difficulty was generational. Katselas was one of the new internal, "method"-based directors coming out of the Actors Studio.[63] Barr, on the other hand, used an external, intellectual "Wellesian" approach, presenting through image and theatricality. Katselas used rehearsals to help actors explore and improvise the "impulses, the feelings and behavior" of the play and "to free them up." Later, he sculpted and simplified their work, stripping away behavior in order to illuminate inner life. The young director felt that there was no reason for "things to have escalated the way they did" and insisted that he stay through the opening, despite what others said, including stage manager Mark Wright.[64] Katselas believed the play was "the advent of a great American writer," and he was grateful "to contribute to the experience." He later directed the award-winning off-Broadway production of *Call Me by My Rightful Name*, was nominated for a Tony Award for his direction of *Butterflies Are Free* on Broadway, and established a well-respected acting studio in Los Angeles.

Despite experiencing some regret, Barr felt strongly about the serious artistic differences between himself and Katselas. After the opening, he wrote Katselas a harsh letter relieving him of his duties. He thought Katselas's interpretation of *The Zoo Story* "lacked tension" and permitted the actors to "go too far in the direction of comedy," which he felt killed "the essential struggle" of the play. Barr agreed to pay Katselas's royalties and give him credit but took him out of any further casting or redirection of the play.[65] The letter "provoked a storm," and Katselas's agent, Helen Harvey, protested the "general tone" of Barr's letter, which she felt was "harsh or thoughtless." Albee was also disturbed by the tone of the letter and wrote to Barr that he "must go on the record as saying that no such summary dismissal of Milton was agreed to." Barr, for his part, believed that Katselas was "a gentleman" about the entire experience. Shortly before Katselas had his "first big hit," he contacted Barr and thanked him for helping his career by giving him the credit for directing *The Zoo Story* "without mentioning the behind-the-scenes contretemps." Katselas concluded that the producer had acted "fairly and decently," and Barr acknowledged that Katselas developed into a "fine director."[66]

The previews of *Krapp and Zoo* felt bumpy. Audiences struggled with *Krapp's Last Tape*, and several walked out of Albee's play. Schneider believed that *Krapp* should not have been first in the evening, which went against "his instincts and desires," and he was also unsure about the direction of *The Zoo Story*, which seemed to be inducing laughter in the audience.[67] According to Mel Gussow, "Barr and Albee rushed back stage and said, 'You're getting laughs. Don't do that.'"[68] Barr was "somewhat" surprised that during the paid admission previews, Albee's play projected what seemed to be unintentional comedy, but, as it turned out, he realized Albee's plays were "very funny," though they rarely depended on jokes. Characters were caught in absurd, difficult circumstances and said "very, very amusing" things. This previewing process became integral to Barr's producing, especially when he produced Albee's *Who's Afraid of Virginia Woolf?* Previewing also allowed Barr to close shows quickly if they were sinking and before they lost too much money.[69]

The opening night on 14 January 1960 was well attended, and the actors played well. Afterward, Barr, Albee, Howard Atlee (the Theater 1960 press agent), Lutz, Schneider, and Brown went to Barr's apartment for what Barr termed the "wake." Barr did not invite the actors to this opening night "party," as it was really a business meeting for his staff to arrange for promotion, based upon the reviews of the show. His staff members could handle bad news, since they did not have to "perform the next day for the public." Inviting actors to this was a "form of senseless masochism," as a particular performer could be critically skewered in front of friends, cast, and family.[70] Barr believed that a show could be saved if the actors were left out of the bloodletting.

The first reviews from Brooks Atkinson of the *New York Times* and Walter Kerr of the *New York Herald Tribune* were mixed, and Atlee read them to the group at 1:00 A.M. in "his mournful voice, which was to haunt me for years." Barr felt that the reviews were "scarcely raves," immediately "went into a slump," and "threatened again to quit the theatre."[71] After hearing the reviews, Barr and Albee left the room, and Brown concluded they were devastated: "We had thought with this little production we had something important, but the reviews had only equivocated, and Albee walked off into the night. The next afternoon every afternoon paper appeared with an unqualified rave, as did the magazines; and Atkinson and Kerr, having had time to think it over, came back with Sunday articles on the plays, and we had the wonderful feeling of having a big hit."[72] Atlee, who had spent the evening reading the reviews, believed that the plays were doing fine and that Atkinson's review, which though tepid in its enthusiasm, was not solely negative.[73]

Atkinson encouraged audiences to take in the production despite its challenging material: "After the banalities of Broadway it tones the muscles and freshens the system to examine the squalor of Off-Broadway." The critics complimented Schneider's direction, praised Beckett for *Krapp*, and offered strong approval for both Katselas and Albee for *The Zoo Story*. Though Atkinson was annoyed with the evening's existentialism, thinking Beckett and Albee "write on the assumption that the human condition is stupid and ludicrous," Schneider noted that other reviews were "positive enough to keep us going a season or more."[74] For his part, Kerr seemed to finally understand Beckett's work, writing, "And while en garde is the proper spirit in which to approach the avant garde, I think you will find that each of these curios creates a genuine and tantalizing mood."[75] Though not "money" reviews, both critics acknowledged something important was being said by talented authors and presented by a gifted theatre ensemble.

Barr was "really despondent" by 3:00 or 4:00 A.M. but decided to get up and go to the Blaine Thompson Agency to salvage positive quotes for a display ad, believing that you don't give in "until you know you're licked."[76] Freddie Golden, one of the key account executives, greeted him with an enormous grin on his face: "Boy, have you got a hit!"[77] Barr asked him, "Where?" Golden exclaimed, "At the Cherry Lane! Have you seen the afternoon papers?"[78] The afternoon reviews by Richard Watts of the *New York Post*, Charles McHarry of the *Daily News*, Henry Hewes of the *Saturday Review*, and Jerry Tallmer of the *Village Voice* were all raves. Watts led the pack, noting that while Beckett's play was the "most human" of his stage works, it was *The Zoo Story* by the "unknown Mr. Albee" that was the "major event" of the evening, writing that Albee "is a dramatist who writes with powerful skill and freshness, and he is clearly a man with a claim to attention."[79] Watts "went crazy for it," Atlee recalled, "and that helped an awful lot." Atlee used the *New York Post* for most of his advertising thereafter and immediately arranged for Watts to interview Albee. The *Post* later sponsored the Vernon Rice Award (now the Drama Desk Award), which went to Barr and Clinton Wilder in 1961.[80]

Barr and Howard Atlee used the reviews to establish Albee as the first major American writer from off-Broadway to embrace the "Theatre of the Absurd."[81] Atkinson and Kerr helped their efforts with their Sunday weekly reviews. Both had had sudden changes of heart and came out with very strong praise for Albee's work. Schneider noted with pleasure that "with such a response, it was not difficult for the Messrs. Barr, Lutz, and Brown to parlay the production into a big off-Broadway success."[82] To Schneider's delight, *Krapp's Last Tape* and *The Zoo Story* won a small flood of *Village Voice* Obie Awards, including Distinguished Performances for Donald Davis and William Daniels and Distinguished Plays for both Albee and Beckett. Schneider noted that it "broke *The Iceman Cometh*'s record as the longest running show off-Broadway."[83]

Barr now required Atlee to include a picture of Albee in all the ads large enough to contain it. This decision would set him apart from other producers presenting off-Broadway vanity showcases for stars.[84] He insisted that "the play is the important thing and the playwright is the most important thing. That's what you promote."[85] Barr wanted "none of the confusion that existed on Broadway with regard to the identity of the real boss." At the same time, he moved very quickly to negotiate an ongoing agreement, making Albee an extraordinary offer: "I realize that it is customary for the author of a first successful play to offer the producer—if he does not already have an advance option—the author's next play. I'll make a deal with you. I want your next work and all your future work as long as you seriously believe that I am the best person to produce it. Further, I will promise to produce anything you write."[86] Barr and Albee kept to this simple agreement. Barr produced all of Albee's work, with a few exceptions, for twenty years, until Albee's *The Lady from Dubuque*. It became one of the longest producer-playwright relationships in the American theatre, though, as Barr observed, it was not always a "smooth" one.

The first bump in their ongoing operation was theatre rental. The Provincetown Theater was leased out for Gilbert and Sullivan operas and children's theatre, and Barr could not convince the owner to keep his show there. So *Krapp/Zoo* had to close at the Provincetown on 21 May 1961 after 582 performances but reopened almost four months later at the East End Theatre on 12 September. In addition, Barr learned an important lesson in advertising. Though he budgeted the show at $9,000 and brought it in at $5,500, he had overspent $1,000 on the advance advertising. Barr came to believe that advance advertising off-Broadway was a waste of money because "off-Broadway does not build on advance sales, so why make the *New York Times* rich?" Still, *The Zoo Story* paid back its investment within its first five weeks, and Barr revived the show eight times between 1960 and 1965. It had 1,064 performances off-Broadway, more than any other of his productions, including *The Boys in the Band*, which played for 1,000 performances.[87] While the show continued to be a moneymaker for Barr, particularly during his years at the Cherry Lane, Harry Joe Brown Jr., whom Barr describes in his memoirs as increasingly "cantankerous and egotistical," was determined to be the sole producer and made an offer to buy him out. Barr accepted. Brown, for his part, remembered the experience this way: "In the ensuing months, Barr made a series of proclamations to the newspapers, in which he gave himself all the credit for the production. It was this in our relationship that I blamed him most for, for it was unnecessary and untrue; and, when later that spring and fall Barr said that he needed me and asked me to go on with him and be his partner in Theatre 1961, I declined for that reason."[88] Barr was ready to go on to other projects, but Brown appealed to Albee to keep the show running, and that was why Barr sold him his rights. The show continued to run with the cast and director receiving their share of the profits. Brown's relationship with Albee ended in London, when after two days, Albee fired him as director and replaced him successfully with Hank Kaplan, a friend of Donald Davis's.[89] Barr was grateful to be done with Brown and to get back to building a theatre dedicated to the work of new playwrights and new plays.

Albee decided to travel after the success of *The Zoo Story* but wrote frequently to Barr to check on its status in New York. Having already penned *The Death of Bessie Smith* in May 1960, he wrote that he was finishing his play *The American Dream*.[90] It is striking how affectionate Albee is in his letters to Barr. The public perception of Albee, even to some of his closer colleagues and theatre artists, was one of a certain catlike detachment. However, there is a very different Albee expressed in these letters, one that is playful, charming, and deeply affectionate. At several points, Albee asks in his correspondence, "Do you miss me?," expressing an almost father/son relationship. Despite the storms to come—Barr's drinking and lack of sobriety eventually became a central issue in their gradual separation—this deep loyalty and warmth between the two never changed.

At this point, Barr did two things as he waited for Albee's first evening-length play. He cemented Theatre 1962's ties to the European absurdists and began his American playwrights workshops, what would become the heart of his operation. Albee had been toying out loud with the idea of his first evening-length play as early as 1960, just after the opening of *The Zoo Story*.[91] With Albee's play forthcoming and the Albee-Beckett success as the wind in his sails, Barr decided to experiment with Ionesco's *The Killer*, the second evening-length play Ionesco had written. Unfortunately, *The Killer* set in motion a series of serious "flops," as Barr called them, experiments in workshop production that ironically led to Barr and Albee's Playwrights Unit. Even as he was "waiting for Albee," Barr continued to connect Albee with the absurdist movement, taking advantage of its intellectual grip on the American theatre zeitgeist as a successful marketing tool. In the process, he created an operation that worked on, off-, and off-off-Broadway, producing new work in a small avalanche of material that changed the American playwriting scene for years to come.

7

PRODUCERS AT WORK

On Broadway, Off-Broadway, and Off-Off-Broadway

Barr's production of Eugène Ionesco's *The Killer* off-Broadway at the Seven Arts Theatre on 22 March 1960 allowed him to experiment with the new multimedia, interdisciplinary "Happenings" of the 1960s, using Wellesian visual imagery from his versions of *Richard III* and *Macbeth* in the new work of the absurdists. With *The Killer*, Richard incorporated all the arts into theatre, as Stuart Little relates: "The abstract painter Ilse Getz did a collage backdrop of New York City. Allan Kaprow, the artist and composer, built a special sound filter to run metropolitan static through on his electronic sound track giving off a continuous urban hum. And Todd Bolender, the dancer and choreographer of the New York City Ballet, worked out movement while Barr himself directed the production over all."[1]

The Killer is the first of Ionesco's Bérenger plays. Bérenger was Ionesco's everyman character and appears in several of his plays, including *Rhinoceros* and *A Stroll in the Air*. In this play, Bérenger discovers a "radiant city" that holds a deadly secret—a serial killer who threatens the lives of all who dwell within. As director of *The Killer*, Barr experimented in ways that resonated with his experiences at the Mercury Theatre: "To begin with, it was the first evening-length Ionesco play produced in the United States; it was the first to use electronic music . . . it was probably the first to use the work of a modern sculptor as a backdrop, and it was certainly one of the first to use

Artaud's theory that the action of the play should surround the audience (not unlike Orson's *Danton's Death*! Did I steal the idea?)."[2]

Barr used one of the Mercury performers, Hiram ("Chubby") Sherman, to be the "star" of the production. Though fairly "mystified" by all of the artistic "embellishments," Sherman was "game and patient."[3] *The Killer* received some kudos for the high-minded effort to bring Ionesco to New York audiences, though critics "hated the play."[4] At this, Richard lost his temper and wrote a vituperative letter to the *New York Times* attacking the Ford Foundation for giving grants to regional theatres rather than to playwrights, noting that "actors and communities do not make theatre; playwrights do" and pointing out that none of the regional theatres given these grants produced any new playwrights of distinction. In the letter, Barr made a plea that the Ford Foundation consider supporting playwrights' work "in professional productions in the theatre capital of the country" so that commercial theatre managers might see how the productions would finance these shows to offset the Ford Foundation's costs.[5] Barr's frustration with the lack of federal support for commercially produced new work led to his idea of a completion fund for new play production on Broadway. This in turn became the seed idea for the Theatre Development Fund. Barr's fury with critics continued throughout his producing career, and, in this case, he went so far as to attempt to explain Ionesco's play to the press, ironically describing the metaphor of his own producing struggles: "Berenger's effort to recapture this transcendence of the world brings him to the Radiant City where all is perfection—much like the vision—except that the Killer is terrifyingly present. Berenger's commitment to find, reform, or overcome this Killer represents to me Ionesco's positive attitude about the worth of Living. Unfortunately Berenger is no Einstein or Picasso, whom the Drunk mentions, and he is overwhelmed."[6]

In his own attempt to overcome the "killer" of theatre arts—commerciality and lowbrow tastes—Barr, too, was overwhelmed. But he believed that audiences could be educated and could evolve to accept the new if it was as well written as it was challenging and provocative. Ever the would-be Princetonian scholar, Barr approached the production of new plays from his own literary sensibilities. His was a conscious intellectualism that led him to link his Theatre of the Absurd Repertory at the Cherry Lane Theatre to Martin Esselin's book *The Theatre of the Absurd*, a study that came to define the absurdist movement. The backlash to this cerebral approach came as Barr became pigeonholed as a producer of "rear-guard" absurdist works.[7] Worse, his high-handed attempts to educate the critics ended up provoking them to attack his major playwright, Edward Albee.

Barr developed a reputation as a producer with something of an attitude. In the article "Barr Boos 'Cavalier' Critics," he lashed out against his adversaries: "I don't care if they [the critics] didn't like it, but the cavalier dismissal several gave it was disgraceful. . . . Ionesco is an important, major playwright and there aren't very many of them around either."[8] Still, Richard Watts of the *New York Post* gave *The Killer* a favorable review, as did a few other critics, but the production folded on 3 April 1960 after less than a month of performances.

Nursing his wounds, and "to keep busy," Barr joined with Lucille Lortel to produce a single evening of short plays by Albee, Beckett, and a playwright by the name of Harry Tierney Jr. on 25 October 1960. *Nekros* by Tierney, *Embers* by Beckett, and *Fam and Yam* by Albee were performed as part of the fifth season of the ANTA Matinee Series, created to showcase new work at the Theatre de Lys. Barr had originally directed the plays at Lortel's White Barn Theatre in Westport, Connecticut, and the show featured James Pritchett in *Embers* as a kind of "Krapp without his tape recorder or banana."[9] Barr had produced the show to keep the flow of news about Theater 1960 moving along while he waited for Albee to finish *The American Dream*. The *New York Times*' Arthur Gelb gave Barr mixed reviews on his directing, noting that he did "a good job for the most part but his touch is anything but sure." Yet *Fam and Yam* revealed to Gelb that Albee had an "ability to laugh at himself," and Beckett's play demonstrated that he could be "vivid about life's ugliness." Tierney's play was "just vivid" and "an overwrought case study."[10] Though not wildly successful, the production was an important opportunity for Barr to direct and gave Albee adequate time to complete his next major work.

The Theatre 1961 season began with Richard Hepburn's historical comedy *The Sudden End of Anne Cinquefoil* on 10 January 1961. It was Barr's first unmitigated off-Broadway flop, "a one night disaster."[11] Though "stung" by the failure of *The Killer*, Barr had felt "feisty" and produced it simply because he liked it, and perhaps he had hoped to lure Hepburn's sister Katharine off-Broadway.[12] Barr had offered a special 60/40 split of profits to his limited partners, an arrangement that he repeated when dealing with challenging new work, and tried to involve Clinton Wilder, his future partner.[13] Wilder took "a rain check," though he noted that Barr was crazy about the play. Howard Taubman, the *Times* reviewer, predicted accurately that it would live up to its title and have a "sudden end." While Hepburn had attempted to write a "witty comedy about feminism," he ended up with a "wordy, wearisome affair."[14] Despite the play's weakness, William Ritman's sets for *Sudden End* expertly accentuated the play's dramaturgy on a limited budget, and Ritman received a litany of praise for his fidelity to playwrights' visions throughout his career.

Sudden End also established the off-Broadway ensemble of actors and staff that Barr used later, including those at the Cherry Lane Theatre and at his off-off-Broadway workshop, Playwrights Unit. During the production of *Sudden End*, Joseph Cali joined Barr's staff as a house manager; he later described its family-like atmosphere: "I don't know if Richard intended this to happen, but it did happen; we became a family. . . . There was an atmosphere in the theatre, at the Cherry Lane itself, where everybody knew everyone else. The back of the house was never cut off from the front of the house, so that there was never any separation. And it all has to do with the way that Richard ran a show."[15] It was this openness among his actors and staff that permitted Barr to open and close shows quickly and was key to his success in producing new work. In this case, Theatre 1961 quickly moved on to Albee's *The American Dream*, though the playwright was pushing for production of *The Death of Bessie Smith*.

Richard had mixed feelings about *The Death of Bessie Smith* and was not alone in his concerns. Albee sent it to Pinkas Braun, who had been instrumental in the Berlin premiere of *The Zoo Story*. Initially, Braun rejected *Bessie Smith*, feeling that Albee let the audience off too easily and that the characters were "exceptions to the rule, so near the edge of being abnormal, that the average citizen in the audience would never agree to identify himself with them."[16] But like *The Zoo Story*, *The Death of Bessie* Smith had a Berlin opening, this one on 21 April 1960 at the Schlosspark Theater. Still, Barr thought it was "a race play" and not the "appropriate follow-up to *The Zoo Story*." It was a weaker, episodic "workpiece" of what Albee realized in a much more developed form in his *Who's Afraid of Virginia Woolf?*, containing characters living in a world of illusion: "The black orderly thinks he has successfully bridged the problem of prejudice, and believes he can move easily in both black and white worlds; he can't. The intern has political illusions, which convince him he should be over in Spain fighting for the Loyalists; but he makes no move to go. Jack, Bessie's friend, believes Bessie can make a great comeback up north and that he is the one to engineer and effect it; he can't. The nurse, the leading character, had social illusions, believing herself to be a 'southern lady.'"[17]

Barr's larger context for his feelings about *The Death of Bessie Smith* was his placement of Albee within the framework of Eugene O'Neill, Tennessee Williams, and Arthur Miller. Barr believed that O'Neill wrote characters who have illusions and accept them as reality; that Williams's characters have illusions, which result from their "psychological problems"; and that

Miller wrote characters who blame society for the reality with which they struggle. Albee "moved into a new world" in Richard's estimation by writing characters like *Virginia Woolf*'s George and Martha, who knowingly create the illusion in which they live. This theme was "objective, imaginative, and closely related to man's awareness in the twentieth century," and it was at the heart of Barr's postmodernist producing sensibility. Barr was interested in plays that were self-conscious and self-referential and recognized themselves as stage fictions.

Though Albee "did not entirely agree" with Barr's opinion of *The Death of Bessie Smith*, he was willing to have *The American Dream* produced first. He pressed Barr into producing a new short opera, *Bartleby*, based on the short story by Herman Melville, as a companion piece. William Flanagan, Albee's partner of several years, was the composer. Albee himself, with James Hinton Jr., had written the libretto. Barr was intrigued by pairing *The American Dream* with an original opera, especially after his success with *All in One* on Broadway. He was sold on *Bartleby* upon hearing it at Albee's apartment with Flanagan playing and singing all the music and roles.

The American Dream was the result of Albee's reimagining an earlier play, *The Dispossessed*, which he had written before *The Zoo Story*. In the process of writing *The American Dream*, he had sketched out an early version of it, which became *The Sandbox*. He used the same characters of Mommy, Daddy, and Grandma but changed the Young Man into the Angel of Death.[18] Though written for Gian Carlo Menotti for his Festival of Two Worlds at Spoleto, Italy, H. B. Lutz first produced *The Sandbox* on 15 April 1960 at the Jazz Gallery, Lutz's new theatre cabaret in St. Mark's Place.[19] Barr read *The American Dream* and was struck by Albee's interpretation of Ionesco's absurdist style, with just a dash of Burr Tillstrom's Kuklapolitan Players. Oddly enough, Albee was a huge fan of Tillstrom's puppetry and the comedy of his Kuklapolitan world.[20] But Barr had no luck raising funds for the production. Harry Joe Brown Jr., was unreliable, and Whitey Lutz had lost money with his Jazz Gallery and pulled out of producing entirely. However, Roger Baker, a painter friend, had Barr contact Clinton Wilder on the project. Barr had approached Wilder in the past but without success. This time, however, Barr knew *The American Dream* would interest Wilder, a wealthy jet-setter who was curious about the European absurdists.

Through Baker, Barr made arrangements to travel to Europe and connect with Wilder in Paris. He thought of Wilder as a "much more successful" producer than himself, since Wilder had enjoyed several Broadway hits, including Marc Blitzstein's *Regina* (the musical adaptation of Lillian Hellman's *The Little Foxes*), *The Tender Trap* by Max Shulman and Robert Paul

Smith, Gore Vidal's *A Visit to a Small Planet*, and a hit show in London, *The World of Suzie Wong* by Paul Osborn. In reality, Richard was by far the more experienced hands-on producer; Wilder was mostly the "deep pockets" of projects he invested in. But having recently pulled out of producing after his 1957 production of *A Visit to a Small Planet*, he was not "enthusiastic" about participating in any Broadway venture. He hadn't seen *Krapp's Last Tape* and *The Zoo Story*, though he knew of the show's success, and hadn't read any plays that interested him enough to "return to the battle" of producing on Broadway. A few years younger than Richard, Wilder was very curious about the newly hip off-Broadway scene. The two men connected personally, and since both were planning for a visit in Paris, they agreed to meet there to discuss their mutual interest, producing off-Broadway.

At a small bistro on the Place St. Michel not far from the Latin Quarter, Barr and Wilder talked "for hours." They joked about the incident at Princeton when they first met, when Barr was tossed in a bathtub (after the success of his *Falstaff*), and shared stories about mutual acquaintances they knew from the Mercury Theatre and about their experiences with Jean Dalrymple and the City Center. Both had worked on the war film *Winged Victory*: Barr had worked on casting the movie at Fort Roach, and Wilder had actually appeared in it. Wilder also expressed interest in Barr's "off-Broadway" experiment with *Krapp and Zoo* and, fulfilling the purpose of Barr's Paris meeting with Wilder, agreed to read Albee's *The American Dream* when he returned to the States.[21]

Back in New York, Barr dropped the play off at Wilder's home on East Seventy-Fourth Street. Though concerned about Barr's disastrous financial turn with *The Sudden End of Anne Cinquefoil*, Wilder, after giving *The American Dream* a first reading, was enthusiastic.[22] He met with Barr at Sardi's after he had finished the play: "I said to Richard, 'I like that little play you showed me.' We decided to produce it. That's how our whole partnership began. We've never had a contract. We don't have one with Edward. We simply ask each other first."[23]

The informality and camaraderie of their partnership was the consequence of similar Ivy League backgrounds and literary taste in theatre. Both producers disliked the "compromise and corruption" they met on Broadway. They felt that off-Broadway could be a training ground for a new generation of American playwrights.[24] Though not impressed by Flanagan's opera, Wilder agreed that the "evening as a whole" had possibilities. They planned a very frugal yet artistically ambitious season off-Broadway that fall. Wilder believed it would be a "kind of marriage between economics and art," something akin to "reform," a change from the way things happened on Broadway. Both producers provided the bulk of the funding out of their own pockets, keeping risk minimal for their partner investors.[25]

Barr's financial arrangements on the show were as important as his selection of play and coproducer. He capitalized the production at $13,000 and offered units of $260 to backers, with each unit receiving 1 percent of the profits. Once again, profits were to be divided, with 60 percent to the backers and 40 percent to the producers, far more generous than the usual 50/50 arrangement. Richard figured his gross would be $5,000 weekly and budgeted the weekly operating costs at $3,490. With this financing, he could repay the investors within seven weeks. The royalties for the author were to be "the usual 6% of the gross," with the director's royalties not to exceed 2 percent of the gross. He budgeted the management with a $50 weekly fee, office expenses at $50 per week, and all the preproduction expenses not to exceed $200. Wilder immediately wanted to cast the shows and select an available theatre, but Barr struggled to raise his half of the funds. Wilder, at this point, according to Barr, "said one of the nicest things I ever heard in my years in the theatre." He told his new partner somewhat mysteriously not to "worry about the money. Somehow it is always found!" When pressed for specifics, Wilder simply repeated himself, and when Barr realized what it meant, "the partnership began."[26]

Richard Barr assembled his usual team of managers and artists, including Mark Wright, his production stage manager; Michael Kasdan, his general manager; Bill Ritman; and Alan Schneider. With the advent of *The American Dream*, Schneider became Barr's "most favored director."[27] He was the quintessential playwright's director: probing with a myriad of questions, ever mindful of the playwright's presence, and coaxing performances out of actors who might not understand this absurdist, nonlinear work.[28] Barr described his reasoning for anointing Schneider this way: "We had known of Alan's work, but we had not met him, nor had we known how faithful a director he was to a playwright's intention, as opposed to the many directors who superimpose their own personality, distort, and actually change texts without the playwright's permission, even though he is present. Alan will have none of this and we were impressed with the way he worked."[29] Though told that he was the producer's "most favored director," Schneider demurred, noting that he was frequently so busy with other shows outside of Albee-Barr-Wilder productions that "no matter how hard I tried, I wasn't."[30]

Barr procured the York Playhouse at Sixty-Fourth and Lexington Avenue for a limited booking, and Schneider, working with Albee, had extraordinary luck casting the show. He used Barr's ever-present "magic list" to bring together "one of those casts for which authors and producers pray." Before Barr produced Albee's *The Sandbox*, he had seen Sudie Bond in the title role of a Living Theatre production of Kenneth Koch's tiny play *Bertha*, about a slightly deranged queen of Norway. Richard thought the play "a mad and wonderful creation" and took Albee to see it.[31] Albee was entranced with Bond. Though only in her early thirties, she had a brilliant way of conveying age, and for Albee she brought a "wild antic humor" to the role, as a well as a "depth and poignancy of characterization that is absolutely staggering."[32] She became Grandma, having already played a similar role in *The Sandbox*. Along with Bond, Schneider cast Gladys Hurlbut as Mommy, Jane Hoffman as Mrs. Barker, John C. Becher as Daddy, and a young actor friend of Albee's, Tom Hunter, as the Young Man. This casting continued to change as Barr revived the play in later productions, and though Barr would always be a resource, he gave Albee and Schneider final say on casting on Albee's plays.

Schneider felt "his life and sanity" was saved by the call from Albee to direct *The American Dream* and was excited to work again with Barr and Wilder. However, in an attempt to pick up work to support his family, he had agreed to direct a new play, *Twinkling of an Eye*, for the Actors Workshop in San Francisco, which would cause him to miss the first few rehearsals. The plan was for Albee to begin rehearsals with the actors in the interim. Just before returning, Schneider called Albee from the San Francisco airport and told him, "Please, just let the actors read the play and, for heaven's sake, don't discuss it or say anything profound. Whatever you do, don't *explain* anything! Just tell them they are great and send them home. I promise you I'll be there tomorrow."[33] Schneider recalled that Albee was "nervous and excited" even as he promised to follow the director's instructions. To assist Albee's thinking about the play, Schneider wrote down his private character descriptions, calling Mommy "a tumescent monster" and Daddy an "acquiescent blob." Chaos was to ensue.[34]

A day later, Albee and Barr picked him up at the airport, and Schneider noticed their grim demeanor in the hired car, which, "considering the expression on their faces, . . . could have been a hearse." He was told that Gladys Hurlbut had withdrawn from the cast because "she was offended by some of her character's dialogue."[35] In reality, because of his inexperience, Albee had borrowed some thoughts from Schneider's private notes and had called Hurlbut's character a "tumescent monster." Schneider deduced that Hurlbut must have researched what the word "tumescent" meant and, realizing that it meant "bloated" and "glowing with sexual desire in the dark," pulled out of the show.[36] By talking to the cast at his apartment for the first read-through of the play, Albee had the unfortunate result of "generally frightening everyone," as Barr recalled, and "gave no sign of the talent he was later to demonstrate as a director."[37]

The situation was quickly righted when Jane Hoffman took over the role of Mommy and her understudy, Nancy Cushman, went on to successfully play Mrs. Barker. Because of "a growing uncertainty" about Tom Hunter's ability to play the role of the Young Man, Schneider cast Ben Piazza, whom he had worked with in his production of *Kataki* on Broadway.[38] This "family" of Hoffman, Becher, Bond, Piazza, and Cushman "replayed" together as *The American Dream* cast for several years, becoming "very good friends in the process."[39] Once Schneider settled in, and despite his bursts of temper (which he regretted), the show moved rapidly toward its opening.[40]

One serious scheduling problem arose, as Jane Hoffman was cast as the housewife in Zero Mostel's production of Ionesco's *Rhinoceros* on Broadway at the same time. Because she was only in the first act of *Rhinoceros*, Barr supplied her with a car and a driver to bring her downtown to play in *The American Dream*. Interestingly, the driver was the late Godfrey Cambridge, who was to become a comedic star in his own right years later.[41] The only serious mishap occurred on a Saturday when Hoffman was to play a double performance of *The American Dream* in the evening. On the opening night, Hoffman nearly missed the show because of a snowstorm.[42]

William Ritman's set was a "simple formal arrangement of arches and some heavy gilt and brocade furniture"; Schneider added a few empty picture frames to the set, which he felt were "a bit symbolic but funny."[43] The overall effect was to transfer the European absurdist style "into a genuine American idiom."[44] Because Ritman also worked on Burr Tillstrom's *Kukla, Fran and Ollie* television show, his design of *The American Dream* was conceived in tandem with Albee's own Tillstrom influence.[45] Barr's producers' notes on the *Playbill* program acknowledged his desire to thrust the American theatre toward the European absurdist avant-garde:

> Our purpose is to present new plays, preferably by American authors, off-Broadway, because of the increasingly severe artistic and commercial limitations of Broadway production.
>
> A further purpose is to introduce new actors, designers, composers and directors whose understanding and illumination of contemporary truths will push the horizons of the theatre a little further along the road which painting, sculpture, music, architecture, literature, and the dance have already travelled.
>
> To aid in effecting the above, we plan to use young American painters, composers and choreographers, not normally associated with theatre, to supplement the work of the theatre designers and directors chosen.
>
> It is our further intention to tour these plays through the colleges of the country.[46]

This statement set forth Barr's ultimate goal for Albarwild Theatre Arts, Inc., to be the premier development and producing organization for new plays in the United States. Albee himself contributed to this expectation, using an interview, "Dramatist in a Troubled World," to note that playwrights' work from the 1930s "sounds silly today. Art had to be propaganda and their work became a kind of pamphleteering." For Albee, all the modern playwright could do was "give his vision of the world," without the propaganda and without the kind of "self-consciousness" that had become the norm among American playwrights.[47] Albee added, "Look, the most important influence in the theatre today . . . is the European influence, especially the French."[48] Albee and Barr were clearly trying to change the course of American playwriting, moving it from its roots in 1930s socialist realism and pushing it toward a postmodernist sensibility built upon the European absurdists. The success of *The American Dream* was the early engine of a change in American playwriting that was followed by Barr's production of new plays off-off-Broadway by the Playwrights Unit.

The American Dream and *Bartleby* opened at the York Playhouse on 24 January 1961 in a blizzard, and *The American Dream* got "blockbuster" reviews, according to Barr. But Howard Taubman of the *New York Times* equivocated, "It is agreed that Albee has talent. 'The Zoo Story,' still running, established that point. 'The American Dream,' which arrived last night at the York Playhouse, reinforces it, even as it raises questions as to the willful manner in which it is employed." Taubman went on to describe Albee's gift for the "bitter comic current of free association" and noted that he "begins brilliantly," but by the end of the review, Taubman expressed concern that the play became "disaffectingly brittle," and "the nonsense at times comes perilously close to being the gibberish it is mocking."[49] Despite Taubman's mixed review, the afternoon papers once again pushed for Albee as New York's best and brightest playwright with Richard Watts of the *New York Post* leading the charge, calling the play "entirely delightful" and noting that the play was "packed with untamed imagination, wild humor, gleefully sardonic satirical implications and overtones of strangely touching sadness." He pointed out that *The American Dream* had confirmed what *The Zoo Story* had suggested, that Albee was "a playwright of fresh and remarkable talent."[50]

Other reviews had equally superlative remarks. Walter Kerr provided the final spur toward Albee's sudden success, writing that he didn't know "what wicked little germ" had set Albee to write the play but that "Mr. Albee has taken a good, nasty look at most of our success images and found them marvelously empty. Those who are following the young playwright's finger-poking progress will want to incorporate this one into their travels."[51]

Even though audiences were somewhat "mystified" by *The American Dream*, they were laughing and enjoying the show. Schneider, for his part, noted that the reviews were "beautiful to behold" but wondered if Albee would not have been "better off not to have wowed the critics 'so violently and so early in his career.'" Albee wrestled with this issue himself, since the ax came soon after the glory, but there was still more glory to come, and Albee's success would seismically change American playwriting.

William Flanagan and Albee's opera *Bartleby*, however, was roundly panned by the critics, and in Barr's opinion, "we were in trouble." It was decided that *Bartleby* had to be scrapped. Albee's *The Death of Bessie Smith* could replace it—a tragic blow to Albee's lover, Flanagan. However, in the interim, Barr presented the Valerie Bettis Dance Company's production of *Domino Furioso: A Commedia in Four Acts.* The show was a refurbishing of a previous work, done at Barr's request, and it proved to be popular with the audiences. The script was written by John Malcolm Brinnin with a musical score by Bernardo Segall and featured Valerie Bettis as Columbine, Sylvia, Harlequin, and Pierrot. Barr was able to lower prices to $2.50 a seat for a limited run, and Bettis got very good notices, giving Barr time to pull together his production of *The Death of Bessie Smith.*

Though Barr felt *Bessie Smith* didn't "work," Clinton Wilder felt strongly that they should do it. Barr was also busy planning to produce several more new plays and needed for *The American Dream* to sustain itself while he raised capital for other works, so he agreed.[52] In the meantime, Barr had sold the rights to *Bessie Smith* to John Eyre, an independent producer, and now gave him a partnership in the production, which Eyre "graciously" accepted after being paid $150. But Barr needed more money, at least $10,000. This he was able to procure from Wilder as a loan, with the cost of producing *The American Dream*, *Bartleby*, *Valerie Bettis Dance Company*, and *The Death of Bessie Smith* totaling $23,000. Rather than seek priority payment as a creditor, Wilder combined his loan with all production costs so that he was paid back along with the investors. Albee also agreed to extend the subsidiary rights when they expired so that all costs of the production were recouped—no one made a profit, but "every cent was repaid to the nice people who had faith" in Theatre 1961.[53]

It was a wise investment. The addition of *The Death of Bessie Smith* "turned the trick" on the production, and the shows began to sell out. The reviews for *Bessie Smith* were more mixed than for *The American Dream*, but they were strong enough to turn Albee's plays into the hottest off-Broadway ticket in New York. Howard Taubman wrote, "Because of the tightness and allusiveness of the writing, 'The Death of Bessie Smith' is not an easy play to encompass. One comes away hopeful that this cast eventually will master its intense brooding spirit. In any event, the play is worth seeing. It is further proof of Mr. Albee's unusual gift for the theatre."[54] Richard Watts was, in Barr's opinion, "far more prescient" in his review, in which he pointed out that "you are in the presence of an enormous and still unplumbed talent, and the talent is literally throbbing through this dramatic sketch."[55]

Before *The American Dream* and *The Death of Bessie Smith* were to leave the York Playhouse, and in accordance with Theatre 1961's contract, Barr presented *Way Out at the York*, an evening that represented the initial stirrings of his Playwrights Unit. It was an evening of theatre, film, and sound effects, and Alex Atkinson described its complexity: "Two ears came onto the stage of the York Playhouse . . . and engaged in conversation. They were over six feet high, and rather unexpected. . . . An item later in the program . . . was called Poem I and concerned a number of pink-and-white-striped boxes, inside which some characters made tapping sounds, but did not speak. After about ten minutes, a person came slithering across downstage bearing a skull, and that was the end of it. Some members of the audience now let it be known that they were more than a little uneasy . . . others . . . were deep in thought. Many had gone somewhere else."[56] Included were two short plays, *The Abstract Wife* and *The Tourniquet* by novelist and translator Ursule Molinaro. While Barr did not consider the plays "significant in themselves," he felt that the decision to present the works led to the creation of the Playwrights Unit, later the heart of the Albee-Barr-Wilder (ABW) operation.

The Theatre 1961 season ended on 18 April with Jack Richardson's *Gallows Humor*. Richardson was the first new playwright of substance, besides Albee, to be produced by the ABW partnership. *Gallows Humor* had already been in the process of cast selection and preproduction with producers Norman Twain and Helen Kamber, but Barr and Wilder were able to move in and take over with the three-person cast of Vincent Gardenia, Julie Bovasso, and Gerald Hiken intact.[57] Richardson's caché was clear. His *The Prodigal*, a modern retelling of the story of Orestes, opening a few months before Albee's *The Zoo Story*, had riveted its audiences, winning Brooks Atkinson's admiration.[58] *Gallows Humor* was an ironic triptych of dramatic stories, all of which explore the life of an executioner in a modern prison. The performances of Bovasso and Gardenia received strong praise, and the show as a whole garnered respectful if not glittering reviews, with the *Times*' Howard Taubman pronouncing it "fresh and incisive," though for him it was "not deep."[59] *Gallows Humor*'s lackluster reception contributed to Barr's awareness that his producing career rested solely upon the success of Albee's plays. He desperately needed to discover another star playwright, something he was never able to do. Still, he was pleased with *Gallows Humor*; both he and Wilder "loved it" and thought that it was "a biting, brilliant, hilariously amusing work with serious intentions."[60]

In May 1961, Barr and Wilder won the Vernon Rice Award (later the Drama Desk Award) "for devotion to new American playwrights and new ideas."[61] Though Theatre 1961 had not been one of their busier seasons, they had established a reputation for producing new plays and new playwrights with a certain consistency of success. Also, by this point, Barr knew Albee had completed the first two acts of *Who's Afraid of Virginia Woolf?* and felt a major success coming, even if Albee wouldn't give Barr a completion date on its third act. Though Barr and Wilder were once again "waiting for Albee," there was another possibility on the horizon, a new Beckett play. It would become one of Beckett's most frequently performed pieces.

On 17 September 1961, ABW's Theater 1962 premiered Beckett's *Happy Days*, directed by Alan Schneider at the Cherry Lane Theatre. Schneider had brought *Happy Days* from Beckett himself to a Barr-Wilder producing team "riding high as off-Broadway impresarios." Despite the intrinsic difficulties of premiering a Beckett play, the production was a critical success, though not a commercial one. Schneider was impressed by how Barr tightly managed the economics of the production: "The producers—and Edward [Albee]—came to one of our occasional runthroughs and loved it. So did our audiences for the five previews we were allotted. Our producers were economy-minded, as usual; they had announced at the start of rehearsal that they were bringing in our production for $2,200, and they stuck to their budget. This was at a time when off-Broadway productions cost around $10,000 at least."[62] Though the budget was minuscule, ticket sales were only fair, and to Schneider's disappointment, Barr cut back the *Happy Days* shows.

Regardless, Barr was delighted with the performances by Ruth White as Winnie and John C. Becher as Willie. White came to be one of the quintessential actresses of Barr's "playwrights' theatre"; she was thoughtful, adventurous, and text-oriented. He had discovered her while working on *The Boy with a Cart* at the Chapel Players with Bill Penn. Though Barr withdrew from the production, White stayed in New York to continue working. By the 1960s, she had become a character actress in much demand. She worked for Barr on, off-, and off-off-Broadway. He regretted that Beckett never saw her play Winnie, since he felt that "as in everything she touched, her work was definitive." White died from cancer in 1969 at a very early stage in her career. "Her early death," writes Barr in his memoirs, "deprived us of one of the great actresses of the generation."[63]

During the Theater 1962 season, Barr decided to go "mad" and produce nine absurdist plays in four weeks. The Theatre of the Absurd Repertory performed Samuel Beckett's *Endgame*, Kenneth Koch's *Bertha*, Jack Richardson's *Gallows Humor*, Edward Albee's *The Sandbox*, Jean Genet's *Deathwatch*, Fernando Arrabal's *Picnic on the Battlefield*, Albee's *The American Dream* and *The Zoo Story*, and Ionesco's *The Killer*.[64] Simultaneously, he took a five-year lease on the Cherry Lane Theatre, producing new American plays in Monday workshops, typically an evening off for Actors' Equity productions. He had chosen the absurdists because, as Stuart Little points out, "they were there, they were good, and not enough good American playwrights were around."[65] Barr's success with the absurdists leveraged his ability to bring new American playwrights to the attention of New York critics and to build a "rolling out" of absurdist work in preparation for the opening of *Who's Afraid of Virginia Woolf?* Ironic about his reputation as a producer of absurdist drama, Barr told *Village Voice* theatre critic Michael Smith, "I consider this the rear-guard theatre, not the avant-garde," adding, "We are doing this because most of the public hasn't seen these plays, and to put a period on this so-called 'movement.'"[66] Barr believed that the absurdists pointed to a new direction in American drama, "abstract realism," the name he gave to the playwrights' style of the 1960s.

Barr focused again on the practical logistics of producing his repertory, opening and closing shows in his usual militaristic manner—"quickly, quietly, and with a minimum of confusion."[67] Part of his efficiency was keeping costs down, and once again, advance advertising could be completely eliminated. A simple listing in the *Times*, a good review, and, most important, word of mouth were the only ways to draw audiences off-Broadway. He pointed out that "you can't have a hit without good notices, but you can have a flop with them." More efficiency was achieved by scheduling—"by organizing a split second timetable, filling every nook and cranny of the village with rehearsals."[68] Barr also contained actors' and directors' salaries and worked closely with designer William Ritman and his general manager, Michael Kasdan, which cut set and other design costs while keeping production values high.

The reviews were once again supportive, though the only real audiences came for Albee's plays, including *The American Dream* and *The Zoo Story*. Barr was proud of the extraordinary efficiency of his and Wilder's well-oiled Cherry Lane producing machine: "The result of this experience is that 'The Theatre of the Absurd,' a spectacularly ambitious project, will cost only $6,500 irrespective of returnable cash—bonds and advances. This is less than half what many less difficult, less professionally managed productions presently cost."[69] This smooth operation, while certainly protecting investors' returns, permitted Barr to produce his first series of Monday night new play workshops at the Cherry Lane Theatre, a priority for him: "Well, we have always had the idea in the back of our mind right from the beginning and actually started a year after we began off Broadway to present new playwrights, but on a very, very limited basis in the sense that we would use our theater on occasion, on Monday nights, which is the dark night off Broadway, to present productions that are a good deal more than workshops but weren't fully costumed and mounted—they were between a workshop and an off Broadway production."[70] Richard budgeted approximately $2,000 to $3,000 for three to four evenings of workshops featuring talented "unknowns" whose work was not ready for regular performance.

The first evening, presented as *Playwrights 1962* on 13 November 1961, consisted of *Sweet of You to Say So* by Page Johnson, *The Audience* by Michael Wilkes, *The Blueberry Affair* by Gudrun Powers, and *And He Made a Her* by Doric Wilson, all directed by Barr. Wilson, a well-known gay activist and playwright and later Barr's close friend, struggled with Barr's direction of his play at Cherry Lane: "This is typical Richard Barr. In his stupid pompous theories, he killed my play, killed it, dead as a doornail, killed it. First of all, the play had already been done [at the Caffe Cino]. I didn't go to rehearsals; I was working. All that we were doing was transferring it onto a stage with some new people. Paxton, who had directed it at the Cino, was the lead there. So what were we losing? We weren't losing anything. Whatever he did, I knew it didn't work, but I was too young, I didn't know why."[71] In distress over Barr's direction of *And He Made a Her*, Wilson went out to a bar for a drink after its dress rehearsal. At the bar, Wilson was, in his own words, "entrapped by a plain (ill-fittingly) clothed policeman who rammed a gun into my larynx and arrested me for sexual (I was innocent) whatever. All part of a . . . campaign to clear the queers out of the Village. . . . Richard Barr got me out of jail."[72]

Though Barr had been unsuccessful with the play, it was his generosity that represented his true character: "That was Richard. He fucked over my play, out of stupidity and pomposity and ignorance; but out of incredible courage he was right there, right on the line. He stayed with me all the way throughout the court thing, we got it finally all taken care of . . . I don't even know how it was all done. That was Richard Barr."[73] One of the early Caffe Cino playwrights, Wilson created a major gay activist theatre, TOSOS (The Other Side of Silence), and remained close friends with Barr for many years. He became Richard's de facto personal secretary, helping him with mundane household chores, sorting through the mountain of scripts that arrived daily.

Wilson believed that Barr had opportunities denied to him because of his homosexuality—and there may be some truth to Wilson's concerns. In the closeted world of the late 1950s and early 1960s theatre, Barr's sexual orientation was known but not openly accepted, particularly by his uptown Broadway colleagues. According to Wilson, Lincoln Center was so close to offering Barr the artistic directorship of the Theatre Forum at Lincoln Center that "they practically brought him to measure the toilets." But despite that, Barr was dropped from consideration for this role, and Wilson felt, "It's not going too far to think they didn't give it to him because of his sexual orientation."[74] Wilson also suggested, though, that Barr may have passed on Theatre Forum because he sensed it would be a difficult house to fill. Regardless, Wilson believed Barr felt slighted by the decision not to use him to direct Lincoln Center's Theatre Forum—especially because Barr thought his sexual orientation was his own business. Albee noted in 2009, "Richard didn't feel his sexual orientation had much to do with his intellectual capacity."[75] Lincoln Center remained on Barr's mind, however, and having this door closed to him because of his sexual orientation rankled the producer's ego.

At any rate, there was no hiding Barr's sexual orientation. Large parties held in his Eighth Street apartment nearly every Sunday were "ostensibly gay," according to Wilson, and everyone in the theatre community attended.[76] Richard Foltz, Barr's production secretary, believed that Barr and his operation were marginalized by the New York theatre community and considered a kind of "gay mafia." Foltz didn't have to hide his sexual orientation while working for Albee, Barr, and Wilder but felt that the group was denigrated for this same orientation.[77] Bruce Hoover, a stage manager and longtime employee of Barr's, confirmed that ABW was considered a "gay operation" by other producers, but as a straight person he always felt like a member of the ABW "family."[78] If Barr sensed this hostility—and at times both he and Albee were subjected to open homophobic baiting—he ignored it and continued to produce new plays by new writers, many of whom were gay.

Regardless of Barr's private travails, the *Playwrights 1962* evening was a success, as recalled by actress Alice Drummond: "Everybody was standing up, yelling bravo. I was already upstairs taking my makeup off because I was going to be in the next play, and I was halfway through my makeup for the next play and there was still yelling. They were yelling down there. So I came back. We thought it was pretty good."[79] With this success, Theater 1962 presented another evening of short works, *Playwrights 1962, Series 2*, on 11 December 1961, using the set and properties available from the current show.

The evening consisted of Gene Feist's *A Toy for the Clowns*, C. Skrivanek Atherton's *Chit Chat on a Rat* (directed by Gene Feist, later the cofounder of Roundabout Theatre), and *Prometheus Rebound* by Lawrence Wunderlich, directed by Richard Barr.

On 1 January 1962, Richard produced a third evening, *Playwrights 1962, Series 3*, which included Terrence McNally's *This Side of the Door* and Megan Terry's *Ex-Miss Copper Queen on a Set of Pills*. This early McNally play was staged by Martin Fried and featured Estelle Parsons. McNally, inarguably one of the most prolific and commercially successful of Barr's playwrights outside of Albee himself, remained one of his most vocal supporters.[80] Megan Terry, later a major feminist playwright, founder of Omaha Magic Theatre, and a member of the Open Theatre, was struck by how professional her production was and that Barr had optioned her work just as she was emerging as a writer.[81] She remained on the Playwright Unit's roster, considering ABW's production of her play one of the turning points in her career.[82]

In August 1962, when Barr and Wilder took a five-year lease on the Cherry Lane Theatre, confident of their record off-Broadway, they decided to experiment.[83] Rather than have a subscription season, they "put things on and let them run their course, then put something else on."[84] This "non-season" policy allowed Barr and Wilder to sublet the theatre or coproduce to cover rent and other expenses. As Theater 1963, they produced William Hanley's two short plays *Mrs. Dally Has a Lover* and *Whisper into My Good Ear* at the Cherry Lane on 1 October 1962. Hanley's writing personified the kind of radical yet accessible realism Richard was trying to promote, dealing with sensitive, even explosive issues. Estelle Parsons, whom Barr had discovered during his early years at the John Drew Theater and who had recently been in McNally's *This Side of the Door*, performed the title role of Mrs. Dally. Playing opposite Robert Drivas, Parsons gave an "outstanding performance" that began a major theatre career, and she won the 1963 Theatre World Award. *Times* critic Howard Taubman, particularly engaged by Hanley's use of language, rewarded Barr's support of a new writer with an excellent review: "The double bill is welcome not only for itself but also as a herald of what a fine new writer should accomplish in the theater."[85] *Mrs. Dally Has a Lover* later appeared on Broadway in September 1965 starring Arlene Francis.

While "waiting for Albee," Barr began his long producing relationship with the Paul Taylor Dance Company. He had been alerted to Taylor's work by Rouben Ter-Arutunian and attended a rehearsal where he saw a "work of great beauty"; he then persuaded his partners to produce Taylor's company that November after producing Albee's *Who's Afraid of Virginia Woolf?*[86] Barr felt that Paul Taylor "in his field was as exciting to me as Albee in his."[87] Taylor rejoiced in the support that Barr was able to give him, not only monetarily but administratively, since the producer offered Taylor the use of the Barr-Wilder offices and helped in the most mundane of office duties.[88] Barr struggled to produce dance on Broadway, because the raising of capital became just as hefty as for a regular Broadway musical with a full live orchestra. But Taylor believed that Barr "was a grand master at cost cutting and good at shoestring productions," and Richard Barr loved the world of dance and continued to have an interest in Paul Taylor and other dance artists, including the first Broadway performances of Twyla Tharp, Yvonne Rainer, Meredith Monk, and Don Redlich.[89]

Though Richard's interest in dance was also predicated by his need to "wait for Albee," by early 1962 he had to wait no longer: Albee completed *Who's Afraid of Virginia Woolf?* after a typically long gestation process.[90] Once Albee's first draft was written, Alan Schneider and Richard Barr read the play in the "late spring" of 1962, sitting at either end of a kitchen table at Barr's Eighth Street apartment, handing off pages to each other hurriedly and heatedly, getting ahead of the other in a scramble to finish the script.[91] Schneider described the task "as though I were being hit over the head with a succession of concrete blocks" or "being hit by a big granite boulder."[92] After reading the play in which a married couple, George and Martha, battle "like dinosaurs battling on a cliff of emotional survival," Schneider and Barr "tiptoed" out to Barr's living room and struggled to say anything to each other. After a moment's thought, Richard told Schneider that he thought the play "was remarkable . . . perhaps too remarkable for Broadway."[93]

With that began Barr's long odyssey to decide whether he would produce the play on the Great White Way or off-Broadway. He arranged for a full reading of the script in his apartment, the unofficial Theater 1962 offices, and cast Albee as George, Clinton Wilder as Honey, and Ben Piazza as Nick. Richard played Martha himself. He invited his staff, including Mark Wright and Michael Kasdan, to hear the new work, and the reaction, according to Barr, "was not mixed. No one liked the play!" While he felt the show could go ahead "with some reservations," Wilder thought it needed several more months of work, and his other staff members believed that it shouldn't be done at all. However, Wright, Albee, and Barr thought that the play should be produced. Wright was struck by the play's humor and believed it would sell the show.[94] In particular, Barr and his staff struggled with the notion of producing the early script's full assortment of "fucks" and "motherfuckers," which had been heard off-Broadway but "had not yet made their Broadway debut." Ironically, Albee took out all the obscene language when it opened on Broadway, only to return it all to the page when he directed the show himself in the 1970s (tat which point the audiences hardly noticed).[95] Though Barr was concerned that the "sensationalism of breaking the 'word-barrier'" would disgust Broadway audiences, he considered taking "one 'fuck' uptown!"[96] But no matter—even though Albee removed all the "blue" language, audiences perceived the play to be "dirty" anyway, and so even without a single obscenity in the play, *Who's Afraid of Virginia Woolf?* acquired the reputation of being obscene.

Barr immediately sent the play to theatre impresario Billy Rose, who was known mostly for "girlie shows" like *Aquacade*; his production of *Jumbo* with Jimmy Durante; and his Casa Mañana club, which featured stripper Sally Rand. Rose had recently acquired the old National Theatre (now the Nederlander) just south of the Broadway theatre district on Forty-First Street and had refurbished it, mostly as a tax write-off. The theatre was often empty and seemed to be the perfect venue for Albee's new work. According to Barr, Rose "flipped" over the play and felt it would be a hit, "if we produced it properly."[97] The theatre was particularly significant to Barr—he had had his first professional audition there with Maurice Evans's company, and it was where Orson Welles's *Five Kings* had rehearsed. Four blocks south of prime theatre district real estate on Forty-First Street, it was considered "too large for a straight play and too small for a musical," according to Schneider.[98] But it was an available Broadway house, a rare commodity for a non-musical drama. Yet even with Rose's support and a decent venue, Barr and Wilder were not sure Albee's latest play would succeed. It was too "downtown" in subject and style. At that point, Barr came up with his "insurance" policy. He would produce the show on and off-Broadway simultaneously. The cast was small; the costs would be easy to contain. That way, if the show wasn't a success on Broadway, he could continue the show off-Broadway and thumb his nose at Broadway audiences for their philistine tastes. Barr felt "fairly certain" that off-Broadway, "we could get a decent twelve week run out of it"—even with the costs of financing and organizing two casts, two directors, and really "two of everything"— and that "it might soften the blast" of the regular Broadway press.[99] However, Billy Rose quickly put the kibosh on the idea, since he thought it was a stunt (something he would know about) and would demean what he believed was an important play. At any rate, he refused to allow Barr to use his theatre if Barr "did anything so foolish."[100]

After the idea of duo productions quickly went by the wayside, Barr had another desire: to move the set and lights onto the empty stage of the Billy Rose Theatre and rehearse the cast there, the way he would have done it off-Broadway. Rose agreed, and this decision created one of the most vibrant productions of a new play on Broadway to be seen in years. For an actress who was as specific about the "reality" of her acting environment as was Uta Hagen, who played Martha in the production, it was a godsend. Rose was completely behind the idea and even wanted to invest in the show, but Barr refused to allow him to do so since "we didn't want any of the control taken out of our hands."[101]

Barr and Wilder were still concerned enough about their ability to capitalize the show themselves that they decided to take on a powerful partner. The Actors Studio had decided to produce a show on Broadway, and Albee had been a member of its Playwrights Unit since 1956. His *The Zoo Story* saw its first performance at the Actors Studio, and there was a certain connection there for Albee's work.[102] Barr and Wilder knew the studio had the financing they needed and a pantheon of stars; Albee and Barr wanted Geraldine Page and Rip Torn for the play. Both were important, influential members of the studio; it seemed a perfect match. The Actors Studio's Cheryl Crawford and Michael (Mendy) Wager attempted to bring Roger Stevens, the producer who would eventually finance the production, on board, but Stevens balked at the language of the play and refused to produce it, despite Crawford's best attempts to convince him otherwise. Paradoxically, arguing most fiercely against the production was Geraldine Page, who did not want to play Martha. Page felt the play was "intensely ugly" and would be a disastrous first choice for the studio, which she thought most people regarded as having "a widespread reputation for being sweaty smelling scratching beatniks who do God Knows What behind closed doors."[103] For Page, the production of *Who's Afraid of Virginia Woolf?* would have been fine if it had been "surrounded . . . by at least three or preferably five positive plays." Page confessed later she was glad the studio never produced the play: "It would have put the stamp on us of bitterness, hostility, and infantilism that would take us years to struggle out from under."[104]

The question of the Actors Studio's involvement in *Who's Afraid of Virginia Woolf?* continued through that summer, and in the end, the studio did make an offer to coproduce. But when Barr inquired as to who would be "signing the checks" on the production and was told it would be Roger Stevens, he passed on the offer. He knew that whoever controlled the purse strings would control the show. Barr felt that "Edward would be better served in the long run by surrounding him with the staff he knew . . . [and] by the people he trusted."[105]

While Barr and Wilder decided to forgo the Actors Studio involvement for logistical reasons, Albee passed on working with Page for artistic reasons, in order to protect Alan Schneider as the director of the production: "I asked Gerry Page to play Martha first. She read the play, liked it a lot and said that she had to ask Lee Strasberg. Why she had to ask Lee is her own business. I got a message back saying that Gerry would be very happy to do the play, but Lee had to be at all the rehearsals as a kind of supervising eminence. That indeed was the situation. She wanted Lee to be there. Alan was already set to direct it, and it struck us that you would have two directors. Besides I had seen Strasberg's work as a director, and I wasn't terribly happy with it."[106] So at that point, Albee and Schneider had to move quickly to cast the show on their own. It was to be an ordeal because, once again, the script was off-putting to traditional stars—and worse, to their agents.

Richard sent scripts immediately to Dame Judith Anderson and Henry Fonda, but both of their agents refused to pass them along to the stars. Fonda was particularly perturbed that his agent hadn't shown him the script, so Richard attempted to cast him in later productions of the play, but Fonda was never available. Anderson was an even greater loss for Barr. He had known her while they both worked for Welles and had become "quite friendly" with her as they often dined together in Hollywood.[107] However, both Fonda and Anderson would have been somewhat old for the roles of George and Martha. Other actors passed on the parts as well, such as Richard Burton (who later played George in the film version) and Katharine Hepburn, who stated that "she wasn't good enough."[108]

But in the end, the actress that Barr, Albee, Wilder, and Schneider agreed upon was Uta Hagen. Hagen, at forty-three, was at the start of an important career as an acting teacher, having taught since 1957 with her husband, Herbert Berghof, at his HB Studio. Though actually about ten years too young for Martha, her stage presence and powerful vocal ability were perfect for the demanding role, and while she was not a star in the conventional sense, Hagen was a well-respected actress with the right mix of discipline, volatility, and emotional range to play the role. Barr knew Hagen well, having worked with her at City Center in the days when he partnered with her former husband, José Ferrer. She agreed to perform Martha, despite some reservations. The problem was not the script; Hagen was immediately taken with the play, noting that "from the first time I read the first act I felt that it was going to be a huge success. I felt that success all the way through."[109] Hagen also confessed in a note to Barr and Wilder as early as November 1961 that she was interested in reading any of Albee's plays and was happy to work with Schneider and the entire Albee-Barr-Wilder team.[110]

Though she told Barr and Wilder she was "happy" to work with Schneider, she expressed later that she had serious reservations about working with him, and Schneider had concerns of his own. He had experienced difficulties previously working with Hagen's husband, Herbert Berghof, and was concerned that these past problems might color Hagen's decision to take the part. Recalling in his autobiography his attempt to convince her to take on the role of Martha, he remembered Hagen's initial reluctance: "I spent, I think, about five hours talking her into accepting. She evidently had a bad time with one of her directors, Michael Redgrave; quite apart from my 'entanglements' with her husband, whatever she had heard about my methods and personality had not entirely reassured her that I wouldn't be equally impossible."[111] What Schneider doesn't discuss was that his reputation for being difficult with women on stage had preceded him, and though he insisted that he did not bring "a riding crop to rehearsals . . . or had ever hurt an actress physically," he did admit that the "whip I . . . carried to rehearsals was a verbal one."[112]

For her own part, it was clear that Hagen wanted the role, regardless of Schneider's direction: "I had the reputation for being unbelievably choosy. I don't mean this to be true without exception, because mostly I can tell within ten minutes whether a play is going to interest me. I wondered how many playwrights know that. It's like an actor's audition; when I audition I can tell within thirty seconds whether there's going to be interest in me or not. In the first four pages of the script, I knew I wanted to play *Virginia Woolf*."[113] However, the tensions between Schneider and Hagen were to continue throughout the run of the rehearsals. Though Schneider was known for finding an actress to attack in every show he directed, he knew better than to go after Hagen.[114]

Without Henry Fonda, the role of George still presented a problem. Wilder suggested Arthur Hill, whom Schneider knew from the Pulitzer Prize–winning play *All the Way Home* by Tad Mosel, in which Hill had played Jay Follet. Hill, who was then in London making the film *In the Cool of the Night* with Jane Fonda, accepted the role but was delayed as he finished shooting. For the role of Honey, Schneider wanted to cast Lane Bradbury from the Actors Studio, and both Hagen and Schneider knew that George Grizzard would be a wonderful Nick. Grizzard was hesitant about the role—partly because it was small and partly because Nick was in essence the play's villain—though he was "rhapsodic about the play."[115] The other issue with Grizzard was his height. He was not the large "bruiser" that the script required.

One other headache took place: Alan Schneider, once again, had overbooked himself and had agreed to direct Harold Pinter's *The Dumbwaiter* and *The Collection* off-Broadway. The producer, Caroline Swann, refused to allow Schneider out of his contract or to change dates, despite the fact that she did not yet have a theatre to produce the Pinter plays. Finally, an agreement was made to allow her the use of the Cherry Lane Theatre, and Schneider was released to start rehearsals on *Who's Afraid of Virginia Woolf?*[116] The opening of the show loomed, 13 October 1962, and it was clear the rehearsals would have to begin without Hill, who was still finishing work on *In the Cool of the Night*. Luckily, Barr bought some extra time by making an early and influential decision about how he would "try-out" the show: he would stay in town and focus on preview performances. So instead of "risking the considerable loss which might occur if we toured this unconventional play," Richard had five free preview performances and five "low priced" performances before the show opened. While he did not "invent" the preview, he reinvigorated the practice by inviting a special audience to these initial performances: "We broke precedent by inviting actors and everyone else in the theater who wished to come, people who usually you don't want anywhere near your show until it's opened and critics have had their say. We did the opposite, and it helped us find a few necessary changes. Very, very few were made in either the text or the performances, which were pretty damn good from the beginning."[117]

The need for an intelligent and sophisticated audience was imperative—even though an audience of theatre "wiseacres" could potentially be "devastating." Having "theatre people" in the audience allowed Barr, Albee, and Schneider to "sense immediately and acutely any sections of the play that sagged, or missed their point."[118] Having the actors rehearse on the show's set in the Billy Rose Theatre with their actual props and costumes facilitated this preview "try-out": "We had the set about ten days after we started rehearsing, so while we did change some furniture here and there, the actors were on the stage with the set and the general blocking and the furniture, and to a great extent the lighting, and in some cases the costumes."[119] Having the set, props, and costumes made the impossibly short "summer stock" rehearsal period workable, even with a script that most of the actors found thicker than most dictionaries. Uta Hagen described the experience and importance of having the set, props, and costumes so early in the production: "To me, that was not only precedent-setting, I have never heard of anything like it since. . . . To start a play of that length and that difficulty *without* the props and scenery, we would have had to rehearse eight weeks longer. To me, this was one of the unique experiences of my entire life in the theater, starting with the things that are food for the play being alive on the stage—every little ice cube, every little clinky glass. I found this the most useful circumstance of any production I've ever been in."[120] Barr's decision to rehearse actors this way was an extension of working off-Broadway, and it was a technique he continued when he produced *Sweeney Todd* nearly twenty years later.

Hill arrived a few days after rehearsals started ("just before everyone could commit suicide," according to Schneider), and the rehearsals continued with only one major interruption. Schneider had been "hound[ing]" Lane Bradbury as Honey until she was so battered that she had to be replaced with Melinda Dillon.[121] According to Schneider, Bradbury, who had been championed by Albee, was colorless, and "her quality was all wrong for Honey." However, the decision to replace Bradbury, who was petite, with the lanky Dillon was profoundly disturbing to Grizzard, who was then the shortest member of the cast—and who had to play the "bruiser" Nick, a former football player. Having given up an opportunity to play Hamlet at the Guthrie to play Nick on Broadway, Grizzard was furious and initially threatened to leave the show. Schneider spent "endless hours" coaxing Grizzard back into the role, and rehearsals began to succeed—brilliantly.[122]

Despite the fact that the script was "unconventional," to say the least, Barr had no difficulties financing it. In the time Albee had taken to complete *Who's Afraid of Virginia Woolf?*, Barr had built the Albee "brand" sufficiently enough to attract many investors. Clinton Wilder also had many "satisfied" investors of his own to bring to the table. One of the first signs of how quickly Barr was to raise the money occurred when Milton Sperling, a Hollywood producer (and a former screenwriter who understood the quality of a great script), offered Richard a $15,000 investment on the show.[123] The show was capitalized for $75,000; however, nearly $20,000 was for the required bonds. In the end, the actual cost came closer to $45,000. The investors were paid off in a few weeks and in the end made over thirty times their original investment.[124] The show earned a net profit of $1,352,528.54 by 1969, and Albee, Barr, and Wilder parlayed that success into their Playwrights Unit, which was in business for another ten years.[125]

Just before the opening of the show, Richard Barr had dinner with Edward Albee and Clinton Wilder at his Eighth Street apartment. Albee made a request: he wanted a share of the profits of the *Virginia Woolf* venture in addition to his normal royalties. Barr and Wilder agreed that Albee would be a full producer with 20 percent of the profits of all first-class productions in the United States and Canada. However, since he already held 60 percent of subsidiary rights, Albee would not receive additional profits there. With this in place, Albee, Barr, and Wilder stood to receive 20 percent each of the show, and the backers retained a 40 percent interest. What this agreement did was give Albee a historic and important new voice in producing new plays by other playwrights. Not since the Playwrights Company in the late 1930s had there been a playwright coproducing his own work on Broadway.[126] The agreement allowed Albee the freedom to write new plays for the theatre without the commercial pressures facing other writers. Albee never went to Hollywood or wrote for television. His focus was always the American theatre. Allowing Albee to become a full producing partner made it possible for him to remain a major influence in the field of playwriting for years to come.

After the first two weeks of rehearsal, Schneider invited Wilder and Barr to a run-through of the show. Until then, following their usual policy, Barr and Wilder kept away from the production to give Schneider a chance to work with the actors and Albee in private. The producers sat in the back of the empty theatre and were quietly "astonished, excited and ineffably moved" by what they saw, as Barr relates: "At the end of it we were so shaken, that outside of a few mumbled words of conventional necessity, we left the theatre at once for his [Wilder's] house on East Seventy-Fourth Street, where we finally exploded. We both knew that something very, very special was happening on the Billy Rose stage; so we resolved to keep our heads and allow nothing to interfere with the presentation of the new work as we all had planned it."[127]

The rehearsal process had been largely uneventful, though Schneider played an uneasy cat-and-mouse game with Hagen, who neither wanted nor needed Schneider's interference. The director gently gave Hill the support he needed and pulled Grizzard and Dillon into the wild fray as the helpless prey for George and Martha's astonishing assortment of cruel games and assaults. There was one major impasse: Hagen was wrestling with the idea of the imaginary baby. In Albee's opinion, Hagen was being "self-indulgent, romanticizing the story instead of describing it somewhat objectively as he intended." Schneider could not reach her and "things were getting unpleasant," so Barr broke a cardinal rule and allowed Albee to discuss what he had intended with Hagen directly.[128] The impasse was broken but only barely, because Hagen had lost a child herself and suffered terribly when dealing with that material.[129] Hagen later complained that she had no problems establishing the notion of the imaginary child for herself and that her questions to Schneider and Albee about it were simply "totally unanswered."[130]

Despite the relatively minor struggles that went on in rehearsal, the previews were very successful. Barr made a suggestion that a scene at the beginning of the third act be cut, and there were "a few cuts and word changes" elsewhere in the script. Otherwise, the script remained intact. And on 13 October 1962, *Who's Afraid of Virginia Woolf?* opened on Broadway after its previews. Alan Schneider, director of the production, succinctly describes *Virginia Woolf*'s opening night success: "With Uta's 'Jesus H. Christ' entrance, I felt the audience fused into rapt attention, punctuated by machine-gun bursts of New York laughter. And two minutes into the performance, the actors on stage, unable to produce anything other than perfection, I knew—from my usual pacing position beside the playwright at the very back of the orchestra—that nothing could stop us. Whatever happened tomorrow or next day, that audience was as one, absorbing Edward's 'dark legend of truth and illusion' into their blood and bones. It was absolutely terrific to be part of that communal experience, to watch and listen and feel eleven hundred transported and transformed, knowing that it was their own guts that were being kicked around on that stage."[131]

Richard had arranged to have the house planted with "some carefully chosen enthusiasts," but the audience was riveted, and the evening turned out to be "one of the most exciting in Broadway history." Barr and Albee stood in the back of the house for three hours, pacing back and forth, and at the final curtain the audience cried for the author, but Albee refused to go up, insisting, "This is the actors' night." Since the opening night was a Saturday, unusual for the Broadway stage, the reviews weren't out until later on Sunday, so a long period of waiting set in. Recalling the experience of opening on a Saturday, Barr offers that "unless you have nerves of steel, I do not recommend the practice."[132]

On Saturday night, Hagen threw an informal get-together at Sardi's to celebrate the opening. Sunday afternoon, Barr and Albee met with Wilder at Wilder's apartment to wait out the reviews, along with Michael Kasdan, Mark Wright, Bill Ritman, and Howard Atlee, the press agent. There wasn't any news to be had, and Billy Rose, who was getting "nervous," according to Barr, asked to come over. By late afternoon, Atlee's "spy" at the *Mirror* was ready to "sing," and notices were starting to come in from other sources, all press connections who were willing to read the reviews over the phone. Billy Rose had made it over to Wilder's home, and Richard asked him to transcribe the reviews in shorthand (Rose had been the Gregg notation world champion as a young man and was able to transcribe two hundred words forward or backward). Rose took the dictation over the phone and read back Robert Coleman's review for the *Mirror* to Barr and company: "Edward Albee's 'Who's Afraid of Virginia Woolf?' is a sick play about sick people."[133] Rose's countenance grew even darker as he took more dictation, as Barr notes: "Billy Rose's face in repose was not exactly conducive to laughter."[134] It only became worse with John Chapman's shocking response to the play, writing for the *Daily News* under the headline "A Play Lies under the Muck in 'Who's Afraid of Virginia Woolf?'": "It is three and a half hours long, four characters wide and a cesspool deep. It's a pity about the depth for it could have gone deeper and become a notable drama. If only somebody—the producers or the gifted director or even Uta Hagen—had taken young Albee out behind a metaphorical woodshed and spanked him with a sheaf of hickory switches, he might have grown up to the responsibility which should come with his being an uncommonly talented writer."[135]

With this review, Richard vowed, once again, to quit the theatre and had a few more drinks. "As the tensions mounted," he took a walk around the block to settle his mind. After a few moments of fresh air, he returned to Wilder's apartment, "sneaked upstairs" to Wilder's library, and fell asleep on the couch. Albee "pretended the virtue of calmness," according to Schneider, and waited until the reviews by Taubman and Kerr.[136] Richard was awoken by Albee reading him Kerr's review in the *Herald Tribune*: "'Who's Afraid of Virginia Woolf?' is a great many things. It is a horror play written by a humorist. It is a western, a decline-of-the-western. It is an evening in the parlor with people who play nothing but games, war games. It is a brilliant piece of writing, with a sizable hole in its head. It need not be liked, but it must be seen."[137] Richard was not thrilled with Kerr's review, even though it signaled the fact, as did most of the reviews, that despite whatever "shocking" flaws it had, *Who's Afraid of Virginia Woolf?* was the debut of a major writer and that audiences should flock to see the show. Billy Rose, realizing that the glum producers might not think they had a hit on their hands, offered to buy them out. Barr held firm, though, and by the next morning "there was a line of about one hundred people" at the box office for the theatre.[138] Even the negative press hadn't hurt; titillating the New York audiences with promises of smut was a surefire way to fill a house. John Chapman titled his follow-up review in the next week's *Sunday News* "For Dirty-Minded Females Only," which actually boosted sales for the show.

Billy Rose also took an initiative in selling the show to these "dirty-minded females" by hawking the wares to the New York City secretaries who would then drag their bosses to see the show. He wrote an advertisement that was published in the *New York Times* titled "The Literate Are Seldom Rich." It pointed out that Rose was offering a special low-price ticket to the intelligent but poverty-stricken stenographers of rich bosses and ended his ad with a warning for their employers: "Last: a word of warning to the Proust-reading stenographer's Boss who used to smirk at the naked tootsie at my Diamond Horseshoe nightclub a few years back. Pass this one up, sire. Edward Albee and 'Virginia Woolf' are not your cup of oolong."[139] After the initial "dailies," the more important *New York Times* review by Howard Taubman and the follow-up articles by Walter Kerr in the Sunday *Herald Tribune* built momentum for the show. Even John Chapman's wife, who read her husband's "dirty-minded female" article, booked tickets for her "Westchester garden club," so Richard felt "home free."[140] It seemed that everyone, even the most acerbic New York critic's wife, wanted the opportunity to see *Who's Afraid of Virginia Woolf?*

But there were to be complications. Barr had planned for only six performances per week as the show was so strenuous for the performers. But Rose demanded eight performances and planned to charge Barr and Wilder for all eight at full houses, at 27.5 percent of the gross. Barr thus conceived of an idea of creating a "matinee" company to handle the earlier shows on Wednesday and Sunday. This was an idea that had never been done before, but the costs of hiring the actors to play the roles was less than Billy Rose's "alimony," so Kate Reid and Shepperd Strudwick were hired, along with Bill Berg and Avra Petrides. The matinee company opened on 27 October 1962, only a few weeks after the "evening company." Even these performances sold out, and Richard was able to book the matinee company to do shows at local universities and colleges to help pay for the additional costs. Richard even made a profit of $20,000 on the arrangement, preserving the energies of his "evening company" of actors while making money!

To his dismay, Barr noted that Billy Rose's cronies were collecting "ice" on top of the box office sales from ticket scalpers, carrying it up in suitcases to Rose's offices. The scalpers sold tickets to the ostensibly sold-out show, gouging the rate of the regular price. Though Barr and Wilder knew about it, they didn't participate in it, and this was confirmed by Jerome Cline, the accountant who handled the Albee-Barr-Wilder finances.[141] Still, this was a sign that the show was an unmitigated hit. The crowds were coming, even if they didn't entirely understand what it was they were seeing.[142] Barr parlayed the success of the show into a London production, a national tour, and eventually productions all over the world. Edward Albee had been added to the rank of coproducer for all the productions under the new Albee-Barr-Wilder leadership. This remarkable relationship was a historic event on Broadway; Thomas B. Morgan, in *Life* magazine, described Albee's control: "He dominates casting and the selection of other professionals; he revises his works to suit himself; his criticisms of performances, lighting and the rest are heard respectfully: he makes no concession to theater owners or investors. In short, Albee exercises more power, perhaps, than any other playwright in the history of the American theater."[143] Albee exerted his new influence by championing absurdist plays, and it was at Albee's suggestion that the first play of the Theater 1964 season was Ugo Betti's *Corruption in the Palace of Justice*, produced on 8 October 1963 at the Cherry Lane.[144]

For producing this rarely seen European work, once again Barr, Wilder, and Albee were rewarded with a particularly warm welcome from Howard Taubman: "The maturest and deepest play in town is 'Corruption in the

Palace of Justice' which arrived at the Cherry Lane Theater last night. . . . Granted that this Italian dramatist wrote subtly, even enigmatically. But he dealt with profound issues, and his work is too significant to be neglected in a theater that cares for something more than overnight sensations."[145] Though *Corruption*'s critical approval did not generate commercial success, it managed to stay open, even though its production coincided with the Kennedy assassination.[146]

Between the successes of *Virginia Woolf* and *Corruption*, the first meeting of the ABW Playwrights Unit was held on Sunday, 29 September 1963, led by Edward Parone, newly hired as the unit's managing director. Richard had been gathering names of new playwrights for many years before the founding of the unit, reading all plays that were brought to his attention, either solicited or unsolicited, and from this, Barr was able to cull a substantial "stable" of writers. Operating outside of the purview of the Actors' Equity Association, the Playwrights Unit became the heart and soul of the ABW operation.[147] It existed within the context of the 1960s off-off-Broadway theatre community—the noncommercial, semiprofessional café theatres of Greenwich Village—and the work presented there was often wildly experimental. Many unit playwrights had been produced earlier at off-off-Broadway's famous venues, including at Caffe Cino, Cafe La Mama, Theatre Genesis, and the Judson Poets Theatre, and many continued to produce work there after their productions at the Playwrights Unit. Thirty-six playwrights were invited, and twenty-six decided to participate, bringing twenty scripts to start the season; these included Bill Amidon, Otis Bigelow, Coe Bridges, Lewis John Carlino, Donald Dewey, James Dey, Edward K. Evans, Frank Gagliano, Morton Golde, David Graeme, John Guare, Arthur Hadley, Robert Heide, Jan Holm, Eric Hughes, Page Johnson, LeRoi Jones, Lee Kalcheim, Adrienne Kennedy, Kenneth Koch, Arthur Kopit, Terrence McNally, Ursule Molinaro, Howard Moss, Tom Oliver, Lawrence Osgood, Harvey D. Perr, Don Peterson, Jack Richardson, Megan Terry, Stuart Richard Townsend, Jean-Claude van Itallie, Deric Washburn, Arnold Weinstein, Doric Wilson, and Lawrence Wunderlich.[148]

Richard believed that these off-off-Broadway playwrights were not being served in their bohemian storefront theatres with amateur productions and coterie audiences. Therefore, he conceived of the ABW Playwrights Unit as a professional theatre workshop dedicated to emerging playwrights. Unlike other venues off-off-Broadway, including the Playwrights Unit of the Actors Studio, which was run by actors and directors, the ABW Playwrights Unit was to be run by playwrights. It became a safe haven for writers learning their craft and a model for other playwrights' theatres and workshops.

Many of the unit playwrights saw their plays performed in a professional, fully equipped theatre for the first time, instead of in cafés, church lofts, or storefronts. Albee, Barr, and Wilder made a conscious decision to take a low-profile, hands-off approach, hiring a manager to handle its day-to-day administration: "'We hope the playwrights themselves will dictate the operation,' he [Albee] said. 'What we're going to do is to provide a theatre to work in, a stage, actors, a director, whatever we can do to be helpful. We are not going to say anything about the kind of work that should be done. If a man wants to do something that seems completely incomprehensible to us, fine . . .' Mr. Albee stressed the fact that the unit will not be a course in playwriting—'You can't teach that,' he said—but he will be on hand to discuss, analyze and advise any writer who wants his help."[149]

The producers' low profile was a double-edged sword; while there was no commercial pressure put on the playwrights by the producers, neither was there much of the hoped-for advice, good or otherwise. Albee's presence, however, was felt, whether he was physically at hand or not. Playwright John Guare, whose early play *To Wally Pantoni We Leave a Credenza* was produced at the unit, felt that Albee was the unit's playwright-hero who had battled the forces of Broadway and won.[150] Though not always able to be physically present, Albee's sponsorship gave the unit its unique notoriety in the milieu of the off-off-Broadway movement.

A total of $23,232.88 from the profits of *Virginia Woolf* was dedicated to the operating costs of the Playwrights Unit, and with those funds, Barr leased Village South Theatre at 14 Vandam Street, a 199-seat theatre located off of Sixth Avenue, for a year. The main expenses for the unit were its rent, utilities, and small staff. Because the unit was a showcase, artists provided their services without payment, a common off-off-Broadway arrangement. The unit was to be divided into two branches, a workshop playing to invited audiences and a playwrights' series that was free and open to the public. Unit playwrights were under no obligation to sell their scripts to the ABW organization after production.

With Parone as the unit's managing director, Lawrence Wunderlich was chosen as its theatre manager and Johnny Dodd as the lighting designer/janitor. Initially, these were the only paid staff members of the unit.[151] Wunderlich wrote the only major account of the unit's activities, often taking a contrary view about its achievements. Parone managed the unit independently, without interference from Barr, Wilder, or Albee—and it was not to be a school but a fully operational theatre, as Wilder describes: "We would rehearse there—our basic, permanent set is a simple one and there are few props, which can be easily moved off stage—then give four or five previews before the official performance. . . . There will be absolutely no restrictions on the kind of thing the playwrights can do. It may be a three-act play, a single scene or an act or two from a work in progress. Admission will be free and, after allowing for people the playwrights themselves want to invite, it will be on a first come, first served basis."[152] The unit's function was grounded in producing theatre, not discussions. "We were not there to talk about plays," Wunderlich writes. "We were there to see that plays were cast, rehearsed, produced, and to see that audiences came."[153]

A total of twenty playwrights of the twenty-six who decided to participate had twenty-one evenings of twenty-six plays produced at the ABW Playwrights Unit under the aegis of Theater 1964. The first play was Lee Kalcheim's *A Party for Divorce*, on Sunday, 17 November 1963, at the Village South Theatre. While Kalcheim, a Yale School of Drama graduate, later wrote the Emmy Award–winning television sitcom *All in the Family*, the realistic style of this early effort came as a surprise to some unit members. Linda Feinfeld Magyar, the first production secretary for ABW Productions Inc., confirmed that *A Party for Divorce* was "a complete and utter shock": "It was like a television sitcom . . . like a bad television sitcom. And no one could believe how awful it was. And everyone, and I mean everyone—Michael Kasdan, Larry Wunderlich, Joseph Cali, all of them—kept saying that he [Kalcheim] was in the unit because his father or his uncle was some big agent at William Morris . . . and it was not as if we were snobs or anything. Except for Larry, who was a snob, and he was furious from the start. . . . It was a scandal."[154] But the play was clearly representative of Barr's growing taste for the tense, menacing Pinteresque realism of Albee's *Virginia Woolf*. And it was a shift away from the nonlinear style of the absurdists toward a more politically committed, humane theatre, according to Barr: "I have a feeling that the new playwrights are moving back toward a much more conventional form than Ionesco or Beckett, toward a recognition of man as an intuitive animal at a new level of awareness. What we're interested in is human beings, human behavior, human feelings. The best new plays are pleas for a recognition of man as a dignified animal, man as man. The playwrights strip man bare of his pretensions and try to merge the intuitive and the rational. The 'absurd' playwrights, reacting against rationalism[,] have left out reason altogether."[155] Though Albee himself had misgivings about Kalcheim's play, Barr's move away from the absurdists was part of a larger trend taking place off-off-Broadway in reaction to the radicalism of the Living Theatre and to the growing orientation of avant-garde theatre away from text.

Over the next six months, a new play was produced at the Playwrights Unit nearly every Sunday, and though much work was excellent, some scripts were patently unadventurous or weakly imitative of Albee's "absurdist" style. Still, the writers were chosen not because they were absurdists but because they demonstrated talent—if there was a page of brilliance, Richard produced the play. The unit was intended to train playwrights and give them room to fail. Barr's ability to procure well-known, talented professional actors to work gratis was key to this process. Playwrights could learn about their plays by having great actors and directors bring them to life. Because the unit offered actors a low-commitment opportunity to perform roles not available to them in the commercial theatre, the unit's experimental work drew the enthusiastic participation of a growing pool of major performers like Frank Langella, Viveca Lindfors, Marian Seldes, James Coco, Alice Drummond, John S. Becher, Ruth White, Jane Hoffman, and many others.

The next important work produced by the Playwrights Unit as part of Theater 1964 was *War* by Jean-Claude van Itallie, who became the principal playwright of the seminal performance group the Open Theatre. The play was given two performances on 22 December 1963 at the Village South Theatre and was directed by Michael Kahn, his first major production in New York. Kahn had met van Itallie in Europe and went on to direct van Itallie's *America Hurrah. War* featured actor Gerome Ragni, one of the creators of the tribal rock musical *Hair.* It was a "thrilling debut" for the young playwright, and when the audience cried, "Author! Author!" after the production, van Itallie was "ecstatic."[156] Yet van Itallie was not totally satisfied, writing that he "loved the production, but it was only on for two days. I wanted it more in the world."[157] At the Playwrights Unit, van Itallie felt he was being treated as a neophyte in a "nursery school" operation. This reflected the opinion of other off-off-Broadway playwrights who regarded the unit as a somewhat patronizing attempt of the "establishment" to take advantage of their talents.[158] Sam Shepard, whose work was first produced at the unit, expressed a similar point of view, though he also desperately sought Albee's affirmation.[159] Shepard's and van Itallie's responses reflected the distrust of a generation who viewed the "Establishment" producers and theatre owners as part of "the problem" against which they sought to rebel. But despite their misgivings, they still took full advantage of the opportunities Barr, Wilder, and Albee had to offer.

Following *War* was *Dutchman* by LeRoi Jones (later Amiri Baraka), produced at the Playwrights Unit on Sunday, 12 January 1964. Jones was a leading "beat" poet at the time and founder, with his wife, Hettie Jones, of the influential poetry journal *Yugen*. He became the voice of a generation of radical African American writers as well as a founder of the Black Arts Movement. The play was directed by Edward Parone and featured Al

Freeman Jr. and Jennifer West. The production of Jones's *Dutchman* at the unit was explosive; audiences had a visceral response to the play, both of outrage and fierce admiration—reactions that the play continues to evoke. Lawrence Wunderlich offered his impression of the production: "There was 'audience participation' of the sort that I had often read or heard about but never witnessed before. Shouts of 'Yes, sir!' and 'You said it!' and 'Hallelujah!' and 'A-men!' rose up from all over the theatre and punctuated the play. At the end, there was a standing ovation and the author was called to the stage."[160]

Wunderlich's impressions were confirmed by Parone. The director had a remembrance of Leontyne Price, "who lived in the neighborhood, suddenly bursting out with 'Right on!' and 'Say it!' several times."[161] Amiri Baraka offered his point of view regarding the audience's reaction to *Dutchman*: "Works really feed on their time and take their strength from that time. And *Dutchman* really reflects the things that were happening during that period. So most of the power in that play is just what I was able to get from what was happening."[162] Barr's selection of *Dutchman* reflected a movement away from the abstraction of absurdist drama to a more tangible, explosive theatre directly related to the issues confronting 1960s audiences. Baraka was pleased with the unit production, with Parone's direction, and in particular with the acting of Jennifer West.[163] *Dutchman* became the first play from the Playwrights Unit to actually move from off-off-Broadway to off-Broadway and was a transformational production for Baraka. He was subject to both great admiration and pointed criticism for the play's fiery politics.

Shortly after the opening of *Dutchman*, Theater 1964 presented *Funnyhouse of a Negro* by Adrienne Kennedy on 14 January 1964 at the East End Theatre. The play was Albee's favorite, and he remains particularly proud of its production.[164] Michael Kahn, who directed the play, immediately connected with the script: "They were so supportive of it; and I knew Adrienne was completely enamored of Edward in the best sense of the word. I was teaching at the Circle in the Square and Edward was teaching at [the] Circle in the Square and the secretary who was running the Playwrights Unit, Joyce Small, sent me a play saying 'Could you think of a director for it?' And I read it and I said, 'Well, I think I actually understand it, so probably I should direct it.'"[165] *Funnyhouse of a Negro* and *Dutchman* opened within days of each other off-Broadway, a reflection of those turbulent times. Though Kahn struggled to give life to the play in such a short time frame, he did not change the script, as it was clear Kennedy needed to see the play as it was. He was struck by how well this short play worked with its off-Broadway audiences: "And that was a big thing—that Edward saw this play and they decided to really sponsor it. And it was one of the first plays off-Broadway that was really short, so they did it twice in an evening—it was way before a play that would last an hour and a half and people would be happy with it, but they did. And they were way ahead of their time."[166] Kennedy's play received a perceptive review by Howard Taubman, who described it as "an overflowing portion of the hallucinated horrors that torment the last hours of a Negro girl."[167] It once again emphasized the influence that Albee wielded over the ABW producing organization. Kennedy remained on the Playwrights Unit roster and went on to an important career as an experimental African American playwright influencing later writers such as Suzan-Lori Parks and Ntozake Shange.

On 24 March 1964, the ABW production of Fernando Arrabal's *Two Executioners* joined Samuel Beckett's *Play* at the Cherry Lane and LeRoi Jones's *Dutchman*. Parone directed both plays in an evening of works titled *Three at the Cherry Lane*. Beckett specifically requested that his short *Play* be performed three times in a row, but the producers expressed concerns about this, and it was one of the few instances that Beckett's instructions were not expressly followed.[168] And *Dutchman* exploded off-Broadway as it had at the unit, confounding the author himself: "They called me names, said I was crazy, that I needed to be locked up. As I was walking back from the newsstand, I was thinking, 'Well, I can see now they want to make me famous for some reason. If they do that, I could kind of like it 'cause I have a lot of things to pay them back for.'"[169] *Dutchman* drew criticism for its implied anti-white rhetoric, for its similarity to Albee's *The Zoo Story*, and for its inflammatory dialogue. Despite this criticism (or perhaps because of it), Barr later paired it with Albee's *The American Dream* on 21 April 1964 at the Cherry Lane, where it was successful with audiences. And this was the high-water mark of Barr's producing volume. In his memoirs, he documents forty-eight hours during this time frame, starting on 23 December 1963. In addition to the work at the Cherry Lane, he was also producing off-off-Broadway at the Playwrights Unit, the Paul Taylor Dance Company, and *Who's Afraid of Virginia Woolf?* on Broadway. Richard denies being compulsive, defending his "mad rush of producing" this way: "The plays existed; the dance companies existed; and it was a part of the excitement of the time that pushed us on. The United States, as a nation, was growing up. People had begun to recognize art as a part of their lives. Television had not yet become the well of nothingness that it now represents, so the theatre and dance began to fill in the void."[170]

On 16 May 1964, the Broadway production of *Who's Afraid of Virginia Woolf?* closed after 660 performances, having grossed $2,585,166 since it had opened at the Billy Rose Theatre on 13 October 1962. The profits from the production were valued at more than $750,000, including film rights.[171] While Barr's productions of *Virginia Woolf* were on tour and in Europe, its Broadway closing ended a dependable source of income, and ABW scrambled to replace it.

After the high-volume first year of their Playwrights Unit, Parone, Barr, Wilder, and Albee discussed new directions to take to improve it. The producers were keeping tabs on what was being done, as can be observed in Clinton Wilder's detailed notes, and were intent on its success.[172] Though Richard had his hands full with ABW's off-Broadway and Broadway productions, he kept trying to improve its operation and attended nearly every production at the unit over its ten years of existence. The next season, the unit was able to afford, in addition to a theatre manager, two stage managers, Walter Cavalieri and Rilla Bergman, with Cavalieri doubling as a lighting designer. This stage manager setup was similar to the Cherry Lane operation and added to the unit's efficiency. With two plays in continuous rehearsal at the unit, one in the theatre and another in the lounge underneath, having two stage managers was a necessity.[173] Another change was the replacement of Edward Parone, who went on to a career as a successful professional director. His career was given a boost by his direction of Jones's *Dutchman*, and he became the creator of the Mark Taper Forum's new play program.

Parone was succeeded by Charles (Chuck) Gnys. Gnys, the manager of the Playwrights Unit from September 1964 through May 1970, was its longest and most important influence, outside of Albee, Barr, and Wilder. On Broadway, Gnys served as the company manager of *Camelot* and was a production assistant for three shows, *The Perfect Setup*, *Viva Madison Avenue*, and *The Poker Game*. Gnys was excited by the prospect of managing the unit, believing that it was going to be the most important venue for new plays in New York City.[174] Theater 1965 began its fall season with the unit's production of Tom Oliver's *Mr. Altschuler's Tree* on 11 October 1964, followed by Lee Kalcheim's *Don't Call Us* on 18 October 1964 and *The Folding Green*, an Albee-esque farce by poet and *New Yorker* poetry editor Howard Moss, on 9 November 1964.

Theater 1965's off-Broadway production of Otis Bigelow's *Giant's Dance* at the Cherry Lane on 16 November 1964 was a flop. Bigelow, a unit stage manager, was one of Barr's close friends, having shared a room with him during his Mercury days. Albee deeply disliked the play and made several attempts to convince Barr not to produce it. The letters exchanged between the two, starting with Albee's (below), reveal a mutual admiration but also a serious difference of taste that later erupted further with Barr's production of Mart Crowley's *The Boys in the Band*:

> I have just finished reading and mulling THE GIANT'S DANCE, and feel I should, as a good partner, give you my feeling about it. I find the play verbose, arch and unbearably tedious. Perhaps the author thinks he is Shaw, but to my mind what he has accomplished is—if reworked—the book for an age 8–12 children's musical. Worst of all, the play—if I recall our conversations of the past few years correctly—has nothing whatsoever to do with what our theatre is supposed to be about.[175]

Richard was stunned by Albee's reaction, having taken quite a liking to the play and deeply connected not only to the script but to the playwright himself. Barr's response to Albee highlights his close friendship with Bigelow but also the generational difference between himself and Albee:

> First, I cried when I read the play. This may be no acid test, but I do not cry often. There is, I believe, a deep sadness and a serious truth in that one of war's causes lies in the restlessness of armies; or in the build-up of munitions; or in the aimlessness of vacillating masses. . . . Otis has written an idyll. He illustrates well my notion that the current trend of American playwriting very often expresses itself through myth/fantasy and satire.[176]

The letter reveals that there was a good deal of negotiating going on between the producers. Each tried to give the other support for pet projects, but money was becoming a growing concern. Still, Albee wrote back with an intensity that made it clear he was not willing to promote work he considered to be pedestrian:

> The play remains arch and tedious. I have—God help me—read it again. I do not think it is ready for serious production. You say Bigelow writes prose very well indeed. If this is so, why does the play stop, sigh, and sit on its ass every time one of the prose paragraphs of "writing" comes along, waiting for it to get the hell over so it can move on? Bigelow may well be the first playwright you ever encouraged, and I certainly hope he won't be the last. . . . I cried over GIANT'S DANCE too, Richard: I cried over the prospect of our having to do it.[177]

Regardless of Albee's serious concerns, Richard decided to produce the show, which lasted only six performances. Howard Taubman, in his *Times* review, though suggesting that "on the fringes of *The Giant's Dance* . . . are diverting intimations of fantasy and humor," criticized the production for "too much Disney-like cuteness and second-hand philosophy for comfort."[178] The critical and commercial failure of *The Giant's Dance* meant an uphill battle to win approval for the new plays to come. It also signaled the growing difference of taste between Albee and Barr.

The next important work produced by the Theater 1965 Playwrights Unit was Sam Shepard's short play *Up to Thursday*, produced with Otway Crockett's *The Burial Committee* on 23 November 1964. *Up to Thursday*, which was personally selected by Albee from a suitcase of scripts Shepard had deposited in his arms, was directed by Chuck Gnys. It was first play Gnys directed at the unit and featured a young Harvey Keitel and Kevin O'Connor, a regular off-off-Broadway performer.[179] Shepard's *Up to Thursday*, though a fascinating first attempt, was the unfinished work of a developing theatre artist. At the same time, it was the work of a brilliant theatrical mind, given over to a musical structure of rock and framed by a rootless adolescent terror. The reaction by the other unit playwrights was one of awe; as Harvey Perr states, "Shepard knocked us out."[180] Though Shepard struggled at the Playwright Unit, as did many off-off-Broadway playwrights, with the notion of "selling out," it was exactly this kind of professional production that Richard Barr was trying to give to playwrights at the unit. He was helping them transition out of their small theatre groups into the larger theatre culture.

Theater 1965's major production was Albee's *Tiny Alice*, produced on Broadway at the Billy Rose Theatre on 29 December 1964 and directed by Alan Schneider with settings by William Ritman. Albee had written the first two acts and then pressed Barr for a production date and to have John Gielgud to play the lead role of Julian. Barr read the play and, liking what he read, immediately sent it on to Gielgud, writing: "Perhaps this is a bit premature, but Edward returned from Europe last evening with the announcement that he is going to write TINY ALICE (a play which he is writing with you very much in mind) as his next play instead of THE SUBSTITUTE SPEAKER on which he had been working."[181] Gielgud's response was quick and positive. He was interested, and by 13 October 1964, his agent, John Perry, was working out the details of Gielgud's contract. This included a clause permitting Gielgud first refusal on the role for the London production, signaling Gielgud's faith in the play and Albee's growing fame. Gielgud also recommended Irene Worth as Miss Alice for the production, and the team was quickly assembled. Schneider directed the production with Ritman designing and Wright stage-managing, and the cast filled out with William Hutt as the Lawyer, Eric Berry as the Cardinal, and John Hefferman as the Butler.

The key to Richard Barr's efficiency as a producer was the presence of the entire company, including the carpenter, at the outset. He set up a team meeting for *Tiny Alice* at Ritman's home to examine and discuss the model for the set. This included Schneider, Albee, Wright, the master carpenter, and the head of the scenic shop where the set was to be built. There were three "complicated" sets, which had to be mechanized so as to be manipulated by only one additional stagehand. The sets "flew in or out from the fly spaces of the theatre as required," and in order to facilitate this, the furniture had to be placed exactly. Ritman designed each of the sets "to the inch," and Wright, Barr's stage manager, was then able to plan all the movements of each set piece or hand prop in advance.[182]

Richard then initiated a reading of the play with actors who were excellent but "totally unsuitable" for the roles so that Albee could hear "an intelligent approximation of the play." This made it possible for scripts to go into production with minimal rewrites after rehearsals began. Just about two weeks before the first rehearsal, Barr had a full staff production meeting. This was something that he had insisted upon since his Princeton college days and his work at the Mercury Theatre. At the meeting, every day of the production schedule was discussed, including photo calls, costume fittings, days off, changes of rehearsal spaces, dress rehearsals, and the schedule of preview performances. Richard took a decidedly institutional approach to producing. Because of this, "everyone knows about every other department's special requirements or problems."[183] The schedule didn't change unless there was an emergency.

The production team convened next in a restaurant meeting after the first dress rehearsal. Barr allowed each department to make "comments, corrections or mutual admiration." Then each night Barr met with the department heads, who were "still correcting their work" until the production was complete. Before the first rehearsals, Barr arranged for the actors to meet with each other for cocktails, since "there is nothing more terrifying," according to Barr, "than the first meeting with his colleagues on a bare stage, usually poorly lit." Because of this process, there was rarely the "backstage tension, unreasonable temperament, or general technical chaos" of many productions. Barr scheduled the hysteria out of the show, even with the difficult, complex plays of Albee, Beckett, and his other writers.[184]

Yet the difficulties with *Tiny Alice* weren't technical; they had to do with the script itself, with Gielgud, and with Barr's own absence from the rehearsal process. Confident in his production team during *Tiny Alice*'s rehearsals, Barr left for a week to attend his mother's seventieth birthday celebration in Portugal with his sisters, Carol Fischer and Barbara Luchs. He also took some time to see the London production of *Who's Afraid of Virginia Woolf?* By the time he returned, several problems had arisen. Gielgud was struggling with the final monologue of the play, which he felt was overly long, and with understanding the play in general. He also wasn't entirely thrilled with Schneider as a director or Ritman as a designer and was having difficulty with Albee's language: "Everything is done through

Schneider, who has been most patient and tactful, but is not Peter Brook. The other three men [actors in the play] are only so-so, but no doubt they will pass in New York—the lawyer especially indifferent—a poor man's Vincent Price. Irene is splendid, though."[185] Gielgud was never entirely comfortable in the role of Julian, who was many years younger than his actual age, and Schneider agreed with his assessment. Albee insisted that he had written the role for Gielgud, and according to Schneider, "eventually, the idea of John (then about sixty) playing a youthful, sexually obsessed priest was accepted by everyone—except John."[186] Despite these issues, Barr worked with Schneider, Albee, and Wilder on a few script changes at their normal "restaurant production meeting" of the show and attempted to fix whatever issues were at hand. Despite being, as Schneider believed, "baffled by the play itself, totally puzzled by the character he was supposed to play, and completely bewildered by what he called 'surrealist theater,'" Gielgud held "steadfast" to his promise to Albee to play the role.[187]

The production of *Tiny Alice* represented the turning point in the fortunes of ABW Productions and its Playwrights Unit. Schneider believed that no one, including the author, really understood what the play was about and thought it needed work: "Still in his mid-thirties, he [Albee] had written his 'big, philosophical play,' his Lady from the Sea, his Dream Play, his Tempest. Perhaps if he had waited to rewrite it once or twice before we went into rehearsal . . . but he would not."[188] From Albee's point of view, however, he simply preferred that his colleagues learn from the play itself rather than from his explanations of what the play should be.[189] In hindsight, perhaps *Tiny Alice*, an important, provocative experimental work by a serious playwright, should not have been first produced on Broadway. But Barr did not want to take a step backward from Broadway. Once Albee had made it there, Richard felt it signaled a retreat to move him back off-Broadway. Still, James Prideaux, who worked at the ABW offices, believed that Albee was hurt by Barr's decision to keep the show on Broadway. In his opinion, Barr should have been more protective of Albee's work by moving the show off-Broadway.[190] *Tiny Alice* represented the serious downside in making one playwright the unquestioned center of the producing paradigm. This was especially the case when the playwright was Edward Albee, who was remarkably protean in his talents as a writer and singularly uninterested in writing plays for commercial value. And, at any rate, Albee was not going to write the "son of *Who's Afraid of Virginia Woolf?*," as he has expressed it many times, as his next major offering on Broadway.[191]

Tiny Alice opened to not unfavorable reviews; Howard Taubman of the *New York Times* gave it this respectful mention: "In 'Tiny Alice' Edward

Albee has moved into the difficult, mysterious, ever tantalizing realm of faith. . . . He has written with the literacy of a man who knows that the word itself can be charged with drama and with a gift for making a scene on a stage reverberate with subtle overtones."[192] While Taubman's review was deferential, it emphasized the more inscrutable aspects of the play, a point stressed by other reviews of *Tiny Alice*, and this conspired to scare away audiences. During the previews, audiences seemed to understand the structure and narrative of the play. Yet after the reviews had "instructed" them that *Tiny Alice* was incomprehensible, the audiences began to pull away.[193] Barr was furious with this response and pushed Albee to call a press conference on 22 March 1965.

Sitting alone on the set in the Billy Rose Theatre, surrounded by five television newsreel cameras and speaking to an audience of 150 press representatives, Albee lamented the critics' inability to support new and difficult plays on Broadway and then carefully explained *Tiny Alice*'s narrative.[194] Barr recalled that "the paraphernalia was so thick, Albee was almost hidden from the audience. I think Edward did very well in a thankless situation."[195]

Alan Schneider believed that the conference set into motion a long-lasting feud between Albee and the newspaper critics, one that ultimately shortened the run of *Tiny Alice*, curtailed the producing life of ABW Productions, and nearly ended the career of Albee himself.[196] Barr ironically notes that "the idea did not backfire, but it did not improve business."[197] The production lasted 167 performances, a respectable run, but the problem for ABW Productions was that *Tiny Alice* had been an extraordinary expense, and one that had eaten into the reserve created by *Virginia Woolf. Tiny Alice* had been groomed as Albee's next big hit, and a cash cow to boot, but instead, *Tiny Alice* set the pattern that, with the exception of *Delicate Balance*, would lead toward the collapse of the ABW firm. Each year Albee brought out an entirely different play, which was promptly trampled by the critics. Audiences stayed away, and the production costs contributed to the gathering financial cloud.

The next important play produced by the Theater 1965 Playwrights Unit was Lanford Wilson's *No Trespassing*, a one-act play, directed by Milton Katselas and opening 31 January 1965. Wilson was already a well-established off-off-Broadway playwright whose career took off shortly after his unit productions. Albee's response to Wilson's *No Trespassing* offers some insight into how playwrights were chosen for participation in the unit: "Attached, NO TRESPASSING, by Lanford Wilson. I have the feeling this fellow's dramatic instinct is, at the moment, pretty superficial . . . or, to put it better, second-hand. And, unfortunately, the play doesn't go anywhere except toward a revelation; the characters do not develop, and the piece is an incident, or a short story. But there's a deep-down kind of wildness, and I think we should encourage him, so let's put him in for a year and see what happens to him."[198] For most of the playwrights, including Wilson, the attitude was "watch and see what happens." Rather than look for a perfect script, Albee seems to have been looking for a certain spark of talent, "a deep-down kind of wildness," to nurture within the writer.

Yet despite the poor showing for *Tiny Alice*, and in celebration of the fifth anniversary of Albee's *The Zoo Story*, Theater 1965 then produced, over the course of twelve weeks, eight new playwrights, most of whom were first presented at the Playwrights Unit. Titled the *New Playwrights Series*, each evening of theatre was to be given eight performances. The first evening opened on 10 February 1965 at the Cherry Lane Theatre and consisted of Sam Shepard's *Up to Thursday*, Paul Foster's *Balls*, and Lanford Wilson's *Home Free*. Wilson speaks of the experience of having *Home Free* produced in the New Playwrights Series: "*Home Free* [at the Cherry Lane] was the first professional thing I had ever had done. . . . [It] had been done at La Mama earlier but [at the Cherry Lane] it was for money! I got a percentage of the house; it was fabulous! Who had ever heard of such a thing—what a concept! It certainly made you feel professional. I mean, we were reviewed, for crying out loud, at the Cherry Lane. Most of them had never been reviewed before. At the Cherry Lane it was for real—it was for a limited run—but it was for real."[199]

The Playwrights Unit and the productions given at the Cherry Lane were a validation of the artistic experimentation these playwrights were attempting. The first play presented was Shepard's *Up to Thursday*, a Playwrights Unit production directed by Gnys, with Harvey Keitel and Kevin O'Connor. Paul Foster, a La Mama regular, had previously produced *Balls* at La Mama and at Caffe Cino, where Wilson's *Home Free* had also been produced.[200] Although Barr was not fond of *Home Free*, Albee insisted upon its production.[201] The reviews of the productions were respectful, and there was encouragement for both the playwrights and the producers. Leonard Harris of the *New York World-Telegraph* wrote: "Five years ago Barr and Wilder discovered Albee. Now they are on another talent hunt. I suggest you join them. There aren't too many Albees extant, but the woods still yield some rare fauna."[202] Most of the reviewers embraced the evening of neophytes, reporting on it rather than offering a traditional review, though several found the language, form, or content of the plays enigmatic.

While the New Playwrights Series was running at the Cherry Lane, the Playwrights Unit continued its regular season. The next important work produced there was John Guare's play *To Wally Pantoni We Leave a Credenza*, directed by Edwin Patrick Aldridge on 21 February 1965. The experience had a profound effect on Guare: "A movement called Off-Off-Broadway was beginning. You'd stop by the Barr-Wilder-Albee workshop to see what was on this week, to argue its merits, its flaws, how to fix it, how to protect it, to drink in this fabulous sense of the new. Who was in the play or who directed the play was not as important as the fact that what you were seeing was a new play written by a new American playwright."[203] *To Wally Pantoni We Leave a Credenza* was produced on NBC Television in 1969.[204] Guare considered it a seminal work in his own development, having tried out in one-act form the devices he used in later plays like *The House of Blue Leaves*.[205] In an article in *New Theater Review*, Guare talks about Albee's importance: "At the hub of this new Off-Off-Broadway fringe, dominating it all, indeed personally sponsoring it, was Albee, who was one of us, yet apart from us, who only wanted to create a world where new playwrights could function and develop with the near-sacred trust that language could joyously carry the truth's wriggling burden. The entire Off-Off-Broadway movement, which has become the mainstream of today, can trace its roots back to Albee's generosity of the sixties."[206] The combination of this prestige, the professionalism and competence of the unit staff, and the freedom to fail without commercial or aesthetic pressures made the ABW unit, in one playwright's words, "a very hot place to work."[207]

The New Playwrights Series at the Cherry Lane continued with a second evening of plays: *Pigeons*, a one-act play by Lawrence Osgood, directed by Edward Parone and featuring Geraldine Fitzgerald, and *Conerico Was Here to Stay* by Frank Gagliano and directed by Melvin Bernhardt, both of which had been previously produced at the unit. The plays opened on 3 March 1965; *Conerico* garnered the better reviews, though neither play received the strong, if somewhat mystified, reviews of the first evening. On 30 March 1965, Theater 1965 sent a letter to the members of the Playwrights Unit announcing that operations at the Village South Theatre were to be discontinued on a weekly basis. With the closing of *Virginia Woolf* in May 1964, the failure of *The Giant's Dance*, and the abbreviated run of *Tiny Alice*, funding for the unit had reached its lowest ebb.[208]

The third evening in the New Playwrights Series included Kenneth Pressman's *Hunting the Jingo Bird*, directed by Chuck Gnys, and *Lovey* by Joseph Morgenstern, directed by Edward Parone. The evening was viewed as "less promising" by *Post* critic Richard Watts, and Walter Kerr of the *Herald Tribune* clearly preferred Morgenstern's play to Pressman's.[209] Both plays were "far less avant garde than those that have preceded them yet they seem to shun the conventional and, as a result, fall between two schools."[210] The fourth evening of the New Playwrights Series was the Pinteresque *Do Not Pass Go* by Charles Nolte, produced by Theater 1965 with coproducer Frith Banbury at the Cherry Lane on 19 April 1965. The play, which follows a structure similar to Albee's own *The Zoo Story*, was well received by the *Times*' Howard Taubman: "Of the new plays introduced by Theater 1965 at the Cherry Lane this season 'Do Not Pass Go' is far and away the best. It is, in fact, one of the better new plays presented this season—not a vintage one, it is true—on or off Broadway."[211] *Do Not Pass Go* ran for sixteen performances, more than any other evening in the series. The New Playwrights Series had been a litmus test for Theater 1965's ability to produce new writers.[212] The cost of the series, particularly after the failure of *The Giant's Dance* and *Tiny Alice*, was beginning to pull at ABW's financial fabric—a result, perhaps, of the series having been promoted as "plays you haven't seen by playwrights you haven't heard of yet."[213]

The Theater 1965 season was a turning point in the fortunes of the Playwrights Unit and ABW Productions. Though Barr continued producing Albee on Broadway and new plays off-off-Broadway and experimenting with repertory, his Playwrights Unit never again presented as many plays. Following the mixed results of the Theater 1965 season, Barr and Albee were invited to the first National Playwrights Conference at the Eugene O'Neill Memorial Theatre Foundation, where they were grilled in question-and-answer sessions. George White, the founder of the conference, had gone to Barr and Wilder to help him select playwrights for this first summer event. The conference had begun on a dark note, with playwrights complaining about a lack of opportunities for their work. Luckily, for White and his fledgling conference, the visit from Albee and Barr had a "leavening effect" on the writers and "saved the first playwrights conference from total chaos."[214] Offering a reality check, Albee pointed out that most Broadway plays are totally forgettable: "It's kind of like watching the television. It's a parentheses around life, rather than an underlining of some point of life. Now if that's the kind of theater that's wanted, it's the kind of theater that we'll get and it'll turn out to be the kind of theater we deserve. Which isn't so hot, is it?"[215]

Albee was adamant that playwrights not abnegate their responsibility to question the status quo in an effort to "entertain" audiences rather than to "engage" them. His feeling was that off-Broadway was a better venue for these writers. Barr was queried on the details of how scripts were selected and, in particular, what made a play producible in his mind. His response was typically upbeat and, at the same time, fairly rebellious: "What we look for is someone who is making an observation on the human situation, on the world today as he sees it in a way that is original and provocative and exciting. . . . Whether they're producible or not doesn't, strangely enough, concern us as much as that first point."[216] While Barr retained his relentlessly positive demeanor, both he and Albee were wrestling with the problems of critics and audiences—and also with ABW's internal operations.

Serious morale problems at Barr's Playwrights Unit led to a letter from Albee, who was genuinely disappointed that the writers were not supporting each other's plays: "A very important thing was the fact that I wanted each of the playwrights to involve themselves in the work of the other playwrights, on the understanding that you learn not only from what happens to your work but from following through what happens to another playwright's work—you might learn something constructive and useful about revision or lack of revision or digging your heels in. I wanted them to be helpful to one another, not only to themselves."[217] It remained then for the unit's third season to solve some of these problems, particularly those that were based on the growing financial obstacle of the producers having to support the unit's efforts from their own pockets. The solutions, financial and administrative, came with the establishment of ABW Productions' not-for-profit entity, Albarwild Theatre Arts, Inc., and, shortly thereafter, new funding and a new proactive stance toward the unit's playwrights and plays.

Richard Barr in drag, as the Countess of Sessex, in the 1937 Triangle production of *Fol-De-Rol.* Billy Rose Theatre Division, The New York Public Library for the Performing Arts, Astor, Lenox, and Tilden Foundations.

Richard Barr as Archer in the 1938 Theatre Intime Production of Farquhar's *The Beaux' Stratagem*. Princeton University Library.

Orson Welles (*left*) and Richard Barr in the RKO Pictures production offices of *Citizen Kane*, 1940. Billy Rose Theatre Division, The New York Public Library for the Performing Arts, Astor, Lenox, and Tilden Foundations. © Warner Brothers.

Lieutenant Richard Barr in uniform, Germany, 1945. Billy Rose Theatre Division, The New York Public Library for the Performing Arts, Astor, Lenox, and Tilden Foundations.

Richard Barr (*rear*), Paula Laurence, and Charles Bowden on a lounge chair at Laurence and Bowden's home, 1959. Billy Rose Theatre Division, The New York Public Library for the Performing Arts, Astor, Lenox, and Tilden Foundations.

Edward Albee and Richard Barr in Barr's Broadway offices in 1959. Alix Jeffry photograph (MS Thr 416). © Harvard Theatre Collection, Houghton Library, Harvard University.

Original cast of *The Zoo Story*: George Maharis (Jerry) and William Daniels (Peter), 1960. Alix Jeffry photograph (MS Thr 416). © Harvard Theatre Collection, Houghton Library, Harvard University.

Donald Davis as Krapp in Samuel Beckett's *Krapp's Last Tape*, 1961. Alix Jeffry photograph (MS Thr 416). © Harvard Theatre Collection, Houghton Library, Harvard University.

Sudie Bond (Grandma) and Ben Piazza (The Young Man) in *The American Dream*, 1961. Alix Jeffry photograph (MS Thr 416). © Harvard Theatre Collection, Houghton Library, Harvard University.

At the 1963 Tony Awards ceremony, at which *Who's Afraid of Virginia Woolf?* won Best Actor in a Play (Arthur Hill), Best Actress in a Play (Uta Hagen), Best Director (Alan Schneider), Best Play, and Best Dramatic Producers (Richard Barr and Clinton Wilder), with (*left to right*) Edward Albee, Richard Barr, Alan Schneider, Clinton Wilder, Uta Hagen, and Arthur Hill, 1962. Photo by Friedman-Abeles, © Billy Rose Theatre Division, The New York Public Library for the Performing Arts.

Al Freeman Jr., LeRoi Jones (Amiri Baraka), Edward Parone, and Jennifer West (*clockwise from left*) on the set of Jones's *Dutchman*, 1964. Alix Jeffry photograph (MS Thr 416). © Harvard Theatre Collection, Houghton Library, Harvard University.

Clinton Wilder, unidentified actor, Richard Barr, Edward Parone, Edward Albee, and unidentified actor on the set of LeRoi Jones's *Dutchman* at the Playwrights Unit 1964 (Village South Theatre). Alix Jeffry photograph (MS Thr 416).

Edward Albee on the set of *Tiny Alice*, Billy Rose Theatre, 1964. Alix Jeffry photograph (MS Thr 416).

William Hutt (Lawyer), John Gielgud (Julian), and Irene Worth (Miss Alice) in *Tiny Alice*, Billy Rose Theatre, 1964. Alix Jeffry photograph (MS Thr 416).

Kenneth Nelson (Michael), Keith Prentice (Larry), and Cliff Gorman (Emory) in the off-Broadway production of *The Boys in the Band*, 1968. vAlix Jeffry photograph (MS Thr 416). © Harvard Theatre Collection, Houghton Library, Harvard University.

The iconic cast photo from the off-Broadway production of *The Boys in the Band*, 1968. *Top row (left to right)*, Peter White (Alan), Leonard Frey (Harold); *second row*, Kenneth Nelson (Michael), Keith Prentice (Larry), Laurence Luckinbill (Hank); *bottom row*, Cliff Gorman (Emory), Reuben Greene (Bernard), Frederick Combs (Donald), Robert La Tourneaux (Cowboy). Alix Jeffry photograph (MS Thr 416). © Harvard Theatre Collection, Houghton Library, Harvard University.

Edward Albee and the cast of *All Over*, 1971. *Front row (left to right)*, George Voskovec (The Best Friend), Colleen Dewhurst (The Mistress), Edward Albee, Jessica Tandy (The Wife), Madeleine Sherwood (The Daughter); *top row*, Neil Fitzgerald (The Doctor), James Ray (The Son), Betty Field (The Nurse). Photo by Martha Swope, © Billy Rose Theatre Division, The New York Public Library for the Performing Arts.

Edward Albee, Richard Barr, and Barr's assistant, Linda Magyar, at Albee's home in Montauk, 1970s. Photo by Friedman-Abeles, © Billy Rose Theatre Division, The New York Public Library for the Performing Arts.

Cast and crew of James Duff's *Home Front*, 1984. *Standing (left to right)*, John Falabella (costume design), unidentified person, Don Walters (production stage manager), Michael Attenborough (director), Richard Barr, James Duff, Hugh O'Connor, Chris Fields (Jeremy), Jeff Knepper; *center*, Carroll O'Connor (Bob), Frances Sternhagen (Maurine); *seated on floor*, Peter Cromarty, Shirley Herz (press representative), Linda Cook (Karen), Clark Bason.

Richard Barr on set for production, 1980s. Photo by Friedman-Abeles,

8

EXPERIMENTING WITH EDWARD

Malcolm to *All Over*

After Barr's production of *Tiny Alice*, there were to be many bright spots for the ABW production team. These included a Pulitzer for Albee's *Delicate Balance*; a brilliant showing of new plays at the Playwrights Unit and at Barr's off-Broadway operations at the Cherry Lane Theatre, including some Thornton Wilder one-acts; and a complete showing of the Theatre of the Absurd Repertory on Broadway. Still, from the Theater 1966 season to the 1971 production of Albee's *All Over*, ABW Productions struggled with a series of setbacks. These resulted from escalating production costs, brutal reviews, difficult producing and budgetary decisions, and the loss of key individuals in its organization. These issues precipitated ABW's decline into dissolution in 1971. Despite these challenges, beginning in 1965 with a tightening of the budget for its Playwrights Unit, the organization kept producing adventurous new plays for six more years as new nonprofit funding became available.

On 2 August 1965, the members of the Playwrights Unit received a positive missive from Barr, Wilder, and Albee, which announced that the unit had received a grant from the New York State Council on the Arts (NYSCA).[1] With his usual show of optimism, Barr was doing everything humanly possible to keep the unit afloat in spite of Theater 1965's poor showing at the box office. His first move was to swiftly shift the unit's operations from the Village South Theatre to the Cherry Lane as a cost-saving measure. Because

Barr ran his business as a commercial producer, outside of the not-for-profit framework, he didn't answer to a board and could adapt his organization according to his instincts. But because of this same independence, Richard constantly scrambled for funds. Commercial producers, unlike the new regional theatres, were being left out of the not-for-profit funding equation.[2]

Not-for-profit funding was regarded with some contempt by commercial producers in the late 1960s. Even so, Richard realized he had to swallow his pride and start applying for grants. In the winter of 1965, through the prodding of Alan Schneider, ABW established a not-for-profit entity, Albarwild Theatre Arts, Inc., in order to receive private and public funding. Though the $5,000 grants Barr received from the NYSCA and the Music Corporation of America (MCA) were not enough to keep the unit going, they helped. Costs above the $10,000 raised by the grants were to be shared among the partners, with each shouldering approximately $7,000.[3] It was remarkable that ABW Productions, established along the old lines of the independent producer, adapted so well. This was noted by Bruce Hoover, co-manager of the unit in 1971: "They [ABW Productions] had to have been in the right place at the right time; they only got small amounts of money. The idea of money from foundations and corporations was bizarre. Raising money for playwrights? Nobody had ever done that before. So they really scored with that funding—and it was a sign of how Richard could adapt."[4]

It was just in time. Both the individual budgets of each unit production and the unit's overall budget increased by 1970. The unit shifted to fewer but better productions, doubling the number of performances from two or three to five or more. Near the end of his tenure, Chuck Gnys directed nearly all the plays, giving the season a stylistic unity, and with a passion for professional, high-quality productions, Gnys used expert lighting skills to offset the unit's minimal production values.[5] The 1966 unit playwrights had more writing experience; many had already received grants and other awards for their writing. Reflecting these changes was the Theater 1966 unit production of Sam Shepard's one-act *4-H Club*, directed by Gnys and produced at the Village South Theatre on 9 September 1965. Shepard had made substantial growth as a playwright since his first unit workshop offering, *Up to Thursday*. *4-H Club* is a more complex play, hinting at Shepard's later claustrophobic "family" dramas such as *Buried Child* or *True West*. Richard Barr was proud of these early workshop productions of playwrights who became the major writers of the 1970s and 1980s. Without his support, many would have remained unknown. He writes in his memoirs: "We, as a team, were never very interested in making money, though we rejoiced over a commercial success as delightedly as the next fellow. We felt, as a team, that the Theatre was an expression of our maturity as a nation; we felt that the Theatre as presented by our new, young playwrights, was as exciting a moment in art history as the advent of abstract expressionism in painting. It was time for the Theatre to catch up to the other American arts, so we dug in."[6]

Digging in meant more productions, including A. R. Gurney's *The Rape of Bunny Stuntz*, which opened on 13 November 1965 at the Cherry Lane and was directed by Chuck Gnys. Gurney, one of the unit's more distinguished veterans (author of *Love Letters*, *The Cocktail Hour*, and *The Dining Room*), was, at the time, a recent graduate of the Yale School of Drama and an assistant professor of English at the Massachusetts Institute of Technology. Gurney pointed to the Playwrights Unit production of *Bunny Stuntz*, his first show ever in New York City, as a turning point in his career: "I didn't call myself a playwright or anything; I was a teacher without a Ph.D., holding on by my fingernails, trying to support this family of mine. I was writing for WGBH, the local television station, doing journeyman work for them, and I did some work for Harcourt Brace editing drama for high school texts, but I really didn't see myself as a playwright. It took me a long time to see myself that way. So this was probably the first time. It's very important to be able to call yourself a writer rather than a dabbler. It was very gratifying to have that call from Chuck Gnys in New York."[7] Even in the midst of their busy Broadway and off-Broadway season, the unit was "functioning fully," and Richard felt he had a "corner on the market" producing these young writers.[8] Even so, by November 1965, all the resources of Theater 1966 were being funneled into Albee's new play, *Malcolm*, which was an adaptation of the cult novel by James Purdy.

Directed by Alan Schneider and designed by William Ritman, *Malcolm* was supposed to be the next big Albee hit.[9] It was not. Barr's own reaction to the production was that "*Malcolm* was a mess. Albee wrote the play with a sword instead of a pen."[10] At $126,055 (originally projected for $150,000), the *Malcolm* budget was by no means unusual for Broadway production of a non-musical drama ($125,000 was the 1962 average). However, compared with that of *Who's Afraid of Virginia Woolf?* ($49,922), it was out of step with ABW's normally prudent financing.[11] The budgetary problem was exacerbated by Barr's use of treadmills in the production. He had seen them in a Jeanne Moreau production in Paris and was wildly excited about the possibilities. The results, though, were disastrous, according to Alan Schneider, as was the "confusing and inconsistent lighting."[12]

Adding to these issues were serious casting problems. Albee had written a role for a dwarf and had convinced Michael Dunn, who had played Cousin

Lyman in Albee's adaptation of Carson McCullers's *Ballad of the Sad Café* in 1963 and 1964, to play the role of Kermit in *Malcolm*. Unfortunately, Dunn backed out, and Albee decided to change the role to "a man who claims to be 192 (though he is only 97)." John Hefferman was then cast. Though Heffernan did well, "the substitution really didn't work." Matthew Cowles (son of producer Chandler Cowles) was cast from his graduation performance at the Neighborhood Playhouse to play the title role. Though Cowles went on to a career on Broadway and in film and television, he was, at the time, "fairly green in *Malcolm*."[13]

Richard allowed critics to attend *Malcolm*'s previews rather than its opening, his normal off-Broadway policy. But this decision gave the critics added time to crush *Malcolm*, and crush the show they did. The blame for the production was passed around. Barr thought Albee's adaptation was "undramatic," and though he admired Purdy's book, he did not think it "could be effectively adapted by anyone." Albee believed that at least some of the blame should rest on Schneider's shoulders. Schneider felt that Albee was "not as involved in the production as he was in other projects" and left much of the decision-making to the director, who was not thrilled with the adaptation himself.[14] Even though he knew the show wasn't working, Schneider was alternately praying for "a magical transformation" that would make the show a success or for Albee to cancel the production.[15] In the end, it was Richard's pure faith in Albee's work that drove the production, despite doubts about its success. And he ran the ABW operation as a family, so all were willing to support the playwright's vision. Normally an Albee fan, the *Post*'s Richard Watts began the bloodletting, panning the show. Stanley Kauffmann at the *New York Times* called *Malcolm* "arty hugger-mugger" with "a superciliousness" that expected the audience to supply its own meanings.[16] Having been chided by Barr and Albee as philistines, the reviewers were hungry for blood, and this combative relationship with the critics added to ABW's spiraling financial woes.

Still, Richard kept producing new work, even as *Malcolm* was sinking. The last production of the Theater 1966 Playwrights Unit was James Prideaux's *Postcards*, directed by Barr himself. *Postcards* was Prideaux's first produced play, and he was one of the unit's most enthusiastic supporters. Prideaux called the experience "the most exciting night of my life."[17] *Postcards* was later produced on Broadway by Barnett Wolfe Plaxen, and Barr produced Prideaux's *The Last of Mrs. Lincoln* on Broadway as well. An ABW office worker, Prideaux was the ultimate insider. His unpublished memoirs reveal much about ABW's development process, particularly as Barr struggled financially to keep producing new work.

With a fiscal disaster looming, ABW had a sudden nonprofit cash infusion, though the amounts that it received differ somewhat in the reporting. On 1 June 1966, Sam Zolotow of the *Times* reported that Albarwild Theatre Arts was to receive a grant of $197,000 from the Rockefeller Foundation; this grant was to be matched by $65,000 from other sources.[18] Some $32,500 was earmarked for the unit, the balance for the production of new plays and revivals at the Cherry Lane. By 1966, Barr, Albee, and Wilder had spent nearly $135,000 of their own money keeping the Playwrights Unit alive, and while the money was tax deductible, they were not bringing in enough income to justify the expense. According to Barr, the Rockefeller fund was to provide three years of financial support with $10,000 per year for the unit and $55,666 per year for the Cherry Lane Theatre.[19] However, the actual grant disbursement to Albarwild, based on documents from the Rockefeller Foundation, was to be $100,000 from 1966 to 1967, $40,000 from 1967 to 1968, and $25,000 from 1968 to 1969. This was to be matched from other sources with increasing amounts from 1966 to 1967 at $35,000, from 1967 to 1968 at $95,000, and from 1968 to 1969 at $110,000 (see table).[20]

Grant Disbursement to Albarwild Theater Arts, Inc.

Source	1966–67	1967–68	1968–69
Rockefeller Foundation	$100,000	$40,000	$ 25,000
Other sources	$ 35,000	$95,000	$110,000

Source: J. Kellum Smith Jr. to Edward Albee, 25 May 1966, Richard Barr–Clinton Wilder Papers, *T-Mss 1987-008, Series I: Administrative Files–Playwrights Unit, box 1, folder 8 (Rockefeller Foundation correspondence), Billy Rose Theatre Division, New York Public Library for the Performing Arts.

With this funding, Richard took a three-year lease of the Village South Theatre, which was renamed The Playwrights Unit.[21] The theatre was given a full renovation, including painting, a new marquee, a new sound system, more lighting equipment, and a new set of masking flats. The stage was raised to improve sight lines and made more flexible in order to allow for varying levels.[22] The Playwrights Unit workshop became much more focused and professional. Fewer plays by experienced playwrights with more performances was a better formula. It was the formula that produced Mart Crowley's *Boys in the Band*.

On 6 September 1966, Theater 1967 began its Festival of American Plays with the production of three one-act plays by Thornton Wilder: *The Long Christmas Dinner*, *Queens of France*, and *The Happy Journey to Trenton and*

Camden. Wilder had never seen these plays onstage, and with them Barr was trying a new tack, celebrating the work of a great American playwright. Wilder was an important innovator in American drama and fiction, an early mentor for Albee, and a friend of Alan Schneider's.[23] The producing choice was a happy one. The three plays, directed by Michael Kahn, were a hit at the box office and provided just the right note to start the Theater 1967 season. Dan Sullivan of the *New York Times* was particularly taken with *The Happy Journey*.[24] Barr felt the performances by John Beal, Leora Dean, and Paula Trueman provided "one of the best evenings we ever presented at the Cherry Lane." Wilder himself "sneaked down to the Village unannounced one night." The theatre was so packed that he had to be seated on the steps, and he was "delighted" by the experience.[25] The Wilder plays moved to the Orpheum, a larger house on Second Avenue, and played until 2 October 1966.[26] Motivated by this success, Richard wanted to produce Wilder's *The Alcestiad*, but the author demurred, embarrassed that the play was like a "loaf of bread" that had been "pulled out of the oven too soon," and thus ended the possibility of Wilder's further collaboration with ABW.[27]

Next, Paul Zindel's *And Miss Reardon Drinks a Little* was produced by the Playwrights Unit on 8 September 1966. Zindel was a self-confessed Albee "stalker" who aggressively pursued the opportunity to work with Barr. Zindel noted that ABW was a family created by the producers with elements of "fun, adventure, and love" that made the unit and all of its productions special.[28] The one-act play, starting with its unit production, made a five-year developmental journey during which it was transformed into an evening-length event. In February 1970, *Miss Reardon* moved to Broadway with the stellar cast of Julie Harris, Estelle Parsons, and Nancy Marchand. Parsons won the 1971 Tony Award for Best Actress for her performance in the Broadway production of *And Miss Reardon Drinks a Little*, and Rae Allen won the 1971 Tony for Best Featured Actress for her performance. Later, Zindel sent Richard a letter that was particularly touching, thanking him for his production at the unit and expressing gratitude for the developmental opportunity in a production that was "largely for the benefit of the playwright."[29]

Albee's *A Delicate Balance* then opened at the Martin Beck Theatre on 22 September 1966. It was his fifth play to open on Broadway within five years. Albee started the rehearsals in his "deep spacious dwelling on West 10th Street," and it was clearly an ABW family affair. William Ritman was the designer, Alan Schneider directed the show, and Mark Wright and Michael Kasdan served as stage and business managers respectively.[30] Richard felt it was "the easiest production of all of Edward's plays," and in the end it won the Pulitzer Prize. After their private reading of the play, their "in-camera" read-through, Barr felt that the character of the husband "seemed to erupt too suddenly" in the final act and that there should be some "hint of the nature of his strength" earlier in the play. He was pleased that his criticism resulted in Albee's writing of the "cat story" in the play, not unlike the "dog story" in the earlier *The Zoo Story*.[31] Part of the success was tied to the talent of husband-and-wife team Hume Cronyn and Jessica Tandy as Tobias and Agnes. Rosemary Murphy was also wonderfully cast as Agnes's alcoholic sister, Claire, as was the talented Marian Seldes playing Agnes and Tobias's neurotic daughter, Julia. Seldes would become one of the most important interpreters of Albee's women.

While mostly favorable, the reviews—as for all Albee productions—were mixed. Walter Kerr pronounced it "the sort of play that might be written if there were no theater" and that "it exists outside itself, besides itself, aloof from itself, as detached from the hard floor of the Martin Beck, where it opened last night, as its alarmed characters are detached from themselves."[32] Richard Watts in the *New York Post*, reliably positive, wrote that *A Delicate Balance* "has all the quality of brilliantly corroding and lacerating wit that marked his previous work" but noted that "amid the mutual exchange of biting insults in his dialogue, there is a sympathetic feeling for the embattled characters that represents an advance in the understanding of human inner-torment."[33] Alan Schneider offers this memory of *A Delicate Balance* in his autobiography: "Although the response, as in previews, could not match the thunderclap intensity of that first head-on collision with a new writer, it filled the Martin Beck. Then the reviews came out. Everyone liked us. Almost everyone, that is. . . . Walter [Kerr] analyzed it to death, sounding as though he was trying hard to rationalize a personal distaste."[34] Schneider's frustration with Kerr's review was perhaps the only damper on the Theater 1967 season. It was busy, eclectic, and particularly fruitful for the Playwrights Unit. In spite of Kerr's review, *A Delicate Balance* ran for a total of 132 performances and received the Pulitzer Prize in May 1968, though Barr acknowledges that some thought it was given as a consolation prize for the decision not to award the Pulitzer to *Who's Afraid of Virginia Woolf?*[35]

Barr's Festival of American Plays at the Cherry Lane continued with a revival of George Kaufman's *The Butter and Egg Man*, produced on 17 October 1966 and directed by Burt Shrevelove. With Kaufman's "granddaddy of all show-biz blockbusters," as Kerr noted in his review of production, Theater 1967 linked itself with the unabashed showmanship of earlier American theatre, and the play, while not commercially successful, provided momentum for the Cherry Lane season. Richard Barr felt that this "profusion of production" was ABW's peak as a producing organization.[36] In the midst of this heady mix of plays, on 26 December 1966, Barr presented the Paul Taylor Dance Company at the ANTA Playhouse. Taylor remained a close friend and a frequent guest at his home, and Barr continued to produce Taylor's work throughout his career.[37]

ABW next produced unit playwright Frank Gagliano's *Night of the Dunce* at the Cherry Lane on 28 December 1966. Kerr's review for the *Times* was not encouraging, lamenting that while "Gagliano contrives a few passages of moderately effective melodrama," the writer was "never able to resolve the split personality that is the essential personality of his play."[38] However, impatient as he was with the Albee/Pinter menace that characterized many of ABW's new American plays, Kerr was at least reviewing the play and not the process, as had been his wont with the New Playwrights Series. Barr's Playwrights Unit followed this with Louis Auchincloss's *The Club Bedroom* on 12 January 1967, directed by Chuck Gnys. Auchincloss, a well-established writer, author of such novels as *The Great World and Timothy Colt* and *Pursuit of the Prodigal*, was brought to the unit through connections with Chuck Gnys's longtime companion Perry Knowlton. Knowlton was the distinguished agent and owner of the literary agency Curtis Brown, Ltd. *The Club Bedroom*, Auchincloss's only work for the theatre, dramatized the woes of a society matron down on her luck.

One of ABW's most important off-Broadway productions was Lanford Wilson's *The Rimers of Eldritch*, which opened at the Cherry Lane Theatre on 20 February 1967. *Rimers* was directed by ABW regular Michael Kahn, who had also staged Adrienne Kennedy's *Funnyhouse of a Negro*. Kahn felt that he owed much to Barr for his career, noting that he had enormous freedom as a young director and was treated with professionalism and respect: "They [Albee, Barr, and Wilder] were very hands-off, and once I got into rehearsal, there was no artistic interference of any kind. And it was a big thing for me to be the 'other' director with Alan Schneider. . . . Alan was the director of Pinter and of Beckett, and I was one of the bright things from La Mama. That was a very important thing in my life, that I would be working with someone like Alan."[39] Barr had plucked up Wilson's *The Rimers of Eldritch* after its initial production at Ellen Stewart's La Mama Experimental Theatre Club. He noted that Wilson's *Our Town* technique of having all the actors onstage all of the time grew out of the lack of space for entrances or exits in Stewart's tiny theatre.[40] *Rimers* was, after LeRoi Jones's *Dutchman* and Kennedy's *Funnyhouse of a Negro*, the most critically successful new play yet produced off-Broadway by ABW Productions.

Dan Sullivan's review in the *Times* was typical in its praise for Wilson's skill as a writer, pointing out that though there wasn't anything "new in the fragmented voices and fractured time sense" of the play, he felt Wilson handled the "collage technique so beautifully" that no other style worked "half so well."[41] The play's success was important because it was the first time that a veteran off-off-Broadway playwright had achieved an important off-Broadway success. *Rimers'* success paved the way for Circle Rep, Lanford Wilson's future home off-Broadway, which became an important training center for actors and playwrights. The production won the Vernon Rice Award, and, as Wilson confessed, "it sort of put me on the map" and prepared him for the complexities of the American commercial theatre.[42]

Newly funded through the Rockefeller Foundation, Barr and his Playwrights Unit took a somewhat more conservative approach to producing new plays by forging a link between older, established American plays and the new American playwrights. The Theater 1967 season had seen a new luster in the work of ABW's star playwright, Edward Albee, with his Pulitzer Prize for *A Delicate Balance*. Barr had produced six plays off-Broadway and eight new plays, several of them evening-length, at the Unit. Notably absent from the Theater 1967 season were the absurdist European playwrights. ABW Productions continued in this more realistic vein until 1969, when, somewhat anachronistically, it presented the plays of Albee, Beckett, and Ionesco in absurdist repertory at the Billy Rose Theatre on Broadway.

On 8 October 1967, ABW produced Mary Mercier's *Johnny No-Trump* on Broadway at the Cort Theatre, directed by ABW veteran Joseph Hardy.[43] Chuck Woodward, who eventually became Barr's business partner, agreed to participate in the project, and ABW quickly went into production. Previously presented in a reading at the developmental organization New Dramatists, where Mercier was a member, *Johnny No-Trump* was her first play. However, neither the play nor the production was well received by the critics. Clive Barnes, now the lead critic for the *Times*, offered a conciliatory but killing review. Barnes felt the play wasn't "good or bad," instead terming it "schizophrenic": it had moments when the characters spoke with "absolute truthfulness" but sounded at other times like a TV situation comedy's "slick gibberish."[44] It the first time ABW had ever premiered a first play by a brand-new playwright on Broadway. Even Albee's first plays were initially presented off-Broadway. The play included a stellar cast—Pat Hingle, Sada Thompson, James Broderick, and Bernadette Peters—and had excellent direction and an exceptionally beautiful set by William Ritman.

In a historic act of anger and frustration with the critics, Richard Barr, perhaps unfairly, closed *Johnny No-Trump* without a second performance. The play was such a phenomenal flop, even by Broadway standards, that its name became synonymous with failure: a play that closed suddenly on

Broadway was Johnny No-Trumped.[45] Ironically, Barr loved Mercier's play, calling it "engaging, literate, and funny," and Wilder loved it as well, though Albee didn't and had passed on the project. But despite his fondness for the script, Barr felt the show "failed totally" and closed it quickly in order to save his investors' money. He was in a bind financially, as he had no advance sales and took in only three hundred dollars after the opening. In his mind, it was "better business" to close the show immediately and return his backers' investment rather than to "wage a losing battle against the notices."[46]

Ironically, the *Johnny No-Trump* fiasco resulted in an important connection between Richard Barr and Clive Barnes. After the critic's review, Barr had wired him, "I am very, very angry." Barnes responded by wire, "I, too, am angry. A producer who opens a play for one night should run it a month. Have more faith in your product."[47] The resulting skirmish lasted until the two met and worked out their differences, though Barnes was certainly not entirely to blame. Barr had moved the play too quickly to Broadway, and the script had suffered from late changes, some at his request. Mary Mercier felt he had closed the show out of anger and wasn't thinking clearly at the time. Even though Barnes became much more receptive to Barr's shows after this incident, sadly *Johnny No-Trump* was the sacrificial lamb, and Mercier's writing career was destroyed. For Mercier, Richard "had forgotten his own policy as a producer, which is that the play you option is the play you're going to do." Mercier continued her career as an actress but felt that she had been betrayed by Barr.[48]

Johnny No-Trump was followed by the Playwrights Unit production of James Prideaux's *Lemonade*, which had been rehearsing at the same time. Prideaux was working in the ABW office during *Johnny No-Trump*'s production period and was horrified to see that Mercier, under the pressure of a Broadway opening, was never given the chance to solve the play's ending: "Richard had made a mistake in not taking the play out-of-town for a run of previews before coming into New York. But Richard didn't take plays out-of-town and there was a reason for that. *Who's Afraid of Virginia Woolf?*, his biggest hit and the high point of his career, hadn't gone out-of-town. And *Woolf* was the criterion in that office for ever after. 'This is the way we did it with *Woolf* and this is the way we do it,' I heard him say a hundred times. He was to pay a price for that."[49] Prideaux was particularly incensed because the play worked up to the last five minutes, when, in his words, "a hit became a flop," and his feelings were echoed by Mercier.[50] Barr's aggressive attempt to move the play to Broadway failed because his organization had neither the financing nor the organization to produce a new playwright on Broadway as well as it could off-Broadway.[51]

Prideaux's *Lemonade* went into rehearsals with Mitchell Nestor as its director and actresses Charlotte Rae and Irene Dailey. Prideaux then, perhaps foolishly, left the rehearsals and continued his administrative work on *Johnny No-Trump*. He returned only to discover that his "delicate little play had become a kind of vulgar, rowdy farce." He immediately asked Chuck Gnys to cancel the production. It was the first production ever canceled at the Playwrights Unit. Barr was infuriated by this decision, which he was informed about during the first paid preview of *Johnny No-Trump*: "As I came down the street toward the Cort Theatre . . . Richard saw me . . . [and] he suddenly turned and said the very words I dreaded to hear. 'How are things going downtown, Jimmy?' he asked. I took a deep breath. 'Richard, I canceled that production this afternoon. It wasn't doing justice to my play.' He walked right over to me and put his nose almost up to mine. He had been drinking heavily. His eyes narrowed into slits. 'Well, I am . . . very . . . very *angry*!' he snarled."[52] Prideaux noted that Barr was fine in the mornings, but after his lunch at Sardi's, he often returned to his office drunk. But the story had a happy ending. Barr contacted Prideaux the next morning, "perfectly sober and very cheery," and told Prideaux, "I just want to say, Jimmy, that you did exactly the right thing. It's such a good play. We'll do it later. And we'll do it *right*."[53]

Barr's temper and drinking, coupled with chronic underfinancing, were contributing to the collapse of the Albee-Barr-Wilder producing partnership. Still, Barr moved ahead with his next Broadway production, Albee's *Everything in the Garden*, an adaptation of a play by English playwright Giles Cooper. It was at this point that "the organization began to change." Wilder had seen the play in London and had "loved it, and thought it would be a simple matter" for Albee to adapt it to an American idiom. Albee agreed and did the adaptation, feeling, according to Barr, that "he could add a great deal to the play other than mere word or place changes."[54]

With Albee as the adaptor, the production "took on an entirely different perspective," and so, with Alan Schneider passing for the first time on an Albee project, Peter Glenville was invited to direct it. In a lucky stroke of fate, word of the project reached the ears of Twentieth Century Fox, which bought the rights and funded Barr's entire production. Glenville cast Barry Nelson in the lead role, with Robert Moore playing the critical role of Jack. Extra star power was added when Barbara Bel Geddes joined the cast, along with a very young Richard Thomas. Settings were by William Ritman. But despite a strong cast, the reviews were mixed, and the audiences didn't come. The production struggled, closing after eighty-four performances, eleven weeks after it opened. Clive Barnes's response was typical: "The theme of the play, from beginning to end, is entirely Mr. Cooper's. Mr. Albee has added nothing but points of differing emphasis. . . . Mr. Albee's play is *not* so good as the original. It lacks cool, it strives too hard to be a hit—which Mr. Cooper's play . . . quite definitely was not. . . . This is a monstrously heavy handed account by Mr. Albee of a stealthily subtle play. If Mr. Albee wishes to sing us a song of social significance he should not choose such a shrill and hysterical falsetto."[55] Barnes's review reflected a growing homophobic response to Albee's work. Along those same lines, William Goldman wrote famously in *The Season*, his "candid" view of a year on Broadway, that *Everything in the Garden* was really a "statement of homosexual mystique" and that the message it gave was that "all wives were whores" and "all husbands were panderers" and the only wisdom to be found was from "bachelors and young boys."[56]

Everything in the Garden was not the success needed after Mercier's play. And its failure was exacerbated by the critics' homophobic response. Yet Barr capitalized on the critics' hysteria regarding homosexuality when he produced *The Boys in the Band*. It satisfied the curiosity of homophobic critics like Goldman, and later Stanley Kauffmann, who were aware that "the homosexual is here, and he's not going anywhere," and what they wanted to know was "what's really on his mind."[57] With *The Boys in the Band*, Barr was going to show them, and rumblings of his independent streak were beginning to try the patience of both Clinton Wilder and Edward Albee.

Ironically, it was at this moment, not long before it was dissolved, that the triumvirate of Albee, Barr, and Wilder gained national recognition with a major feature in the *New York Times Magazine*. Barbara La Fontaine, the *Times* reporter on the ABW partnership, noted the "cheerful vagueness with which Albee, Barr and Wilder describe the way they work" and "the general peace and quiet" with which ABW "goes about the business of producing plays."[58] Yet even as "peace and quiet" reigned in the producing partnership, economic realities were rising to ABW's glossy surface. This included the loss of the lease on the Cherry Lane Theatre, forcing Barr to move the Playwrights Unit.

In March 1968, with the closing of *Everything in the Garden* and on the cusp of La Fontaine's article in the *Times*, Clinton Wilder withdrew as a partner. According to the brief *Times* mention of the event, Wilder was pulling out to attend to family investments. The same announcement disclosed that Barr was planning to produce Mart Crowley's *The Boys in the Band* with Charles Woodward, a Buffalo insurance agent, who was to replace Wilder.[59] Barr confesses in his memoirs that Wilder's main "gripe" about him was his impatience and impulsiveness and his tendency to move forward with new ideas "without properly consulting others." Though Richard admits that his modus operandi was "scarcely diplomatic," it was more efficient to move quickly on projects when necessary. Also, he kept "regular office hours," while Wilder dropped by only when needed. Even though Barr did not ever make substantive decisions without Wilder, his decisions were often "of sufficient importance" to annoy Wilder "considerably." Yet the end of the partnership was without "animosity," and there was "no great fight; nothing, in fact, that would make a good story."[60]

But several ABW staff members believed that Wilder's decision to leave the partnership was based primarily on Barr's decision to produce *The Boys in the Band*.[61] Barr was aware that Wilder "disliked both the subject matter and the play" and felt strongly enough about it that he wanted to "remove his name from the production."[62] While all three ABW partners were gay, only Barr seemed comfortable with the subject matter of the play—as well as saw a potential commercial hit. Albee's own nonparticipation as a producer may be explained by a self-confessed dislike for the play: "I didn't get involved with it because it's a play that does serious damage to the public perception of homosexuality. Richard didn't produce it because he thought it was good; he produced it because he thought it would make him money. And he was in a financial hole and he needed a way out. The play may have its significance in terms of historical and political reasons, but not for artistic reasons. It is a poorly written play that set back the public's understanding of what it means to be gay—and I couldn't be a part of that."[63] Albee's point of view was perhaps buoyed by his own career-long insistence not to be pigeonholed as a "gay" playwright and by his opinion that other writers who happen to be gay shouldn't be so narrowly categorized, either. For Albee, one's sexual orientation was "totally irrelevant."[64] His consistent viewpoint on this subject, tied to his fears of gay writers being "ghettoized" by their sexual orientation, raised controversy within the gay community.[65] But he was not without good reason for his fears. Both Albee and Tennessee Williams had been attacked by critics for writing female characters that many suggested were really men in drag and for pursuing a secret gay agenda in their writing.[66]

But the reality for Barr was that he was compelled to do the play for some of the financial reasons Albee mentioned and also because he felt Crowley was talented: "My goal going off-Broadway was to discover and present new playwriting talent, and here was a built-in natural."[67] For other writers, including Tony Kushner, Barr's production of Crowley's play was an act of bravery. Even Barr acknowledged the risk at that time of presenting "an open, but somewhat distorted, treatment of a homosexual's birthday party."[68] Still, Albee would not be alone in his criticism of *The Boys in the Band*; many others in the gay community remained guarded in their acceptance of the play and protested against the original showing of the film version.[69] But ever loyal to Barr and despite his grave concerns, Albee agreed to discuss the play with Crowley, including his "reservations" about the play.[70]

Barr's decision to produce *The Boys in the Band* damaged the producing partnership built on his and Clinton Wilder's uniquely complementary personalities. Wilder was more experienced and wealthy than Charles Woodward and proved a necessary foil to Barr's unbridled enthusiasms. Woodward didn't challenge Barr's sometimes-disastrous decisions, and this became a problem.[71] But Barr needed a new partner, and Woodward was a known quantity, having invested in his productions starting with *Hotel Paradiso* in the late 1950s. And to his credit, Woodward seemed to know "what was playing at every theatre in New York, the grosses, the amount of profit hits had accumulated and the exact figures on the losses of flops," despite the fact that he was an out-of-towner hailing from upstate New York. Woodward's "small syndicate" in Buffalo invested in Broadway shows, and after years of his running a successful insurance business in Buffalo, he had fairly deep pockets.[72] Though he was not as experienced as Clinton Wilder, he demonstrated a "nose" for the business. Woodward and Barr were to have phenomenal financial success with *The Boys in the Band*, which turned out to be nearly as profitable as *Who's Afraid of Virginia Woolf?*

Mart Crowley originally had written *The Boys in the Band* in response to Stanley Kauffmann's famous 1966 article in the *New York Times* "Homosexuality and Its Disguises," which called for gay authors to write openly of their lifestyle instead of hiding behind a screen of heterosexuality: "The conditions that force the dissembling must change. The homosexual dramatist must be free to write truthfully of what he knows, rather than try to transform it to a life he does not know, to the detriment of his truth and ours."[73] Crowley, an unemployed screenwriter at the time, wrote the play both to answer Kauffmann and in defiance of Kauffmann's veiled homophobia.[74] It was a raw, funny exploration of a small gathering of gay men celebrating a birthday party for their friend Harold and hosted by a bitter, self-loathing alcoholic, Michael. At times outrageously funny and at other moments brutally sad, the characters enact cruel games on each other, attempting to come to terms with their homosexuality. Once he completed the play, Crowley struggled to find a producer. Luckily, he was living with director Robert Moore, who had been starring as Jack in Albee's *Everything in the Garden*. From Moore he learned about Barr's support of Albee's work and that of other experimental new writers at his Playwrights Unit. Crowley thought Barr might be crazy enough to do *The Boys in the Band*, but he needed an agent to make the connection.[75] At the time, he worked as an assistant to Natalie Wood, the screen legend, and her fiancé was Richard

Gregson, a co-owner of London International, a literary agency. Wood was a close friend and enabled Crowley to get a hearing with agent Janet Roberts at London International. When he brought the play to Roberts's office, she sent Crowley away for three hours so she could read it. When he returned, Roberts was "steaming":

> She said, "I don't know what to do with this play. This is outrageous! This is like some weekend on Fire Island!" And I said, "Well, exactly, that's what it's like; that's what it is." It was at this point, more or less, [when] I knew that she was just about to dump me, that I said, "Do you know Richard Barr?" She said, "Of course I know Richard Barr. Why do you ask me that?" And I said, "I don't know, but it just occurred to me that anybody that had the guts to put on *Who's Afraid of Virginia Woolf?* wouldn't blink at this type of material." Those were my very words. And I said, "Would you send it to him?" And she said, "Well, you know, since you're a friend of Richard Gregson, you know, I've got to do something." Well, it was less than twenty-four hours, I think, when I heard from her—from one afternoon to the later morning the next day when she called me at my friend's apartment and asked to speak to me. She said, "I've heard from Richard Barr, and I'm just stunned, and I don't know what to say to you, I can't believe this, but can you have a drink with him and Edward Albee at 5 o'clock this afternoon?" And I said, "My God, of course I can!"[76]

Barr offered Crowley a Playwrights Unit workshop production of *The Boys in the Band* but was not without his doubts about the play. While it was "too risky" for off-Broadway, it was "hilariously funny."[77] Despite Barr's admiration for the play in his memoirs, Albee felt privately that "Richard thought it was a piece of shit, too."[78] These issues aside, Barr desperately needed the money and felt this might be the hit to save his Playwrights Unit.

Robert Moore, who was starring in *Everything in the Garden*, was to direct the show at the Playwrights Unit, and Crowley worked on *The Boys in the Band* to trim it down to a cohesive whole. Crowley also knew Chuck Gnys at the unit, and according to Perry Knowlton, Gnys's partner and CEO of Curtis Brown, Ltd., Crowley revised parts of the play at his and Gnys's home in Andes, New York. Interestingly, Crowley based the characters of Larry and Hank on Gnys and Knowlton, one of the few positive, long-term gay relationships in the play.[79]

After the revision, Barr deemed the play ready to be produced. *The Boys in the Band* opened on 23 January 1968 at the Vandam Street Theatre, directed by Robert Moore. The cast included Kenneth Nelson, Frederick Combs, Cliff Gorman, Nicholas Cortland, Laurence Luckinbill, Chuck Daniel, Robert

La Tourneaux, Peter White, and Keith Prentice, with settings by Peter Harvey. The audience reaction, like the reaction to Jones's *Dutchman*, was visceral. Crowley didn't remember anyone attending the first night of the unit production, but by the second night, "there was a line around the block. The New York intelligentsia [began to] descend on the play. And suddenly it was famous."[80] Barr called it "an almost uncontrollable smash hit," because the line that stretched past Sixth Avenue became "disorderly" when customers learned there just weren't any more seats.[81] The gay community came out in droves; it was a "Stonewall" event before the famous Stonewall riot. Luckinbill, who played Hank in both the original play production and in the film, recalled seeing a gay audience lining up to see the production:

> I remember that . . . morning after we had opened the workshop production. It was a bitterly cold January. I was crossing the street and I saw this huge crowd around the corner of Sixth Avenue, and I thought there must have been an accident or something going on. And as I got closer I realized that it was not just a crowd, it was a line, and the line was heading down Vandam Street and back up to Houston Street, and I thought this was unbelievable, and I realized everyone in the line was gay. And every age, every color, every size and shape, and there they were, stamping their feet and laughing and just having a grand time. And I thought, this is astounding; I've never seen so many gay people in one place. I've never seen so many openly gay men who seem to be laughing and joyous.[82]

Gnys turned away more than three hundred people but could not extend the run due to actors' commitments and Actors' Equity rules forbidding more than ten performances.[83] Crowley recalled his nerves from the opening of the show: "I just remember one moment of opening night. . . . Bob Moore suddenly loomed before me, and I stopped him, and I was dry-mouthed and white-lipped and ice-cold, and all I said to him was, 'Do you think they'll think it's funny?' And Bob Moore said back to me, 'Listen, they've been laughin' at fags since Aristophanes, and they're not going to stop tonight.'"[84] The play was moved to Theatre 4, a 299-seat house on West Fifty-Fifth Street; two parts were recast; and it reopened on 14 April 1968 and settled in for a run of 1,001 performances off-Broadway.

Casting the show had been a challenge, finding talented actors willing to perform in a gay play. Peter White, the original Alan in *The Boys in the Band*, initially struggled with the idea of auditioning for the show: "I was touring with actress Myrna Loy in *Barefoot in the Park*, and things were sort of really moving for me; I was doing so well, and I thought, 'I don't need this kind of risk.' I talked to Myrna. She became my mentor. And she said,

'Peter, if you are going to be an actor, you are going to have to take some risks in your life.'"[85] White auditioned, was cast, and connected well with the company during the Playwrights Unit workshop production. But with the move to off-Broadway came serious issues for the cast: "We all had pretty well bonded, and certainly wanted to do it because it had been a success, but we had to wait three months to see who was being dropped and who was being kept. By the time we did get offered to do it, those of us lucky enough to be a part of it . . . lost our agents because the agents said if we did it, we'd never work again; . . . it would kill our careers. Larry [Luckinbill] and I had commercials on the air at the time, and after the play became such a success, we were both dropped from the commercials."[86] While Luckinbill confessed that he had no trepidations about playing a gay role, it took an incredible leap of faith for the actors, many of whom were not gay, to play these roles. Several of the straight actors in the cast later struggled to escape identification with the characters. Cliff Gorman, who played Emory, the flamboyantly gay character, later famous for his portrayal of Lenny Bruce in the Broadway play *Lenny*, went to great pains to point out that he was straight and married. On the other hand, Robert La Tourneaux, who played the hustler in the play, died of an AIDS-related illness after taking on the real-life role of a hustler.[87] By 1993, most of the gay actors who had played in the original production had died of illnesses related to AIDS. And for several members of the cast, including Kenneth Nelson, Frederick Combs, and Leonard Frey, there was a price to be paid as they struggled to find work after *The Boys in the Band*, having been typecast as being gay.

Barr encouraged critics to come to the previews, as often as they liked, but not to opening night. Instead, the opening night audience consisted of backers (Barr had sold $17,000 of the $20,000 capitalization by then), family and friends of the cast and crew, and "friends of friends." Barr gave a brief curtain speech, noting that there were no press members in the audience. This gave the audience permission to laugh, which was crucial, since word of mouth off-Broadway meant much more than reviews. Of the reviews, though, many were quite positive. Perhaps Harold Clurman's in *New York Magazine* was the most eloquent:

> It is skillful and amusing in its dialogue, frank in attitude, casually obscene in speech, kind at heart, sentimental at bottom.
>
> Though full of camp fun, *The Boys in the Band* is not a cheap exploitation of its subject. It aims to show the guilt and self-loathing . . . from which many homosexuals, like members of all minorities, suffer. Within the restricted area of its material . . . *The Boys in the Band* is a legitimate comedy whose author should be identified as a playwright to be watched.[88]

Buoyed by such reviews, *The Boys in the Band* went on to a London production, two national tours, and a successful film. According to Joseph Cali, the production made more money, at least initially, than *Who's Afraid of Virginia Woolf?*[89] Barr had spent only $10,500 on the original production and so was making back the capitalization very quickly, even though the tickets were originally only $5.95.[90] And even after he discovered scalpers were selling tickets for $25, he raised the ticket price only to $10, which quickly cut into the "black market" sales. At the new price, the show grossed $17,000 per week, and since the weekly costs were only $9,000, the show was making $8,000 a week. With the film rights, the play earned over 3,000 percent on the original investment. Barr's choice to keep the play off-Broadway with limited seating built demand and turned the production into a hit. He negotiated a deal for $100,000 of the profits from the production, and once again the savvy producer had saved his Playwrights Unit.

It was shortly after the success of *The Boys in the Band* that Albee, who owned a home on the beach in Montauk, Long Island, convinced Barr to build a home there on two acres. With $75,000 of inheritance money from his aunt and the income from *The Boys in the Band*, Barr built a home that was "not only a joy" but a "very wise investment."[91] It was also around this time that Barr became involved with Anthony Constantine (also known as Antony Gallactides), who began as Barr's lover and companion but later became an investor in Barr's various business deals. Constantine, also known as "Tino," was neither trusted nor liked by Albee nor by Barr's other business partners. Barr says nothing about their relationship in his memoirs and remained mum about his other lovers. Even Albee, who knew Barr well, wrote that he "wasn't sure that I knew whether or not he ever had a lover." Barr had any number of sexual encounters, but Albee "never saw him behave toward anyone as if it were an intense, emotionally involving relationship." For Albee, Constantine was "bad news," and he took Barr "to the cleaners" because by that point in his career, Barr was drinking so much that he didn't have "sufficient control over his life to handle it properly."[92] However, the house that Barr shared with Constantine became a centerpiece of his financing for several productions. It was the house that Barr was forced to hock when all else failed.

The Playwrights Unit continued through the spring of 1968 with three productions. *The Golden Fleece* by A. R. Gurney, a modern send-up of the myth of Jason and Medea, was produced on 22 February and directed by Jered Barclay. Howard Moss's *The Palace at 4 A.M.* was produced on 25 April and directed by Chuck Gnys. James Prideaux's *The Autograph Hound*, which was produced on 9 May, was based on the celebrity-obsessed frequenters of Sardi's and was directed by Barry Plaxen. Barr later produced the play at Lincoln Center's Forum Theatre, and it, along with Prideaux's *Lemonade*, remains a popular show with community and regional theatres.[93] Theater 1968's smash hit, *The Boys in the Band*, had reinvigorated the Playwrights Unit's outlook and justified its existence. The audiences were at near capacity, and the unit was auditioning new actors regularly and interviewing new directors, designers, and stage managers. Script readings were increasing, according to Gnys; five or six more productions were planned before the unit broke for the summer. The Theater 1968 Playwrights Unit had been one of its most productive and rewarding seasons since it had begun five years earlier.[94]

Bitten by the repertory fever particularly virulent in 1960s New York theatre, Barr had planned in the fall of 1967 to run a six-week absurdist repertory on Broadway at the Billy Rose, consisting of short works he had premiered off-Broadway, eventually titling it the *Theater 1969 Playwrights Repertory*.[95] He felt that by moving his Cherry Lane operation onto Broadway, his off-Broadway absurdist hits would be "exposed up town" along with new works, justifying his principle that the playwright is master of his product.[96] Barr hoped to achieve his dream of a playwrights' theatre by changing the very nature of what was considered Broadway fare. He wanted to break down the "meaningless" distinctions between Broadway and off-Broadway. Yet his process of breaking down these distinctions was a fairly improvised, if not quixotic, quest, reflecting his own restless nature.[97]

Keeping to his usual anti-subscription policy, Barr put together a series of twin bills on Broadway at off-Broadway prices, citing a $4.95–$5.95 ticket price.[98] Though interested in name performers, he kept salaries low at the $200 maximum on two-week flexible contracts so the actors could pick up film and television work and continue in the repertory. But his ambitious Broadway plan was stymied when Harold Pinter refused to give Barr the rights to *The Lover* and *The Collection*. Because of this, by January 1968, Barr was rethinking the entire project, now interested in the Billy Rose Theatre project becoming more of a performing arts center with a program of dance, avant-garde films, folk concerts, and modern chamber music, perhaps competitive even with Lincoln Center.[99]

Once again, Richard Barr wanted complete flexibility, which included no subscriptions, "the freedom to change the bill as often as necessary," and $4.95 as a top price for all presentations.[100] He could boast of a healthy start-up fund of approximately $150,000 from Clinton Wilder's Fanton Foundation, the Rockefeller Foundation, and the David Merrick Foundation. The program, scheduled for September 1968, would hypothetically include Sam Shepard's

Chicago, Lanford Wilson's *This Is the Rill Speaking*, Albee's *The Sandbox*, Samuel Beckett's *Happy Days*, Frank Gilroy's *Who'll Save the Plowboy?*, and even possibly Mary Mercier's *Johnny No-Trump*.[101] On 5 August 1968, he announced that his ticket prices would be $5.50 a seat, still the lowest ticket prices on Broadway, with the goal of reaching "the largest audience available." His repertory season was set to begin on 30 September 1968 at the Billy Rose Theatre. Modern dance performances were scheduled to start in January 1969, including the companies of Alvin Ailey, Merce Cunningham, and José Limón. And included were three weeks of avant-garde films scheduled as well. Mercier's *Johnny No-Trump* was mentioned again in advanced publicity, as the playwright stated she needed only "to change four pages of the sad ending," but it never received a production.[102]

The plays actually produced were Albee's *Box*, *Quotations from Chairman Mao Tse-Tung*, *The American Dream*, *The Death of Bessie Smith*, and *The Zoo Story* and Samuel Beckett's *Krapp's Last Tape* and *Happy Days*. William Ritman designed the sets and lighting.[103] *Box* and *Quotations from Chairman Mao Tse-Tung* were to have an out-of-town run in Buffalo, New York. This was the first time Barr had premiered an Albee play outside of New York City, breaking with his own *Virginia Woolf* rule. In spite of all the planning, however, his absurdist repertory on Broadway was not a hit with the critics. Clive Barnes's respectful, tepid review of Albee's *Box-Mao* production did nothing to drum up an audience: "I don't say I understood it—actually I presumed, perhaps wrongly, that there wasn't very much to understand—but I let the words lap over me, like creative foam over a more than usually receptive stone, heard some of them, let them run around in my mind, and this way or that gathered an experience."[104] Though Barnes's lukewarm review encouraged his *Times* readers to attend, audiences stayed away in droves. The entire operation closed before the dance or films could be presented.[105] Barr was dismayed: "We didn't expect this kind of a disaster, what with favorable notices, low prices, and the caliber of plays presented."[106] In a revealing letter to the Rockefeller Foundation, Barr struggled to make the best of the situation and tried to come up with a new play project that would make use of regional theatres, starting at the Mark Taper Forum, and stock settings.[107] He realized that the American regional theatre, rather than Broadway, would become the next important place for the development of serious drama and for new theatre audiences. Though it never came to fruition, Barr's idea was prescient. Later, others would conceive of the National New Play Network, an alliance of not-for-profit professional theatres that champions the development, production, and continued life of new plays for the American theatre within the regional theatre.

The Playwrights Unit had also run into a dilemma. The theatre on Vandam Street had been sold to Allen Boretz, a playwright, so the Playwrights Unit had to find a new home.[108] ABW expected to lease a facility on West Nineteenth Street that Chuck Gnys had managed for Jerome Robbins at the same time he was managing the Playwrights Unit.[109] On 27 February 1969, however, Barr announced new facilities for his Playwrights Unit at 84 East Fourth Street, previously the home of New Dramatists. The building was bought for $77,000 with monies from Barr, Woodward, and Albee. Additional funds were to be raised with a revival of Ben Hecht and Charles MacArthur's *The Front Page*. The unit had never owned its own building before; extensive alterations were planned.[110]

The Front Page was a last-ditch effort to keep the unit alive after the expensive failure of the *Playwrights Repertory*. Recently staged in Long Island, *The Front Page* was a ready-made production. Robert Ryan, its star, pressed Barr to consider a Broadway transfer. The actors agreed to perform at the Equity minimum, and Barr was struck by their willingness to do so to "further the cause of new playwrights in the professional theatre."[111] Directed by Harold J. Kennedy with settings by Will Steven Armstrong and costumes by Sara Brook, ABW's revival of *The Front Page* was a hit, with a rave review from Clive Barnes in the *Times*: "There are many bad bad plays, a few good bad plays, and just one or two positively great bad plays. I suggest that 'The Front Page' by Ben Hecht and Charles MacArthur, joyously restored on Saturday night to Broadway, albeit for a miserably limited run, is of that number."[112] Buoyed with good reviews, the production ran for eight weeks profitably, raising needed funds for the unit's new facilities, which were renovated at a cost of approximately $25,000. The building, now called The Playwrights Unit, had three floors, two playing areas, an open floor for rehearsals, and a modern 150-seat theatre (slightly smaller than the 199-seat Village South), as well as rehearsal, office, and storage space. The cost of these new facilities, in addition to new steeper maintenance costs, were falling more and more upon Albee, Barr, and Woodward.

The Playwrights Unit began the Theater 1970 season at its new address. Philip Magdalany's two short plays *Watercolor* and *Criss-Crossing* led off the season, both opening on 31 October 1969, and then subsequently transferred to the ANTA Playhouse on Broadway. Directed by Chuck Gnys with sets by Peter Harvey, *Watercolor* and *Criss-Crossing* were the only plays brought directly to Broadway from the Playwrights Unit. They received a respectful review by *New York Times* critic Clive Barnes, who sang the praises of the unit's activities and noted that "Mr. Magdalany's duo is not entirely successful, but it is just the kind of work that should be encouraged by such workshop performances."[113] *Watercolor* and *Criss-Crossing* were capitalized at approximately $33,000, and the production was the only one produced by Theater 1970 under an Actors' Equity contract.

About this time, the beginning of February 1970, Mel Gussow wrote an article on the unit in the *New York Times*, which is helpful in understanding how it functioned. He pointed out that Albee's concerns about the internal operations of the unit, about the quality of the work, and how plays were chosen for production led him to submit his own short play *Box* to the unit under the assumed name of "Rayne Endars." Chuck Gnys's subsequent rejection of this script (which Gussow dismissed as unimportant) was the primary reason for Albee's decision to remove Gnys from his position.[114] Only a few months after the Gussow article, Gnys left the unit under anything but amicable terms.[115]

Gussow turned to Barr for answers to the essential questions of how the unit functioned and selected plays. The unit didn't do "unfinished work," Barr explained, and didn't "develop an idea with a playwright." The primary consideration for work produced was its "literacy" and whether the play was "really part of our time." Also, was the work interesting? Was the writer developing, or was the current script a "one-shot venture"? Gussow reported that the plays were staged with "first-rate" actors, directors, and designers, working for free, with budgets of no more than two hundred dollars and running for a total of eight performances. When Barr's competitors accused the unit of being a "cheap tryout," he insisted this was not their objective. Still, he quipped, "What's the matter with a cheap tryout?" According to Barr, of the seven hundred scripts submitted every year, 98 percent were "worthless." And if one strong voice among the producers was either for or against a particular script, it was "enough to outweigh the others." By February 1970, the unit had produced over eighty-seven plays, one-third of which had been done off-Broadway or in regional theatres.[116]

The Theater 1970 season was an exciting yet difficult time for the Playwrights Unit, with a much-expanded facility but, at the same time, a larger financial burden. With just the single Broadway production of Philip Magdalany's *Watercolor* and *Criss-Crossing*, it was clear that Theater 1970 was financially beleaguered. Still, by the Theater 1971 season, the Playwrights Unit had replaced the Cherry Lane as Barr's locus of activity and, quixotically, plans for its activities were redoubled, with preparations for ten plays, ten staged readings, and twenty play readings. The slate was filled, unfortunately, with more readings and staged readings than with full workshop productions.[117] Bruce Hoover and Robert Moss became the Playwrights Unit's new managing directors. Moss later capitalized on his work with the unit to create Playwrights Horizons, which exists today. Hoover had been a stage manager for the APA Repertory, had directed several plays at the unit, and went on to an important career as a major Broadway stage manager.

Despite a busy schedule, it was clear that funding for the Playwrights Unit was reaching bottom, and on 14 December 1970, Hoover and Moss sent out a letter soliciting funds.[118] Richard also attempted a somewhat flashier, more "Hollywood" style attempt to raise money; he hosted a huge opening party for Albee's *All Over*, ABW's next major Broadway production. Audiences attending the production of *All Over* were invited, at the cost of $50–$100 per person, to spend an evening dancing to rock music at the unit's facilities. Barr hoped to raise $8,000–$10,000 by this means. Among those attending the event were Albee's own mother, John Gielgud, Colleen Dewhurst, members of the cast of *All Over*, and, oddly enough, Princess Lucie Shirazi, the Belgian widow of an Iranian Prince.[119]

On 28 March 1971, Theater 1971 presented Albee's *All Over* on Broadway at the Martin Beck Theatre. The play, intended to resurrect Albee's career, had the opposite effect. The casting had been a problem; John Gielgud, who directed, had great difficulty assembling a cast of the right age and temperament for the roles. Edward Cohen, whose play *The Breeding Ground* was in production at the Playwrights Unit, described the May 1971 failure of *All Over* and the dissolution of the unit:

> That was the irony; it was a totally miscast production—no one near the level of stardom Edward wanted, no one near the age that was required to play it. It was absolutely a compromise cast from day one. . . . What happened was *All Over* opened and was a disaster. The reviews were very bad, and business was worse. . . . It created enormous panic in Edward and in Richard Barr, because the expectations were so high. . . . When you have a humiliating failure, given all the hoopla that preceded it, their response was immediately, "Close up, we got to pull back everything, there's no money, there's no nothing. . . . We're going to have to put [in] every penny we've got to keep thing this going. . . . We'll have to shut the Playwrights Unit."[120]

Moss and Hoover, the Playwrights Unit managers, corroborated the effect of *All Over*'s failure with the closing of the Playwrights Unit.[121] *All Over* had been given the full Barr-Woodward treatment, with Michael Kasdan serving as the general manager, set and costume design by Rouben Ter-Arutunian, and lighting by Richard Nelson. The review by Clive Barnes was duly reverential: "Mr. Albee has reached that strange and solstice age, that middle moment, when a man first gets glimpses of his own death, those first intimations that mortality includes him. The result is this obituary play."[122] Doing what he could to intrigue his readers, Barnes inadvertently pigeonholed the play as intellectual art, a death knell for Broadway audiences. Walter Kerr, never an Albee aficionado, wrote some of his most acid criticism regarding *All Over*: "He is off form, seriously. Having surrendered his vituperative energy, once the best thing about him, he has turned placid to no purpose but to overdecorate his prose."[123] If Clive Barnes's faint praise condemned the play to a highbrow grave, Kerr's criticism nailed down the lid.

All Over struggled to find an audience and closed after forty performances, even after its director, actors, and playwright agreed to salary cuts. The failure of *All Over* was the straw that broke the back of the entire ABW producing operation. Barr writes emotionally of this moment in his memoirs: "We left the Martin Beck Theatre not waiting to see the second night and wander[ed] up Eighth Avenue in silence. After a block or two, I turned to Edward and said: 'What did we do wrong?' Then I cried! All of my instincts and training told me that this play was superb—head and shoulders above any written by an American in many years; that the cast chosen had performed with impeccable taste; that the direction by Gielgud, and startling set by Rouben Ter-Arutunian were consistent with Albee's intentions; and yet, we were obviously going to fail." Richard suffered an emotional collapse, and after a "sleepless night," he awoke feeling almost "autistic."[124] He lost his ability to speak and had his companion, Anthony Constantine, call Albee, who came immediately. Both Barr and Albee had to struggle physically and emotionally after the failure of *All Over.* Barr required, by his own admission, sedation and companionship. Still, both recovered, both continued their work, but everything had changed.

On 14 April 1971, about two weeks after the opening of *All Over*, the Playwrights Unit offered its last production, Edward Cohen's *Breeding Ground*, a triptych including *Bumper to Bumper*, *Rats*, and *Sitting Shiva*, directed by Peter Frisch. After the show, the unit closed its doors permanently on 5 May 1971. It was a tremendous personal loss, as Robert Moss, the unit's manager, recalled, but its closure led Moss to the founding of Playwrights Horizons: "We closed the Playwrights Unit, and on my last day there, I noticed the cardboard shoebox that had the mailing list in it on three by five cards, and I looked at it and, without any prescience of what I might or might not do, I thought—I'm going to take this. So I took this shoebox. It contained the mailing list for the Playwrights Unit. It was the smartest thing I ever did. It was a list of ordinary people who loved going to the theatre. And that's the incredible value of that shoebox. And that's how Playwrights Horizons had its start."[125] Moss brought with him from his years at the Playwrights

Unit a philosophy of providing a service to playwrights, without charge, to further the art of playwriting. Since there had been no charge for the use of the facilities at the unit, Moss didn't charge at Playwrights Horizons. Like Barr, Moss felt if there was a page of brilliance to a script, he would produce it, regardless of whether the play would fail. Moss was concerned not with the development of plays but with the development of playwrights.

The failure of *All Over* and the subsequent closing of the Playwrights Unit was a bitter loss for both Richard Barr and Edward Albee, who retreated to Montauk to rethink his nearly ten years in the limelight of the New York theatre. Albee still had great fans in Clive Barnes and Harold Clurman but left many others "feeling befuddled, bothered and belligerent." Audiences did not know what to make of the playwright who had electrified them with the emotional fireworks of *Who's Afraid of Virginia Woolf?* but then left them with the cold, removed *All Over*. In kind, Albee no longer knew what to make of his audiences, and even less of the critics. His raw feelings about this experience were included in a *New York Times* article, "Edward Albee Fights Back," on 18 April 1971: "There is a syndrome in this country. The critics set somebody up, maybe too soon—underline *maybe*—and then they take great pleasure, the only pleasure critics *do* take—except possibly with their wives and mistresses—in knocking him down. . . . The majority of our critics are best qualified to cover brush fires in New Jersey. There *have* been good reviews for this play—Elliot Norton and Clurman and Clive—but the vituperation of the *bad* reviews exceeds any *rational* opinion of the play. . . . Richard and I and Chuck Woodward down at The Playwrights Unit wonder if it's really possible to have a serious commercial theater."[126]

Albee attacked realistic drama and belittled agitprop theatre, struggling to place his work in a different aesthetic. Barr joined the fray: "A major work by a major playwright—you don't just kick it down the toilet that way."[127] But then, surprisingly, Albee's tirade about the critics ended on a remarkably bright note: "Here I am, Edward Albee, entering into my middle age, and I think of it as a *beginning*. Life is absolutely super and wonderful. There shouldn't be any sadness in it. People should be aware of all things at all times, they should experience the extremities of life, fulfill themselves completely. Why does everyone want to go to sleep when the only thing left is to stay awake?"[128] True to his word, Albee, though certainly wounded by the failure of *All Over*, broadened his support of new work by assisting artists of every background and media.

Within three months, he established the William Flanagan Center for Creative Persons in a rehabilitated stable above Montauk's sand dunes. Included in its initial summer were works by Philip Magdalany, author of

Criss-Crossing and *Watercolor*, and Robert Moss. In addition to theatre professionals, the "Stable," as it was nicknamed, became a retreat for sculptors, painters, and composers. Albee spent $45,000 to purchase the property, $45,000 to renovate it, and nearly $30,000 a year for its operations. Barr handled the paperwork of selecting artists, although Albee was the final arbiter of which artists actually used the facilities. The "Stable" has continued as a retreat for over forty years. Albee was once asked why he involved himself in such idealistic work. He responded, "Work in progress in the theater, in painting, excites me. The unfinished keeps moving, changing, hopefully growing."[129]

Barr's and Albee's efforts furthered the notion of a playwrights' theatre in America, one that has been slowly disintegrated by notions of actors' theatres, directors' theatres, and performances that discard the text entirely. Subsequent to their partnership, a small army of new play development opportunities arose to counter the decline of playwriting and drama in the United States. Many, like the National Playwrights Conference at the O'Neill Theatre Center, Playwrights Horizons, and the new play program of the Mark Taper Forum, were created in direct imitation of Barr and Albee's Albarwild Productions. In recent years, the Cherry Lane Theatre, under its innovative artistic director, Angelina Fiordellisi, has created a mentorship program for young playwrights in honor of the work done there by Albee and Barr and their tiny yet enormously important Playwrights Unit.

9

HOCKING THE HOUSE

Seascape to *Sweeney Todd*

By July 1972, Albee and Barr were busy at the John Drew Theater in East Hampton, producing Thornton Wilder's *The Long Christmas Dinner*, Albee's *The American Dream*, Joe Orton's *What the Butler Saw*, and Howard Moss's *The Palace at 4 A.M.* Though they were at work on the summer season, they both still felt the wounds of *All Over*'s commercial and critical failure. Barr complained: "The American theater is the only one in the Western World that is not subsidized. And some kind of subsidy is inevitable to insure its survival. I don't see why dance companies and symphony orchestras are subsidized and theater is not."[1] As president of both ANTA and the League of New York Theatres and Producers, and a member of the advisory board of the NYSCA, Richard was busy promoting the theater as a subsidized art form, a project he continued until his death in 1989.[2]

All Over, despite its debacle in New York, ran successfully in London, as well as in The Hague and in Munich. The London cast featured Dame Peggy Ashcroft and Angela Lansbury. A later production at the Hartford Stage Company in 1976, under the direction of Mark Lamos, its artistic director, became one of the first Albee plays to be staged for television, on the PBS series *Theater in America*. *All Over* has continued to be revived regularly, both nationally and internationally. In 2002, an Obie-awarded production of *All Over* transferred to the Roundabout Theatre from McCarter Theatre, directed by Emily Mann and featuring Rosemary Harris and Michael

Learned. With Albee's success with *Three Tall Women* in 1994, many of his "unproducible" and "unsuccessful" plays, previously premiered by Barr, were revived as both critical and commercial successes on and off-Broadway.

After the disaster of *All Over*, Richard plunged ahead with what he termed be his "saga of seven failures," of which he counted *All Over* as the first.[3] He immediately opened another unmitigated disaster, *Drat!*, a new musical, on 18 October 1971 at the McAlpin Rooftop Theatre. It had first been developed at the Goodspeed Opera House in Connecticut, which considered it one of its "most successful productions," running for two summers there.[4] The show featured the book and lyrics by Fred Bluth, a children's author and illustrator, and the music of Steven Metcalf and starred Bonnie Franklin. After seventeen preview performances, it closed the day after it opened. Clive Barnes of the *New York Times* gave it the worst review of any Barr production, writing that "it had all the taste of a wedding staged in a funeral parlor."[5]

Barr was not one to linger over his failures; he made his living by producing plays, after all. And he was ready for his next major challenge—his first major Broadway musical, *The Grass Harp*. Based upon the novel by Truman Capote, it is a fanciful version of Capote's childhood in the South and revolves around Dolly Talbo, an eccentric old maid who abandons society to live in a tree house in order to protect her "gypsy dropsy potion" from her tyrannical sister, Verena. Dolly is joined in the tree house by her nephew, Colin; their housekeeper, Catherine; and other lost souls and outsiders. A wistful bit of southern whimsy, the novel was first adapted for the stage as a non-musical play in March 1952 by Arnold Saint-Subber and was directed by Robert Lewis.[6] Poet Kenward Elmslie and composer Claibe Richardson then adapted the play into a musical. Elmslie had met Capote years before, when the original play version of *The Grass Harp* had arrived on Broadway.[7] The show had debuted at Trinity Square Repertory Company in 1966, with Elaine Stritch as Babylove Dallas, but stopped there, and the two collaborators struggled to raise money for a New York production.[8] Kermit Bloomgarden first optioned the show, but Mary Martin, who had been wooed to star, turned it down, and with that Bloomgarden pulled out.[9]

Barr and Chuck Woodward then came into the deal. The show was going to be a challenge from the outset, but they loved the music and devised a way to do it by collaborating with the University of Michigan, which had, in 1971, opened its new Power Center for the Arts. *The Grass Harp* was its premier production. A major problem struck at the outset. The Martin Beck Theatre on Broadway, where *The Grass Harp* was to debut, did not have a fly loft. According to Russ Thacker, who starred as Colin Talbo in the show, the set consisted of an enormous metal tree, and because the director, Ellis Rabb, wanted all the other scenic elements to be flown in, a special fly system had to be built. At the opening of the show, disaster ensued: "Barbara [Cook] said, 'Do you hear?' And I go, 'Hear what?' And she says, 'Granddad's voice, singing through the trees.' And I said, 'Do you hear?' and we hear ripping, grinding noises and the whole fly board fell on us—everything came down, all those stairs and windows, and the piano, every scrim and all the pipes. Luckily, that tree was made like a big gymnasium, like a big jungle gym—nothing hit us—but Barbara screamed, 'Oh, Jesus Christ!' We were just frozen in fear. Everything splintered and shattered and broke. The whole show just collapsed. I didn't know what to do, so I said, 'Hear what?' And the audience was stunned and then they laughed."[10] The next day a new fly system was built and the show continued on, and as far as Thacker could tell, "Dick didn't bat an eye about the money."[11] But the crash of the fly system was only the beginning of the disaster that was coming.

This original production at the University of Michigan was not well received, and so began "road work." This is the repair of a show on the road before it can be brought to New York. There were several issues to be resolved. Celeste Holme, who was "badly miscast" as Babylove, was replaced with Karen Morrow; Barr took on this unpleasant task. He also thought the show's book needed work. Truman Capote was brought in, but Thacker felt he only added to the problems: "Truman was impossible and wouldn't stay away, and was tinkering constantly with the book, which he didn't write [he wrote the novel on which the book was based], and was driving us crazy. He came every night for the show and walked up and down the aisle. We would hear applause going on, and Barbara Cook said to me, 'What *is* that?' And I said, 'I think that's Truman Capote walking up and down the aisle.' The book killed the show."[12] Another issue was the set; designer James Tilton's "cast-iron tree, about thirty feet wide and twenty feet tall" had to be "torched into pieces" and welded back together in the Martin Beck Theatre. There were orchestration problems, casting issues, and ongoing book problems—all of which Barr and Woodward were able to solve.[13] Barr also had to convince the director, the distinguished Ellis Rabb, to work with less rehearsal time and to persuade a demoralized cast that the show would do well in New York.[14]

The Grass Harp opened in New York on 2 November 1971, about a month after *Jesus Christ Superstar*, and received strongly positive audience reaction during the previews. Thacker remembered that "the audiences loved it, absolutely loved it," with standing ovations and "screaming bravos," and the cast felt that they were safe. But there wasn't enough front money to handle the setbacks, and when *Jesus Christ Superstar* became a hit, the show was doomed. The gentle little southern musical disappeared in the flash of the mega success of *Jesus Christ Superstar*, and audiences stayed away. As it became clear that the show was failing, Thacker recalled that Barr gave them an option: "Richard Barr said to us, 'We have a choice: we can run this out another week, and hope that we catch fire, or we can make an album.' And we all opted for the album, and thank God, because I don't think a week... would have been enough."[15] Though Richard brought the musical in for the "incredibly low figure" of $165,000, it closed on 6 November 1971, not even a week after it opened. The reviews were a mix of abysmal and genuinely positive, but both investment and operating costs were a loss.

Martin Gottfried of *Women's Wear Daily* was particularly brutal, as he continued to be throughout the 1970s, writing, "'The Grass Harp' is an hour and a half long, which is short for a musical but, in this case, nowhere near short enough."[16] Richard Watts of the *Post* was supportive, although not overly so, calling the show "a charming little fantasy" that had been adapted into a "modest little musical" that was "tasteful and unpretentious," though "it never engenders any excitement and grows fairly tiresome although it is brief."[17] Barr and Woodward lost $30,000 each on the venture, and though the investors were protected, the producers had to personally cover the losses. Richard remortgaged his house in Montauk and borrowed money from his mother in order to meet his "share of the obligation." His personal sacrifice was somewhat mitigated by the success of *The Grass Harp* recording. It became a collector's item, according to Barr, "not because of its scarcity, but because of its beauty."[18] Ken Mandelbaum, author of *Not Since "Carrie": Forty Years of Broadway Musical Flops*, notes that the show had a "ravishing score" and was one of a "special breed" of great flops that were "particularly glorious—and sometimes foolhardy—in the ambition."[19]

Richard jumped into his next project, James Prideaux's *The Last of Mrs. Lincoln*, with Charles Woodward. Despite Prideaux's strong script about a fascinating historical figure and the brilliant performance of Julie Harris as Mary Todd Lincoln, the play was "smothered" by overproduction. Wanting to workshop the play before going into full production, *The Last of Mrs. Lincoln* was initially presented in a "gypsy rehearsal," using a bare stage, with actors in street clothes using rehearsal props, and in work lights.[20] It was an extraordinary experience, according to Maureen Anderman, the actress who played Mary Harlan in the show and became a regular in the Albee-Barr production family: "I remember those gypsy run-throughs—they're always so wonderful—and I don't know if you can do them anymore, because you can't rehearse in a theatre anymore, but you get these pure moments acting, and you know you're about to lose it, [about to] take four giant steps backward, because the next step is costumes and settings. So what you've got is the best of—the peak of—what you worked on in three or four weeks of rehearsal."[21]

The gypsy performance was a "smashing success," and audience members thought the producers should "forget the sets and costumes, and perform the show in this skeleton manner."[22] Barr should have followed this advice. *The Last of Mrs. Lincoln* opened in Washington, D.C., at the Opera House in the Kennedy Center, and the performance space itself was, according to Anderman, something of a shock: "We were the first play to open the Opera House at the Kennedy Center, which is enormous. We were the first and maybe one of the only plays to play the Opera House. . . . The last few times I've been there . . . I've looked at that place and I think of little Julie up there; you know, it's hard to believe we actually played there."[23] Richard struggled to rein in production costs, but it was too late. Even with William Ritman's "splendiferous" sets, Noël Taylor's "exquisite" costumes, and the stellar performances by Julie Harris and Leora Dana, who won Tony Awards for their performances, the show was "undoubtedly overproduced and failed."[24]

The Last of Mrs. Lincoln opened in New York at the ANTA Playhouse on 12 December 1972. The critics were enthused about Harris's portrayal of Mary Todd Lincoln, and the show ran for sixty-three performances. Douglas Watt of the *Daily News* wrote, "As the second half of 'The Last of Mrs. Lincoln' begins, Mary Todd Lincoln is well on the way to recovery, and so is the evening." Like other critics, Watt found the first half of the evening slow. But, he noted, "at the end it is hard to resist both a tear and a cheer for its gallant heroine and actress Julie Harris, in that order."[25] The script did not appeal to all the critics, however, and Martin Gottfried, dependably negative, complained in *Women's Wear Daily* that "James Prideaux has written research rather than drama, his dialogue is capable, if without distinction, and he has provided actors with historical figures to play, rather than characters."[26] Richard considered his inability to simplify the production of *The Last of Mrs. Lincoln* to be "the most serious error in judgment we have made as producers."[27] In Washington, the grosses came in at $90,000 in the last week, and in New York, he was able to bring in just $27,000 per week for only one or two weeks.

Struggling with this second flop, and in an attempt to reproduce the success of *The Front Page*, Barr and Woodward produced Sidney Kingsley's *The Detective Story*. Harold J. Kennedy directed the production, which featured Rita Moreno, Walter Flanagan, and Barry Nelson. Richard knew Kingsley well and even brought him in to work with the cast. But the production struggled with a series of bizarre cast problems. Renee Taylor, who was to the play the shoplifter in the production, threatened to pull out of the play because there wasn't a pickle in the sandwich she was to eat onstage. Kennedy scrambled and had his prop man find a pickle on a Sunday night, when the stores were closed, so that Taylor could play the role.[28] Another actress refused to stay at the company hotel, obsessing over an imaginary stalker. Kennedy, who also played Endicott Sims in the production, wrote a book about the experience, aptly titled *No Pickle No Performance*. Other disastrous incidents plagued the show, and Barr closed it out of town at Kingsley's request. The show ended, Kennedy observed, as it had begun, "on kind of a crazy note."[29]

Richard found his next "flop," *Noël Coward in Two Keys*, in London. It turned out to be such a negative experience that it nearly drove him from the stage. He had produced Noël Coward's *Fallen Angels* before with Nancy Walker and had maintained a close relationship with Coward over the years. The short plays featured in *Noël Coward in Two Keys* were *Come into the Garden, Maud*, and *A Song at Twilight*. Both took place in a private suite in a luxurious hotel in Switzerland. The stronger of the two plays, *A Song at Twilight*, is much darker and therefore more satisfying. The play focuses on Sir Hugo Latymer, a writer and a pompous bore. Coward acted in the original production as Latymer, the first openly gay character he ever played—a point that was not lost on its audiences.

Both plays, accompanied by a third Coward piece, *Shadows of the Evening*, had been produced in London at the Queen's Theatre, directed by Vivian Matalon, as *Suite in Three Keys* in April 1966. Coward starred in all three pieces. *A Song at Twilight* was played as the long piece, alternating with *Shadows of the Evening* and *Come into the Garden, Maud* on separate nights. Richard connected with Vivian Matalon in the winter of 1973, shortly before Coward's passing. He felt that the third piece, *Shadows of the Evening*, a dark comedy about cancer, did not work with the rest of the show and asked Matalon to drop it. The director agreed, and after consulting with Coward himself, he cut *A Song at Twilight* to the length of a "longish one-act" and trimmed *Come into the Garden, Maud* as well.[30] The entire evening was renamed *Noël Coward in Two Keys* and featured Hume Cronyn and Jessica Tandy.

Barr opened the show in Philadelphia, but there was some indecision about whether to end the evening with *Come into the Garden, Maud*, favored by Barr and Woodward because it was hilarious in rehearsals, or with *A Song at Twilight*, which was the stronger of the two pieces and favored by the director. Matalon had tremendous affection and admiration for Barr but felt that putting *Maud* second would have an adverse reaction in the reviews. And there was still another looming issue: Barr's drinking, which had worsened by the 1970s. Matalon noted, "I thought Richard was a wonderful producer, and I would say arguably the best I ever worked with, provided you got him before lunch. He was simply brilliant and astute and I was very, very fond of him. But I learned to completely ignore anything he said after he went to Sardi's."[31] Richard's drinking also became the major dividing issue between himself and Albee, each accusing the other of being worse. Barr thought Albee was "a terrible drinker" because his "personality would change" and he became "sullen and abusive." The differences between Barr and Albee over drinking came to a head later during *Seascape*.[32] Thankfully, Barr decided to review *Noël Coward in Two Keys* closely in Philadelphia, sober, and then agreed with Matalon to change the order of the show so that *A Song at Twilight* ended the evening. The reviews in New York justified the change.

While Richard included the production as one of his "seven failures," it opened on 28 February 1974 after four preview performances and ran for 140 performances before going on tour. Clive Barnes, in the *New York Times*, gave the show a money review, writing, "It was part of Sir Noël's genius always to be able to give you a soufflé and to send you out feeling as though you have had a meal." Barnes was taken by Ritman's "plush Swiss hotel suite" and was complimentary of Matalon's direction of the actors, noting in particular the actors' ability to take on wildly different characters over the course of the two-play evening.[33] Richard Watts of the *New York Post* agreed, writing, "The two plays were wonderfully entertaining themselves, but they have the important additional value of showing the scope of Sir Noël's talent as a dramatist." He noted that "when he comes to the subject of homosexuality, he proves how shallow current plays on the topic usually are." Martin Gottfried was less sanguine, calling the evening "predictable," though he pointed out that *A Song at Twilight* "is touching for an unintended reason, because it shows Coward coping, at life's end, with his secret homosexuality." But despite positive notices and a production that was on budget, *Noël Coward in Two Keys* still lost money and was not able to repay its original investment.[34]

Barr, struggling to make sense of the critical success of *Noël Coward in Two Keys* and its financial failure, writes, "Don't ask me why, because I don't know."[35] Though he ignores the topic in his memoirs, there was a growing perception among New York theatre critics, peers, and audiences that Barr's and Albee's sexual orientation influenced their highbrow tastes. While William Goldman and others made tacit comments about this issue, the lines in the New York theatre had been drawn long ago, although they were never openly discussed. This was especially true after Barr produced *The Boys in the Band*. In this regard, Mel Gussow recalled one bare-knuckled fight between Albee and Barr's fellow producer Joseph Papp in Gussow's own home. Papp considered Albee's work to represent "intellectualism and an aesthetic arrogance that debilitated . . . the societal demands of the-ater."[36] Albee attacked what he considered to be Papp's middlebrow producing choices. But in the 1970s, Papp's working-class, social realist (and homophobic) sensibilities were on the rise in the New York theatre; Barr's and Albee's high-aesthetic, absurdist sensibilities were behind the times. This fact was not lost on the critics. The openly gay activist and theatre artist Doric Wilson believed that Barr and Albee were targeted, particularly when Richard produced shows like *Noël Coward in Two Keys*, which dealt openly with homosexuality. It was not the last time New York critics would attack Barr's producing choices as being a tacit endorsement of homosexuality.

While Richard waited for and "mulled over" Albee's next major offering, *Seascape*, he stepped into the role of director again, taking on *Butley* by Simon Gray. The show had premiered on Broadway in October 1972, featuring Alan Bates in the title role as the acerbic T. S. Eliot scholar and intellectual bully. Richard directed the play at the Coconut Grove Playhouse in May 1973, featuring the television actor James Daly. Anderman had high marks for Barr, remembering that "it was a wonderful production."[37] Several other major actors starred in the production, including Swoosie Kurtz and Barbara Lester, and Richard received strong notices for his direction.[38] It was a well-deserved break from Barr's series of "flops," which were to continue, even with an Albee play that would earn the Pulitzer Prize.

Though Albee was soon ready with his script for *Seascape*, Richard thought the show was "one of the most difficult of Albee's plays from a producer's point of view." It underwent a substantial revision process, unlike any other of Albee's plays. *Seascape* was developed from *Life*, one of two one-acts Albee had written titled *Life* and *Death*. The second of the two plays, *Death*, grew into *All Over*, which Barr had produced earlier, the reception of which had "almost defeated both of us."[39] Recovering from that experience, it took Albee three years to develop *Seascape*.[40] It had its world premiere in Europe in a three-act version that never made it to the United States; it had been "gobbled up" by other producers before Barr could get his hands on it. The reasons for Richard's deep misgivings about the play were complex. Having read it, he contacted Albee by letter, a form of communication reserved only for "crisis" moments between the two. He pointed out "structural changes" and even edited the text, highlighting "non-sequiturs and repetitions." This was a sea change in their relationship. Barr had rarely challenged Albee's writing, but Albee was continuing to struggle with alcohol in the 1970s. His long-term partner, Jonathan Thomas, felt that the drinking had especially affected *All Over*, *Seascape*, and *The Lady from Dubuque*, and because of the drinking, Albee "was too isolated to be creative."[41]

Despite these differences, Barr was willing to go out on a limb with Albee, who was not only his major writer but also a friend who needed his support. Richard sent a selection of "pensées" he had written "á la Pascal" for Albee that resonated on the structure of *Seascape*: "Even as the fish evolved from the acute pressure of the sea, and suffered the relatively less painful pressure of the land, so do we in our 'sea of oxygen' struggle upwards to space to escape the air pressure." Though Albee "apparently . . . did not" find this brief haiku of dramatic structure helpful, he took Barr's letter and his script of *Seascape* with him to California, where he was scheduled to continue on a relentless lecture schedule. Albee's lecturing was another source of tension between the two. Richard wondered why he spent so much time teaching when he should be writing plays. Still, Albee returned from the trip with a "seriously revamped version" of *Seascape*. Though he claimed he had barely revised it, Barr believed "the structure changed greatly." Albee had "clarified his intention," and the script was "quite ready" to be rehearsed and produced.[42]

Upon submitting *Seascape* to Barr after this revision, Albee also requested that he alone should direct the play. Though he had directed many of his plays after they had been on and off-Broadway by 1975, he had never directed a Broadway premiere. Richard had no qualms about this, feeling that "the old cliché that a playwright should not direct his own play because of lack of objectivity is simply not true."[43] Albee continued to direct due in large part to Barr's encouragement and fundamental belief that the director was an interpretive, not a creative, artist whose touch should be "invisible," at any rate.[44] With Albee in place as director of the show, Richard sought out stars whose participation could help bankroll the production.

The two major roles of Nancy and Charlie had been originally written for an elderly couple. Barr and Woodward forwarded the script to Henry Fonda, who was very interested and had been a fan of Albee's work since he had been considered for George in *Who's Afraid of Virginia Woolf?* But Fonda had been sent a major new one-man show, *Clarence Darrow*, and passed, regretfully, on *Seascape*. Helen Hayes was also sent a script and "most politely" turned down the role, having not performed on Broadway since playing Veta Louise Simmons in a revival of *Harvey* in 1970.[45]

The roles turned out to be too demanding for two elderly performers. Richard suggested that Albee reduce the ages of the actors ten to fifteen years so that the characters were no longer facing the end of their lives. Instead, they were "merely at the turning point in a long, successful marriage," deciding how to live out the remainder of their lives. Barr immediately arranged for a reading that summer at Albee's Fifth Avenue apartment with Maureen Stapleton playing Nancy. Maureen Anderman, who had recently performed in Barr's production of *Butley*, read for Sarah. George Grizzard read for Charlie, and James Ray, who had played the son in *All Over*, read for Leslie. After the reading, and clearly not interested in the role, Stapleton confided with Anderman, saying, "What the hey was that about?"[46]

Instead of Stapleton, Barr was able to procure Deborah Kerr, the graceful and distinguished Scottish film actress who had not acted on Broadway in twenty years, since she starred in Robert Anderson's play *Tea and Sympathy*. Barry Nelson was cast as Charlie and Frank Langella as Leslie, the lizard opposite Anderman's lizard Sarah. Albee had some trepidation about the casting, particularly about Deborah Kerr, who had some doubts herself after so many years away from the stage.[47] What was more alarming was the size of the production, which was driven by Albee's request for a realistic set with a real sand dune running along the ocean's edge. Worse, the second act (there were three acts at this point) took place *under* the sea as Charlie and Nancy descended into the deep to see Leslie and Sarah's world. Though in the European productions the designers created an underwater set, complete with undersea creatures, Richard didn't feel this act worked. But he thought that Albee had to understand on his own the structural reason for eliminating the second act. So the show went into rehearsal with the second act intact. One day, as they left rehearsal on their way to their usual drinking establishment, Albee let Barr know he was thinking of cutting the second act. Barr asked if he could stop work on the set in the shop, and Albee asked for an evening to think about it. Barr gave it to him, and the next day the second act was gone.[48]

The cast had its own concerns—about Albee's directing. Though Maureen Anderman was friendly with Albee and his partner, Jonathan Thomas, she did not know what he would do as director, and she wasn't alone: "I was at the theatre one night before rehearsals and Deborah Kerr was at the theatre, and I nervously went up to her to introduce myself to her and she took my hand and was shaking, and she said, 'Oh, darling, I'm so happy to meet you—I'm so nervous about this.' So I knew we were all in the same boat."[49] Anderman felt that Kerr achieved "a beautiful performance," and the cast's concerns about Albee's direction during the show were quickly allayed. He was, according to Anderman, "very gentle and very kind," and "we had a very enjoyable rehearsal period; it was a lot of fun." A movement expert, William Rhys, came in to help with the lizards' movement. This became one of the high points of the production, especially the work of Frank Langella. Albee directed the show with humor and a sense of fun and innocence.

"There was a lot of silliness" because, as Anderson explained, "we were both crawling around as lizards."[50] Sometimes, however, this sense of fun was not always a good thing. Langella, as Leslie, the large male lizard, stole the show in a somewhat reckless manner and even "bedeviled" the cast with upstaging during *Seascape*'s tryouts at the Kennedy Center.[51] Still, Langella received rave reviews as well as his first Tony Award for his performance.

Seascape opened on Broadway on 26 January 1975 and ran for sixty-five performances before closing on 25 March. The production designer was James Tilton, who had designed the tree house set for Barr's *The Grass Harp*. Costumes were by Fred Voelpel, who, though a Barr favorite, was designing his first and only Albee production. Mark Wright served as the production stage manager, and Clinton Wilder joined Barr and Woodward in the financing of the production. The reviews, with the notable exception of Clive Barnes's, were mixed. Martin Gottfried of the *New York Post* predictably wrote, "'Seascape' starts out looking like a Pinter play on a Beckett set, but it proves just another shovelful of phony art, fake sensitivity and ersatz eloquence from Edward Albee."[52] But Clive Barnes began his review with a triumphant, "Hats off, and up in the air! A major dramatic event," and followed with a strong, positive review of Albee's play, calling it "a comedy rather than a farce, and it is a curiously compelling exploration into the basic tenets of life." Barnes also noted that Albee's direction had been done with "self-evident skill and ease."[53]

Richard Watts of the *New York Post* and Brendan Gill of the *New Yorker* both gave the show rave reviews, and Barr was overwhelmed by the critical response: "One would think with a send off like that we were home free, but not so!"[54] Both the local New York television and radio reviews were brutal, with Kevin Sanders at WABC-TV sounding one of the darker notes of the season.[55] Aggravated, Barr believed that these TV critics were "simply not qualified to review major works." Though the magazine critics were far more supportive of the production, "by the time their reviews arrive on stands, the tidal wave of television has swept the play away."[56]

Richard did everything he could to keep the show going, including keeping the play's most unusual characters a mystery. No photographs of the lizards were allowed outside of the theatre or in the press. Finally, he decided to "flee" to California to see if he could do business with the show at the Shubert Theatre in Los Angeles, where "it did a good deal better, but not well enough." Ironically, Albee's *Seascape* was awarded the Pulitzer Prize for Drama a day after the show closed in California, even as the set was being broken down and burned.[57] Anderman recalled, "I do remember distinctly leaving the theatre the night we closed; it was like the *Cherry Orchard*, they were chopping down the set. And the next day, we were sitting around the pool with Edward, and Edward came over and said we got the Pulitzer."[58]

Barr hardly waited after the closing of *Seascape* in March 1975 to open his next major show, *P.S. Your Cat Is Dead*, a wild sex farce written by James Kirkwood, who wrote the book for *A Chorus Line*. It was directed by Vivian Matalon, who had directed *Noël Coward in Two Keys*, and featured Keir Dullea as Jimmy Zoole, a hapless, out-of-work actor who is abandoned by his girlfriend on New Year's Eve and catches a burglar, Vito, played by Tony Musante, robbing his apartment.[59] Matalon had encountered Kirkwood at the same party where he had met Barr. After a first reading, Matalon had found *P.S. Your Cat Is Dead* "touching and a very, very funny play." His direction of the production would receive strong reviews, as did the acting and design. Keir Dullea had played in Barr's first off-Broadway production, *Season of Choice*, and starred in *Butterflies Are Free* on Broadway (directed by Milton Katselas, the first director of *The Zoo Story*). Dullea had become a Hollywood film star with his portrayal of David Bowman in *2001: A Space Odyssey*, but by 1975, he was trying to build a career in the theatre.

What was controversial about the comedy was its cheerful exploration of the nature of love between two men; it seemed to advocate for homosexuality. Mary Hamill, the actress who played Janie in the production, remembered Zoole's somewhat kinky capture of Vito as being one of the selling points of the production for audiences, and perhaps one of the reasons why the producers became uncomfortable about the production: "There's a scene in it where Tony Musante has burglarized Keir Dullea's apartment and Keir Dullea catches him and ties him atop a sink, which was planted center stage. And at some point, his character has to pee, and so his pants are cut off. So he's up there . . . with his butt hanging out throughout the entire play. So people came to see the show for that reason. And the producers got frightened about that kind of PR."[60] Vito spends much of the play explaining his homosexuality to Zoole; in the end, Zoole becomes sympathetic and releases Vito. The two go on a crusade together to revenge the injustices in their lives. It was tough and foul-mouthed like *Who's Afraid of Virginia Woolf?* but lacked the intellectual or lyrical power of that play. It was as challenging and intense as *The Boys in the Band*, but in its cynicism it lacked the humanity of that show. Richard closed the show quickly once he saw it struggle to find an audience.

Despite these later misgivings, Tony Musante remembered Barr being excited about the script and asking him to read it as early as the late 1960s.[61] Richard cast Musante, who had started as an assistant stage manager for ABW management at the Cherry Lane and had been cast in a number of plays there, including *Match Play, Party for Divorce, Night of the Dunce*, and *Mrs. Dally Has a Lover.* By the time Barr finally asked him to star in *P.S. Your Cat Is Dead*, Musante had become a television star on the series *Toma* and had also appeared in the hard-hitting film *The Incident*: "My personal story about *P.S. Your Cat Is Dead* involves *Toma*, the television show. In that entire decade, I did a lot of work at the Cherry Lane, and at one point—it had to be the late sixties, early seventies—the script for *P.S.* came to me from Richard. Would I be interested in reading for this role? But it never came to fruition for whatever reason; it just didn't happen. I did the pilot for *Toma* in '72–'73. I read the script shortly before I went into *Toma*, and it was a big hit. And now I received the script again: 'Would you like to do the role of Vito?' So I have to tell you I owe my Broadway role to a television series."[62] Musante's success in *Toma* brought him to Barr's attention. Richard wanted actors who could approach the play with intelligence, sensitivity, and a strong sense of comedy, and Musante's performance in *Toma* confirmed this for him.

Richard arranged with Neal Du Brock at the Studio Arena Theatre in Buffalo to produce the world premiere of *P.S. Your Cat Is Dead.* He had rehearsed and produced Albee's *Box-Mao* at his theatre in 1968. Du Brock covered all production expenses, including the building of sets and costumes, as well as a portion of the director's and designer's fees. The play was, according to Barr, a "triumph" in Buffalo. Musante recalls the excitement: "We leave town and we go up to Buffalo, . . . a hockey town, and we open to smashing reviews, and at one point in the local paper, somebody was offering two tickets to a hockey game for two tickets to *P.S. Your Cat Is Dead*! And this is in Buffalo, blue collar, hockey town. I mean, we were just sailing; we did standing room only for four weeks."[63] The cast was elated and traveled to New York City for the show's previews, which began 3 April 1975. Throughout the previews, the audiences howled with laughter and, according to Mary Hamill, were "wildly appreciative." Tony Musante remembered: "Then we roll into in Manhattan in the middle of a blizzard. And we went into rehearsal and we opened at the Golden. And I'm thinking, 'My God, isn't life great?' And three weeks later—I'm laughing now, but I wasn't laughing then—it closed. And I won a Drama Desk Award, and people loved the show."[64]

The poor reviews revealed a distinct edge of homophobia. Clive Barnes, however, despite deep misgivings, tried to be generous and connected to the show's comedy: "It would get few prizes for dramatic credibility, its basic (and extremely cute) situation is overprolonged, and it is a play with an immoral moral. But only the very up-tight will fail to get a few raucous chuckles from the wonderful show-biz dialogue that crackles with bitchery like campfire."[65]

Barnes praised the production for its "first-rate" cast and called Vivian Matalon's direction, particularly his "timing and pauses," "perfect for the play." But Barnes struggled with the play itself, noting that "this is the first public-public play that appears to be actually proselytizing for homosexuality."[66] Martin Gottfried of the *New York Post* complained about the implausibility of a gay man converting a straight man to homosexuality: "The point is that instead of being 'square' and unadventurous he 'should take a chance' because homosexuality 'might work out.'"[67] Though both Dullea and Musante were trying to play against stereotypes, the critics were not impressed.[68] Mary Hamill confirmed: "They weren't gay, and they weren't playing gay."[69] But the critics ignored the actors' work because the play seemed to be promoting homosexuality, and the language was "raunchy" and aggressively sexual.

Barr's reaction was swift and predictable: he closed the show on 20 April 1975, after only sixteen performances. Though some felt that he and Woodward did so prematurely, "it was better for the majority of the investors to close the show quickly, save what money was available, and hope for the future revenue from motion pictures or stock."[70] Having opened without an advance sale in New York, the box office was "wrapping" only $1,000 a day when it really needed at least $5,000 a day to stay afloat. It was a typical Richard Barr flop; the show had "preview audiences howling with it, and later the New York critics howling at it." Despite the grim critical response, *P.S. Your Cat Is Dead* was awarded the Drama Desk Award for Outstanding New Play, and Tony Musante received a Drama Desk Award as well. Ironically, it was successfully revived off-Broadway at the Promenade Theatre in 1978, only three years after its original production, and ran for 301 performances. Terry Spiegel, a coproducer on the original production, was the producer of this revival and had been particularly unhappy when Barr's show had closed so quickly.[71]

In his memoirs, Richard wrestles with what he termed his seven failures of the 1970s.[72] Why did he produce these plays? Barr had to make a living, and he made money only when he was producing shows. Despite what others may have believed, he always lived on the edge of financial ruin and was never the deep pockets of his operation. He had been able to buy his home in Montauk only because of a family inheritance and some of the profits from producing *The Boys in the Band*; this was the same house he had to hock to help finance *The Grass Harp*.

Despite this string of flops, Richard did have two more major productions in the 1970s. The first was Robert Wilson's *I Was Sitting on My Patio. This Guy Appeared. I Thought I Was Hallucinating*, which he produced at the Cherry Lane Theatre on 22 May 1977. The circumstances around Barr's decision to produce the piece were somewhat haphazard. Sitting around the office one day, he received a call from the former co-manager of his Playwrights Unit, Bruce Hoover, who had stage-managed several of Barr's Paul Taylor dance productions. Performance artist Robert Wilson had called him, looking for a producer for his show, and Hoover asked if Barr was interested. Richard was "certainly" interested but wanted to meet Wilson because he had never seen his work. The two immediately took a liking to each other. Barr found Wilson to be "appreciative, bubbling, inquisitive," and though he confessed that he did not readily comprehend Wilson's intentions, Barr did believe that "Wilson is one of the most creative men I have ever met."[73] He produced Wilson's *I Was Sitting on My Patio* for a limited engagement of fourteen performances "on a hunch" and points out that "there is a smell about genius and I recognized it."[74] Clive Barnes wrote the rather whimsical *New York Times* review of the production: "Did I enjoy—forgive the familiarity—'Patio'? Well, at times, I thought I was hallucinating, and at others I wondered about my foot—but by and large, yes, I suppose, I did. I like watching other people's boredom—it enables me to comprehend better my own. Also the whole thing looked—at any moment, second, instant—beautiful: a frigid picture of an inner landscape."[75]

It was not surprising that Richard produced Wilson's work. It was theatre, dance, visual art, and music encompassed into a single production, not unlike Barr's other eclectic shows. The only surprise was that Wilson sought out a commercial producer like Barr. But Richard saw how he could help Wilson; he "simply organized everything for him, surrounded him with capable people." By doing that, Barr felt that Wilson was "protected and he knows he doesn't have to make every single decision."[76] Once again, Richard was able to bring the show and the tour in for a capitalization of $30,000, with the most expensive part being Wilson's metallic chairs, which were later sold as artwork to the investors after the production. Actors' Equity picketed the theatre, however, because Wilson was a non-Equity performer. Irritated, Richard publicly stated that Equity should stop policing off-off-Broadway, since the union had already "destroyed" off-Broadway. The League of New York Theatres and Producers, for which Barr still served as president, was unhappy with his comments, especially as Broadway contracts were up for renegotiation by 1 June. But never one to kowtow to the unions, Barr ignored Equity's request that Robert Wilson and his co-performer, Lucinda Childs, be forced to join the union.

The last show Barr produced in the 1970s was Stephen Sondheim's *Sweeney Todd: The Demon Barber of Fleet Street*, and it was to be his last, most important, most critically successful, and, sadly, least remunerative production.

It was a stunning theatrical achievement on par with his production of *Who's Afraid of Virginia Woolf?* but without the benefit of that show's financial success. He first discovered the Christopher Bond adaptation of *Sweeney Todd*, which became the basis for Sondheim's musical, through three accidental encounters. The first was a meeting in the early 1970s with the actor Werner Klemperer at Sardi's, one of Barr's usual haunts. Klemperer dropped the news that the three Noël Coward comedies in *Suite in Three Keys* were being considered for a summer stock tour in 1974. Richard quickly contacted Coward's agent and asked for the summer tour to be canceled so that he might acquire the Broadway rights to the show, which would become the basis for his own production of *Noël Coward in Two Keys*.

He immediately sent Chuck Woodward to Switzerland to meet with Coward's heirs and to negotiate exclusive producing rights. Woodward decided to stop in London to persuade Irene Worth to star in the New York production of the show. Here another "accident" occurred. During his visit in London, Woodward was "plagued" by Blanche Marvin to see a play written by one of her clients, Christopher Bond, titled *Sweeney Todd: The Demon Barber of Fleet Street*. Writing the show for himself, Bond had cobbled the play from such sources as Alexandre Dumas, Jacobean drama, Shakespeare, and the Bible, adding to it a touch of Cockney slang. In his own words, he "crossed Dumas' *The Count of Monte Cristo* with Tourneau's *The Revenger's Tragedy* for a plot."[77]

The Bond production had opened at the Victoria Theatre on 17 April 1970 in one of London's suburbs, Hammersmith, and was a word-of-mouth success.[78] Woodward saw the show at Theatre Royal Stratford East in 1973, was entranced by the production, and contacted Barr immediately. Coincidentally, Stephen Sondheim saw it as well and was attracted to the larger-than-life characters, which, despite their melodrama, had the quality of real human beings.[79] Sondheim loved the language that Bond had created for the production, which was "elegantly written, part in blank verse"; he also noted that "the language was so rich and thick without being fruity."[80]

Woodward acquired the rights to Coward's plays, but Richard became intrigued by Bond's *Sweeney Todd* and the possibility of producing the play with evocative musical numbers placed in between scenes. He immediately contacted Flora Roberts, Bond's American representative, to acquire the rights to his *Sweeney Todd* and discovered (and here was the third "accident") that Roberts was also Sondheim's agent. Sondheim was also interested in acquiring rights for the production as a musical theatre project for himself. Barr made it clear to Roberts that working with Sondheim on the project "interested the hell out of us," and so he immediately contacted Sondheim.[81]

Though Sondheim was "most receptive," according to Richard, he had just committed to writing the musical score for *Pacific Overtures* for Harold Prince. He wouldn't be able to work on the project until *Pacific Overtures* was completed. Barr was willing to wait, if Sondheim agreed to write the show. Sondheim agreed, but without "the usual monetary advance to which he would normally be entitled." Instead, Barr negotiated a "gentleman's agreement," and in a single afternoon on Montauk, Barr and Woodward had acquired both book and music for a new hit musical. Sondheim admitted later that he "didn't really get around to starting work on 'Sweeney' until the summer of 1977," so the producers had to be patient for four years.[82] Par for the somewhat bizarre course the production took, the show didn't open until 1 March 1979, nearly six years after Barr first became interested.

From the outset, Richard knew that Sondheim was essentially writing an "opera" themed around "rape, revenge and cannibalism." But Barr's respect for Sondheim was "so great" that the challenges of the show seemed to him and Woodward to be "as sensible a venture as some of those dared in the past," and so Barr and Woodward took on the project. Sondheim wanted Harold Prince to direct, his collaborator on his shows since Prince's production of Sondheim's *A Funny Thing Happened on the Way to the Forum*. Prince was reluctant and had to be persuaded to get on board with the project for a number of reasons. He found Bond's script to be "a little on the campy side, about serving meat pies at intermission and hissing the villain and applauding the hero."[83] Worse, Prince couldn't connect to the period, pointing out, "I really couldn't see beyond Sherlock Holmes."[84] But Prince also had other concerns. Sondheim was a notoriously slow writer, and knowing that, Prince wanted Sondheim to complete the entire score before rehearsals began. Making matters worse, Sondheim insisted on writing not only the music and lyrics but the book as well. Having had "little experience with musicals," Barr and Woodward naively agreed to all of Sondheim's requests.[85]

Sondheim finished with *Pacific Overtures* on 26 June 1976, and after he and Prince completed the filming of *A Little Night Music*, he began work in earnest on *Sweeney Todd*. The first public mention of the show was in a brief paragraph in the *New York Times* on 30 April 1976: "Imagine a barber who butchers his customers and makes them into mincemeat pies . . ."[86] Oddly, Richard used the advertisement to impose his sense of the show's period. Throughout the production, he struggled to no avail to convince Prince and his designers that the show belonged in the eighteenth century. And despite their somewhat carnivorous advertising, Barr and Woodward were also concerned that audiences might think *Sweeney Todd* was some kind of "slasher" horror show. So the show was advertised as being "very high comedy" and "Grand Guignol," noting in particular that "it does not try to scare you. It's a comic musical."[87]

The first major challenge occurred when it became clear that Sondheim, who had been working on the score of *Sweeney Todd* as early as October 1976, became overwhelmed by the "very tightly constructed Christopher Bond adaptation."[88] Trying to write *Sweeney* as a virtually uninterrupted musical score, Sondheim realized he was only on page 5 of the original Bond script, and "at that rate, the show would possibly have been nine hours long." Barr brought in Hugh Wheeler, Sondheim's collaborator on *A Little Night Music*, *Candide*, and *Pacific Overtures*, to take on the book at Harold Prince's request.[89] It was "a happy choice," and for Sondheim, Wheeler was the perfect pick because "he had written mysteries and he was British and he would understand the tradition of the play."[90]

In terms of casting, Len Cariou was the first choice for Sweeney, and British actress Patricia Routledge was the original choice for Mrs. Lovett. Routledge had just played every first lady from Abigail Adams to Eleanor Roosevelt in the short-lived Leonard Bernstein musical *1600 Pennsylvania Avenue*. However, as Sondheim and Wheeler further developed the mercurial comedic role of Mrs. Lovett, it became clear that Routledge was the wrong type. Angela Lansbury, with her strong musical theatre skills and enormous comedic talents, was a better fit for the show. Lansbury was about to perform at the Hartford Stage Company in *Counting the Ways* and *Listening*, written and directed by Edward Albee. The show, if it came to New York, would have made it impossible for Lansbury to participate, but fortunately, Richard knew that the Albee plays would not transfer to Broadway. With Lansbury signed on, Sondheim and Prince were much more confident about Mrs. Lovett's portrayal, and the show moved ahead.[91]

Before taking his family to Majorca, Spain, in the summer for a month of rest, Prince read Hugh Wheeler's script out loud, and Sondheim performed the music for Woodward, Barr, and Eugene and Franne Lee, the set and costume designers. Richard felt the first act was "in readable and playable form." But then the designers presented the producing team with a nineteenth-century poster that they felt personified the show's style. Barr was livid; he argued that Bond's *Sweeney Todd* "explicitly states that the time is that of George II, which was the first half of the 18th Century, nearly one hundred years earlier." Though assured by Franne Lee that she and her husband would make the play "periodless," Barr knew that both Lee and Prince "had other ideas." Prince felt the show could be "ambiguously the Victorian Age" but agreed that scenery should represent an eighteenth-century foundry.[92]

Eugene Lee saw *Sweeney Todd* as an environmental theatre "movie set" through which the audience would walk, "accompanied by the necessary light changes."[93] Richard thought the idea was possible. Another idea for Lee's sprawling set design for the show included tearing out the Vivian Beaumont Theatre and adapting it into an environmental space.[94] Because of his own lingering desire to control Lincoln Center's Beaumont, Barr actually explored this idea, especially after Joseph Papp had failed to make it a success. However, without enough seats in the house to justify its use, Barr couldn't make the "necessary gross" to cover the renovation expense.[95] He struggled with Eugene Lee's extravagant ideas, which included using a defunct airplane terminal on New York City's west side and a television sound stage, but was willing to listen.[96]

While these ideas were being explored, Prince had settled into Majorca and asked that Sondheim, Wheeler, and the two Lees come to Spain to discuss further plans with him. Barr and Woodward were somewhat shocked at the request for four airfares, with no front money at that point. The issue pressed against a larger problem. The budget for *Sweeney Todd* stood at $900,000, and that money had yet to be raised. There had been several backers' auditions, with Sondheim presenting the show's music, and not a single investor had signed on.[97] But now that the principals were in place, including the stars, Cariou and Lansbury, along with the creative team, Sondheim, Prince, and Wheeler, the money could be raised. Barr and Woodward moved swiftly to cover the mounting expenses. In order to do so, the producers needed to post an investment advertisement in a major New York newspaper. Public advertisement for investors was frowned upon among Broadway producers, as raising money for shows was traditionally handled privately, but after success with a similar investor advertisement in the *Wall Street Journal* for *Seascape*, they decided to try it again. Using the Sunday *New York Times* to make their appeal, they placed their advertisement in a prominent spot, by the ABC theatre listings.[98]

The response, according to Barr, was "startling." Over 1,500 requests by mail and phone were made to purchase shares in the show. Within a few months, over 150 investors had sent checks, including "one gentleman who walked in the office the next day and gave us a check for $18,000." By the end of Barr and Woodward's advertising campaign, they had raised $225,000 and had made history with their financing achievement.[99] In the end, there were 271 investors, an unusually large number for a big Broadway musical in the 1970s.[100] This initial money was placed in certificates of deposit at the Irving Trust Company because no funds could be spent until the show was fully capitalized. Because the certificates of deposit had an interest rate of

9.5 percent, however, Barr and Woodward raised enough money in interest to pay for the creative team to meet with Prince in Majorca.[101]

While the creative team was meeting, Richard received a request from Prince to secure the Uris Theatre (now the Gershwin Theatre). One of the largest theatres on Broadway, it had the stage and seating capacity that could accommodate the size of the show and could produce enough revenue to justify its expense. Barr and Woodward immediately procured the space from owner James Nederlander. In 1976, it was the first new Broadway house to have been built since 1929 and was one of the most impressive theatres on Broadway. However, the designs for the show were not ready, and Barr and Woodward wanted to know how Lee would handle the set, since he was notorious for cost overruns. After the creative team had returned from Majorca, Prince made assurances at an evening party that he did not intend to "overwhelm the musical" with production and that "the strength of the book . . . [and] the marvelous contribution of Steve's music and lyrics made it unnecessary for him to do more than put it on the stage."[102]

Of course, both Barr and Woodward were delighted with this decision, having been told that Lee had been "working upstairs" at Prince's home. But when asked to see the designer's preliminary sketches for the show, Prince insisted it would "embarrass" Lee to show his unfinished work. The reality was that Lee's designs were not ready to go into production for some time, which forced Barr and Woodward to keep the Uris Theatre empty, though now secured for the show, despite what seemed to them an interminable amount of time in development.[103] By 23 December 1977, Richard spoke to the press about *Sweeney* opening in Boston in the fall of 1978 and then transferring to New York.[104] But in reality, Richard was deeply frustrated by the "eccentric" Lee and his wife, Franne, feeling that the designers ignored the cost of their design decisions and that Prince accepted their "tempestuous and taciturn" attitude as a matter of course. One of the most stunning requests was for actual Rhode Island foundries that Lee had found near his home and had shipped to New York. The foundry parts had come in at $7,000, which was dwarfed by the shipping costs totaling over $100,000, with the total set budget at a "preposterously high" $200,000.[105]

Their financing woes seemed to have been solved when Columbia Pictures bought a $450,000 stake in the show for first refusal rights. Unfortunately, just as Richard celebrated the near-completion of the financing at his home in Montauk, he received a call from a "disgruntled Columbia executive" telling him that Columbia Pictures was backing out of the deal.[106] And with only about half of the money raised, Barr needed more partners on the project. He contacted "The Producers' Circle 2, Inc.," which included Robert

Fryer, Mary Lea Johnson, and Marty Richards. The organization's partners agreed to cover the rest of the capitalization as long as they were assured a "commensurate interest in our share of the profits." Richard was desperate, especially as costs mounted on the set production, and accepted the offer.[107]

But even with Barr's raising of additional money, set costs were "alarmingly over budget."[108] As previews were set to begin on 19 February 1979, he was compelled to raise even more money.[109] Barr asked for and got nearly all of a 10 percent overcall, a total of $87,000. Still, he brought in new potential partners to view run-throughs of the show. This raised an additional $290,000 in addition to the original $900,000. Even with this, the show lost money in previews. To prevent the crew from quitting, Barr had to borrow to meet payroll.[110] Rather than hocking his house, Barr went directly to friends and coproducers. He borrowed $15,000 from his partner Anthony Constantine and another $25,000 from Judy Manos, their "front-money friend," receiving the money without any security, interest, or a percentage of the show's profits. He also managed to scrounge an additional $35,000 from his, Woodward's, and the Producers' Circle partners. All these loans and special limited partners were paid first as the show began to recoup its costs, but at a major cost to Barr and Woodward's stake in the profits, which shrank from the initial 25 percent to 6.5 percent.

The rehearsal and preview process had gone well because the show had previewed in New York and rehearsed on the ANTA stage on a "rough mock-up" of Lee's set. Still, many technical problems had to be solved in previews.[111] The rolling platform holding Sweeney's famous barber chair, which sat immediately above Mrs. Lovett's pie shop, was the first issue. The building material for the platform was switched from light aluminum to steel, to be strong enough to hold actors on top as well as move. But then, according to Len Cariou, "it weighed a ton and nobody could move it."[112] Other issues included an infestation of wood lice in the Italian Barber's caravan and a sweater for Mrs. Lovett that had been so hastily "distressed" in Romano cheese and tomato sauce that it nearly caused Angela Lansbury to vomit during her musical numbers. Finally, and perhaps most horrifying, Sweeney's blade spurted an unconscionable amount of blood during the neck-slashing, splattering preview audiences and sending them, nauseated, to the bathrooms. Prince had also made the decision to tear out the theatre space and replace it with the factory setting so that the focus was actually on the wagon, and thus it would "confine your eyes to the story."[113] But the huge set overwhelmed the actors, and audiences walked out during the intermission; investor Martin Richards felt the "show got lost in its set."[114] The producers decided to step away from the production to give

Prince room to reassess and restage the production, and he successfully did so within two days.

During the previews, Barr also interceded in what he considered to be anachronistic elements that were adding unnecessary time to the show. Prince listened to his complaints and made the cuts. The Judge's flagellation scene was incorrect for the period; "people were not flagellating themselves during the 19th century," Richard pointed out, and Prince couldn't find a way to make the scene work.[115] Also cut was a child-hanging scene; the dummy had come apart during the first test run, with straw "splattering" all over the stage below. Finally, Barr insisted that an anachronistic dentist's song, though "very funny," be trimmed, and it was finally cut in the London production.[116]

Despite the protestations of Sondheim and Prince, Barr brought Albee, a trusted friend, to see the show in previews. Sondheim's and Prince's concerns were not unjustified; Albee had "serious reservations" about the show. Barr humorously notes, however, that Albee rarely liked any show Barr produced that wasn't Albee's.[117] Tension was rising between the partners themselves. A great deal of money had been invested in the production, and the consensus was that the show had been overproduced to serve Prince's spectacle and Sondheim's music.[118] To mitigate these tensions, the producers met continually but without engaging with either Sondheim or Prince, in order to protect their creative vision. Though the author and director understood the producers' anxiety, both felt like audiences were "getting it."[119] Richard was proud that "none of us lost our nerve," even as the show lost $100,000 in previews and the response was "sluggish," because the cast and crew were performing "superbly."[120]

The relationship between Barr and Prince was that of mutually respectful colleagues. Prince trusted Barr's producing experience, and conversely, Prince was the premier musical theatre producer on Broadway. When Barr and Woodward brought their show into Prince's territory, they "walked softly." Though initially nervous about working with Prince, Barr believed that he was so organized in his approach that though the producing process was not easy, neither was it "difficult, nor unpleasant." Prince did take Barr's concerns into consideration and "never overruled" his producers' decisions. But he also wasn't shy about making "casting and advertising" decisions on his own.[121] And though he reduced his royalties as negotiated by his lawyer, Frank Weissberg, until "the show could catch on with the public," he could not, in Barr's opinion, control Eugene Lee's extravagance. Consequently, Lee took "considerable advantage" of the situation by not completing his plans; his sets could not be built efficiently to contain costs. Always the elder "gentleman" producer, Richard was not always comfortable with Prince's brash style, noting that Prince executed his work "noisily" and that he was "voluble, mercurial." Prince insisted that his staff not only keep up with him but be "several steps ahead of him." He accepted criticism and suggestions but "demanded perfection—sometimes in a very loud voice." He was a genius director/producer of Albee's generation, and Richard worked with Prince the same way he did with Albee: he took a fatherly, statesmanlike, and somewhat academic approach, with a businessman's attention to the financial details.[122]

Though Barr handled Prince with kid gloves, he was utterly delighted by Sondheim, and his memoirs reveal an affectionate, touching side to his admiration of the composer/lyricist. He acknowledges that more than the design, the book, or the original play by Bond, it was Sondheim's "dazzling score and lyrics" for *Sweeney Todd* that captivated him. Though he thought of Sondheim as a "mature little boy" who liked to play "games" and who was "vulnerable in the area of his genius," he was impressed by Sondheim's confidence in his own talent. This, coupled with a humility and intelligence, made him, in Richard's estimation, "the greatest creative artist working in the musical theatre today."[123] And Sondheim's ability to come in under budget gave Barr special reasons for finding him so endearing.

Sweeney Todd opened on 1 March 1979, after nineteen previews. Though Barr had attended many opening nights on Broadway, he felt it was "the most exciting I had attended since the Albee opening of *Who's Afraid of Virginia Woolf?* in 1962."[124] Until the advent of *Sweeney Todd*, the Broadway musical theatre season had been something of a critical wasteland, with crowd-pleasers such as *The Best Little Whorehouse in Texas* and *They're Playing Our Song* being the major draws. So "the audience was primed" for the success of *Sweeney Todd*. Barr broke one of his own "cardinal rules" and invited his family from Washington, D.C., to be a part of the opening. The evening was thrilling. *Sweeney Todd* opened just before the Tony Awards, and the tension in the air was palpable. By the end of the evening, when Sweeney Todd slammed shut the massive iron door on Mrs. Lovett and the horrors of their bloody deeds, there was a roar from the audience. A "shout went up in that enormous 1,890-seat theatre" that Barr believed "will be heard for years."[125]

Richard Eder's review for the *New York Times* was typical of those that not only raved about the production but offered "pseudo-intellectual stabs" that rebuked it for its ambition.[126] Eder wrote: "The musical and dramatic achievements of Stephen Sondheim's black and bloody 'Sweeney Todd' are so numerous and so clamorous that they trample and jam each other in that invisible but finite doorway that connects a stage and its audience; doing themselves some harm in the process."[127] While lauding the brilliance of the lyrics and beauty of the musical score (which Eder deemed "extraordinary"), the "powerful" staging by Harold Prince, and the performances of both Len Cariou and Angela Lansbury, Eder was uncomfortable with the Brechtian style married to the Grand Guignol content.[128] Several other critics struggled with this stylistic blend, including Clive Barnes of the *New York Post* who noted that "the show will almost certainly be compared with *The Threepenny Opera*" because of the "Brechtian nature of the piece, and its staging, to say nothing of the declamatory ballad which opens and closes the show that is reminiscent of Kurt Weill."[129] For Barnes, Lansbury was "magnificent as a comic cockney of musical comedy" and was equaled by Cariou's performance, which was "magnificent as the doomed haunted killer." But for Barnes, the show's fatal flaw was in this odd coupling of styles, and because of that it was "less of a crafted piece of integral theater and more a vehicle for Miss Lansbury."[130]

Many of the critics remarked on the operatic style of the production. Howard Kissel of *Women's Wear Daily* noted that the "choral writing is particularly stunning, building as it often does from some monochromatic lines into glorious chords." For Kissel, the large Uris Theatre was made strangely intimate with the use of the factory/foundry setting, which "fairly assaulted" its audience "on entering the theater by the ashen interior of some Victorian factory." This setting was complemented by "Franne Lee's imaginative costumes," which Kissel thought were "quite realist, often giving the piece a surreal, nightmare quality, especially in Ken Billington's macabre lighting."[131] But for Walter Kerr, the show had an "uncomfortable void" with a story that "leaves us restive and unabsorbed" and ultimately "puzzled as to why its creators went to so much trouble to tell it."[132]

The audiences, which had struggled through the previews with many of the "blue-haired matinee ladies" leaving at the intermission, slowly came to life after these mixed reviews and "were beginning to respond."[133] Ticket sales didn't really pick up until the awards started coming in, beginning with the Drama Desk Awards, for which *Sweeney Todd* received nine. The Tony Awards followed; *Sweeney Todd* was nominated for nine awards and received eight: Best Musical, Best Book of a Musical, Best Original Score, Best Actor in a Musical, Best Actress in a Musical, Best Scenic Design, Best Costume Design, and Best Direction of a Musical. By 1989, Barr had paid $1,000,000 toward an outstanding capitalization of $1,200,000 to his investors. Within a year, both Cariou and Lansbury completed their contracts and left the show and were successfully replaced by George Hearn and

Dorothy Loudon. Unfortunately, business was hurt by the subway strike shortly thereafter, beginning on 1 April 1980, and *Sweeney Todd* never recovered its audiences. Barr and his partners closed the show on 29 June 1980 after a total of 557 performances.

Within a week, the show opened in London, on 2 July 1980, at the Drury Lane, without Cariou or Lansbury, who were already busy in other roles. Once again, *Sweeney Todd* received several standout reviews, but the London critics attacked the show's vapid message. Barr was particularly irked by James Fenton of the *Sunday Times*, who wrote, "*Sweeney Todd* the musical is, if one can imagine such a thing, a tissue of bullshit from start to finish."[134] The show played in London for nearly five months, despite the mixed reviews, and won Olivier Awards for Best Musical, Best Music and Lyrics in a Musical, and Best Actor in a Musical. But even as *Sweeney Todd* was playing in London, Barr was negotiating a road tour (with trepidation after his experiences with *Auntie Mame*) and struggling to find a Mrs. Lovett. He offered the role to Estelle Parsons, but she was busy with *Miss Margarida's Way*, which became a major vehicle for her.[135] Instead, though it was unusual for the time, Richard successfully negotiated a contract with Angela Lansbury, who agreed to star, once again, as Mrs. Lovett in the national touring company. It was to start in Washington, D.C., and end in Los Angeles with "Miss Lansbury's bank account bulging from a hefty percentage of the grosses."[136] For her part, Lansbury told Barr, "You know you've hired an athlete. It takes an athlete in very good condition to play this musical properly."[137] Understanding this, Barr and Woodward allowed her to perform in only seven instead of the usual eight shows a week, as long as the size of the houses justified fewer performances.

Prince objected to Lansbury's request because he believed this would cost him money, and he already had cut his royalties for the tour. Barr defended her request, explaining why he thought that it helped the production. His creative financing of the tour demonstrated to Prince his commitment and ability. He signed a loan of $500,000 with Buffalo-based Manufacturers and Traders' Trust Company at a 2 percent plus prime rate.[138] In addition, he invested $45,000 of his own money, with Woodward adding $20,000 as well. The Theatre Development Fund provided $40,000 to cover a bond for Lansbury, and then Barr borrowed an additional $30,000 from the Independent Booking Office. The producer made it clear to Prince that "pushing this work of art across the country is quite a feat!" and that "it has not been lucrative" for him to present works "which, though risky, have pushed the American theatre in the direction I assume we would all like to go."[139] In the end, the fact that the Barber Road Company cost less than $700,000 to produce and that Barr had paid Prince back before and would do so again made Barr's case for him. Prince finally relented and accepted the seven-performances-a-week schedule.

The road production of *Sweeney Todd* opened in Washington, D.C., to rave reviews. According to Barr, James Lardner of the *Washington Post* lauded the production as pristine and "seen for the first time as it should be seen."[140] But despite critical success, it did not return its investment, and as late as 1989, Richard still owed over $300,000 of the original loan. He struggled publicly with *Sweeney Todd* investors who demanded a return for their investment—and who even complained about not being invited to an opening party or receiving a cast album.[141] The decision to fund the show with the massive loan from Manufacturers and Traders' Trust Company forced Barr to wind down his producing career.[142] Still he soldiered on, producing his last Albee play, the haunting *The Lady from Dubuque*, and his final major Broadway production, James Duff's *Home Front*.

By the late 1970s, the relationship between Barr and Albee became strained. Albee was recovering from years of alcoholism with the help of his partner, Jonathan Thomas, but Barr was still drinking heavily. The undercurrent of Albee's growing discomfort with Barr's drinking continued throughout the last years of their friendship and professional relations. Also, producing *Sweeney Todd*, a musical of major significance in the American musical theatre, without Albee involved had changed Richard. A producer, Barr felt, was akin to being "an editor in a publishing firm," and he began to take on that role with Albee's next work. Often accused of giving Albee far too much freedom, Richard now felt he was more of a "Maxwell Perkins," an editor who would "prod the author into dramatizing the *author's* own intentions."[143] Perhaps because of Barr's newly developed notion of the "producer as editor," *The Lady from Dubuque* was the last Albee play he produced.

Originally titled *The Substitute Speaker*, *The Lady from Dubuque* "gestated" in Albee's mind for nearly twelve years before his first draft in 1977, which Barr produced finally in January 1980.[144] Albee struggled with this play, even as he grappled with his own drinking issues, during a time that Gussow refers to as Albee's "down" period.[145] The play begins after an evening of drinking. Three couples play parlor games in the home of one of the couples, Sam and Jo. Jo, we discover, is dying—most likely of cancer. A strange, elegant woman appears and explains that she is Jo's mother, from Dubuque. An equally elegant black gentleman named Oscar accompanies her and does her bidding. Over the course of the play, Sam is forced to accept Jo's death and to give her over to the Lady and her assistant.

In the writing of the play, Albee had been influenced by the 1973 book *On Death and Dying* by Elisabeth Kübler-Ross, which had tremendous cultural impact at the time.[146] According to Albee, there had been three drafts of the play. He completed the first in 1978, and it was not his habit to move much beyond the original draft, especially as the show was going into production.[147] Reading through the initial script of *The Lady from Dubuque*, Barr felt it was "brilliant up to a point" but had real problems, and to his mind, "emergency measures were needed." Following his Princeton training, Barr decided the play needed "an obligatory scene." As in the past when he had difficulties with Albee, Barr wrote Albee a letter spelling out his concerns in a thoughtful and forceful manner. He did not think the central problem of the play could be corrected "with a few changes" and pointed out that his past suggestions had affected Albee positively, as Albee was able to successful revise *Seascape*, winning the Pulitzer Prize in the process.[148]

In his letter, Richard outlined the major elements of Albee's plays, starting with *The Zoo Story* and ending with *The Lady from Dubuque*, suggesting that Albee might facilitate something more of a "denouement" in *The Lady from Dubuque*. The problem with the play was in its ending. The intruders are not true characters but only metaphors. Barr noted that the style of *The Lady from Dubuque* necessitated the kind of naturalism that Albee's other plays had required, and he felt the play needed a denouement that provided not only the "subtlety" Albee required but also a sense of real ending for its audience, so it could "go home, puzzled, thinking, or satisfied, or all three."[149] Barr made it clear that if Albee could meet him halfway, he'd be able to procure a star to perform the title role. Agreeable to some of Barr's ideas, Albee worked further on the play. One major change was the characters' direct address to the audience, which hadn't existed in previous drafts.[150] It was time to find a star to play the Lady from Dubuque herself.

There were two requests made by Albee for the production. The first was to have Irene Worth, the star of his *Tiny Alice*, play the Lady, and the second was that Albee wanted to direct the show himself. Barr felt that Albee's direction was a strong point for the production, especially after Albee's capable direction of *Seascape*. However, when Albee approached Irene Worth about the play, she was uncomfortable with an author directing his own work. Albee was stunned and hurt by Worth's response and responded with a terse letter reflecting his irritation with her.[151] Though Worth later apologized to Albee and remained interested in the script, she was still uncomfortable with Albee directing and so passed on the play.[152] Albee then pursued Ingrid Bergman, but she also passed on the play. Instead, oddly enough, she expressed a deep desire to play one of the lizards in *Seascape*.[153] Others considered for the role included Katharine Hepburn, Geraldine Fitzgerald, Colleen Dewhurst, Elaine Stritch, and Lauren Bacall, each to no avail. Barr could not raise money without a star and finally went back to Worth, a year after Albee and Worth's original conversation, and asked if she would do the role if Albee did not direct. She agreed, and Albee immediately suggested Alan Schneider as the director. Though Schneider was busy directing Michael Weller's *Loose Ends*, when Barr asked him when he could read Albee's script, Schneider replied, "This afternoon."[154] Schneider arrived at Barr's office within an hour and read the script, and by five o'clock that evening, both Schneider and Worth were committed to the project. Barr and Woodward could set about raising money for the production.

It proved to be a difficult and frustrating process. Albee's reputation on Broadway had diminished, and Richard was forced to take on several partners, several of whom had worked with him on *Sweeney Todd*. Barr once again had to advertise in the *New York Times* to raise funds, which brought in $35,000. The play was capitalized at $400,000, without an overcall. Barr struggled to raise the last $85,000–$100,000.[155] The play was "beautifully produced" with a suitably gray set by Rouben Ter-Arutunian, costumes by John Falabella (with Irene Worth's gorgeous gown designed by Pauline Trigère), and a magnificent cast starring Earle Hyman as Oscar, Frances Conroy as Jo (at Schneider's request), Maureen Anderman as Carol, and Tony Musante as Sam. Musante felt the show would be such a success that it would run for several years and thus negotiated a release so that he could get film work. Anderman recalled receiving special casting consideration as a member of the Albee-Barr acting family, having also worked with Schneider in *Moonchildren*: "Of course I would have liked to play Jo, but Alan wanted Frances Conroy. So then I was being considered for Lucinda, and I said, 'You know I'd love to play Carol,' but Alan was interested in Swoosie Kurtz for that role. Anyway, so we're out in California, and we went out to dinner one night, some place out in Malibu. Edward handed me the script, and he had written inside the cover 'to Carol,' and I knew I had the role. So I was part of it; I was part of the family."[156] Albee knew and trusted Anderman from her work in *Seascape* and knew she was right for Carol. Barr's "magic list" continued to prove helpful even in his final production of an Albee play.

The Lady from Dubuque began its previews on 25 January 1980, and the actors felt that the audience was engaged. Much of the play, though dark at its core, was very funny and connected with its viewers. Yet, as the actors checked in with friends attending the previews, the response was mixed, as Anderman noted: "The audience response was totally split fifty-fifty; some people were crazy about it, just crazy about it. And other people thought, 'Oh, that's just

Edward,' you know, 'what is he writing about, what is he talking about, all this death and this Elisabeth Kübler-Ross.' It was kind of mysterious and wonderful and funny, and harrowing. And I always thought that it was ten years ahead of its time, before AIDS, before the specter of death was hanging over everyone. It was heartbreaking . . . devastating when the critics just creamed it."[157] Tony Musante also thought audiences were enjoying the show before the critics let the ax fall: "When we were in previews, a very dear friend, an actress, came backstage and said to me, 'I'm so glad I could get tickets to a preview, I know that after you guys open I will never be able to get tickets.' Well, she was wrong, I was wrong, so I could understand how Edward felt."[158]

The play opened on 31 January 1980, following eight successful previews, but the reviews were scathing. Walter Kerr led the assault: "Edward Albee's 'The Lady from Dubuque' is a play in two acts and three questions, none of which—as Irene Worth points out in an aside to the audience—is ever answered." Kerr immediately attacked the heart of Albee's writing, his dialogue, pointing out that "Mr. Albee is still working in an ornately convoluted 'literary' style that has no conversational feel to it, so that when we *are* given a snatch of characterization to cling to, it's apt to come out as, 'I am his only friend whose every virtue embarrasses him.' By the time we've got the syntax unraveled, the play has moved on to new difficulties."[159] Howard Kissel of *Women's Wear Daily* was also unhappy with the development of the characters. He then focused on what was to be one of the pet peeves of the critics, the fact that the characters addressed the audience directly: "To make the heavy artifice heavier, Albee has his characters address the audience, as if to imply intimacy. It only alienates us more."[160] The poor reviews forced Barr to shut down the show to save what he could of his investors' money. Albee was infuriated by this decision and called Barr and his producing partners "the seven dwarves."[161]

There was tremendous emotional loss when the show closed. Tony Musante articulated it best: "It was very sad for all of us involved, and I still think it's one of his most brilliant plays, and I'd still be willing to be involved with it today." The actors enjoyed the script, despite its "harrowing" subject matter, and were rewarded for their performances. Earle Hyman and Maureen Anderman won Tony Awards for Best Featured Actor and Actress in a Play.[162] *The Lady from Dubuque* did not receive a major production again until 2007, when Seattle Repertory produced it under David Esbjornson's direction. The show that Walter Kerr decided was a "sort of philosophical speculation" that he found to be "thinnish and familiar" and written in "an ornately convoluted 'literary' style that has no conversational feel to it" has joined the Albee oeuvre and gone on to many more productions.[163]

With the failure of *The Lady from Dubuque* and the financial obligations remaining from *Sweeney Todd*, Barr would not produce another show on Broadway until 1985. More significant than his financial straits in this final fallow period was his struggle to find another Albee. Though his producing career had already given American theatre a cornucopia of new playwrights, he was not satisfied. As altruistic as his intentions were, the quest to find the next Albee would prove to be his undoing. Yet, as the president of the League of American Theatres and Producers, Richard Barr would change the very nature of New York's Broadway theatre scene.

10

Brightening Broadway's Lights

Barr's Legacy to the American Theatre

Richard Barr's last Broadway production was *Home Front* by James Duff, produced in 1985, the culminating effort of a producer who had struggled mightily against the tide of mediocre Broadway theatre. Barr, who had spent years championing the work of major experimentalists like Edward Albee, LeRoi Jones, Lanford Wilson, Sam Shepard, Samuel Beckett, Robert Wilson, Paul Taylor, Stephen Sondheim, and others, was desperate to pay off debt and to find a way to continue to support himself. During the "strange interlude" of five years before he produced *Home Front*, he kept busy with his work as president of the League of New York Theatres and Producers and continued to direct. He worked with stars like Elaine Stritch and Barry Nelson at the Paper Mill Playhouse in *Noël Coward in Two Keys*. Alvin Klein of the *New York Times* called Barr's direction "scintillating."[1] But Barr had no new plays he was in the position of promoting.

It was during this time, the early 1980s, that Albee brought *The Man Who Had Three Arms* to Broadway.[2] Richard was not involved with this, the first Albee play to hit Broadway without Barr's involvement as a producer. The production was roundly (and brutally) dismissed as an angry, indulgent diatribe that had more to do with Albee's drinking than it was a dramatic work with any intrinsic value. Though not involved in *The Man Who Had*

Three Arms, Richard remained very interested in Albee's next work, *The Marriage Play*, and hoped to produce it.[3] However, the estrangement between Barr and Albee remained, particularly after the abrupt closing of *The Lady from Dubuque* in 1980.[4]

On the prowl for new work, Richard was at a crossroads in his career. Broadway in the 1980s was itself swiftly changing, driven by commercial concerns, and the Great White Way featured Las Vegas–style musicals appealing to tourists. The non-musical theatre crowd was dwindling, and so, listless and without a production to give him focus, Barr explored some of the bars around the Broadway theatre district. Barr and Chuck Woodward often had lunch at Mildred Pierce, on West Forty-Sixth Street, just off the beaten path for theatregoers. Managed by David Bixler, later a business partner of Barr and Woodward's, the restaurant was also a popular lunch spot for Lee Minskoff, who was working with them at the time. On one visit, Richard became friendly with the bartender, "an attractive young man with a decided Texas accent," and chatted with him for a while. This was James Duff, the playwright whose play, *Home Front*, Barr eventually produced.

Duff had been born in New Orleans and, adopted by a family in Texas, had grown up in exactly the kind of suburban home that he depicts in his play. Because of his father's job as an executive in the Sears Roebuck organization, his family moved around frequently. James had gone to five elementary schools, three junior high schools, and three high schools before his family finally moved to Arlington, Texas. Because of the sudden changes and his own need to rebel, he left Arlington to return to Lubbock, where the family had lived previously, because he "resented being jerked around."[5] After moving to New York to be a professional actor, James began writing plays, deciding that writing was his best means of attaining success.[6] *Home Front* was Duff's reaction to the treatment of Vietnam veterans after the war, treatment that was not particularly sympathetic.

After meeting Duff for the first time, Richard was invited by Gammon Sharpley, a waiter at Mildred's, to have dinner, and Barr accepted, as it was "an uncommon occurrence" for waiters to invite Broadway producers to dinner. The invitation was actually a ploy to convince Richard to read Duff's play. It was not the first time that James had aggressively pursued a producer. In fact, he had once been so insistent that a producer had threatened to have Duff arrested.[7] Barr "ordered an expensive dinner" but waited until "after the main course" to agree to read the script. Sharpley convinced Richard to attend a workshop performance of Duff's play at a small theatre in the Carter Hotel. Barr rarely attended showcases, fearing that he would be "trapped" at an awful performance. Sharpley was "a very bright persuasive fellow," however, and the dynamic young James Duff intrigued Barr, so he agreed to see the play, which was then titled *The War at Home*.[8]

At the Carter Hotel production, which was on "one of New York's most dismal streets," Barr was astonished at Duff's "skill and literacy" and at "the sensitivity and humor." More important, Barr emotionally connected with the show, writing, "I laughed; I cried; I applauded." At the end of the evening, he told James, "I would like to present your play on Broadway." James and his off-off-Broadway colleagues invited Richard for a sip of champagne at the Back Stage restaurant, not far from the hotel. It was the beginning of "one of the strangest, most stimulating, most tragic, most rewarding, most disappointing" producing experiences of Barr's career, one that took nearly four years to come to fruition.[9]

Even at the outset, there were problems. As it turned out, James had already agreed to a producing partnership, DWD Productions, which included Duff; a lawyer, Raymond De Marco; and the director of the Carter production, Robert Windslow. Frustrated, Richard could not get an option for the play and decided to try "an end run" around the legal contract that James had signed with De Marco and Windslow. De Marco told Barr he had $100,000 to invest in an off-Broadway production of the show. Richard declined; he wanted to produce it independently on Broadway. In his opinion, it was the best play he had seen or read since he had produced *Who's Afraid of Virginia Woolf?*, and Duff was, to his mind, the next Albee.[10]

Barr took De Marco aside and over lunch explained that unless De Marco hired him as a professional consultant, he would discover there were serious business "pit-falls" in producing off-Broadway. Barr was willing to take the job for $100, handling all business and artistic decisions for an off-Broadway production. De Marco, who had very little experience in the professional theatre, was "very pleased" with Barr's offer, and Richard immediately began his usual "magic list" casting process and seeking a director for the show.[11]

Richard immediately contacted Alan Schneider, since Barr considered him to be "the best director for authors young or old," and Schneider responded with "extraordinary enthusiasm." De Marco had never heard of him and questioned the decision to hire Schneider.[12] Horrified at De Marco's naïveté, Richard immediately called his lawyers to see if De Marco could be "bought out." Because of the weak "work-in-progress" production De Marco had given to Duff's *The War at Home*, Barr had to pay off De Marco and Windslow with $4,500 because of the producing partnership agreement Duff had signed.[13] Afterward, Barr, Woodward, and Lee Minskoff then began their preparations to produce the show on Broadway. The name of the show was also changed to *Home Front*, since the title *The War at Home* had been used for an Academy Award–winning documentary by Glenn Silber in 1979.

The team began to cast stars in Duff's play. Christopher Fields, the young actor who played Jeremy in the Carter Hotel production, was retained at Duff's request (though Schneider worried about Fields's lack of Broadway experience). James also wanted Linda Cook to play the role of Karen, and both Fields and Cook were eventually in the 1985 Broadway cast.[14] For the starring roles of the fundamentalist mother, Maurine, and the complicated, sympathetic father, Bob, Barr and Schneider decided on Frances Sternhagen and Philip Bosco. Duff had wanted Sternhagen for the role from the beginning.[15] But even with these stars, it was very difficult to raise funds. Barr sent Duff and Chuck Woodward down to Texas to see if they could raise money in the Dallas community, and investment advertisements for the production appeared in the *New York Times*.[16] Barr was looking for groups of small investors who could put in $500 to $1,000, similar to how he had raised money for *Sweeney Todd*.[17] But Woodward and Duff returned empty-handed, leaving Barr to scrounge for enough funding to convince the Shubert Organization to rent him a theatre. Richard found this funding and also procured "front money" to help raise an additional $155,000 from interested investors. But unfortunately, "there the money stopped." Without at least another $40,000, Richard wasn't going to be able to rent a theatre from the Shubert Organization, which thought his budget for Duff's play was too small.[18] Barr had posted a bond for Sternhagen and Bosco, who were ready to start. But without the money and interest in the show, the "money was lost."[19] Without going further, the money was returned to the investors, per New York state law, and the show wasn't able to open.

Not long after this, Alan Schneider brought the play to Margaret Ramsey, a play agent in London whom Barr knew from Albee's adaptation of the Giles Cooper play *Everything in the Garden*. Ramsey immediately recommended the script to the Hampstead Theatre, one of the top "fringe" theatres in London that produced new work. Several shows had transferred from the Hampstead to London's West End and then to Broadway. If Richard could have the Hampstead produce the play, transfer it to London's West End, secure strong notices, and then bring the show to Broadway, he'd realize huge savings in production costs.[20] It was a "novel idea" that not only could work for Duff's play but might serve for any number of future productions.[21] Ramsey sent the script to Michael Attenborough, the managing director of the Hampstead Theatre, who quickly decided to produce it with Alan Schneider directing. Attenborough agreed to use Frances Sternhagen as long as a work permit could be procured and she consented to the typical "fringe" salary of $150 per week. Sternhagen was interested but less than thrilled to leave her husband, Tom Carlin, and six children for a period of two months for a salary that would barely cover her expenses. To offset this, Barr negotiated with British Actors' Equity to permit a British actor, Ian Bannon, to perform on Broadway, allowing the two actors to perform in each other's native country. The Shubert Organization covered the difference in Sternhagen's English "fringe salary" and Bannon's Broadway salary.

Richard was pleased with the English cast, particularly with the casting of David Threlfall (*Nicholas Nickleby*'s "Smike") as Jeremy and Timothy West as the father. Schneider, his schedule tight as always, was to come back to New York to direct a series of Beckett plays before they were to go to the Edinburgh Fringe Festival. Rehearsals for the London premiere of *Home Front* were to take place in June when Schneider and both the English and American actors were available. Barr and Duff planned to be in London during the last week of rehearsal so that if Schneider had any additional changes to the play, James would be there to assist.

Before the production began in England, Schneider and Duff worked closely on the play for several months, reshaping the script, with Schneider peppering James "on every page, every character, and every intention." During this time, James stayed with Barr in Montauk and traveled to Schneider's apartments in East Hampton. Over the course of the development and productions of *Home Front*, Duff developed a strong and close friendship with Barr. Schneider then left for London, after having opened Harold Pinter's *A Kind of Alaska* at the Manhattan Theatre Club.[22] During that summer of 1984, Richard initiated another private reading of the play at his Montauk home to help James time the script's duration. The reading took place on a late afternoon in May, and Duff and Barr were thrilled that despite the initial financial setback, they had successfully negotiated all "technical, artistic, and financial problems" and were finally on their way to an exciting London premiere.[23]

Within a few hours, however, the entire situation changed. At eight o'clock that evening, Richard received a phone call from Michael Attenborough, the managing director of the Hampstead Theatre. Alan Schneider was dead, killed by a motorcyclist as he crossed a London street to post a letter to his great friend and artistic associate Samuel Beckett.[24] Barr immediately considered postponing or canceling the show; without Schneider, it was unlikely that the show would go on. Schneider's wife and son immediately flew to London, and Richard returned to New York City from his Montauk home. He was greeted by Chuck Woodward, and they immediately contacted Margaret Ramsey. She recommended Attenborough as a reliable director to substitute for Schneider. Attenborough was really their only choice, as an outsider would not have been well received by the Hampstead company members.

Barr and Duff immediately made plans to go to London, although there was another problem: James did not have a passport, and he and Barr were to leave within forty-eight hours. By sheer force of personality and making use of every connection he had, Richard procured a passport through the help of Connecticut congressman Stewart McKinney.[25] Barr and Duff left for London and upon arrival were taken to the Hampstead Theatre, where rehearsals were to take place. There they were met by Jean and David Schneider, Alan Schneider's wife and son, along with Michael Attenborough. In the midst of these preparations, Barr was deeply impressed by the "dignity and courage" with which the Schneider family dealt with "an agony of the deepest kind" following Alan Schneider's untimely death.[26]

The rehearsals went smoothly at the Hampstead Theatre. Duff assisted the British actors on their Texas dialects to help them find consistency and accuracy. Barr was thrilled with how accurate the accents ultimately became. He was even more pleased with the staff members at the Hampstead Theatre, which, to his surprise, were "almost all women." Michael Attenborough was also clearly the right director for the show, and while not in the same league as Alan Schneider, he was attuned to the script and Duff's sensibilities. The show opened four weeks later to very strong reviews, including a *Sunday Times* review that called the show "a stunning first play." The *Sunday Express* pronounced it "a first play by a prodigiously talented young man," and it was called "an extremely well-written first play by an experienced actor" in the *Standard*. In the *Times*, however, a review by Irving Wardle was closer to the eventual response in New York. Wardle called it "an erratically talented variation on a well-worn American theme."[27]

On some level, Barr didn't want to see the play for what it was, a strong first outing by a new writer that should have been premiered off-Broadway. Even a West End production would have been better but was unlikely because of the limited run at the Hampstead and the subsequent lack of available British performers. So as to avoid letting "the momentum wither away," Barr and Woodward planned for an immediate Broadway transfer, holding on to only Frances Sternhagen for the New York production. Richard had been thrilled with trying out a show in the London "fringe" theatre. Much like his off-Broadway experience, it was particularly gratifying because Barr "did not have to raise a nickel" for the Hampstead production.[28]

With the London success of his play, Barr negotiated somewhat more generous terms to extend Duff's contract. The Shubert Organization agreed to open up a theatre, and Barr was also able to negotiate a "buy" of tickets by the Theatre Development Fund, which also agreed to cover the Actors' Equity bond necessary to hold on to performers. Capitalized at $400,000, Barr had to come up with at least three-fourths of the total budget to hold the Shubert-owned theatre.[29] At this point, Barr and Woodward lost their coproducer, Lee Minskoff. However, David Bixler, who had worked with Duff at Mildred Pierce's and was an early supporter of *The War at Home*, contributed $10,000 to the *Home Front* project and was hired by Barr to be an assistant in his and Woodward's office. Bixler was successful in raising an additional $35,000 from his own parents and moved from being an assistant to a partner. Bixler remained Barr's partner until Richard's death in 1989 and actually kept the Barr-Bixler offices open two years after Richard passed away.[30]

In terms of finding stars to attract investors, Barr set aside his "magic list" for a change and worked with Lionel Larner, a British-born agent known for a strong "A" list of clients. After a few false starts with various Hollywood stars, Larner suggested Carroll O'Connor, who was exactly right for the role of Bob. Despite his involvement in a recent Broadway flop, *Brothers* by George Sibbald, which he had directed as well, O'Connor agreed to play the role. The role in *Brothers* had been seen as too close to O'Connor's famous Archie Bunker role in the television series *All in the Family*. After *Brothers*' failure, it seemed unlikely that he would agree to perform on Broadway, but Duff's script appealed to him, as did acting with Frances Sternhagen, and he felt he might "redeem the blunders of the year before."[31] O'Connor's willingness to work at low wages, for a Hollywood star, made the production possible.

With O'Connor and Sternhagen in hand, Richard could begin seeking investors in earnest, and he decided to advertise in the *New York Times* once again. Barr was successful in raising $50,000, but still more money was needed, and Bixler, like the Shuberts, believed that even at $400,000 the show was underbudgeted. By November 1984, the situation was, as Barr put it, "tense." Michael Attenborough, who had come over from London to direct *Home Front*, contacted his father, Sir Richard Attenborough, who then invested $25,000 of his own funds into the production. The senior Attenborough was filming the Twyla Tharp film version of *Hair* in a Broadway theatre; both father and son were directing on Broadway at the same time. Even with this financial boost, however, there was still not enough money. Richard decided to turn the annual Barr family Thanksgiving holiday into a fund-raising venture for *Home Front*. Barr raised $25,000 from his brother-in-law S. Greenhoot ("Greenie") Fischer and another $25,000 from his mother, with both using the contribution as a tax write-off. Richard contacted Chuck Woodward and told him that rehearsals could begin on the following Monday. Once again, the Baers had come to the rescue of their New York producer relative.[32]

Broadway rehearsals got underway at the Michael Bennett Studios, which were beautiful and roomy. Frances Sternhagen and Carroll O'Connor were very comfortable with each other, having appeared together years before in *Ulysses in Nighttown* off-Broadway. They also worked well with the actors playing the minor roles, Linda Cook and Christopher Fields, and Michael Attenborough had a firm directorial hand. Per their usual policy, Barr and Woodward didn't visit the production rehearsals after the first read-through, and when they returned, they were very pleased. Richard believed that the production had a "strong" script and an excellent director and cast. Though the show was running long "despite cuts from the London production," Barr planned to do additional minimal cuts during the previews.[33]

Home Front began its previews on Christmas Day, 25 December 1984. Audiences, according to Barr, were delighted with the show, "laughing, crying, cheering, and standing." Barr and Woodward felt they had a major Broadway hit in the making—the best of the season. The opening night on 2 January 1985 was equally well received; all was going well "until the reviews came out." *New York Times* critic Frank Rich set the major discordant theme in later reviews. The play was too much like a television sitcom: "Much like Norman Lear, Mr. Duff has tried to revivify old formulas (sitcom and melodrama) with a social conscience. His play contains slick, professionally polished scenes and jokes, and it tells the serious, if shopworn, tale of an embittered Vietnam veteran's homecoming. . . . If the ostensible topic of debate is 'the war,' Mr. Duff so trivializes the Vietnam era that everyone might just as well be arguing over the car keys."[34]

Worse was Rich's concern that Carroll O'Connor was cast, yet again, as another version of Archie Bunker. This was to be a recurrent theme with many of the critics. Richard Corliss in *Time* magazine wrote, "Are these the Cleavers or the Bunkers, this family of four preparing for an ordinary Thanksgiving in 1973?"[35] Not all the reviews were negative; Douglas Watt of the *Daily News* called the show "a first-rate play," noting that O'Connor "wholly erased" his Archie Bunker persona and that the script itself was "an extraordinary piece of work, a major event in any theater season."[36] Walter Kerr was perplexed by the humor in *Home Front* and blamed Michael Attenborough, not James Duff, for his inappropriate use of it: "As things stood, even so fine an actress as Frances Sternhagen (mother of the family) had been forced to giddy up the proceedings until she seemed a calliope in hair-curlers."[37] Mel Gussow noted a serious structural problem with the play: "The truth is that the play splits in two; there is a definite disparity in tone between the first act frivolity and the second act crisis."[38] Disappointed, Barr particularly disliked Frank Rich's "lecture" and felt that the critic was "not qualified for his powerful position."[39] The show struggled on for two weeks. Though he closed it on 12 January 1985, Barr was still pleased with how tight its budget had been at $315,000 and that he had sold the amateur and stock rights for $40,000 to help cut losses. The cast was dismayed that Barr closed the show so quickly. David Bixler recounts: "In a way, Dick almost took a perverse pleasure in just ending it all as quickly as possible. He put so much work into it, but then, it's not going to work, [so] cut your losses and just move on. And it was also strange because . . . there was no money set aside for an opening night party. There was only going to be a party if the show ran. So Carroll O'Connor footed the bill for Sardi's that night, and though it was a small cast and the crew, it wasn't a small deal to pay for all that."[40] Despite the show's closing, James Duff was catapulted into a major television and film-writing career. *Home Front* was later made into a 1996 film, *The War at Home*, featuring Emilio Estevez (who also directed), Martin Sheen, and Kathy Bates. Duff went on to become the writer/producer of *The Closer*, the Emmy Award–nominated and Golden Globe Award–winning series featuring Kyra Sedgwick.

Home Front was Barr's last Broadway show, after which he entered into a final "strange interlude." He kept busy and became involved with Paramount Studios, attempting to acquire the Broadway rights to the film *Sunset Boulevard* (later a Broadway hit). He also began preparations to produce Albee's *The Marriage Play*. Neither project flew before his death in 1989.[41] Far more important, and as significant as his own producing career, were his efforts as president of the League of American Theatres and Producers, nicknamed "The Club." The league began in the 1930s when "Broadway theatre operators came together to promote their common interests and negotiate collective bargaining agreements with theatrical unions and guilds."[42] An organization made up of theatre owners and of producers who rented those theatres, the league had the inherent tensions of an organization of landlords and tenants.[43] Barr was elected president of the league on 9 February 1967, filling a vacancy after Harold Prince resigned, and served until his death in 1989.[44]

Between 1967 and 1989, Richard worked closely with the league (which had several name changes during that time), as well as with the Shubert Organization, to address major issues that threatened Broadway's continued economic health and helped develop the Times Square theatre district into the thriving theatre center it is today. His achievements at the league included (1) promoting the notion of Broadway "finishing money" that developed into the Theatre Development Fund (TDF), (2) facilitating the First American Congress of Theatre (FACT) in 1974, connecting the non-profit and for-profit theatre communities, (3) creating a new middle-tier class of Broadway production to mitigate the ongoing increases in costs of production, and (4) establishing the self-imposed league "tax" for programs that improve the health of the theatre industry as a whole.[45] Barr also changed the time shows started, from 8:30 P.M. to 7:30 P.M. (later moving to 8:00 P.M.), and fostered better negotiations with all the trade unions.

The late 1960s and early 1970s was a challenging time for the theatre business in New York City, as the city itself was in decline.[46] In 1967, just as Richard assumed the responsibilities of president of the New York League of Theatres, Actors' Equity members rebelled over the preponderance of British actors working on Broadway. And because British Equity had far more stringent rules regarding their employment in London, American actors found it impossible to perform there, resulting in serious inequities.[47] The situation was aggravated by a growing number of English imports appearing on Broadway. In the fall 1967 Broadway season, sixteen plays were being performed; of these, only five were by American playwrights.[48] Barr advocated for "a free exchange of actors between Broadway and the West End." To spur on more productions of new American work, Richard supported an endeavor to expand the number of new Broadway theatres (even as older Broadway houses were demolished) by appointing league members to a committee to influence Mayor John Lindsay and his administration on the building of new theatres.[49]

Barr had strong cooperation from his colleagues at the league. With a committed executive committee, a youthful board of directors, and an active membership volunteering for the committees that made up the heart of the league's operation, Richard was able to effect major changes.[50] One of Barr's closest associates was Harvey Sabinson, a former press agent who served as his special projects director from 1976 through 1989 and later as league president himself. Another major collaborator in Barr's projects was Irving Cheskin, the executive director of the league and one of the most knowledgeable members of Barr's inner circle. However, it was Barr's close collaboration with Gerald Schoenfeld, the chairman of the Shubert Organization, that moved the league's efforts from that of a small "club" into a serious trade organization that changed the fabric of the Times Square theatre district. Schoenfeld's genius for working with governmental agencies was particularly helpful in moving the league's agenda for continued growth and change. Alexander Cohen, a league producer of countless shows, both great hits and flops, also became an important partner to Barr's ambitious agenda. Cohen was the organization man behind the Tony presentations, coordinated by the league at the behest of the American Theatre Wing. Cohen produced the Tony Award ceremony for twenty years and later was instrumental in the creation of the FACT, which brought together the not-for-profit and commercial theatres.[51] According to Schoenfeld, "Alex Cohen was a great creator of events" and remained so until he left the league in 1985.[52] Sabinson noted that because of Barr's ability to coordinate an organization of strong individuals, "the league grew from just basically a labor negotiation organization into a true trade association doing things that a trade association should be doing."[53]

Richard Barr was initially selected as president of the League of New York Theatres because of the peculiarity of the organization itself, as Sabinson pointed out: "The league was always a battlefield between producers and theatre owners. They're basically an association of landlords and tenants. That doesn't make much sense, does it? But it does work, if they get together, because they have a lot of common enemies. And they do come together at union negotiations."[54] For years, that tension was exacerbated by a rivalry between the Shubert and Nederlander organizations, which controlled the majority of the Broadway theatres. Barr was considered to be a neutral figure in this field of players, and as Cheskin noted, he was trusted because of his own record as a "quality" producer: "He was very well respected by his fellow producers, and he was a good producer. He did not go about elaborately wasting money here or there for publicity or a name or anything like that. He would produce quality stuff. Richard they liked, and they worked with him. And Hal Prince directed for him, and that was quite a tribute to Richard."[55]

With a governing board of volatile personalities such as Harold Prince, Kermit Bloomgarden, Robert Whitehead, Alexander Cohen, and David Merrick, Sabinson felt Barr had a calming influence: "Richard's attitude was always 'Take it easy, take a deep breath, don't let it bother you, that's the way it is.' That was one of the things I admired about him."[56] This attitude combined with Barr's ability to get things done creatively. Schoenfeld believed that Barr's greatest achievement was to encourage a more direct and effective participation of the members of the league. Richard encouraged each of the league's members to apply their unique skills effectively to a growing list of specific functions.[57]

Barr's ability to pull the league together resourcefully was important during the 1970s, when the Broadway theatre and Times Square was suffering. New York City was going bankrupt, and Times Square was considered "dirty, crime-ridden and depressed."[58] The area now called the Broadway theatre district was in physical decay, and older theatres were being torn down regularly. During the 1965–66 season, Barr authorized a study of Broadway's economics, which showed the legitimate theatres in New York had a profit of $3,340,237, after a gross profit of $11,240,396 and a loss amounting to $7,900,159.[59] Barr was concerned enough about these numbers that he asked theatre producers to stop publishing weekly grosses in *Variety*, which sparked not a little controversy.[60] The quality of the work was suffering as well; more adventurous work was being done off- and off-off-Broadway. Even the powerful Shubert Organization was starting to lose money. Of the sixteen theatres controlled by the Shuberts, only eleven of the houses were open and playing to audiences.[61]

In October 1967, Richard was reelected president of the League of New York Theatres, with Louis Lotito serving as his first vice president, Robert Whitehead as secretary, and Morton Gottlieb as treasurer.[62] Barr immediately pushed for a zone shift program by the City Planning Commission to actually create a theatre district, and a public hearing was held for that purpose. Barr and his colleagues in the league pointed out that the Broadway theatres were "in deplorable condition and that there was an exodus of talent to the West Coast."[63] He worked to be a more visible representative of Broadway in general, serving in 1968 as the president of the New York Cultural Foundation, formed by 250 representatives of sixty organizations. The foundation gave Barr a bully pulpit from which he advocated for Broadway.[64] In May 1969, Barr pushed for more involvement by business in the cultural life of the city, declaring that with a "responsible" investment by a major business group, "a quiet revolution" could be effected.[65]

Richard and the league worked with Mayor Lindsay to begin the process of sprucing up Times Square, and, to make theatres and other landmarks easier to find, a sign system was mounted.[66] The league was reshaped into committees geared toward solving the problems, and it assessed itself a "hefty" tax of $400–$600 per week per show to create a new Department of Special Projects under the leadership of Harvey Sabinson.[67] Sabinson's department invested in shows that needed help, refurbished theatres in need of renovation, and put pressure on colleagues to clean up their act and improve the quality of the productions they were pursuing and the theatre district as a whole. Barr sought legal means in order to change the zoning to prohibit the sex trade's growing incursion (including peep shows, sex shops, prostitution, massage parlors, and live sex shows) into the legitimate theatre scene.[68] Though this problem was not resolved until the end of the 1990s, the steady pressure of containment had its beginnings in the 1970s and began to pay off in the 1980s with growing audiences and a real theatre "boom."[69]

One of the major partners in this process of Broadway's revitalization was the Shubert Organization, under the leadership of Bernard Jacobs and Gerald Schoenfeld, both of whom were the major negotiators for the league for the contracts with the actors, musicians, and stagehands unions. With Schoenfeld and Jacobs to lead the bargaining sessions with the unions, there was only one major strike in the twenty years Barr served as the league's president, that of the musicians in 1975 (a minor actors' strike in 1968 lasted only eight days).[70] While there was occasional grousing about the influence of the Shubert Organization, the league continued to give Jacobs and Schoenfeld unusually strong support. Even when there was a legal challenge to Jacobs and Schoenfeld's continued service as trustees of the Shubert Organization, a nearly unanimous league supported them.[71] Schoenfeld was particularly important to the negotiations for his governmental connections, and Sabinson traveled to Washington with him to lobby Congress: "Jerry was superb in getting governmental support locally for the theatre. It was unbelievable what he was able to do with the city, and he remains to this day the chairman of the mayor's midtown citizen's committee, which has functioned under five or six different administrations."[72] Though Schoenfeld's presence created tension with the Nederlanders (James Nederlander quit and then later rejoined the league), Barr pressed ahead with Schoenfeld's expert help. What was important was Schoenfeld's understanding that the not-for-profit theatre (or what he termed the "non-tax-paying" theatre), both in New York and regionally, provided a tremendous opportunity to develop and produce new work that could be produced on Broadway. Schoenfeld and Jacobs, who had inherited a very troubled Shubert Organization, were all too aware that they had to change things, and part of that change was to encourage the city and the nonprofit theatre to join with commercial producers on Broadway.[73]

Richard believed that Broadway's tourist dollars were intrinsic to New York City's economic health, commissioning a study to show exactly what those dollars meant in terms of the city's coffers. Broadway's influence on tourist dollars was not then understood by the government leaders, according to Sabinson: "We did a study on the economic impact of the theatre to the city. It was an enormous figure, and we never realized how important it was—that it was *the* most important tourist attraction. These are all projects that were encouraged by Richard during his administration. They've been used ever since, and every city uses that study around the country now."[74] Internationally respected Princeton economist William J. Baumol worked with the league to clarify the economic realities that Broadway faced at the time. Irving Cheskin called this the "multiplier theory," which was that "for every buck we spent, it was able to create many additional dollars more."[75]

Under Richard's influence, the league sought to reinvent the "square" uptown Broadway theatre by building upon the youthful energy that was creating a firestorm off-Broadway and off-off Broadway. To persuade these economically disadvantaged not-for-profit downtown theatres to transfer shows uptown, Barr negotiated a new "middle" contract that attempted to defray the union expenses. Downtown musicals and plays considered to be "financially risky" had substantially lower ticket prices and a nearly 50 percent reduction in costs from the various theatre unions. The producers operating under the reduced contract were required to lower ticket prices and keep weekly box office grosses below $25,000. In return, the producers received a $150 weekly wage ceiling for all "nonroyalty" personnel. Additionally, theatre owners had to agree to a guarantee of no more than $4,000 against 25 percent of the weekly gross. If the show was a hit, Barr negotiated the contract so that it could move into a "first class" Broadway contract and raise its prices and royalties with relative ease.

The theatre unions, audiences, and performers were enthusiastic about the possibility of significantly lower ticket prices, which meant more people in seats, especially the younger audiences who had abandoned Broadway theatre. The league and the unions unanimously approved the agreement, though off-Broadway producers thought they might be hurt by the terms of the "middle" contract. Theatre owners were also concerned that they might see a migration of producers downtown.[76] Still, by 1971, Barr's middle contract concept, which became known as the "limited gross agreement," went into effect.[77] The plan was implemented and renewed a year later, with several productions taking advantage of its terms. However, it never was fully employed by producers because it did not completely reduce production costs, something that Barr continued to negotiate during his tenure as president of the league.[78]

Richard was also instrumental in the creation of the Theatre Development Fund. He first broached the idea of an organization that added "completion money" to a production, according to Stephen Benedict, the former president of TDF, at a meeting regarding off-Broadway at Radio City Music Hall on 3 June 1963.[79] Having just produced the Paul Taylor Dance Company on Broadway, Barr was deeply frustrated that the Ford Foundation subsidized ballet in the United States to the tune of $8 million, but not modern dance.[80] Chaired by John D. Rockefeller III during the planning period for "Performance Arts: Problems and Prospects," the panel attendees included Dana S. Creel of the Rockefeller Brothers Fund, Judith Malina, Julian Beck, Theodore Mann, David Ross, and Norris Houghton. Barr was asked if he could present any ideas that would result in "a healthier climate for serious theatre on Broadway." In response, he developed the notion of a "completion fund" run by theatre professionals to help risky shows run long enough to find an audience. Having just lost over $4,500 presenting Paul Taylor, Barr believed that if the Ford Foundation gave presenters of modern dance "finishing money" to help cover minimal losses, every modern dance company in the United States could be supported "for twenty years."[81]

Richard wanted funds to provide "continuance of the operation or [to] cover a loss on an approved project," noting that any professional producer understood the reasonable costs on a production and could discern its "practicability."[82] The highlight of the program was that relatively "modest" funds were needed for any one production. Barr's organization could also be run by a small "controlling body" of three members. This committee would consist of a foundation executive, a theatrical producer, and a theatre artist of some renown. The major funding could come from several different foundations interested in producing "new plays by American playwrights."[83] Since the organization could be "extracurricular," it was not an administrative burden to any one foundation and could exist within a larger foundation like the Twentieth Century Fund. And regardless of whether it was a commercial or nonprofit entity, Barr thought the grant should be a loan that would be repaid out of any profits made by the production.

Richard envisioned the completion fund to help three different types of situations: (1) when a show was "worthwhile" but was "faltering" at the box office; (2) as completion money on a capitalization of a risky show at its outset; and (3) to cover any losses for a culturally important show that was forced to close. Barr gave practical examples as well; he thought that the production of *The Subject Was Roses* by Frank Gilroy, for instance, would have benefited from these funds and actually provided a return on the investment. He believed that an off-Broadway show that was capitalized at $15,000 but had only $10,000 could borrow the last $5,000 to cover bonds and theatre rental guarantees, and on a limited run production, funds could be provided to help guarantee the project against a loss, giving an incentive to investors.[84]

August Heckscher and John Booth of the Twentieth Century Fund invited Richard to a series of luncheons where he again discussed his notion of completion money. Heckscher and Booth then looked into the practical application of Barr's ideas and contacted John Wharton, an important theatrical attorney, to take up the notion with his partners at Paul, Weiss, Rifkind, Wharton and Garrison. Barr's idea was "transmuted into a broader range of different methods for encouraging serious theatre than he first envisaged."[85] By 1968, TDF was "born" to become an organization that ultimately allowed "tens of thousands" of theatregoers to be able to afford to see serious theatre. Barr even used TDF "finishing money" himself on several occasions, including on his production of *All Over.*[86]

Another major outcome of Barr's notion of finishing money was the TKTS discount ticket booth in Times Square. Richard felt that TDF was a strong first step toward a subsidized commercial Broadway theatre, one that would be open to risky new plays. Next, he wanted TDF to help sell tickets to shows at half-price in order to bolster the sales on shows that were struggling to stay open.[87] The idea for the TKTS booth was the brainchild of Anna Crouse, the founder of TDF, who first came up with the idea based upon Gray's Drugstore, the "cut-rate arm" of LeBlang's Ticket Agency in the 1930s.[88] There was resistance to TKTS from some members of the league because they thought the discount ticket sales would depress the full-price market.[89] Richard asked Crouse to "use her feminine wiles and good sense" to push the producers to consider the possibilities.[90] Harvey Sabinson noted that Barr negotiated the agreement on TKTS by pointing out its "business sense," despite the glum response by league members: "Richard did have some foresight and it didn't destroy the full-price ticket sale. At all. There were big hits that were not at the booth initially. If you had a big hit and you were selling out, you sent no tickets over to the booth. You used the booth when you had available tickets, so it made sense. That was never a problem."[91] Five years later, the TKTS booth was still an enormous hit with audiences and even with the producers.[92] The producers could decide how many tickets went to the booth and how much of a discount was offered. Even better, the producers could even make this decision on an hourly basis.[93]

Richard also pushed the league to modernize and expedite ticket sales by using credit card sales.[94] Ticket sales had been a strictly cash business handled at the theatre box office where the show was being produced. This inconvenience was one of the most frequent complaints of ticket buyers. Barr worked with William McKinney of Bankers Trust in the early 1970s to jumpstart credit card sales for Broadway tickets. In addition, computerized sales of tickets needed to be established, and Barr worked with the Shubert Organization to establish a system that was open to all theatres.[95] Combined with the use of credit cards, the computerized system was a revolution in Broadway ticket sales, and it was all facilitated by Barr's innovative ideas.[96]

By 1974, the league had reached a major crossing point. Richard had succeeded with several major initiatives to modernize ticket sales and facilitate development in the Broadway theatre district. There were early improvements in the physical decay of Times Square, and Mayor Lindsay had been very supportive of the efforts made by the league to help effect that change. Mayor Ed Koch likewise supported the league's campaign to improve the physical decline of the theatre district. But a larger issue loomed. Along with escalation of costs and loss of audiences, Broadway was considered to be "part of a worn-out, up-tight establishment," and so younger audiences stayed away.[97] Instead of Broadway theatre, young people were going to see rock music, new wave films, and off- and off-off-Broadway experimental productions, if they went to the theatre at all. A few shows like *Jesus Christ Superstar*, *Hair*, *Pippin*, *Grease*, and *Candide*, which had been developed in the nonprofit sector, were taking downtown sensibilities uptown. But these shows were infrequent visitors. A generation of disaffected theatre professionals were "doing their thing" in the off- and off-off-Broadway theatres and refusing to take their wares uptown.[98] It took *A Chorus Line*, an unequivocal hit, to make that change a permanent part of Broadway in 1975.

Broadway was in decline, despite the best attempts by the League of New York Theatres and Producers to change its fortunes. On 4 November 1973, Richard Berkvist wrote an article titled "Why Bring a Show to Broadway at All?," questioning the sanity of bringing any new work to Broadway, where despite good reviews and strong sales out of town, a show was doomed to fail financially: "Broadway! The very name once flashed like some magical marquee in the mind of every producer, playwright, actor and director. It was the place where you were finally recognized for what you were worth, and with that recognition came the rewards of fortune and distinction. But times have changed, and Broadway's luster has dimmed as its costly risks have multiplied. Lately, even well-received shows have been known to sicken and die."[99] Using producer Roger Stevens (later a National Endowment for the Arts chair) as an example, the article was filled with horror stories about shows that lingered on the road to make back at least some of the return to investors before heading to Broadway to die. Berkvist's article touched a nerve. The league's producers felt their backs against the wall, and Alex Cohen had particularly harsh words for Stevens, noting his failures on Broadway, declaring: "Now he's a merchant of mass mediocrity at the Kennedy Center, where he uses government money to subsidize a string of failures."[100] While not as venomous as Cohen, Richard Barr protested Berkvist's accusations and promoted Broadway in the face of its current struggles, writing a letter to the *New York Times* titled "Broadway? Yes, Indeed!" There he noted that without Broadway, there would be no regional theatre, no dinner theatre, and a faster flight of actors, directors, and writers from the theatre to Hollywood. Barr criticized those who were producing road-show revivals as star vehicles and disparaged what he termed the road-show mentality. He also bemoaned the lack of subsidy for the Broadway theatre and pleaded for Washington to consider the plight of Broadway producers.[101]

Despite Barr's advocacy, Broadway costs were escalating out of control, and with risks so high, producers were looking for "safe" scripts to draw audiences.[102] This led to a staleness of material that could not attract new, younger audiences. And the older audiences had long fled for the suburbs during the 1960s, making them that much less likely to attend a Broadway show. One aspect that discouraged "bridge and tunnel" audiences was curtain time. Traditionally, Broadway shows had curtain times at 8:30 P.M., but this had commuters leaving the theatre at 11:00 P.M.[103] In 1971, theatre producers attempted to help mitigate this loss of audience by making theatre curtains earlier at 7:30 P.M. But then David Merrick backpedaled and decided to move his shows from a 7:30 curtain to 8:00, and other producers followed his lead.[104] Barr was not happy with Merrick's decision to break with his colleagues at the league but felt an 8:00 curtain still encouraged commuter audiences to see a show.[105] Regardless of the curtain times, older audiences were not returning to Broadway; it was going to be new work that connected with younger audiences.

In order to attract that new work, the league would need to seek out the younger generation of theatre artists who could be induced to bring their shows to Broadway. Barr encouraged Alexander Cohen to explore the off-Broadway and off-off-Broadway theatres and come up with a plan to encourage new synergies with Broadway.[106] In June 1974, the league decided to put on a full-fledged conference to bring together the world of the nonprofit off-Broadway and regional theatres with that of the Broadway commercial theatres. The conference became known as the FACT, the First American Congress of Theatre, and though contentious, unruly, and barely organized, it ended up being one of the significant events of Barr's administration of the league.

Cohen organized the conference under the auspices of the League of New York Theatres and Producers at Princeton University and received funding from many sources, including TDF and the newly created National Endowment for the Arts.[107] Invitees included Hugh Southern, executive director of TDF; W. McNeil Lowry, vice president of the Ford Foundation's division of humanities and the arts; Richard Schechner, codirector of the Performance Group; Bernard Jacobs, executive director of the Shubert Organization; Joseph Papp, artistic director of the New York Shakespeare Festival; Arthur Storch, artistic director of the Syracuse Stage; Robert J. Buzbee, director of civic affairs for Sears, Roebuck; Robert H. Leach, vice president for marketing services of American Express; Andre Gregory, director of the Manhattan Project; Julian Beck and Judith Malina, artistic directors of the Living Theatre; and Richard Barr, president of the league, among many others.[108] The conference included representatives from professional theatre companies in seventeen states as well as Washington, D.C., and Canada and was made up of government officials, theatre owners, producers, designers, various service agency personnel, critics, playwrights, reporters, and lawyers for the arts.[109] It was the United Nations of the American theatre, and on 2 June 1974, this unlikely mix of nonprofit and commercial theatre artists gathered under sunny skies in Princeton, New Jersey, to begin a dialogue that has continued, unabated, ever since.[110]

Richard Barr was one of the first speakers to present before this congress in the Woodrow Wilson School of International Affairs. Barr focused on the historical significance of the American theatre, which, he pointed out, was only around fifty years old in 1974. He spoke about the significance of off-Broadway, a theatre for which he had a special fondness, but noted the "catch-as-catch-can" nature of this particular commercial theatrical enterprise. Without a true national theatre to support their projects, Barr declared that, for most theatre artists, Broadway was simply the final step for a production that had begun elsewhere. And whether it was regional, off-, or off-off-Broadway, "almost all theatre in the western world considers Broadway . . . the capital of the theatre world. Ask any writer, director, actor, or designer what his eventual goal is, and you will get one answer."[111]

This point was not taken well by the alternative theatre panelists at the conference, and in particular by Gordon Davidson, who pointed out that "I do not try out plays. I do plays. I make theatre. If a play or a production happens to visit another town and that town happens to be New York City, fine."[112] Richard Schechner asked his fellow alternative theatre panelists, "Do we really want to help support Broadway, a ship we have been trying to sink all these years?" and André Breton simply pointed out to Barr that it was no longer true that a Broadway run was the final desired outcome for his theatre's productions.[113] Barr observed that both O'Neill and Albee had had their beginnings off-Broadway but then needed financially and artistically to move to Broadway. Supporting Broadway was not a question of values but a question of financial stability, not just for Broadway but for the American theatre as a whole: "I am not being a propagandist for Broadway because I believe all is well, or because I believe we do better work than others, or because I believe we are presenting the most exciting plays or the most daring or the most worthy. I can say what I have said because it is true, and the reason it is true is that there is more money there, and that is all. The fact that a play is presented on Broadway, if successful, simply creates more money for it elsewhere for the contributing arts. It is as simple as that."[114]

These were fighting words for the alternative theatre panelists who were ambivalent about what they perceived as the real agenda of this "Congress," which they felt was to bail out Broadway commercial theatre with government subsidy. For Barr, the FACT was a plea for the nonprofit theatre to join with the Broadway theatre to lobby Washington as a united front. What Barr and Cohen sought from Washington were very specific things: an abolition of the federal excise tax on theatre tickets, enactment of depletion allowances for theatrical enterprises, tax shelters for income derived from a play's profit, a theatrical investment tax credit, a double deduction for theatrical investment losses, and ultimately the kind of subsidy enjoyed by the English theatre. And this could be done, they believed, with the support of the not-for-profit theatre world.[115]

The Broadway commercial theatre was on its knees in an attempt to connect with the nonprofit world of experimental theatre, the theatre of ideas and visions. The reaction of these far leaner theatre experimentalists was, at least on one level, predictable. Julian Beck, inarguably the most radical theatre practitioner at the conference, along with Judith Malina, his Living Theatre coproducer, famously went ballistic, screaming, "The capitalist pig theatre must go! It must die! We rejoice in its death!" Bernard Jacobs, executive director of the Shubert Organization, oddly enough agreed, stating: "As I see it, there is no future for the profit theatre as we know it. . . . It is very important that all of us remain together. . . . The real issue is do you want theatre to survive, do you want live performances to survive, or do you want the whole thing to die? It isn't a matter of the commercial theatre dying. Each time any part of the theatre, commercial or otherwise, dies, a part of each dies with it."[116]

Interestingly, Joseph Papp came the closest to supporting Barr's initial statements, having made the leap to commercial theatre with the hit *A Chorus Line*, which then subsequently subsidized his nonprofit theatre. As different as Barr was from Papp, both shared a vision of a reciprocal relationship between the two worlds, one that was to become the norm in the Broadway theatre of the present day. At the end of the congress, there were still questions, and still great differences, but as Rocco Landesman noted in his article on the conference, something had changed: "If the Congress sought merely to establish a forum for the exchange of views and the discussion of common problems, it succeeded perhaps even beyond its planners' expectations because the representatives of the two theaters developed respect and in many cases warm feelings for each other."[117]

Barr for his part was satisfied with this outcome for the FACT, writing that "the League had two major considerations in mind. First, we producers wished to change our image in the theatre world from that of 'robber barons' to one more honestly reflective of our serious artistic intentions in a precarious business. We also wished to show the non-profit theatre that it was our intention to cooperate not only by exchanging ideas, but by exchanging material on a completely new financial basis."[118] The cooperation that Barr predicted in 1974 became the norm in the new millennium. In 2000, the Second American Congress of Theatre took place at Harvard University, and despite the differences between the two worlds, the friction was now mostly grousing between those who regularly collaborated and worked closely together. Gerald Schoenfeld, who attended both meetings, pointed out that "you cannot afford the luxury any longer of thinking of two distinct isolated worlds of theater. Economics have been the driving force between profit and nonprofit, or taxpaying and nontaxpaying, as I call it."[119] Producers now move effortlessly between both worlds. Barr was the first of these producers whose involvement in the FACT helped to make these distinctions a function of the kind of theatre one wanted to present rather than the foundation, based on divisive ideological issues.

On 13 December 1982, Richard Barr was given the John F. Wharton Award, named after the famous theatrical lawyer, having been nominated by Edward Albee, his longtime collaborator.[120] In his nomination for Richard, Albee pointed out several aspects of Barr's career that recommended him for this honor: "He, along with a few others, spearheaded the development of Off Broadway as an important creative force in the American Theatre. His dedication to encouraging young, new playwrights is legendary. Indeed, the free experimental theatre group which he, Clinton Wilder, and I financed and moderated for ten years, gave an entire generation of young playwrights (Sam Shepard, LeRoi Jones, Terrence McNally, Leonard Melfi, John Guare, etc.) their first stage performances. As a Broadway producer, Richard's record suggests an enthusiasm for quality however suicidal."[121] Barr was honored at a reception at Sardi's, having been selected "in recognition of his distinguished tenure as president of the League of New York Theaters and Producers."[122]

With all of these innovations, much of Richard's time with the league was tied up with the constant bickering, gamesmanship, and machinations that he summed up as "Tony fever." One of the major and most lucrative functions of the league was its production of the Tony Awards each June for the American Theatre Wing (ATW). The ATW was originally created as a war effort called the Stage Women's War Relief in 1917 for World War I.

After the bombing of Pearl Harbor, the American Theatre Wing became an independent entity, a "War Service Corporation." It was known for its legendary "Stage Door Canteens," where servicemen were fed, entertained, and given a needed break from the war while back in the States for needed rest and recreation.[123] The first Antoinette Perry Awards, as they are formally known, were presented by the American Theatre Wing as a memorial to Antoinette Perry, one of the most energetic and important members of the ATW, on 6 April 1947 in the Grand Ballroom of the Waldorf Astoria hotel on an Easter Sunday.[124] "It was pretty much a loose kind of a framework," according to Irving Cheskin, the former executive director for the league. "There were luncheons mainly for the industry."[125] Helen Menken organized the award ceremony until her death in 1965, at which point the League of New York Theatres was asked to take over the event.[126] In 1967, Alexander Cohen, using his legendary showman's skills, produced the evening for television, and the Tony Awards became a commercial hit. And this is where the troubles began. After winning a Tony Award for Best Play on his own production of Harold Pinter's *The Homecoming*, Cohen's weekly gross went from $14,000 to $40,000.[127] The stakes were suddenly raised, and the ceremony needed to be professionally handled with a scrupulous eye for detail. Still, with this new income for the league, Richard felt that Cohen was the best person to run the Tony Award ceremony, and Cohen stayed in that position from 1967 to 1986.[128]

Barr created the Tony administration committee, composed of the executive officers of the league as well as several officers of the ATW. By 1976, the organization included an eligibility committee of three members, which included a drama critic, a member of the league, and a member of the ATW, to determine the eligibility of each show's roles for specific awards.[129] After that, the administration committee made any addendums to the eligible shows, and the list was then passed on to the nomination committee (approximately thirty members selected by the administration committee). Each nomination committee member made his or her selections by secret ballot. After the nominations were made, the approximately 750 Tony Award voters made their selections.[130]

Despite the care by Richard and his "scrupulously fair" Tony administration committee, the awards continued to be contentious, and because of the nature of theatre people and the business, they are likely to remain so. In 1985, for reasons that he did not "divulge," Alexander Cohen resigned from the league, and his contract ended as producer of the Tony Awards ceremony. Apparently, Cohen had made an obscene remark with regard to critic Frank Rich, as well as one about then governor Mario Cuomo.[131]

The duties of presenting the Tony Awards were then passed on to Don Mischer, a television producer, who took over in 1987 and was producing the Tony Awards when Barr died in 1989.[132] By then, in the late 1980s, Barr's own leadership of the league was being questioned as his health began to falter.

It was clear that by 1985, there was beginning to be something of a divide between the up-and-coming young producers like Fred Zollo (who was producing *Hurlyburly* and *Ma Rainey's Black Bottom*), Rocco and Heidi Landesman (*Big River* and *Pump Boys and Dinettes*), and Michael Frazier (*Lena*, *Grind*, *End of the World*) and producers like Alexander Cohen, Robert Whitehead, David Merrick, and Barr. An organization called the "Producers Group" grew up out of these disgruntled younger producers. Their concern was that ticket prices had grown too high and younger audiences were not coming to the theatre. They disagreed with strategies like the TKTS booth that seemed to be an inconvenience to customers and instead just wanted to charge less at the box office. And they were particularly uncomfortable with the presence of the theatre owners, who they felt were in league with the older generation of producers holding back more adventurous shows. The Producers Group wanted to do marketing research, as Michael Frazier noted: "We all know the yuppies prefer to go out to eat rather than go to the theater, but we don't know why."[133] Harvey Sabinson recalled that the criticism of Barr was tied not just to the inherent tensions between the producers and theatre owners but to Richard's sexual orientation as well: "There was a lot of strife when Richard tried to arrange peace between these warring factions; there was a lot of criticism of him, and I recall . . . a lot of cracks from people about his homosexuality, which I felt was just horrible. And there was even talk toward the end of his life, before he died, that maybe he ought to be replaced, he had been there too long. But at that point he developed AIDS, [and] they couldn't make that move. I visited him at Mt. Sinai hospital many times. He became my friend."[134]

At the same time, in Barr's own producing partnership, two major projects were refusing to come together. Barr and David Bixler had managed to procure the rights to the film *Sunset Boulevard* from Paramount Pictures. Calvin Remsberg was working on the book and lyrics, and Roger Ames was writing the show's music.[135] Barr had capitalized the project at $3.5 million and investors were being sought, but fate was to change the availability of the rights. Within a few days of completion of the score and finalization of the financing, Andrew Lloyd Webber acquired Broadway rights to *Sunset Boulevard*, and the entire project came to a halt.[136]

Still Barr and Bixler kept on, with Charles Woodward now retired, attempting to bring the next play by Edward Albee, *The Marriage Play*, to

Broadway. Having recently negotiated a reduction in playwright's royalties on Broadway, Richard was particularly pleased with Albee earning 5 percent on his projected weekly gross on the show of $250,000, which gave Albee a royalty of $12,500 per week, "a respectable sum."[137] However, Barr was struggling to find funding for the production and had been for several years. He and Bixler had several readings of the play, with stars such as Swoosie Kurtz and Rosemary Harris.[138] Albee had been working on the play since the mid-1980s, and it had been commissioned by the English Theater in Vienna, where it was eventually produced on 17 May 1987.[139] Richard died before the production could come to Broadway; its first major US production was in 1992 at McCarter Theater, featuring Shirley Knight and Tom Klunis.[140]

Despite Richard's worsening physical condition, he remained active in the league and was still a voice advocating for new work on Broadway. He participated in yet another theatre conference in 1986 in Stamford, Connecticut, sponsored by the league, which in 1985 changed its name from the League of New York Theatres and Producers to the League of American Theatres and Producers in order to incorporate Broadway road-show producers. At the conference, Barr also continued in his mission to promote a middle or limited contract for Broadway to reduce costs, recommending that six "endangered theatres"—including the Cort, Belasco, Lyceum, Nederlander, Biltmore, and Ritz—have limited ticket prices no higher than twenty-five dollars and a six-dollar ticket for balcony seats at all times. Richard also recommended that the actors, stagehands, directors, and playwrights work at minimum and allow investors to have a percentage of the gross only in the profitable weeks of the run.[141]

In 1988, Barr wrote a rather passionate letter to the *New York Times*, stating, "If we can make a continuing exchange between the nonprofit professional theater, Off Broadway or elsewhere; if we can make it simple for a talented playwright to be heard . . . if we can do this in a sensible, unselfish, nonegotistical manner, we have, and I do not exaggerate, the possibility of equaling Athens."[142] Despite the fact that Richard had less than a year left to live, he envisioned today's stage alliances, with Broadway building a strong collaboration with nonprofit theatre.

Barr's illness was beginning to take its toll on his ability to effectively run the league, and he began to pull back from his duties. He was also having difficulties with his partner, Anthony Constantine, who had been with him for several years and whose background was still something of a mystery. Barr had tied his finances and ownership of his homes into Constantine's business deals. James Duff, Clark Bason (Barr's assistant), and David Bixler all had mixed feelings about Constantine's involvement with Barr. Bason noted that Barr was rather trusting in his relationships, both personally and professionally: "I think he recognized talent and sparks in people. He always looked to the young people and the future. . . . I think that maybe he believed in some of the wrong people sometimes, and I'm not saying in his professional life, but in his personal life."[143] Later, after Barr's death, a fire broke out in his Eighth Street apartment, and materials went missing—papers and theatre artifacts that should have been donated to the New York Public Library at Lincoln Center per Barr's will. Constantine made assurances that these documents had been destroyed in the fire. However, these items were later discovered in an auction held by Gotham Bookmart and being sold by Constantine, and a suit ensued between the library and Constantine. The library was finally able to receive the materials, where they are now available to all researchers.[144] It was an unfortunate coda to Barr's important contribution to American theatre.

In late 1988, Barr announced to his colleagues that he was struggling with AIDS and would no longer be able to serve as league president, but the league agreed to keep Barr as president until his death. According to his business partner David Bixler, the news was particularly shocking to this group of producers and theatre owners, despite the fact that AIDS was killing one major theatre artist after another in the late 1980s: "I think a lot of people were frankly very shocked that he was sexually active. Knowing somebody is gay is one thing, but then finding out that they have AIDS or HIV is another."[145]

By December 1988, Barr's health was deteriorating badly. And because it was rather unusual that someone of Barr's age could contract AIDS, he was having difficulty receiving proper treatment.[146] Finally, shortly after New Year's Day, Bason received a call from Barr, who was no longer able to leave his apartment on Eighth Street. "One night he called me and told me, 'I cannot be alone tonight.' And I decided right then and there I would be with him. Richard was dying that night, and I saw that things were turning for [the] worse and it was a very unglamorous event, just dealing with the health issues. I got him downstairs, and he did not want an ambulance, so he took one step at a time (sitting down) and I managed to get him into a taxicab and we got him to a hospital on the East Side."[147] Bason was not alone in keeping Barr company. Edward Albee joined him in a nightly watch at the hospital, both taking turns dozing on nearby coffee tables, to try to assure Barr that he was not alone. Others came to see Barr as well, including Harvey Sabinson, who visited the hospital frequently. Barr's HIV infection was complicated by his years of drinking, and he finally died of liver failure on 9 January 1989.[148]

Barr was survived by his mother, Ruth, and his sisters, Carol Fischer and Barbara Luchs. After his remains were interred, a small gathering took place at Sardi's, one of his favorite restaurants and the place of many of his business lunches and postproduction gatherings. The crowd included Edward Albee, Colleen Dewhurst, Frances Sternhagen, Elaine Stritch, Harvey Sabinson, Charles Woodward, and Bernard Jacobs, among many others. The passing of Richard Barr closed the door on a generation of "gentlemen" producers—independent, articulate, sophisticated, and discerning theatre business leaders who had changed the lives of a generation of theatre artists. Dewhurst, at the time the president of Actors' Equity, noted, "We aren't left with many producers like him, who really know what they're looking at and why they chose what they did." Both Bernard Jacobs and Harvey Sabinson stated how important Barr was to young playwrights, and Sabinson pointed out Barr's significant proposal that led to the establishment of the Theatre Development Fund and his tireless advocacy for "noncommercial plays and musicals."[149]

In Barr's obituary in the *New York Times*, Mervyn Rothstein wrote that Barr "as president of the theater league . . . presided in 1971 over a revolutionary change on Broadway." Rothstein noted that Barr's extensive career included his formative years in the Mercury Theatre and his production of the plays of Albee, Beckett, and a generation of young writers, and he quoted Harvey Sabinson, who pointed out that Barr "was one of the great independent and creative producers" who led the league "during the period of its greatest growth and expansion." Albee called Barr "his mentor and one of my dearest friends," and Dewhurst pointed out that "Richard Barr was part of the dream we began with when we were young and building Off Broadway. Somehow, through everything, Richard managed to stay with the spirit that we began with, so that in the end, to see Richard was to remember the dream."[150] Elizabeth Ireland McCann, a more recent producer of Edward Albee's plays, observed that Barr was one of "a generation of men whose presence propelled a critical moment and who sort of get forgotten through time and history." For McCann, whose last memory of Barr was meeting him at Joe Allen's for a drink in 1989, shortly before he died, Barr was part of a cohort of producers who presented some of the greatest work in the theatre but did it with little or no recognition from the general public:

> When one thinks of producers, what comes to mind are the ones like David Merrick or Alex Cohen, the great impresarios who always had such flashy careers on Broadway, and when I think of Dick Barr, especially after he produced *Sweeney Todd* and mortgaged his home to take that production out to California, . . . I think of these men, like Phil Rose,

> who produced *Raisin in the Sun,* who floated in and out of the theater, who had unheard-of courage and quietly produced these masterpieces. I wonder if Broadway would be such a mess today—and I think it is—if we had some of these characters around with these absurd dreams. A lot of people, when they think of producers, think of someone like Joe Papp, who went on to become an icon. But there were others all around. Dick Barr was one of a generation of men who quietly toiled and produced some of the best work on Broadway, and we don't hear of them today.[151]

McCann pointed out that most producers today can't do what Barr did in the past, reading plays, independently choosing shows to produce, bringing in backers to support a vision. Instead, the plays are developed by not-for-profit theatre companies who seem to be "on a mad search to find the new great American writer" and ignore the great American playwrights from the past who are still writing. McCann explained that what separated Barr's management of the league in the past from what it is now is partly based on the size of the league and its constituency. "Dick could walk into a room of his peers, and he would have the respect of those peers," according to McCann, and now because there is not the same populace of independent producers, the league cannot effect the influence on the American theatre it once had. New plays must find their life elsewhere and a different venue for national success. With the passing of Richard Barr and the generation of independent producers, a new support system for American drama must be developed. McCann, who has taken on the mantle of serving as the producer of Edward Albee's work, is hopeful. She notes that while there are not many new plays or playwrights worth producing, they are still out there, and it will take the same kind of vision to bring them to the stage.[152] It will take a new generation of producers, like Richard Barr, who are willing to challenge the American theatre and perhaps even "hock" their own homes for the opportunity.

AFTERWORD

NOTES

BIBLIOGRAPHY

INDEX

AFTERWORD

Well! There it is!

Not all good stories end happily, of course, and Richard Barr was eventually defeated in his endeavors by a combination of his own excesses and diminishings and a power structure determined to win out, even at the cost of destroying its own usefulness.

Was Richard tilting at windmills? Was the wonderfulness of his goals the guarantor of his decline? I won't play "what if?" here, and humanity brings its weaknesses with it, but the goal was worth the journey; the journey was brave, however foolhardy and flawed; and we are all the better for Richard Barr having been among us.

Edward Albee

NOTES

Introduction: "You Have to Hock Your House: The Story of a Producer"

1. Barr, "You Have to Hock Your House," 2C (all references to this unpublished memoir are from the private Edward Albee Theatre Collection).

2. Ibid., 4A.

1. Privilege with a Price: Washington, Princeton, and Early Theatre Efforts

1. Altschuler, *Jews of Washington, D.C.*, xii.

2. Diner, *Time for Gathering*, 31.

3. Nordlinger, "History of the Washington Hebrew Congregation," 11–65.

4. Barr, "You Have to Hock Your House," 49 (all references to this unpublished memoir are from the private Edward Albee Theatre Collection); Fischer interview; Luchs interview.

5. Barr, "You Have to Hock Your House," 36; Fischer interview; Luchs interview.

6. Barr, "You Have to Hock Your House," 37; Fischer interview; Luchs interview.

7. Barr, "You Have to Hock Your House," 38; Fischer interview; Luchs interview.

8. Barr, "You Have to Hock Your House," 40.

9. Ibid., 44; Fischer interview; Luchs interview.

10. Barr, "You Have to Hock Your House," 46.

11. Henry Parker Taylor, "Richard of Bordeaux," *New York Times*, 4 February 1934; Barr, "You Have to Hock Your House," 49.

12. Barr, "You Have to Hock Your House," 50.

13. Ibid., 47–48.

14. "Theatre Intime Facility to Be Renovated," press release, Princeton University, 27 April 2000; Edward W. Borgers, "The Significance of Princeton's Theatre Intime," *Educational Theatre Journal* 4.4 (1952): 308–14.

15. Borgers, "Significance," 308–314; Barr, "You Have to Hock Your House," 51–52.

16. Borgers, "Significance," 310.

17. Barr, "You Have to Hock Your House," 54.

18. Ibid., 55.

19. "Drama Factory," *Time* 68 (20 August 1956), 72.

20. Barr, "You Have to Hock Your House," 56.

21. Ibid., 58.

22. "Fol De Rol," *Time* 30.25 (20 December 1937).

23. Ibid.

24. Barr, "You Have to Hock Your House," 59.

2. Playing with Martians: Stage and Screen with Orson Welles and the Mercury Theatre

1. Barr, "You Have to Hock Your House," 62 (all references to this unpublished memoir are from the private Edward Albee Theatre Collection).

2. Ibid.

3. Ibid., 63.

4. Ibid., 64.

5. Houseman, *Run-Through*, 381.

6. Barr, "You Have to Hock Your House," 65.

7. Ibid., 66.

8. France, *Theatre of Orson Welles*, 143–45.

9. Barr, "You Have to Hock Your House," 68.

10. Bob Groves, "Orson Welles in 1940: Prodigy on the Loose," *Buffalo Courier-Express*, 9 November 1980.

11. Barr, "You Have to Hock Your House," 69.

12. Houseman, *Run-Through*, 364–65.

13. Ibid., 366.

14. Barr, "You Have to Hock Your House," 70.

15. Houseman, *Run-Through*, 393.

16. Higham, *Orson Welles*, 124.

17. Houseman, *Run-Through*, 393; Groves "Orson Welles in 1940."

18. Houseman, *Run-Through*, 394.

19. Barr, "You Have to Hock Your House," 71.

20. Ibid., 71; Houseman, *Run-Through*, 392.

21. Houseman, *Run-Through*, 403; Barr, "You Have to Hock Your House," 71.

22. "Radio Listeners in Panic, Taking War Drama as Fact," *New York Times*, 31 October 1938, 1.

23. Brown, *Manipulating the Ether*, 244.

24. Barr, "You Have to Hock Your House," 71.

25. Higham, *Orson Welles*, 127; Houseman, *Run-Through*, 404.

26. Barr, "You Have to Hock Your House," 72.

27. Ibid., 73.

28. Lubertozzi with Holmsten and Callaway, *War of the Worlds*, 27.

29. Barr, "You Have to Hock Your House," 73.

30. Houseman, *Run-Through*, 403.

31. Higham, *Orson Welles*, 128.

32. Ibid., 131; *Run-Through*, 412–13.

33. *Saturday Evening Post*, 27 January 1940, 51.

34. Houseman, *Run-Through*, 380–89.

35. Barr, "You Have to Hock Your House," 74.

36. Ibid., 74.

37. Ibid., 75.

38. Houseman, *Run-Through*, 382; Barr, "You Have to Hock Your House," 75.

39. Barr, "You Have to Hock Your House," 75.

40. Ibid., 76.
41. Kaiser, *Gay Metropolis*, 6–8.
42. Ibid., 7.
43. Ibid., 7–8.
44. Barr, "You Have to Hock Your House," 4A.
45. Hadleigh, *Broadway Babylon*, 161.
46. Houseman, *Run-Through*, 414.
47. Barr, "You Have to Hock Your House," 77; Houseman, *Run-Through*, 416–17.
48. Barr, "You Have to Hock Your House," 77.
49. Ibid., 77.
50. Ibid., 81.
51. Ibid., 78; Houseman, *Run-Through*, 418.
52. Barr, "You Have to Hock Your House," 78.
53. Houseman, *Run-Through*, 419.
54. Ibid., 420.
55. Barr, "You Have to Hock Your House," 79.
56. Houseman, *Run-Through*, 421.
57. Barr, "You Have to Hock Your House," 80.
58. Houseman, *Run-Through*, 418.
59. Welles et al., *Orson Welles on Shakespeare*, 173.
60. Barr, "You Have to Hock Your House," 82.
61. Houseman, *Run-Through*, 426.
62. Waldau, *Vintage Years of the Theatre Guild*, 325–27.
63. Barr, "You Have to Hock Your House," 82.
64. LoMonaco, *Summer Stock!*, 72–73.
65. Young, *Famous American Playhouses*, 122.
66. Houseman, *Run-Through*, 432.
67. Barr, "You Have to Hock Your House," 83–84.
68. Ibid., 86.
69. Ibid., 87.
70. Callow, *Road to Xanadu*, 460–61.
71. Welles and Bogdanovich, *This Is Orson Welles*, 33.
72. Barr, "You Have to Hock Your House," 87.
73. Houseman, *Run Through*, 436–37; Higham, *Orson Welles*, 142–43; Callow, *Road to Xanadu*, 462–63.
74. Callow, *Road to Xanadu*, 468.
75. Ibid., 470.
76. Mel Gussow, "Dolly Haas, 84, an Actress and the Wife of Hirschfeld," *New York Times*, 17 September 1994.
77. Callow, *Road to Xanadu*, 470; Barr, "You Have to Hock Your House," 87–88.
78. Callow, *Road to Xanadu*, 476–77; Higham, *Orson Welles*, 142; Barr, "You Have to Hock Your House," 89.
79. Barr, "You Have to Hock Your House," 91; Callow, *Road to Xanadu*, 477; Higham, *Orson Welles*, 141.
80. Houseman, *Run-Through*, 437.
81. Callow, *Road to Xanadu*, 459; Higham, *Orson Welles*, 143.
82. Callow, *Road to Xanadu*, 462; Higham, *Orson Welles*, 140.

83. Higham, *Orson Welles*, 140.

84. Barr, "You Have to Hock Your House," 92.

85. Higham, *Orson Welles*, 140.

86. Barr, "You Have to Hock Your House," 92; Eyman, *Ernest Lubitsch*, 207.

87. Callow, *Road to Xanadu*, 481.

88. Barr, "You Have to Hock Your House," 109.

89. Houseman, *Run-Through*, 439; Callow, *Road to Xanadu*, 477, Higham, *Orson Welles*, 144.

90. Houseman, *Run-Through*, 459–60.

91. Ibid., 459.

92. Callow, *Road to Xanadu*, 487.

93. Richard Barr, affidavit, May 1941, Richard Barr–Clinton Wilder Papers, Series III: Productions, 1940–1979, box 7, folder 2B.

94. Welles and Bogdanovich, *This Is Orson Welles*, 495.

95. Barr, "You Have to Hock Your House," 93.

96. Houseman, *Run-Through*, 444.

97. Callow, *Road to Xanadu*, 484.

98. Ibid., 484; Houseman, *Run-Through*, 444.

99. Higham, *Orson Welles*, 146.

100. Barr, affidavit.

101. Houseman, *Run-Through*, 450; Callow, *Road to Xanadu*, 484.

102. Barr, affidavit.

103. Barr, "You Have to Hock Your House," 93.

104. Barr, affidavit.

105. Barr, "You Have to Hock Your House," 94; Groves, "Orson Welles in 1940"; Welles and Bogdanovich, *This Is Orson Welles*, 499.

106. Barr, "You Have to Hock Your House," 94; Welles and Bogdanovich, *This Is Orson Welles*, 498.

107. Welles and Bogdanovich, *This Is Orson Welles*, 495; Carringer, *Making of "Citizen Kane,"* 26–31.

108. Barr, affidavit.

109. Callow, *Road to Xanadu*, 498.

110. Barr, "You Have to Hock Your House," 94.

111. Ibid.

112. Ibid., 95; Callow, *Road to Xanadu*, 498–524; Higham, *Orson Welles*, 160; Kael, "Raising Kane," 74–79.

113. Barr, "You Have to Hock Your House," 95; Callow, *Road to Xanadu*, 507.

114. "Maurice Seiderman, 82, Inventor and Hollywood Makeup Artist," *New York Times*, 22 July 1989, 10; Welles and Bogdanovich, *This Is Orson Welles*, 69–70; Barr, "You Have to Hock Your House," 95–96.

115. Groves, "Orson Welles in 1940."

116. Barr, "You Have to Hock Your House," 96; Groves, "Orson Welles in 1940"; Welles and Bogdanovich, *This Is Orson Welles*, 71.

117. Barr, "You Have to Hock Your House," 98; Welles and Bogdanovich, *This Is Orson Welles*, 72.

118. Barr, "You Have to Hock Your House," 98.

119. Kael, "Raising Kane," 74–79; *Citizen Kane*, directed by Orson Welles (1941; Turner Home Entertainment, 2001), DVD.
120. Barr, "You Have to Hock Your House," 97.
121. Ibid., 99.
122. Carringer, *Making of "Citizen Kane,"* 72.
123. Barr, "You Have to Hock Your House," 99; Callow, *Road to Xanadu*, 522.
124. Callow, *Road to Xanadu*, 514; Higham, *Orson Welles*, 159.
125. Higham, *Orson Welles*, 168–75; Callow, *Road to Xanadu*, 540–60.
126. Carringer, *Making of "Citizen Kane,"* 112–13; Higham, *Orson Welles*, 176.
127. Barr, "You Have to Hock Your House," 100; Higham, *Orson Welles*, 168–69.
128. Ibid., 101.
129. Groves, "Orson Welles in 1940."
130. McBride, *Whatever Happened to Orson Welles?*, 33; Higham, *Orson Welles*, 168–69, 172.
131. Barr, "You Have to Hock Your House," 101; Higham, *Orson Welles*, 167.
132. Higham, *Orson Welles*, 172.
133. Flynn, *My Wicked Wicked Ways*, 170; Madsen, *Sewing Circle*, 105.
134. Barr, "You Have to Hock Your House," 103.
135. Ibid., 104; Higham, *Orson Welles*, 193; Welles and Bogdanovich, *This Is Orson Welles*, 357–58.
136. Barr, "You Have to Hock Your House," 104.
137. Ibid., 107.
138. Callow, *Road to Xanadu*, 4; Higham, *Orson Welles*, 32.
139. Barr, "You Have To Hock Your House," 111.

3. A Theatrical Warrior: Lieutenant Richard Barr

1. Barr, "You Have to Hock Your House," 111 (all references to this unpublished memoir are from the private Edward Albee Theatre Collection).
2. Doherty, *Projections of War*, 40–41.
3. Barr, "You Have to Hock Your House," 112.
4. Koppes and Black, *Hollywood Goes to War*, 1–16.
5. Barr, "You Have to Hock Your House," 113."
6. Hotchner, *The Day I Fired Alan Ladd*, 59.
7. Ibid., 90.
8. Barr, "You Have to Hock Your House," 114–15; Master Sergeant George J. Siegel, "Hollywood's Army: The First Motion Picture Unit, US Army Air Forces, Culver City, California," The California State Military Museum website, http://www.militarymuseum.org/1stmpu.html (accessed 20 October 2008).
9. Barr, "You Have to Hock Your House," 116.
10. Siegel, "Hollywood's Army."
11. Hotchner, *The Day I Fired Alan Ladd*, 90.
12. Barr, "You Have to Hock Your House," 119; Siegel, "Hollywood's Army."
13. Barr, "You Have to Hock Your House," 117.
14. Reagan, *American Life*, 97–100; Barr, "You Have to Hock Your House," 118.
15. Barr, "You Have to Hock Your House," 117–19.
16. Ibid., 124.

17. Siegel, "Hollywood's Army"; Reagan, *American Life*, 98; Barr, "You Have to Hock Your House," 123.

18. Reagan, *American Life*, 98.

19. Cassidy, *What Women Watched*, 159–60.

20. Umstattd, *B.A.U. in Action*, 5, 153–68; Hubert C. Heffner and Stanley Wood, "The Army in the Theatre," *Theatre Arts Monthly* 30 (July 1946): 395–98.

21. Umstattd, *B.A.U. in Action*, 8.

22. Heffner and Wood, "Army in the Theatre," 396; Barr, "You Have to Hock Your House," 127.

23. Heffner and Wood, "Army in the Theatre," 396.

24. Barr, "You Have to Hock Your House," 130.

25. Ibid., 119.

26. Mellow, *Charmed Circle*, 460; Sprigge, *Gertrude Stein*, 260.

27. Bowers, "The Composition That All the World Can See," 142.

28. Stein, *Stein Reader*, 496.

29. Bordman and Hischak, *The Oxford Companion to American Theatre*, 660.

30. Heffner and Wood, "Army in the Theatre," 396; Barr, "You Have to Hock Your House," 132.

31. Corliss Phillabaum, "Review," *Educational Theatre Journal* 28.1 (March 1976): 124–25.

32. Laura Shea, "O'Neill, the Theatre Guild, and *A Moon for the Misbegotten*," *Eugene O'Neill Review* 27 (2005): 76–97; Barr, "You Have to Hock Your House," 132.

33. Murray Teigh Bloom, "Biarritz and 'Richard III'; Some Memories of a GI Version That Started for Broadway by Way of the Celebrated French Resort Town," *New York Times*, 6 February 1949, X3.

34. Barr, "You Have to Hock Your House," 133.

35. Bloom, "Biarritz and 'Richard III.'"

36. Umstattd, *B.A.U. in Action*, 167.

37. Barr, "You Have to Hock Your House," 133.

38. Bloom, "Biarritz and 'Richard III.'"

39. Barr, "You Have to Hock Your House," 133.

40. Ibid.

4. Learning the Director's Craft: Stock, Broadway, and City Center

1. Vaughn, *Ronald Reagan in Hollywood*, 224.

2. Goodell, *Independent Feature Film Production*, 112.

3. Barr, "You Have to Hock Your House," 138 (all references to this unpublished memoir are from the private Edward Albee Theatre Collection).

4. Charles Hoffman, letter to Richard Barr, 8 May 1947, Richard Barr–Clinton Wilder Papers, Series IX: Scrapbooks, 1945–1981, box 40, scrapbook, 1945–1949.

5. "The New Pictures," *Time*, 15 December 1947; J. D. Spiro, "Hollywood Memos: Orson Welles Starts Shooting 'Macbeth'—Turtle's Voice Muted—Other Items," *New York Times*, 29 June 1947, X5.

6. Barr, "You Have to Hock Your House," 34.

7. Ibid., 139.

8. Ibid., 140.

9. Lewis Funke, "News and Gossip of the Rialto; Eva Le Gallienne," *New York Times*, 10 November 1946, 65.

10. Barr, "You Have to Hock Your House," 140.

11. Edwin Schallert, "Streamlined 'Macbeth' Appreciated at El Patio," *Los Angeles Times*, 29 November 1946.

12. "Shakespeare Staged in Smash Hit as GI Show Tours ETO Circuit," undated clipping; program for *Macbeth*, El Patio Theatre, both in Richard Barr–Clinton Wilder Papers, Series IX: Scrapbooks, 1945–1981, box 40, scrapbook, 1945–1949.

13. George Lewin, "Something New's Been Added: War-Tried 'Macbeth' to Open at El Patio," *Hollywood Citizen-News*, 16 November 1946, 8.

14. Schallert, "Streamlined 'Macbeth' Appreciated."

15. Lewin, "Something New's Been Added," 8.

16. Barr, "You Have to Hock Your House," 142; Malvin Wald to Richard Barr, 20 December 1946, Richard Barr–Clinton Wilder Papers, Series IX: Scrapbooks, 1945–1981, box 40, scrapbook, 1945–1949.

17. *Red Channels: The Report of Communist Influence in Radio and Television* was published at the height of the McCarthy era by *Counterattack*, a far right-wing journal, which named 151 actors, writers, directors, and other broadcast professionals as communist sympathizers. Those named in *Red Channels* were subsequently "blacklisted" in the broadcast industry—and were refused employment on the basis of these scurrilous accusations.

18. Benshoff and Griffin, *America on Film*, 310.

19. Dalrymple, *From the Last Row*, 71.

20. Ibid., 72.

21. Ibid., 75–76.

22. Barr, "You Have to Hock Your House," 145.

23. Ibid., 143; Dalrymple, *From the Last Row*, 78.

24. Dalrymple, *From the Last Row*, 78.

25. Barr, "You Have to Hock Your House," 143; Dalrymple, *From the Last Row*, 78.

26. Brooks Atkinson, "At the Theatre: Jose Ferrer and Richard Whorf Inaugurate a Season of Drama with 'Volpone' at City Center," *New York Times*, 9 January 1948, 24.

27. Nathan, *Theatre Book of the Year*, 217–19.

28. Dalrymple, *From the Last Row*, 80–81.

29. Barr, "You Have to Hock Your House," 145.

30. Dalrymple, *From the Last Row*, 80.

31. Brooks Atkinson, "At the Theatre," *New York Times*, 23 January 1948, 26.

32. Nathan, *Theatre Book of the Year*, 219.

33. Brooks Atkinson, "At the Theatre," *New York Times*, 6 February 1948, 29; Nathan, *Theatre Book of the Year*, 254.

34. Dalrymple, *From the Last Row*, 81.

35. Barr, "You Have to Hock Your House," 146.

36. Beckhard and Effrst, *Blueprint for Summer Theatre*, 65–67.

37. Program, "Romeo & Juliet," John Drew Theater, Richard Barr–Clinton Wilder Papers, Series IX: Scrapbooks, 1945–1981, box 40, scrapbook, 1945–1949.

38. Barr, "You Have to Hock Your House," 147.

39. Ibid., 146.

40. Louis Calta, "2 Openings Tonight Start New Season; 'Sleepy Hollow' Arrives at St. James and 'Insect Comedy' Bows at City Center," *New York Times*, 3 June 1948, 29.

41. Beckhard and John Effrst, *Blueprint for Summer Theatre*, 5.

42. Barr, "You Have to Hock Your House," 148.

43. Hubert C. Heffner and Stanley Wood, "The Army in the Theatre," *Theatre Arts Monthly* 30 (July 1946): 396.

44. Barr, "You Have to Hock Your House," 150.

45. Ibid., 151.

46. Frances Herridge, "Across the Footlights," *New York Post*, 5 June 1961.

47. Louis Calta, "Guild Co-sponsor of Heyward Play: Organization to Join Allyn Rice in Doing 'Set My People Free' Next Season," *New York Times*, 21 February 1948, 8.

48. Sam Zolotow, "2 Directing Chores for Miss Webster; She Starts Work Tomorrow for 'Hamlet' and 'Macbeth,' Booked Sept. 27 Till April," *New York Times*, 23 August 1948, 14.

49. Barr, "You Have To Hock Your House," 149.

50. Werdna Finley, "News," *Educational Theatre Journal* 16.1 (March 1964): 90–102.

51. Robert Garland, "An Excellent Revival of a Wise, Witty Play," *New York Journal-American*, 29 November 1948, 10.

52. George A. Leiper, "The Repertory: Boston's Own," *Harvard Crimson*, 27 November 1948; Gaver, *Curtain Calls*, 59.

53. Barr, "You Have to Hock Your House," 156.

54. Elliot Norton, "Richard III Presented at Copley: Whorf Enacts Lead to Great Delight of Audience," *Boston Post*, 18 January 1949.

55. De Banke, *Shakespearean Stage Production*, 151–52.

56. Norton, "Richard III Presented at Copley."

57. Elinor Hughes, "Copley: Richard III," *Boston Herald*, 28 January 1949.

58. Qtd. in Barr, "You Have to Hock Your House," 158.

59. Gaver, *Curtain Calls*, 59.

60. Barr, "You Have to Hock Your House," 159.

61. T. D., letter to the editor, "Canned Music," *New York Times*, 20 February 1949, X2.

62. Barr, "You Have to Hock Your House," 159.

63. Richard Watts Jr., "The New 'Richard III' an Exciting Show," *New York Post*, 9 February 1949, in *New York Theatre Critics' Reviews* 10 (1949): 368.

64. Ward Morehouse, "An Exciting 'Richard III,'" *Sun*, 9 February 1949, in *New York Theatre Critics' Reviews* 10 (1949): 368.

65. Brooks Atkinson, "At the Theatre," *New York Times*, 9 February 1949, 33.

66. Kappo Phelan, "The Stage & Screen: 'Richard III,'" *The Commonweal* 49.20 (February 1949): 493–94.

67. Christiansen, *Theater of Our Own*, 93.

68. Ibid.

69. Vernon Rice, "Summer Theatres: Paula Laurence Discovers a New Meaning in 'Go West,'" *New York Post*, 3 September 1949.

70. Londré, *History of North American Theater*, 438.

71. Barr, "You Have to Hock Your House," 161.

72. Qtd. in Rice, "Summer Theatres."

73. Barr, "You Have to Hock Your House," 162.

74. Parish and DeCarl, *Hollywood Players*, 261–63.

75. Barr, "You Have to Hock Your House," 162.

76. Parish and DeCarl, *Hollywood Players*, 284.

77. Ibid., 286.

78. Barr, "You Have to Hock Your House," 149.

79. Brooks Atkinson, "At the Theatre," *New York Times*, 6 April 1949, 37.

80. Barr, "You Have to Hock Your House," 150.

81. Brooks Atkinson, "The Theatre: Synge Premiere," *New York Times*, 15 December 1949, 51; Brooks Atkinson, "No Classics Allowed: Broadway Is Not Organized for Plays Out of Dramatic Literature," *New York Times*, 25 December 1949, X1.

82. Richard Watts Jr., "Two on the Aisle: A Neglected Synge Masterpiece," *New York Post*, 16 December 1949, 62.

83. Programs from the Comédie-Française and Moscow Art Theatre, Richard Barr–Clinton Wilder Papers, Series IX: Scrapbooks, 1945–1981, box 41, scrapbook, 1949–1954; Barr, "You Have to Hock Your House," 163.

84. Hoare, *Noël Coward*, 384.

85. Barr, "You Have to Hock Your House," 164.

86. William P. Halstead, "Broadway Gets an Arena Stage," *Educational Theatre Journal* 2.3 (October 1950): 235–38.

87. Brooks Atkinson, "At the Theatre; Shaw's 'Arms and the Man' Acted with Francis Lederer and Sam Wanamaker," *New York Times*, 20 October 1950, 34.

88. Otis L. Guernsey Jr., "The Coating Melts," *New York Herald Tribune*, 20 October 1950.

89. Robert Coleman, "'Arms and the Man' Still Highly Amusing Satire," *Daily Mirror*, 20 October 1950.

90. Program, "Design for Living," 23 January 1951, Richard Barr–Clinton Wilder Papers, Series IX: Scrapbooks, 1945–1981, box 41, scrapbook, 1949–1954.

91. Shane, "Plays Out of Town: Woman with Red Hair," *Variety*, undated, Richard Barr–Clinton Wilder Papers, Series IX: Scrapbooks, 1945–1981, box 41, scrapbook, 1949–1954.

92. Claudia Cassidy, "'The Tempest,' Ferrier's Song Cycle, Cantelli, Stern, Others," *Chicago Tribune*, 6 February 1951.

93. "'Tempest' Comes Off in Special Disk Version," undated clipping, Richard Barr–Clinton Wilder Papers, Series IX: Scrapbooks, 1945–1981, box 41, scrapbook, 1949–1954; Barr, "You Have to Hock Your House," 163.

94. Barr, "You Have to Hock Your House," 168.

5. Broadway Beginnings: Ethel Waters, Ruth Draper, and Theatrical Collage

1. Ethel Waters, "Ethel Waters to Re-create Great Songs of Her Career," *New York Herald Tribune*, 20 September 1953, sec. 4, 1.

2. Woll, *Dictionary of the Black Theatre*, 10–11.

3. Brooks Atkinson, "At the Theatre; 'At Home with Ethel Waters' Is a One-Woman Show of Song Numbers," *New York Times*, 23 September 1953, 36.

4. Water F. Kerr, "At Home with Ethel Waters," *New York Herald Tribune*, 23 September 1953, 22.

5. Barr, "You Have to Hock Your House," 168–69 (all references to this unpublished memoir are from the private Edward Albee Theatre Collection).

6. Susan Mulcahy, "Twilight of Miraculous Life," drapermonologues.com, http://www.drapermonologues.com/biography.html#miraculous (accessed 26 November 2008).

7. Warren, *Letters of Ruth Draper*, 313.

8. Brooks Atkinson, "Ruth Draper Announces This Visit as Her Farewell New York Engagement," *New York Times*, 26 January 1954.

9. Warren, *Letters of Ruth Draper*, 313; Barr, "You Have to Hock Your House," 169.

10. Warren, *Letters of Ruth Draper*, 313.

11. J. P. S., "The Theatre: Fry Drama; 'The Boy with a Cart' Presented at Church," *New York Times*, 5 April 1954, 19.

12. J. P. Shanley, "Hit Play in a Broadway Chapel," *New York Times*, 25 April 1954, X1.

13. Sydney J. Harris, "Salt Creek Play Moving—At Times," *Chicago Daily News*, 30 June 1954.

14. "New Play Is Tested," undated clipping, Richard Barr–Clinton Wilder Papers, Series IX: Scrapbooks, 1945–1981, box 41, scrapbook, 1949–1954.

15. "New Musical Tent," undated clipping, ibid.

16. A. G., "Theatre: The Drapers," *New York Times*, 27 December 1954; Barr, "You Have to Hock Your House," 168–70.

17. Warren, *Letters of Ruth Draper*, 323.

18. Susan Mulcahy, "The RCA Recordings," drapermonologues.com, http://www.drapermonologues.com/recordings.html (accessed 2 December 2008).

19. Warren, *Letters of Ruth Draper*, 323.

20. Barr, "You Have to Hock Your House," 170.

21. Mulcahy, "The RCA Recordings."

22. "Ruth Draper, 72, Monologuist, Dies," *New York Times*, 31 December 1956, 13.

23. Barr, "You Have to Hock Your House," 171.

24. Spoto, *Kindness of Strangers*, 197.

25. Barr, "You Have To Hock Your House," 173.

26. "Trouble in Tahiti," *The Concise Oxford Dictionary of Music*, by Michael Kennedy and Joyce Bourne (Oxford University Press, 2007), Oxford Reference Online, http://www.oxfordreference.com/views/ENTRY.html?subview=Main&entry=t76.e9285 (accessed 3 December 2008).

27. John Chapman, "'All in One' a Stimulating Little Evening of Music, Drama, Dance," *Daily News*, 20 April 1955.

28. Brooks Atkinson, "Theatre: 'Trouble in Tahiti,' Draper, '27 Wagons,'" *New York Times*, 20 April 1955; Walter F. Kerr, "'All in One,'" *New York Herald Tribune*, 20 April 1955.

29. Richard Watts Jr., "A Drama, an Opera, and a Dancer," *New York Post*, 20 April 1955.

30. Kerr, "'All in One.'"

31. Atkinson, "Theatre: 'Trouble in Tahiti,' Draper, '27 Wagons'"; Kerr, "'All in One.'"

32. Barr, "You Have to Hock Your House," 173; Lewis Funke, "Rialto Gossip: 'All in One' Sponsors Work for Future Editions—Other Items," *New York Times*, 8 May 1955.

33. Lewis Funke, "Theatre: Satire on the Middle Class," *New York Times*, 25 April 1955.

34. Barr, "You Have to Hock Your House," 175; "Summer Theatres," brochure (Berkeley: University of California, 1957), 18.

35. Barr, "You Have to Hock Your House," 176.

36. Walter F. Kerr, "'Fallen Angels,'" *New York Herald Tribune*, 18 January 1956.

37. Brooks Atkinson, "Theatre: Nancy Walker," *New York Times*, 18 January 1956.

38. Kerr, "'Fallen Angels.'"

39. Qtd. in Barr, "You Have to Hock Your House," 175.

40. Lahr, *Notes on a Cowardly Lion*, 285.

41. Gottfried, *Balancing Act*, 105.

42. Ibid., 106.

43. Edelman and Kupferberg, *Angela Lansbury*, 100.

44. Lahr, *Notes on a Cowardly Lion*, 287.

45. Ibid., 290.

46. Barr, "You Have to Hock Your House," 179.

47. Walter Kerr, "'Hotel Paradiso,'" *New York Herald Tribune*, 12 April 1957.

48. Tom Donnelly, "Lahr Hops into Classic Bedlam," *New York World Telegram*, 12 April 1957.

49. Brooks Atkinson, "The Theatre: Bert Lahr Stars in Farce," *New York Times*, 12 April 1957.

50. Lahr appeared on the cover of *Life* on 13 May 1957 under the title "Bert Lahr as a Bumbling Lover."

51. Lahr, *Notes on a Cowardly Lion*, 291.

52. Vernon Rice, "Curtain Cues: Producers League Rebuilds Road," *New York Post*, 22 February 1954, 20; "11 Producers Unite to Prep Touring Shows," *Show Business*, 22 February 1954, 7.

53. Richard Tyler Jordan, *But Darling, I'm Your Auntie Mame!*, 68.

54. Brian Kellow, *The Bennetts: An Acting Family* (Lexington: University Press of Kentucky, 2004), 378.

55. Barr, "You Have to Hock Your House," 180.

56. Josef Mossman, "'Mame' Wild and Wonderful," *Detroit News*, 18 November 1957; Harlow R. Hoyt, "'Auntie Mame' Role First: Constance Bennett," *Cleveland Plain Dealer*, 3 November 1957; J. Dorsey Callaghan, "'Mame' Sparkles in Riviera Debut," *Detroit Free Press*, 18 November 1957.

57. Barr, "You Have to Hock Your House," 182.

58. Ibid., 183.

6. *The Zoo Story*: Discovering Edward Albee

1. Richard Barr, interview on WCBS-TV, 12 November 1963, Richard Barr–Clinton Wilder Papers, Series I: Administrative Files–Playwrights Unit, 1952–1976, box 2, folder 2.

2. Richard Barr, "You Have to Hock Your House," 184 (all references to this unpublished memoir are from the private Edward Albee Theatre Collection).

3. Ibid., 185.

4. Qtd. in ibid.

5. Ibid.

6. Qtd. in Mervyn Rothstein, "Richard Barr, 71, Stage Producer and Theater League Head, Dies," *New York Times*, 10 January 1989, B7.

7. Barr, "You Have to Hock Your House," 186.

8. Ibid., 187.

9. Brooks Atkinson, "At the Theatre; Tennessee Williams' 'Summer and Smoke' Acted by the Loft Players at Their Circle-in-the-Square," *New York Times*, 25 April 1952, 19.

10. Albert Poland and Bruce Mailman, eds., *The Off, Off Broadway Book* (Indianapolis: Bobbs-Merrill, 1972), xi.

11. Greenburger, *Off-Broadway Experience*, 19.

12. Charles L. Mee Jr., "Off-Broadway: A Limited Engagement: An Interview with Judith R. Marechal," *Tulane Drama Review* 10.1 (Fall 1965): 78–87.

13. Ibid., 78.

14. Barr, "You Have to Hock Your House," 187.

15. Ibid., 189.

16. Ibid., 190.

17. Ibid.

18. Ibid.

19. Gussow, *Edward Albee*, 119.

20. Qtd. in ibid., 120.

21. Albee interview, 12 July 2008.

22. Barr, "You Have to Hock Your House," 191.

23. "Noel Behn, 70, Novelist, Producer and Screenwriter," *New York Times*, 31 July 1998.

24. Barr, "You Have to Hock Your House," 192.

25. Albee interview, 12 July 2008.

26. Barr, "You Have to Hock Your House," 193.

27. Albee interview, 12 July 2008.

28. Katselas interview.

29. Albee interview, 12 July 2008.

30. Edward Albee to Richard Barr, undated note (1971), Richard Barr–Clinton Wilder Papers, Series V: Correspondence, 1950–1986, box 36, folder 11.

31. Richard Barr to David Merrick, 20 November 1959, and Jules Irving to Richard Barr, 7 April 1967, ibid.

32. Louis Calta, "Writer-Producer Critical of Stage; H. B. Lutz Regrets That Off Broadway Is Used as Commercial Medium," *New York Times*, 25 May 1960, 45.

33. H. B. Lutz, "Some Words on *The Connection*," *Village Voice* 4.41 (5 August 1959), 9.

34. Richard Barr to H. B. (Whitey) Lutz, undated (1959), Richard Barr–Clinton Wilder Papers, Series V: Correspondence, 1950–1986, box 36, folder 11.

35. Barr, "You Have to Hock Your House," 197.

36. Ibid.

37. Ibid., 198.

38. Sam Zolotow, "Barr, Lutz Form Production Team," *New York Times*, 16 December 1959.

39. Barr, "You Have to Hock Your House," 198.

40. Ibid.

41. Ibid., 199.

42. Wright interview.

43. Ibid.

44. Barr, "You Have to Hock Your House," 276A.

45. Hoover interview.

46. Barr, "You Have to Hock Your House," 200.

47. Schneider, *Entrances*, 209, 268.

48. Ibid., 268.

49. Ibid., 270.

50. Barr, "You Have to Hock Your House," 200.

51. Schneider, *Entrances*, 272.

52. Ibid., 273.
53. Barr, "You Have to Hock Your House," 201; Schneider, *Entrances*, 273.
54. Schneider, *Entrances*, 274.
55. Barr, "You Have to Hock Your House," 201.
56. Ibid.
57. Ibid., 202.
58. Gussow, *Edward Albee*, 123.
59. Barr, "You Have to Hock Your House," 202.
60. Wright interview; Barr, "You Have to Hock Your House," 202.
61. Katselas interview.
62. Barr, "You Have to Hock Your House," 203.
63. Katselas interview.
64. Ibid.
65. Barr, "You Have to Hock Your House," 203.
66. Ibid., 204.
67. Schneider, *Entrances*, 275.
68. Gussow, *Edward Albee*, 124.
69. Barr, "You Have to Hock Your House," 205.
70. Ibid., 206.
71. Ibid., 205.
72. Qtd. in Jerry Tallmer, "Yes, Virginia, There Is a Richard Barr," *Cavalier*, August 1963, 30.
73. Atlee interview; Tallmer, "Yes, Virginia," 30.
74. Brooks Atkinson, "Theatre: A Double Bill Off Broadway; 'Krapp's Last Tape' and 'Zoo Story' Staged Donald Davis Acts in Play by Beckett," *New York Times*, 15 January 1960, 37; Schneider, *Entrances*, 276.
75. Gussow, *Edward Albee*, 125; Walter Kerr, "*Krapp's Last Tape* and *The Zoo Story*," *New York Herald Tribune*, 15 January 1960.
76. Barr, "You Have to Hock Your House," 206.
77. Atlee interview.
78. Barr, "You Have to Hock Your House," 207.
79. Richard Watts, "Two on the Aisle: *Krapp's Last Tape* and *The Zoo Story*," *New York Post*, 15 January 1960.
80. Atlee interview.
81. Schneider, *Entrances*, 277.
82. Ibid.
83. Ibid.
84. Atlee interview; Barr, "You Have to Hock Your House," 209.
85. Atlee interview.
86. Barr, "You Have to Hock Your House," 209.
87. Richard Barr biography and résumé, Richard Barr–Clinton Wilder Papers, Series IV: Personal Papers, 1974–1982, box 36, folder 1.
88. Qtd. in Tallmer, "Yes, Virginia," 30.
89. Edward Albee to Richard Barr, London, 23 August 1960, Richard Barr-Clinton Wilder Papers, Series V: Correspondence, 1950–1986, box 36, folders 7–8.
90. Ibid.
91. Gussow, *Edward Albee*, 150.

7. Producers at Work: On Broadway, Off-Broadway, and Off-Off-Broadway

1. Little, *Off Broadway*, 222.

2. Barr, "You Have to Hock Your House," 215 (all references to this unpublished memoir are from the private Edward Albee Theatre Collection).

3. Ibid.

4. Sheratsky, "Off-Broadway Theatre," 421.

5. Richard Barr, letter to editor, "In the Drama Mail Bag," *New York Times*, 16 October 1960.

6. Richard Barr, letter to editor, undated, Richard Barr–Clinton Wilder Papers, Series IX: Scrapbooks, 1945–1981, box 42, scrapbook, 1957–1961.

7. Michael Smith, "Richard Barr: Avant-Garde Producer of 'Rear-Guard' Plays," *Village Voice*, 8 February 1962.

8. Henderson Cleaves, "Barr Boos 'Cavalier' Critics," *World Telegram*, undated, Richard Barr–Clinton Wilder Papers, Series IX: Scrapbooks, 1945–1981, box 42, scrapbook, 1957–1961.

9. Arthur Gelb, "Theatre: 3 One-Acters; Plays by Beckett and Albee in ANTA Series," *New York Times*, 26 October 1960, 44.

10. Ibid.

11. This spelling of "theatre" was the only time Barr and Wilder used it in the company's title; in all other years, the spelling was "theater," as in "Theater 1963."

12. Barr, "You Have to Hock Your House," 216.

13. "Barr-Lutz-Brown Seek $13,000 for 'Sudden End'; Off-Broadway Joint Venture," *New York Times*, September 1961.

14. Howard Taubman, "'Sudden End of Anne Cinquefoil' Opens," *New York Times*, 11 January 1961.

15. Cali interview.

16. Gussow, *Edward Albee*, 133.

17. Barr, "You Have to Hock Your House," 218.

18. Gussow, *Edward Albee*, 135.

19. Barr, "You Have to Hock Your House," 217.

20. Gussow, *Edward Albee*, 136.

21. Barr, "You Have to Hock Your House," 221.

22. Jerry Tallmer, "Yes, Virginia, There Is a Richard Barr," *Cavalier*, August 1963, 30.

23. Qtd. in Faye Hammel, "Three for the Play: Theatre '64 Says the Writer Must Be King," *New York Times*, 3 March 1966, 10.

24. Kolin, *Conversations with Edward Albee*, 28.

25. Tallmer, "Yes, Virginia," 29; Little, *Off Broadway*, 223.

26. Barr, "You Have to Hock Your House," 223–24.

27. Sheratsky, "Off-Broadway Theatre," 445.

28. Schneider, *Entrances*, ix.

29. Qtd. in Downer, *American Theatre Today*, 115.

30. Schneider, *Entrances*, 292.

31. Barr, "You Have to Hock Your House," 225.

32. Gussow, *Edward Albee*, 137.

33. Schneider, *Entrances*, 287.

34. Gussow, *Edward Albee*, 142, 143.

35. Ibid., 143.

36. Schneider, *Entrances*, 289.
37. Barr, "You Have to Hock Your House," 226.
38. Schneider, *Entrances*, 288.
39. Barr, "You Have to Hock Your House," 226.
40. Schneider, *Entrances*, 282.
41. Barr, "You Have to Hock Your House," 226.
42. Gussow, *Edward Albee*, 143.
43. Schneider, *Entrances*, 289.
44. Gussow, *Edward Albee*, 142; Esslin, *Theatre of the Absurd*, 302.
45. *Playbill* program, *The American Dream*, 23 January 1961, Richard Barr–Clinton Wilder Papers, Series IX: Scrapbooks, 1945–1981, box 42, scrapbook, 1957–1961.
46. Ibid.
47. Thomas Lask, "Dramatist in a Troubled World," *New York Times*, 22 January 1961.
48. Ibid.
49. Howard Taubman, "The Theatre: Albee's 'The American Dream,'" *New York Times*, 25 January 1961, 28.
50. Richard Watts, "'The American Dream/Bartleby,'" *New York Post*, 25 January 1961.
51. Walter Kerr, "'The American Dream' & 'Bartleby,'" *New York Herald News*, 25 January 1961.
52. Sam Zolotow, "Drama by Albee Will Open Feb. 28; 'Bessie Smith' to Be Part of Double Bill at York Theatre—'Galgenhumor' Planned," *New York* Times, 9 February 1961, 37.
53. Barr, "You Have to Hock Your House," 227.
54. Howard Taubman, "Theatre: Intense Hour; Albee's 'The Death of Bessie Smith' Opens," *New York Times*, 2 March 1961, 19.
55. Richard Watts, "'American Dream' and 'The Death of Bessie Smith,'" *New York Post*, 2 March 1961.
56. Alex Atkinson, "Innocents Off-Broadway," *Holiday* 30 (September 1961): 89–93.
57. Sam Zolotow, "'Gallows Humor' to Open April 18," *New York Times*, 20 March 1961, 32.
58. Brooks Atkinson, "Off Broadway Puts On Play by Talented New Writer," *New York Times*, 21 February 1960, X1.
59. Howard Taubman, "The Theatre: Cutting 'Gallows Humor,'" *New York Times*, 19 April 1961, 35.
60. Barr, "You Have to Hock Your House," 229.
61. Sam Zolotow, "Drama Desk Names Winners of Vernon Rice Awards," *New York Times*, 9 May 1961.
62. Schneider, *Entrances*, 297.
63. Barr, "You Have to Hock Your House," 231.
64. Ibid.
65. Little, *Off Broadway*, 225.
66. Michael Feingold, "Avant-Garde Producer of 'Rear-Guard' Plays," *Village Voice*, 8 February 1962.
67. Barr, "You Have to Hock Your House," 232.
68. Qtd. in Smith, "Richard Barr."
69. Ibid.
70. Richard Barr, interview on WCBS-TV, 12 November 1963, Richard Barr–Clinton Wilder Papers, Series I: Administrative Files–Playwrights Unit, 1952–1976, box 2, folder 2.

71. D. Wilson interview.

72. Doric Wilson, "Everything but the Dates," *Other Stages* 1.12 (March 1979): 7; see also David Carter, *Stonewall: The Riots That Sparked the Gay Revolution* (New York: Macmillan, 2004), 41.

73. Wilson, "Everything but the Dates."

74. D. Wilson interview.

75. Albee interview, 10 August 2009.

76. D. Wilson interview.

77. Foltz interview.

78. Hoover interview, 19 November 1994.

79. Drummond and Johnson interview.

80. Terrence McNally, "In Conversation with Terrence McNally: Edward Albee," *Dramatists Guild Quarterly* 22.2 (Summer 1985): 17.

81. Barbara La Fontaine, "Triple Threat On, Off and Off-Off Broadway," *New York Times Magazine*, 25 February 1968, 46.

82. Megan Terry to Richard Barr, 20 March 1964, and Megan Terry to Edward Parone, 13 January 1964, Richard Barr–Clinton Wilder Papers, Series V: Correspondence, 1960–1969, Playwrights Unit, box 1, folder 2.

83. Jerry Tallmer, "Barr, Wilder Take 5-Year Lease on the Cherry Lane," *New York Post*, 13 August 1962.

84. Ibid.

85. Howard Taubman, "William Hanley Double Bill at Cherry Lane," *New York Times*, 2 October 1962.

86. Taylor, *Private Domain*, 142–43.

87. Barr, "You Have to Hock Your House," 234.

88. Taylor, *Private Domain*, 143.

89. Ibid.; Siegel, *Howling near Heaven*, 22.

90. Gussow, *Edward Albee*, 155.

91. Terrence McNally, "Landmark Symposium: 'Who's Afraid of Virginia Woolf?,'" *Dramatist Guild Quarterly* 19.1 (Spring 1982): 14.

92. Schneider, *Entrances*, 309; McNally, "Landmark Symposium," 14.

93. Schneider, *Entrances*, 309.

94. Wright interview.

95. Gussow, *Edward Albee*, 165.

96. Barr, "You Have to Hock Your House," 236.

97. Ibid., 237.

98. Schneider, *Entrances*, 312.

99. Qtd. in McNally, "Landmark Symposium," 18.

100. Barr, "You Have to Hock Your House," 237.

101. Qtd. in McNally, "Landmark Symposium," 19.

102. Adams, *Lee Strasberg*, 360.

103. Qtd. in Hirsch, *Method to Their Madness*, 270–71.

104. Qtd. in ibid.

105. Barr, "You Have to Hock Your House," 238.

106. Kolin, *Conversations with Edward Albee*, 199.

107. Barr, "You Have to Hock Your House," 239.

108. Schneider, *Entrances*, 312.

109. Qtd. in McNally, "Landmark Symposium," 9.

110. Uta Hagen to Clinton Wilder, 23 November 1961, Grand Hotel in Rome, Richard Barr–Clinton Wilder Papers, Series III: Productions, 1940–1979, box 33, folder 2.

111. Schneider, *Entrances*, 313.

112. Ibid., 313; Albee interview, 10 August 2009; Gussow, *Edward Albee*, 168–69.

113. Qtd. in McNally, "Landmark Symposium," 12.

114. Drummond and Johnson interview.

115. Schneider, *Entrances*, 239.

116. Barr, "You Have to Hock Your House," 240.

117. Qtd. in McNally, "Landmark Symposium," 9.

118. Barr, "You Have to Hock Your House," 249.

119. Qtd. in McNally, "Landmark Symposium," 9.

120. Qtd. in ibid., 10.

121. Gussow, *Edward Albee*, 173; Schneider, *Entrances*, 318.

122. Schneider, *Entrances*, 319.

123. Barr, "You Have to Hock Your House," 241.

124. Ibid.

125. *Who's Afraid of Virginia Woolf?* statement of receipts, disbursements, and expenses, 31 December 1969, Richard Barr–Clinton Wilder Papers, Series III: Productions, 1940–1979, box 33, folder 12.

126. Atkinson, *Broadway*, 267–83; Taubman, *Making of the American Theatre*, 242.

127. Barr, "You Have to Hock Your House," 247.

128. Ibid.

129. Schneider, *Entrances*, 323.

130. McNally, "Landmark Symposium," 10.

131. Schneider, *Entrances*, 326.

132. Barr, "You Have to Hock Your House," 250.

133. Robert Coleman, "The Play 'You'll Love or Loathe,'" *New York Mirror*, 15 October 1962, in *New York Theatre Critics' Reviews* 23.17 (1962): 254.

134. Qtd. in McNally, "Landmark Symposium," 10.

135. John Chapman, "A Play Lies under the Muck in 'Who's Afraid of Virginia Woolf?,'" *Daily News*, 15 October 1962, in *New York Theatre Critics' Reviews* 23.17 (1962): 254.

136. Schneider, *Entrances*, 328; Atlee interview.

137. Walter Kerr, "First Night Report: 'Who's Afraid of Virginia Woolf?,'" *New York Herald Tribune*, 15 October 1962, in *New York Theatre Critics' Reviews* 23.17 (1962): 252.

138. Barr, "You Have to Hock Your House," 251.

139. Billy Rose, undated advertisement, *New York Times*, Richard Barr–Clinton Wilder Papers, Series IX: Scrapbooks, 1945–1981, box 43, scrapbook, 1962–1964.

140. Barr, "You Have to Hock Your House," 252.

141. Cline interview.

142. Barr, "You Have to Hock Your House," 254.

143. Thomas B. Morgan, "Angry Playwright in a Soft Spell," *Life*, May 1967, 98.

144. Frances Herridge, "Edward Albee Turns to Producing," *Variety*, 3 May 1963.

145. Howard Taubman, "'Corruption' Is Offered at the Cherry Lane," *New York Times*, 9 October 1963, 49.

146. Cali interview.

147. See my book *Off-Off-Broadway Explosion*; see also my article "A Paradigm for New Play Development: The Albee-Barr-Wilder Playwrights Unit," *Theatre History Studies* 26 (2006): 31–51.

148. John Keating, "A Producer Should 'Produce,'" *Theatre Arts* (September 1961): X3; Playwrights Unit address list, September 1963, Richard Barr–Clinton Wilder Papers, Series I: Administrative Files–Playwrights Unit, 1952–1976, box 1, folder 9.

149. Keating, "Producer Should Produce," X3.

150. Guare interview.

151. Lawrence Wunderlich, "Playwrights at Cross Purposes," *Works* 1.2 (Winter 1968): 18.

152. Qtd. in Keating, "A Producer Should Produce," X3.

153. Wunderlich, "Playwrights at Cross Purposes," 18.

154. Magyar interview.

155. Qtd. in Smith, "Richard Barr."

156. Phyllis Jane Wagner, "Jean-Claude van Itallie: Political Playwright," *Serif* 9.4 (Winter 1972): 30.

157. Jean Claude van Itallie, "'War' and 'We,'" *Other Stages* 617 (May 1979): 6.

158. Jean Claude van Itallie to Richard Barr, April 1964, Richard Barr–Clinton Wilder Papers, Series I: Administrative Files–Playwrights Unit, 1952–1976, box 1, folder 12.

159. Sam Shepard, "OOB and the Playwright: Two Commentaries," *Works* 1.2 (Winter 1968): 70.

160. Wunderlich, "Playwrights at Cross Purposes," 23–24.

161. Parone interview. See also Vena and Nouryeh, *Drama and Performance*, 877–84.

162. Qtd. in James Hatch, "'Amiri Baraka,' March 30, 1985," *Artist and Influence 1985* (New York: Hatch-Billops Collection, 1985), 12.

163. Ibid., 8.

164. Albee interview, 10 August 2009.

165. Kahn interview.

166. Ibid.

167. Howard Taubman, "Adrienne Kennedy Play Opens at East End," *New York Times*, 15 January 1964, 25.

168. Schneider, *Entrances*, 341.

169. Qtd. in Hatch, "'Amiri Baraka,'" 10.

170. Barr, "You Have to Hock Your House," 277A.

171. Louis Calta, "'Virginia Woolf' to Close May 16: Albee Hit Leaves Broadway after 660 Performances," *New York Times*, 5 May 1964.

172. Clinton Wilder, notes on yellow-lined pad, Richard Barr–Clinton Wilder Papers, Series I: Administrative Files–Playwrights Unit, 1952–1976, box 1, folder 2.

173. Theatre 1965 Playwrights Unit House Rules and General Information, mimeographed flyer, Michael Kasdan Collection.

174. Nash and Nash interview.

175. Edward Albee to Richard Barr, June 1964, Richard Barr–Clinton Wilder Papers, Series V: Correspondence, 1960–1969, Subseries 1: Edward Albee, 1950–1968, box 36, folders 7–8.

176. Richard Barr to Edward Albee, undated, ibid.

177. Edward Albee to Richard Barr, 28 August 1964, ibid.

178. Howard Taubman, "The Giant's Dance," *New York Times*, 17 November 1964, 48.

179. Albee interview, 10 August 2009.

180. Perr interview.

181. Richard Barr to John Gielgud, 2 July 1964, Richard Barr–Clinton Wilder Papers, Series V: Correspondence, 1960–1969, Subseries 1: Edward Albee, 1950–1968, box 36, folders 7–8.

182. Barr, "You Have to Hock Your House," 289.

183. Ibid.

184. Ibid., 291.

185. Mangan, *Sir John Gielgud*, 318.

186. Schneider, *Entrances*, 345.

187. Ibid., 346.

188. Ibid.

189. Magyar interview.

190. Prideaux, "Memoirs," unpublished manuscript, 226.

191. Albee interview, 10 August 2009.

192. Howard Taubman, review of *Tiny Alice*, as performed by Theater 1965, *New York Times*, 30 December 1964, 14.

193. Downer, *American Theatre Today*, 130.

194. "Albee Hurls Tiny Bit of Malice at the Critics," *Herald News*, 23 March 1965, 3C.

195. Barr, "You Have to Hock Your House," 296.

196. Schneider, *Entrances*, 350.

197. Barr, "You Have to Hock Your House," 296.

198. Edward Albee to Richard Barr, undated, Richard Barr–Clinton Wilder Papers, Series I: Administrative Files–Playwrights Unit, 1952–1976, box 1, folder 3.

199. L. Wilson interview.

200. Albert Poland and Bruce Mailman, *The Off Off Broadway Book* (Indianapolis: Bobbs-Merrill, 1972), xvii–xxiii.

201. L. Wilson interview.

202. Leonard Harris, "Trio of 1-Acters at Cherry Lane," *New York World-Telegraph*, 11 February 1965.

203. John Guare, "Guare on Albee: A Figurehead for a Generation of Playwrights," *New Theater Review* 15 (Fall/Winter 1996): 24.

204. John Harrop, "NTQ Checklist No. 3: John Guare," *New Theatre Quarterly* 3.10 (May 1987): 160.

205. Guare interview.

206. Guare, "Guare on Albee," 24.

207. Perr interview.

208. Poland and Mailman, *Off-Off-Broadway Book*, xxxvii.

209. Richard Watts Jr., "Another Pair of New Dramatists," *New York Post*, 26 March 1965; Walter Kerr, "Kerr Reviews 2 New Plays," *New York Herald Tribune*, 26 March 1965.

210. George Oppenheimer, "On Stage: 3rd Part of Theater 1965 Presents 2 Newcomers," *Newsday*, 26 March 1965.

211. Howard Taubman, "Theater: Sardonic 'Do Not Pass Go,'" *New York Times*, 20 April 1965.

212. See in particular Edward Albee, "Where the Action Is, or Notes on the Future," *Sunday Herald Tribune Magazine*, 27 December 1964, 16.

213. Advertisement for Theater 1965 New Playwrights Series, 31 January 1965, Richard Barr–Clinton Wilder Papers, Series I: Administrative Files–Playwrights Unit, 1952–1976, box 2, folder 10.

214. George White, "The First Five Years: 1964–69," Eugene O'Neill Theater Center website, http://www.oneilltheatercenter.org/about/hist2.htm (accessed 2 June 2009).

215. "Albee and Barr Dissect Plays, Playwrights, Critics," *New York Herald Tribune*, 3 October 1963, 10.

216. Ibid., 11.

217. Albee interview, 19 June 1996.

8. Experimenting with Edward: *Malcolm* to *All Over*

1. Lawrence Wunderlich, "Playwrights at Cross Purposes," *Works* 1.2 (Winter 1968): 30–31.

2. Barr, "Twilight for the Great White Way?," 36–37.

3. Theater 1967 budget, Richard Barr–Clinton Wilder Papers, Series I: Administrative Files–Playwrights Unit, 1952–1976, box 1, folder 9.

4. Hoover interview.

5. Rod Nash and Marcia Merrill Nash interview; Knowlton interview.

6. Barr, "You Have to Hock Your House," 277A (all references to this unpublished memoir are from the private Edward Albee Theatre Collection). For a full exploration of all the plays produced by the Albee-Barr-Wilder Playwrights Unit, see my dissertation: David Allison Crespy, "Albarwild's Nexus of New Play Development: The Playwrights Unit, 1963 to 1971," City University of New York, 1998.

7. Gurney interview.

8. Barr, "You Have to Hock Your House," 280.

9. Cline interview.

10. Barr, "You Have to Hock Your House," 300.

11. Cali interview.

12. Schneider, *Entrances*, 373.

13. Barr, "You Have to Hock Your House," 301.

14. Gussow, *Edward Albee*, 249.

15. Schneider, *Entrances*, 373.

16. Richard Watts, "Edward Albee Has a Catastrophe," *New York Post*, 12 January 1966; Stanley Kauffmann, "Theater: Edward Albee's 'Malcolm,'" *New York Times*, 12 January 1966.

17. Prideaux, "Memoirs," unpublished manuscript, 223.

18. Sam Zolotow, "Playwrights' Unit Receives Subsidy for Staging," *New York Times*, 1 June 1968.

19. Barr, "You Have to Hock Your House," 281.

20. J. Kellum Smith Jr. to Edward Albee, 25 May 1966, Richard Barr–Clinton Wilder Papers, Series I: Administrative Files–Playwrights Unit, 1952–1976, box 1, folder 8 (Rockefeller Foundation correspondence).

21. The theatre space known as The Playwrights Unit eventually moved to an East Fourth Street location, so subsequent references to the Playwrights Unit are to the workshop/company, not to the physical theatre space.

22. Wunderlich, "Playwrights at Cross Purposes," 33–34.

23. Schneider, *Entrances*, 234–33.

24. Dan Sullivan, "Theater: Wilder Is Given," *New York Times*, 7 September 1966, 53.
25. Barr, "You Have to Hock Your House," 286.
26. Prideaux, "Memoirs," 223.
27. Barr, "You Have to Hock Your House," 287.
28. Zindel interview.
29. Barr, "You Have to Hock Your House," 268.
30. Howard Thompson, "Albee's 'A Delicate Balance' Goes into Rehearsal," *New York Times*, 16 August 1966, 35.
31. Barr, "You Have to Hock Your House," 303.
32. Walter Kerr, "The Theater: Albee's 'A Delicate Balance' at the Martin Beck," *New York Times*, 23 September 1966, 44.
33. Richard Watts, "Two on the Aisle: Good News from Edward Albee," *New York Post*, 23 September 1966, in *New York Theatre Critics' Reviews* 27.10 (1966): 295.
34. Schneider, *Entrances*, 377.
35. Barr, "You Have to Hock Your House," 303.
36. Ibid., 287.
37. Cline interview.
38. Walter Kerr, "Night of the Dunce," *New York Times*, 29 December 1966, 21.
39. Kahn interview.
40. Barr, "You Have to Hock Your House," 284.
41. Dan Sullivan, "Theater: 'The Rimers of Eldritch' at Cherry Lane," *New York Times*, 21 February 1967.
42. L. Wilson interview.
43. For this production, Richard Barr, Clinton Wilder, and Charles Woodward Jr. were the producers, since Albee was preparing his adaptation of *Everything in the Garden* and was unavailable to participate.
44. Clive Barnes, "'Johnny No-Trump' in Premiere at Cort," *New York Times*, 9 October 1967.
45. Stasio, *Broadway's Beautiful Losers*, 408.
46. Barr, "You Have to Hock Your House," 318.
47. Ibid., 319.
48. D. Brown, *Shoptalk*, 87.
49. Prideaux, "Memoirs," 280.
50. Ibid.
51. Stasio, *Broadway's Beautiful Losers*, 422–25.
52. Prideaux, "Memoirs," 278.
53. Ibid.
54. Barr, "You Have to Hock Your House," 305.
55. Clive Barnes, "The Theater: 'Everything in the Garden' Arrives," *New York Times*, 30 November 1967, 60.
56. Goldman, *The Season*, 234–35.
57. Ibid., 240.
58. Barbara Fontaine, "Triple Threat On, Off and Off-Off Broadway," *New York Times Magazine*, 25 February 1968, 30–31.
59. "Wilder Withdraws as Albee Partner," *New York Times*, 6 March 1968, 34L.
60. Barr, "You Have to Hock Your House," 311.
61. Cali interview; Foltz interview; Plaxen interview.

62. Barr, "You Have to Hock Your House," 320.

63. Albee interview, 10 August 2009.

64. Ibid.

65. Bernstein, *Cast Out*, 186.

66. For a deeper exploration of this subject, please see my essay "Inconspicuous Osmosis and the Plasticity of Doing: The Influence of Tennessee Williams on the Plays of Edward Albee," in *The Influence of Tennessee Williams:* Essays *on Fifteen American Playwrights*, edited by Philip C. Kolin, 216–20 (Jefferson, N.C.: McFarland, 2007).

67. Barr, "You Have to Hock Your House," 322.

68. Tony Kushner interview, in *The Boys in the Band*, directed by William Friedkin (1970; New York: CBS Home Entertainment, 2008), DVD; Barr, "You Have to Hock Your House," 320.

69. Michael R. Schiavi, "Teaching the 'Boys': Mart Crowley in the Millennial Classroom," *Modern Language Studies* 31.2 (2001): 75–90; D. Wilson interview.

70. Barr, "You Have to Hock Your House," 320.

71. Cline interview. See also Barr, "You Have to Hock Your House," 316.

72. Barr, "You Have to Hock Your House," 316.

73. Stanley Kauffmann, "Homosexual Drama and Its Disguises," *New York Times*, 23 January 1966, 93.

74. Kaiser, *Gay Metropolis*, 195.

75. Barr, "You Have to Hock Your House," 320.

76. Crowley interview, 27 February 2009.

77. Barr, "You Have to Hock Your House," 320.

78. Albee interview, 10 August 2009.

79. Crowley interview, 19 February 1995.

80. Wendell Ricketts, "Talking Truth: *Boys in the Band* Author Mart Crowley on His 'Gorgeous Little Monster,'" *Bay Area Reporter*, 8 February 1990, 35.

81. Barr, "You Have to Hock Your House," 321.

82. Luckinbill interview, 2 February 2009.

83. Charles Gnys to Ruth Mayleas, 6 February 1968, Richard Barr–Clinton Wilder Papers, Series I: Administrative Files–Playwrights Unit, 1952–1976, box 1, folder 8 (Rockefeller Foundation correspondence).

84. Crowley interview, 27 February 2009.

85. White interview.

86. Ibid.

87. Judy Klemesrud, "You Don't Have to Be One to Play One," *New York Times*, 16 January 1969, D1, 3; David Ragan, "For Many, the Party's Over; 'The Boys in the Band,'" *New York Times*, 21 November 1993, H4.

88. Harold Clurman, "Comedy about Tragedy," *New York Magazine* 1.5 (6 August 1968): 52.

89. Cali interview.

90. David Rothenberg, "The Boys in *The Boys in the Band*," *Center Stage* (a publication of the Gay and Lesbian Community Services Center, New York City), April 1989.

91. Barr, "You Have to Hock Your House," 154.

92. Edward Albee to author, electronic mail message, 26 November 2010.

93. Prideaux, "Memoirs," 286.

94. Charles Gnys to Ruth Mayleas.

95. Sam Zolotow, "Producing Team Plans Repertory: Albee, Barr and Wilder List 6-Week Season Here," *New York Times*, 5 September 1967.

96. Sam Zolotow, "Repertory Rises Again," *New York Times*, 1 October 1967.

97. Ibid.

98. Ibid.

99. Sam Zolotow, "Play Plan Grows into Arts Center," *New York Times*, 16 January 1968, 25.

100. Ibid.

101. Ibid.

102. Sam Zolotow, "Albee Will Open Repertory House," *New York Times*, 5 August 1968.

103. Sam Zolotow, "Repertory Group Chooses 7 Plays," *New York Times*, August 28, 1967.

104. Clive Barnes, "Theater: Albee's Adventurous Plays," *New York Times*, 1 October 1968, 39.

105. Clive Barnes, "The Theater: 'Krapp's Last Tape' and 'Zoo Story,'" *New York Times*, 11 October 1968.

106. Qtd. in Sam Zolotow, "5 Play Closings Announced in Day," *New York Times*, 15 October 1968.

107. Richard Barr to Norman Lloyd, 30 October 1968, Richard Barr–Clinton Wilder Papers, Series I: Administrative Files–Playwrights Unit, 1952–1976, box 1, folder 8 (Rockefeller Foundation correspondence).

108. Sam Zolotow, "Producer Closes 'The Cuban Thing,'" *New York Times*, 26 September 1968.

109. Sam Zolotow, "'Front Page' Here as Benefit in May," *New York Times*, 8 January 1969.

110. "Playwrights Unit Purchases a Home on the East Side," *New York Times*, 27 February 1969.

111. Zolotow, "'Front Page' Here as Benefit in May."

112. Clive Barnes, review of *The Front Page* as produced by Theater 1969 on Broadway, *New York Times*, 12 May 1969, 54.

113. Clive Barnes, "Theater: A Double Bill with Promise," *New York Times*, 22 January 1970.

114. Mel Gussow, "Playwrights Unit Lifts Curtain on Success," *New York Times*, 4 February 1970.

115. Richard Barr to Chuck Gnys, 4 June 1970, Richard Barr–Clinton Wilder Papers, Series I: Administrative Files–Playwrights Unit, 1952–1976, box 1, folder 3.

116. Mel Gussow, "Playwrights Unit Lifts Curtain on Success"; Albee interview, 10 August 2009.

117. Bishop, *Plays from Playwrights Horizons*, 331–36.

118. Bruce Hoover and Robert Moss to the Playwrights Unit audience, 14 December 1970, Playwrights Unit, clippings folder.

119. Enid Nemy, "'Non-social' Party Aids Playwrights Unit," *New York Times*, 29 March 1971.

120. Cohen interview.

121. Moss, Hoover, and Pressman interview.

122. Clive Barnes, review of Edward Albee's *All Over*, presented by Theater 1971 at the Martin Beck Theatre, *New York Times*, 29 March 1971, 41.

123. Walter Kerr, "Albee's 'All Over'—The Living Are Dead, Too," *New York Times*, 4 April 1971, 11.

124. Barr, "You Have to Hock Your House," 331.

125. Moss interview.

126. Qtd. in Guy Flatley, "Edward Albee Fights Back," *New York Times*, 18 April 1971, D1.

127. Qtd. in ibid.

128. Qtd. in ibid., D10.

129. Patricia Bosworth, "Will They All Be Albees?" *New York Times*, 18 July 1971, D1.

9. Hocking the House: *Seascape* to *Sweeney Todd*

1. Qtd. in Phyllis Stewart, "Albee Directs on LI: Joins Barr at John Drew Theater," *Long Island Press*, 9 July 1972, 14.

2. The name of what is now called the Broadway League changed over the course of several years. It began in 1930 as the League of New York Theatres; in 1973, the name changed to the League of New York Theatres and Producers; in 1985, it became the League of American Theatres and Producers; and in 2007, it became the Broadway League.

3. Barr, "You Have to Hock Your House," 329 (all references to this unpublished memoir are from the private Edward Albee Theatre Collection).

4. Ibid., 334.

5. Clive Barnes, "Stage: 'Drat!,' Musical by Fred Bluth; Melodrama Arrives at McAlpin Rooftop," *New York Times*, 19 October 1971, 53.

6. Davis, *Party of the Century*, 39–40.

7. Robert Wilder Blue, "Kenward Elmslie's World," US Opera Web, 2002, http://www.usoperaweb.com/2002/december/elmslie.htm (accessed 28 January 2009).

8. Thacker interview.

9. Blue, "Kenward Elmslie's World."

10. Thacker interview.

11. Ibid.

12. Ibid.

13. Ibid.

14. Barr, "You Have to Hock Your House," 334. Director Ellis Rabb was known for his brilliant repertory work with his Association of Producing Artists.

15. Thacker interview.

16. Martin Gottfried, "Theatre: 'The Grass Harp,'" *Women's Wear Daily*, 4 November 1971, in *New York Theatre Critics' Reviews* 32.18 (1971): 197.

17. Richard Watts, "Theater: The People Up the Tree," *New York Post*, 3 November 1971, in *New York Theatre Critics' Reviews* 32.18 (1971): 196.

18. Barr, "You Have to Hock Your House," 334.

19. Mandelbaum, *Not Since "Carrie,"* 306.

20. Barr, "You Have to Hock Your House," 336.

21. Anderman interview.

22. Barr, "You Have to Hock Your House," 336.

23. Anderman interview.

24. Barr, "You Have to Hock Your House," 337.

25. Douglas Watt, "Julie Harris Rallies to Win in the 2nd Half," *Daily News*, 13 December 1972, in *New York Theatre Critics' Reviews* 33.24 (1971): 140.

26. Martin Gottfried, "Theatre: 'The Last of Mrs. Lincoln,'" *Women's Wear Daily*, 14 December 1972, in *New York Theatre Critics' Reviews* 33.24 (1971): 141.
27. Barr, "You Have to Hock Your House," 339.
28. Kennedy, *No Pickle No Performance*, 13–21.
29. Ibid., 21.
30. Matalon interview.
31. Ibid.
32. Barr, "You Have to Hock Your House," 273; Albee interview, 10 August 2009.
33. Clive Barnes, "Stage: Hume Cronyn Dances through 'Coward in Two Keys,'" *New York Times*, 1 March 1974, 18.
34. Richard Watts, "'Noel Coward in Two Keys,'" *New York Post*, 1 March 1974, in *New York Theatre Critics' Reviews* 35.6 (1974): 356; Martin Gottfried, "'Noel Coward in Two Keys,'" *New York Theatre Critics' Reviews* 35.6 (1974): 357.
35. Barr, "You Have to Hock Your House," 338.
36. Gussow, *Edward Albee*, 305.
37. Anderman interview.
38. "Grim Butley Script Baffles Audience," *Miami Herald*, 3 May 1973, 12B.
39. Barr, "You Have to Hock Your House," 338.
40. Mel Gussow, "Recalling Evolution of 'Seascape' Play, Albee Sees Tale Not of Lizard, but of Life," *New York Times*, 21 January 1975.
41. Gussow, *Edward Albee*, 302–5.
42. Barr, "You Have to Hock Your House," 339.
43. Ibid., 342.
44. Ibid.
45. Ibid., 340.
46. Anderman interview.
47. Gussow, *Edward Albee*, 291.
48. Barr, "You Have to Hock Your House," 341.
49. Anderman interview.
50. Ibid.
51. Gussow, *Edward Albee*, 293.
52. Martin Gottfried, "Edward Albee's Latest," *New York Post*, 27 January 1975, in *New York Theatre Critics' Reviews* 36.2 (1975): 369.
53. Clive Barnes, "Albee's 'Seascape' Is a Major Event," *New York Times*, 27 January 1975, in *New York Theatre Critics' Reviews* 36.2 (1975): 368.
54. Barr, "You Have to Hock Your House," 342.
55. Kevin Sanders, "Seascape," WABC-TV, 26 January 1975, in *New York Theatre Critics' Reviews* 36.2 (1975): 373.
56. Barr, "You Have to Hock Your House, 343.
57. Ibid.
58. Anderman interview.
59. Kirkwood, *P.S. Your Cat Is Dead*, 9.
60. Hamill interview.
61. Musante interview.
62. Ibid.
63. Ibid.
64. Ibid.

65. Clive Barnes, "Stage: 'P.S. Your Cat Is Dead!' Is Raunchily Funny; Kirkwood Uses Farce for Serious Purpose but You Are Advised Not to Take Aunt," *New York Times*, 8 April 1975, 31.

66. Ibid.

67. Martin Gottfried, "Theater: Going His Way," *New York Post*, 8 April 1975, in *New York Theatre Critics' Reviews* 36.9 (1975): 279.

68. Douglas Watt, "Love Climbs in the Window," *Daily News*, 8 April 1975, in *New York Theatre Critics' Reviews* 36.9 (1975): 278; Gottfried, "Theater: Going His Way."

69. Hamill interview.

70. Barr, "You Have to Hock Your House," 345.

71. John Corry, "Broadway; 'P.S. Your Cat Is Dead!' Is Getting Another Life," *New York Times*, 13 January 1978, C2.

72. The seven shows he considered "flops" were *All Over, Drat!, The Grass Harp, The Last of Mrs. Lincoln, Noël Coward in Two Keys, Seascape*, and *P.S. Your Cat Is Dead.*

73. William Harris, "Off and On," *Soho Weekly News*, 19 May 1977, 64; Barr, "You Have to Hock Your House," 381.

74. Barr, "You Have to Hock Your House," 381.

75. Clive Barnes, "'Patio' Is Staged at Cherry Lane; One Must Suspend All Disbelief," *New York Times*, 23 May 1977, 20.

76. Harris, "Off and On."

77. Qtd. in Secrest, *Stephen Sondheim*, 289.

78. Gerould, *Melodrama*, 47.

79. Ilson, *Harold Prince*, 281–82.

80. Qtd. in Gordon, *Art Isn't Easy*, 210.

81. Barr, "You Have to Hock Your House," 8; Secrest, *Stephen Sondheim*, 290.

82. Robert Berkvist, "Stephen Sondheim Takes a Stab at Grand Guignol," *New York Times*, 25 February 1979, D1; Barr, "You Have to Hock Your House," 8.

83. Ilson, *Harold Prince*, 283.

84. Qtd. in Zadan, *Sondheim & Co.*, 245.

85. Barr, "You Have to Hock Your House," 9.

86. John Corry, "Broadway; Ustinov Gains 'Lear' Role Off Shubert Alley Via 'Audition' at Allen's Alley," *New York Times*, 30 April 1976, 54.

87. Barr, "You Have to Hock Your House," 12.

88. John S. Wilson, "The Composer Turns SoHo Cabaret Performer in 'Broadway at the Ballroom' Series," *New York Times*, 8 October 1976, 58.

89. Zadan, *Sondheim & Co.*, 246.

90. Ibid.

91. Barr, "You Have to Hock Your House," 11.

92. Mel Gussow, "'Sweeney Todd': A Little Nightmare Music; Revenge Possesses," *New York Times*, 1 February 1979, C15; Barr, "You Have to Hock Your House," 12.

93. Ilson, *Harold Prince*, 291; Barr, "You Have to Hock Your House," 12.

94. Richard F. Shepard, "Committee to Seek Beaumont Troupe; A General Overseer Box-Office Support Unions 'Willing to Cooperate' 'A Flexible Theater,'" *New York Times*, 20 June 1978, C3; Ilson, *Harold Prince*, 291.

95. Barr, "You Have to Hock Your House," 13.

96. Ibid.

97. Secrest, *Stephen Sondheim*, 299.

98. Undated advertisement, *New York Times*, Richard Barr–Clinton Wilder Papers, Series IX: Scrapbooks, 1945–1981, box 50, scrapbook, 20 September 1978–4 June 1979.

99. "It Pays to Advertise for Legit Angels: Time Ad Brings 'Sweeney' 225G," *Variety*, 20 September 1975, 103; Barr, "You Have to Hock Your House," 15.

100. Zadan, *Sondheim & Co.*, 252.

101. Barr, "You Have to Hock Your House," 16.

102. Ibid.

103. Ibid., 17.

104. John Corry, "Broadway: Angela Lansbury to Come Back Singing Next Fall," *New York Times*, 23 December 1977, 46.

105. Ilson, *Harold Prince*, 291; Barr, "You Have to Hock Your House," 17.

106. Barr, "You Have to Hock Your House," 19.

107. Ibid.

108. Ibid., 20.

109. "Article 3—No Title; Musical, 'Sweeney Todd,' Due on Broadway Feb. 19," *New York Times*, 16 November 1978, C24.

110. Barr, "You Have to Hock Your House," 20.

111. Gussow, "'Sweeney Todd.'"

112. Qtd. in Secrest, *Stephen Sondheim*, 299.

113. Ilson, *Harold Prince*, 292.

114. Qtd. in Secrest, *Stephen Sondheim*, 300.

115. Ilson, *Harold Prince*, 293; Secrest, *Stephen Sondheim*, 296–97; Zadan, *Sondheim & Co.*, 256.

116. Barr, "You Have to Hock Your House," 22.

117. Ibid., 21.

118. Secrest, *Stephen Sondheim*, 299.

119. Ibid.

120. Barr, "You Have to Hock Your House," 24.

121. Ibid., 22.

122. Ibid., 23.

123. Ibid., 24.

124. Ibid., 25.

125. Ibid., 26.

126. Ibid., 25.

127. Richard Eder, "Stage: Introducing 'Sweeney Todd,'" *New York Times*, 2 March 1979, in *New York Theatre Critics' Reviews* 40.1 (1979): 350.

128. Ibid.

129. Clive Barnes, "Sondheim's 'Sweeney Todd' Is a Bloody Good Musical," *New York Post*, 2 March 1979, in *New York Theatre Critics' Reviews* 40.1 (1979): 351–52.

130. Ibid.

131. Howard Kissel, "'Sweeney Todd,'" *Women's Wear Daily*, 2 March 1979, in *New York Theatre Critics' Reviews* 40.1 (1979): 352–53.

132. Walter Kerr, "Stage View; Is 'Sweeney' on Target?," *New York Times*, 11 March 1979, D1.

133. Barr, "You Have to Hock Your House," 26.

134. James Fenton, "The Barberous Crimes of Sondheim and Prince," *Sunday Times* (London), 6 July 1980, 40.

135. Carol Lawson, "Broadway," *New York Times*, 18 January 1980, C2.

136. Carol Lawson, "Broadway; 'Fifth of July,' More on the Talley Family, Is Due in Early Fall," *New York Times*, 2 May 1980, C2.

137. Qtd. in Barr, "You Have to Hock Your House," 29.

138. The bank's vice president, Peter MacDonell, was Woodward's close friend.

139. Barr, "You Have to Hock Your House," 30.

140. Qtd. in Barr, "You Have to Hock Your House," 31.

141. Robert Kivelson, "'Now That I'm a Hot-Shot Angel . . . ,'" *New York Times*, 13 July 1980, D3; Richard Barr, "Mailbag: The Business of Being a Broadway Angel," *New York Times*, 10 August 1980, D4.

142. Barr, "You Have to Hock Your House," 354.

143. Ibid., 347; Maxwell Perkins, the famous editor for Charles Scribner's Sons, edited the works of Ernest Hemingway, F. Scott Fitzgerald, and Thomas Woolf and famously convinced a resistant Woolf to cut his massive manuscripts for such books as *Look Homeward, Angel* and *Of Time and the River.*

144. Robert Berkvist, "Albee Returns to the Living Room Wars," *New York Times*, 27 January 1980, D1; Mel Gussow, "Albee Prepares Play in 'Woolf' Mold,'" *New York Times*, 23 May 1978, C1.

145. Gussow, *Edward Albee*, 315.

146. Horn, *Edward Albee*, 47.

147. Berkvist, "Albee Returns to the Living Room Wars."

148. Barr, "You Have to Hock Your House," 349.

149. Ibid., 350.

150. Berkvist, "Albee Returns to the Living Room Wars."

151. Gussow, *Edward Albee*, 312.

152. Barr, "You Have to Hock Your House," 351.

153. Gussow, *Edward Albee*, 311.

154. Barr, "You Have to Hock Your House," 352.

155. Carol Lawson, "Albee's Play Delayed," *New York Times*, 19 December 1979, C23.

156. Anderman interview.

157. Ibid.

158. Musante interview.

159. Walter Kerr, "Stage: Albee's 'Lady from Dubuque,'" *New York Times*, 1 February 1980, in *New York Theatre Critics' Reviews* 41.1 (1980): 384.

160. Howard Kissel, "'The Lady from Dubuque,'" *Women's Wear Daily*, 1 February 1980, in *New York Theatre Critics' Reviews* 41.1 (1980): 386.

161. Gussow, *Edward Albee*, 314.

162. Musante interview.

163. Kerr, "Stage: Albee's 'Lady from Dubuque.'"

10. Brightening Broadway's Lights: Barr's Legacy to the American Theatre

1. Alvin Klein, "Scintillating Coward at the Paper Mill," *New York Times*, 27 March 1983.

2. Barr, "You Have to Hock Your House," 375 (all references to this unpublished memoir are from the private Edward Albee Theatre Collection).

3. Bixler interview.

4. Gussow, *Edward Albee*, 328.

5. Enid Nemy, "It's How We Got Where We Are," *New York Times,* 30 December 1984.

6. Ibid.

7. Ibid.

8. Barr, "You Have to Hock Your House," 355.

9. Ibid., 356.

10. Bixler interview.

11. Barr, "You Have to Hock Your House," 357.

12. Ibid.

13. Ibid., 358.

14. Bixler interview.

15. Bason interview.

16. Carol Lawson, "Broadway; Royal Shakespeare to Open 'All's Well' at Martin Beck," *New York Times,* 4 February 1983.

17. Bixler interview.

18. Ibid.

19. Barr, "You Have to Hock Your House," 360.

20. Mel Gussow, "Broadway Tryouts in the West End," *New York Times,* 20 August 1985.

21. Barr, "You Have to Hock Your House," 360–61; Gussow, "Broadway Tryouts in the West End."

22. Frank Rich, "Stage: Three by Pinter," *New York Times,* 18 April 1984.

23. Barr, "You Have to Hock Your House," 364.

24. Mel Gussow, "Alan Schneider, Pioneering Director, Is Dead," *New York Times,* 4 May 1984; Kenneth S. Brecher, "Samuel Beckett: Private in Public," *New York Times,* 12 June 1988.

25. Barr, "You Have to Hock Your House," 365–66.

26. Ibid., 366.

27. Irving Wardle, "Theatre: *The War at Home*—Hampstead," *London Times,* 14 June 1984, 8; other newspapers qtd. in Barr, "You Have to Hock Your House," 367–68

28. Gussow, "Broadway Tryouts in the West End."

29. Bixler interview.

30. Ibid.

31. Frank Rich, "Stage: Carroll O'Connor Is Star in 'Brothers,'" *New York Times,* 10 November 1983; Leslie Bennetts, "Can Carroll O'Connor Shake Off Archie Bunker?," *New York Times,* 6 November 1983; O'Connor, *I Think I'm Outta Here,* 236.

32. Barr, "You Have to Hock Your House," 371.

33. Ibid., 372.

34. Frank Rich, "Stage: Family Strife in 'Home Front,'" *New York Times,* 3 January 1985.

35. Richard Corliss, "A Ghost Sonata in Sitcom Land Home Front," *Time,* 3 January 1985.

36. Douglas Watt, "A First-Rate Play," *Daily News,* 3 January 1985, in *New York Theatre Critics' Reviews* 46.1 (1985): 396.

37. Walter Kerr, "Stage View; Taking Comedy Seriously," *New York Times,* 27 January 1985.

38. Mel Gussow, "Protagonists Who Substitute Self-Pity for Courage," *New York Times,* 13 January 1985.

39. Barr, "You Have to Hock Your House," 373.

40. Bixler interview.

41. Ibid.

42. The Broadway League website, http://www.broadwayleague.com/index.php (accessed 16 March 2009).

43. Samuel G. Freedman, "Harold Prince Quits Theater League," *New York Times*, 7 June 1985, C3.

44. Sam Zolotow, "Living Theater Due Back in Fall; Becks Took Troupe Abroad after 1964 Tax Trouble," *New York Times*, 10 February 1967, 27.

45. Barr, "You Have to Hock Your House," 391.

46. Campbell Robertson, "Broadway, the Land of the Long-Running Sure Thing," *New York Times*, 10 September 2006.

47. Sam Zolotow, "Equity Will Meet on Alien Actors; Members to Air Complaint at Special April Meeting," *New York Times*, 14 March 1967, 53.

48. Louis Calta, "Broadway Lists 21 Shows for Fall; 16 Plays, 4 Musicals and 1 Revue to Have Premieres," *New York Times*, 29 July 1967, 13.

49. Milton Esterow, "City Proposes More Theaters to Revitalize Midtown District," *New York Times*, 1 October 1967, 1.

50. Barr, "You Have to Hock Your House," 403.

51. Alex Witchel, "Alexander H. Cohen, Producer of 101 Theatrical Hits and Flops, Dies at 79," *New York Times*, 23 April 2000, 236.

52. Qtd. in Samuel G. Freedman, "Cohen Resigns from Theater League: Producers," *New York Times*, 5 June 1985, C21.

53. Sabinson interview.

54. Ibid.

55. Cheskin interview.

56. Sabinson interview.

57. Schoenfeld interview.

58. Margaret Croyden, "The Box-Office Boom," *New York Times*, 10 May 1981, sec. 6, 27.

59. "1965–66 Stage Year Had, Survey Finds, Profit of $3-Million," *New York Times*, 30 June 1967, 28.

60. Sam Zolotow, "Theater League Urges Discretion; Asks Members Not to Make Weekly Receipts Public," *New York Times*, 20 October 1967, 56.

61. Croyden, "Box-Office Boom."

62. "Barr Again Heads League," *New York Times*, 13 October 1967, 33.

63. "Zone Shift to Aid Theaters Pressed," *New York Times*, 13 October 1967, 6.

64. "Richard Barr Named Head of City Cultural Foundation," *New York Times*, 30 September 1968, 44.

65. Louis Calta, "Business Called Apathetic toward Arts," *New York Times*, 6 May 1969, 40.

66. Harry Gilroy, "Street Signs in Midtown to Direct Theatregoers: Carney and Zoe Caldwell Mount Ladder to Put Up First of 35 Markers," *New York Times*, 27 September 1968, 39.

67. Croyden, "Box-Office Boom."

68. Murray Schumach, "Prostitutes Are Returning to Midtown, but Their Approach Is Less Brazen," *New York Times*, 29 July 1971, 41; McCandlish Phillips, "Peep Shows and Massage Parlors Are Targets in City's Intensified Drive to Clean Up Times Square," *New York Times*, 13 July 1972, 26.

69. Leonard Sloane, "What Keeps Broadway; Behind the Theater Boom," *New York Times*, 11 May 1980, D1; Carol Lawson, "Theater Enjoys Biggest Boom in Years," *New York Times*, 6 February 1981, C4; Croyden, "Box-Office Boom."

70. Richard F. Shepard, "Strike by Actors Closes 19 Shows along Broadway," *New York Times*, 18 June 1968, 1; Robert D. Mcfadden, "9 Broadway Theaters Are Shut as Musicians Begin a Walkout," *New York Times*, 19 September 1975, 77.

71. Louis Calta, "Producers Back Shubert Trustees; Lefkowitz Bars Comment on Plea for Retention," *New York Times*, 7 May 1974, 52.

72. Sabinson interview.

73. Croyden, "Box-Office Boom."

74. Sabinson interview.

75. Cheskin interview.

76. Louis Calta, "League of Theaters Proposes a 'Middle' Contract," *New York Times*, 27 January 1970, 46.

77. George Gent, "Theaters Adopt Pact to Cut Costs and Prices," *New York Times*, 6 January 1971, 28.

78. Louis Calta, "Theaters' Pact on Pay Extended; Barr Says 'Limited Gross' Plan Needs Further Test," *New York Times*, 18 January 1972, 23.

79. Stephen Benedict, "Richard Barr's Key Role in the Creation of TDF," *tdfsightlines* 3.4 (April 1989).

80. Barr, "You Have to Hock Your House," 394.

81. Ibid.

82. Ibid., 395.

83. Ibid., 396.

84. Ibid., 397.

85. Benedict, "Richard Barr's Key Role."

86. Barr, "You Have to Hock Your House," 401.

87. Ibid., 399.

88. Louis Calta, "Half-Price Tickets Will Go on Sale at Times Sq. Unit," *New York Times*, 22 May 1973, 49.

89. Mel Gussow, "TKTS Is a Hit in Duffy Sq.," *New York Times*, 21 May 1976, 61.

90. Barr, "You Have to Hock Your House," 400.

91. Sabinson interview.

92. Eric Pace, "TKTS, in Fifth Year at the Booth, Is Still a Hit," *New York Times*, 22 June 1978, C17.

93. Barr, "You Have to Hock Your House," 400.

94. Leonard Sloane, "What Keeps Broadway Booming Along?" *New York Times*, 11 May 1980, D1.

95. Barr, "You Have to Hock Your House," 404.

96. Leonard Sloane, "Broadway Is Bringing Box Office to Main Street," *New York Times*, 9 June 1972, 49; Croydon, "Box-Office Boom."

97. Croydon, "Box-Office Boom," 27.

98. Little, *After the FACT*, 15.

99. Robert Berkvist, "Why Bring a Show to Broadway at All?," *New York Times*, 4 November 1973, 159.

100. Qtd. in ibid.

101. Richard Barr, "Drama Mailbag: Broadway? Yes, Indeed!" *New York Times*, 2 December 1973, 186.

102. Baumol and Bowen, *Performing Arts*, 112.

103. McCandlish Phillips, "Broadway Curtains Rise at 7:30; Impact Uncertain," *New York Times*, 5 January 1971, 1.

104. "Merrick Breaks the Front on 7:30 Curtain," *New York Times*, 5 September 1971, 1.

105. Barr, "You Have to Hock Your House," 403.

106. Little, *After the FACT*, 20.

107. Ibid., 20–21.

108. Mel Gussow, "Theater Parley Has a Happy Ending; Cry from Audience Suggestion from Barr," *New York Times*, 7 June 1974, 24.

109. Little, *After the FACT*, 24.

110. Rocco Landesman, "A Report on a Free-for-All Called the First Annual Congress of Theater at Princeton," *New York Times*, 16 June 1974, 101.

111. Qtd. in Little, *After the FACT*, 32.

112. Ibid., 47.

113. Landesman, "A Report on a Free-for-All."

114. Qtd. in Little, *After the FACT*, 32.

115. Landesman, "A Report on a Free-for-All."

116. Qtd. in Little, *After the FACT*, 56.

117. Landesman, "A Report on a Free-for-All."

118. Barr, "You Have to Hock Your House," 390.

119. Qtd. in Robin Pogrebin, "Theater for Fun or Profit," *New York Times*, 15 June 2000, E1.

120. "Richard Barr Wins Theater Award," *New York Times*, 25 November 1982, C14; Edward Albee to Anna E. Crouse, 11 June 1981, Richard Barr–Clinton Wilder Papers, Series V: Correspondence, 1980–1989, box 36, folder 10.

121. Edward Albee to Anna E. Crouse.

122. "Richard Barr Wins Theater Award," *New York Times*, 25 November 1982, C14.

123. "History of American Theatre Wing, Overview, The American Theatre Wing during World War II," American Theatre Wing website, http://americantheatrewing.org/about/history_of_atw.php (accessed 26 March 2009).

124. "Tony Award: Our Legacy," Tony Award website, http://www.tonyawards.com/en_US/archive/index.html (accessed 26 March 2009).

125. Cheskin interview.

126. Patricia Bosworth, "The Drama behind the Tony Awards," *New York Times*, 5 June 1977, D1; Cheskin interview.

127. Bosworth, "The Drama behind the Tony Awards."

128. Barr, "You Have to Hock Your House," 407.

129. Bosworth, "The Drama behind the Tony Awards."

130. "Behind the Scenes: How the Voting works," Tony Award website, http://www.tonyawards.com/en_US/about/awards.html (accessed 26 March 2009).

131. Samuel G. Freedman, "Cohen Resigns from Theater League; Producers Criticize Remarks at Tonys," *New York Times*, 5 June 1985, C21.

132. "Don Mischer to Produce '87 Tony Show on CBS," *New York Times*, 10 December 1986, C30.

133. Qtd. in Samuel G. Freedman, "Producers Group Seeks Theater Crisis Solution," *New York Times*, 6 August 1985, C13.

134. Sabinson interview.

135. Enid Nemy, "Broadway: Sunset Boulevard Detours to Gotham in Spring Musical," *New York Times*, 11 July 1986, C2.

136. Staggs, Close-Up on Sunset Boulevard, 319–21.

137. Richard Barr, "In the Theater, Success Still Means Broadway," *New York Times*, 16 July 1988, 26.

138. Bixler interview.

139. Gussow, *Edward Albee*, 351–52.

140. Alvin Klein, "Albee's 'Marriage Play' in East Coast Premiere," *New York Times*, 23 February 1992, NJ16.

141. Jeremy Gerard, "Conference Confronts Theater's Troubled Times," *New York Times*, 11 November 1986, C14.

142. Barr, "In the Theater, Success Still Means Broadway."

143. Bason interview.

144. "Supreme Court of the State of New York, County of New York: Part 49, Gotham Book Mart & Gallery, Inc., Plaintiff, against the New York Public Library, Astor, Lenox and Tilden Foundations and Anthony Constantine," 11 June 1999, http://www.courts.state.ny.us/comdiv/Law%20Report%20Files/January%202000/gotham.html (accessed 1 April 2009). According to Bason, Duff, and Bixler, many other theatre artifacts were also missing from Barr's apartment.

145. Bixler interview.

146. Bason interview.

147. Ibid.

148. Mervyn Rothstein, "Richard Barr, 71, Stage Producer and Theater League Head, Dies," *New York Times*, 10 January 1989, B7.

149. Qtd. in Andrew L. Yarrow, "Richard Barr, a Figure in Theater, Is Recalled at a Sardi's Gathering." *New York Times*, 21 March 1989.

150. Rothstein, "Richard Barr, 71."

151. McCann interview.

152. Ibid.

BIBLIOGRAPHY

Interviews

Albee, Edward F. Interview with author. Tape recording. New York, 19 June 1996.

———. Interview with author. Tape recording. Montauk, N.Y., 12 July 2008.

———. Interview with author. Tape recording. Montauk, N.Y., 10 August 2009.

Anderman, Maureen. Interview with author. Tape recording. Weston, Conn., 2 September 2008.

Anderson, Arthur. Interview with author. Tape recording. New York, 3 September 2008.

Atlee, Howard. Interview with author. Tape recording. Towson, Md., 6 January 2009.

Bason, Clark. Interview with author. Tape recording. Palm Springs, Calif., 4 September 2008.

Beckwith, Tobias. Interview with author. Tape recording. Las Vegas, Nev., 1 October 2008.

Bixler, David. Interview with author. Tape recording. Woodbridge, Conn., 2 November 2008.

Cali, Joseph. Interview with author. Tape recording. New York, 9 March 1997.

Cheskin, Irving. Interview with author. Tape recording. Scarborough, N.Y., 4 October 2008.

Cline, Jerome. Interview with author. Tape recording. Plainview, N.Y., 2 June 1997.

Cohen, Edward M. Interview with author. Tape recording. New York, 3 May 1995.

Crowley, Mart. Telephone conversation with author. Tape recording. Bloomfield, N.J., 19 February 1995.

———. Telephone conversation with author. Tape recording. New York, 27 February 2009.

Drummond, Alice, and Page Johnson. Interview with author. Tape recording. New York, 2 May 1997.

Duff, James. Interview with author. Email correspondence. 1 October 2008.

Feist, Gene. Telephone conversation with author. Tape recording. 14 March 1995.

Fischer, Carol. Interview with author. Tape recording. Washington, D.C., 7 June 2008.

Foltz, Richard. Interview with author. Tape recording. New York, 29 March 1997.

Gagliano, Frank. Telephone conversation with author. Tape recording. 26 June 1995.

Granite, Judith. Interview with author. Tape recording. New York, 14 May 1995.

Guare, John. Interview with author. Tape recording. New York, 28 March 1995.
Gurney, A. R. Interview with author. Tape recording. New York, 3 April 1996.
Hamill, Mary. Interview with author. Tape recording. New York, 5 September 2008.
Hellman, Libby. Interview with author. Tape recording. Northbrook, Ill., 24 August 2008.
Herz, Shirley. Interview with author. Tape recording. New York, 23 April 2009.
Hoover, Bruce. Interview with author. Tape recording. New York, 19 November 1994.
———. Interview with author. Tape recording. New York, 23 September 2008.
Jacobsen, Stephen. Interview with author. Tape recording. New York, 17 April 1995.
Kahn, Michael. Interview with author. Tape recording. Washington, D.C., 10 June 2008.
Kalcheim, Lee. Interview with author. Tape recording. New York, 3 March 1998.
Katselas, Milton. Interview with author. Tape recording. Beverly Hills, Calif., 8 August 2008.
Kindl, Charles. Interview with author. Tape recording. New York, 2 September 2008.
Knowlton, Perry. Interview with author. Tape recording. New York, 3 May 1995.
Lipsett, Richard. Telephone conversation with author. Tape recording. 27 February 1995.
Luchs, Barbara. Interview with author. Tape recording. Washington, D.C., 29 May 2008.
Luckinbill, Laurence. Interview with author. Tape recording. Washington, D.C., 3 September 2008.
———. Interview with author. Tape recording. New York, 2 February 2009.
Magyar, Linda Feinfeld. Telephone conversation with author. Tape recording. 19 May 1997.
Matalon, Vivian. Interview with author. Tape recording. Glenford, N.Y., 11 September 2008.
McCann, Elizabeth Ireland. Interview with author. Tape recording. New York, 17 December 2008.
Molinaro, Ursule. Telephone conversation with author. Tape recording. 6 March 1995.
Moss, Robert. Interview with author. Tape recording. New York, 2 September 2008.
Moss, Robert, Bruce Hoover, and Kenneth Pressman. Interview with author. Tape recording. New York, 19 November 1994.
Musante, Tony. Interview with author. Tape recording. Washington, D.C., 26 September 2008.
Nash, Rod, and Marcia Merrill Nash. Interview with author. Tape recording. White Plains, N.Y., 2 April 1995.
O'Malley, Glyn. Interview with author. Tape recording. New York, 10 July 2006.
Parone, Edward. Interview with author. Tape recording. New York, 14 March 1995.
Patrick, Robert. Interview with author. Tape recording. Los Angeles, Calif., 21 May 2008.
Peluso, Emanuel. Online discussion with author. 18 April 1995.
Perr, Harvey. Interview with author. Tape recording. New York, 8 April 1996.
Plaxen, Barry. Interview with author. Tape recording. Bloomingsburg, N.Y., 6 May 1996.
Prideaux, James. Telephone conversation with author. Tape recording. 27 March 1995.
Sabinson, Harvey. Interview with author. Tape recording. New York, 30 May 2008.
Schoenfeld, Gerald. Interview with author. Tape recording. New York, 25 September 2008.
Thacker, Russ. Interview with author. Tape recording. Wilton Manors, Fla., 14 March 1995.
Van Itallie, Jean-Claude. Interview with author. Tape recording. New York, 16 February 1995.

White, Peter. Interview with author. Tape recording. Los Angeles, Calif., 1 October 2008.
Wilson, Doric. Interview with author. Tape recording. New York, 28 August 1996.
Wilson, Lanford. Telephone conversation with author. Tape recording. 27 March 1995.
Wright, Mark. Interview with author. Tape recording. Last Frontier Theatre Conference, Valdez, Alaska, 15 June 2000.
Zindel, Paul. Interview with author. Tape recording. Montague, N.J., 21 August 1997.

Selected Archival Collections and Web Resources

Barr, Richard. Papers. Billy Rose Theatre Division, New York Public Library for the Performing Arts, New York.
———. Papers. Theatre Archives, Princeton University Library, Princeton, N.J.
———. "You Have to Hock Your House: The Story of a Producer." Unpublished memoir. Edward Albee Theatre Collection (private).
———. "You Have to Hock Your House: The Story of a Producer." Unpublished memoir. 1989. Richard Barr–Clinton Wilder Papers, Billy Rose Theatre Division, New York Public Library for the Performing Arts, New York.
Richard Barr–Clinton Wilder Papers, 1935–1982. *T-Mss 1987-008. Billy Rose Theatre Division, New York Public Library for the Performing Arts, New York.
The Broadway League. http://www.broadwayleague.com/index.php (accessed 16 March 2009).
Gnys, Chuck. Clippings folder. Billy Rose Theatre Division, New York Public Library for the Performing Arts, New York.
———. Papers. Courtesy of Curtis Brown, Ltd., New York.
IBDB (Internet Broadway Database). The Broadway League. http://www.ibdb.com/index.php (accessed 1 September 2010).
Kasdan, Michael. Collection. Lawrence and Lee Theatre Research Institute, Ohio State University, Columbus.
Lortel Archives—The Internet Off-Broadway Database. The Lortel Foundation. http://www.lortel.org/lla_archive/ (accessed 1 September 2010).
Parone, Edward. Clippings folder. Billy Rose Theatre Division, New York Public Library for the Performing Arts, New York.
The Playwrights Unit. Clippings folder. Billy Rose Theatre Division, New York Public Library for the Performing Arts, New York.
Prideaux, James. "Memoirs." Unpublished manuscript. May 1995.
Wilder, Clinton. Papers. Billy Rose Theatre Division, New York Public Library for the Performing Arts, New York.
———. Papers. Theatre Archives, Princeton University Library, Princeton, N.J.

Books

Adams, Cindy Heller. *Lee Strasberg, the Imperfect Genius of the Actors Studio*. Ann Arbor, Mich.: University of Michigan Press, 1980.
Altshuler, David, ed. *The Jews of Washington, D.C.* Jewish Historical Society of Greater Washington. Chappaqua, N.Y.: Rossel Books, 1985.
Atkinson, Brooks. *Broadway*. New York: Macmillan, 1970.
Barr, Richard. "Twilight for the Great White Way?" In *Theatre I*, edited by Rosamond Gilder, 36–37. New York, N.Y.: The Twelfth Congress of the International Theatre Institute of the United States, 1969.

Baumol, William J., and William G. Bowen. *Performing Arts—The Economic Dilemma.* New York: The Twentieth Century Fund, 1966.

Beckhard, Richard, and John Effrst. *Blueprint for Summer Theatre.* New York: John Richard Press, 1948.

Benshoff, Harry M., and Sean Griffin. *America on Film: Representing Race, Class, Gender, and Sexuality at the Movies.* New York: Wiley-Blackwell, 2004.

Bernstein, Robin, ed. *Cast Out: Queer Lives in Theatre.* Ann Arbor: University of Michigan Press, 2006.

Bishop, Andre. *Plays from Playwrights Horizons.* New York: Broadway Play Publishing, 1987.

Bordman, Gerald Martin, and Thomas S. Hischak, eds. *The Oxford Companion to American Theatre.* New York: Oxford University Press, 2004.

Bowers, Jane Palatini. "The Composition That All the World Can See: Gertrude Stein's Theatrical Landscapes." In *Land/Scape/Theater,* edited by Elinor Fuchs and Una Chaudhuri, 121–44. Ann Arbor: University of Michigan Press, 2002.

Brown, Dennis. *Shoptalk: Conversations about Theater and Film with Twelve Writers, One Producer—And Tennessee Williams' Mother.* New York: Newmarket Press, 1993.

Brown, Robert J. *Manipulating the Ether: The Power of Broadcast Radio in Thirties America.* Jefferson, N.C.: McFarland, 1998.

Callow, Simon. *The Road to Xanadu.* London: Jonathan Cape, 1995.

Carringer, Robert L. *The Making of "Citizen Kane."* Berkeley: University of California Press, 1985.

Cassidy, Marsha Francis. *What Women Watched: Daytime Television in the 1950s.* Austin: University of Texas Press, 2005.

Christiansen, Richard. *A Theater of Our Own: A History and a Memoir of 1,001 Nights in Chicago.* Evanston, Ill.: Northwestern University Press, 2004.

Crespy, David. *Off-Off-Broadway Explosion.* New York: Back Stage Books, 2003.

Dalrymple, Jean. *From the Last Row.* Clifton, N.J.: James T. White, 1975.

Davis, Deborah. *Party of the Century: The Fabulous Story of Truman Capote and His Black and White Ball.* Hoboken, N.J.: John Wiley, 2007.

De Banke, Cécile. *Shakespearean Stage Production: Then and Now.* New York: McGraw-Hill, 1953.

Diner, Hasia R. *A Time for Gathering: The Second Migration 1820–1880.* Baltimore: Johns Hopkins University Press, 1992.

Doherty, Thomas. *Projections of War: Hollywood, American Culture, and World War II.* New York: Columbia University Press, 1993.

Downer, Alan S. *The American Theatre Today.* New York: Basic, 1967.

Edelman, Rob, and Audrey E. Kupferberg. *Angela Lansbury: A Life on Stage and Screen.* Secaucus, N.J.: Citadel Press, 1999.

Esslin, Martin. *The Theatre of the Absurd.* London: Taylor and Francis, 1968.

Eyman, Scott. *Ernest Lubitsch: Laughter in Paradise.* Baltimore: Johns Hopkins University Press, 2000.

Flynn, Errol. *My Wicked Wicked Ways.* Cutchogue, N.Y.: Buccaneer, 1978.

France, Richard. *The Theatre of Orson Welles.* Lewisburg, Penn.: Bucknell University Press, 1977.

Gaver, Jack. *Curtain Calls.* New York: Dodd, Mead, 1949.

Gerould, Daniel. *Melodrama*. New York: New York Literary Forum, 1980.

Goldman, William. *The Season*. Pompton Plains, N.J.: Limelight, 1969.

Goodell, Gregory. *Independent Feature Film Production: A Complete Guide from Concept through Distribution*. New York: Macmillan, 2003.

Gordon, Joanne. *Art Isn't Easy: The Achievement of Stephen Sondheim*. Carbondale: Southern Illinois University Press, 1990.

Gottfried, Martin. *Balancing Act: The Authorized Biography of Angela Lansbury*. Boston: Little, Brown, 1999.

Greenburger, Howard. *The Off-Broadway Experience*. Englewood, N.J.: Prentice-Hall, 1971.

Gussow, Mel. *Edward Albee: A Singular Journey*. New York: Simon and Schuster, 1999.

Hadleigh, Boze. *Broadway Babylon: Glamour, Glitz, and Gossip on the Great White Way*. New York: Back Stage, 2007.

Harbin, Billy, with J. Kim Marra and Robert A. Schanke, eds. *The Gay and Lesbian Theatrical Legacy*. Ann Arbor: University of Michigan Press, 2005.

Heyer, Paul. *The Medium and the Magician: Orson Welles, the Radio Years, 1934–1952*. New York: Rowman and Littlefield, 2005.

Higham, Charles. *Orson Welles: The Rise and Fall of an American Genius*. New York: St. Martin's Press, 1985.

Hirsch, Foster. *A Method to Their Madness: The History of the Actors Studio*. New York: Da Capo Press, 2002.

Hoare, Philip. *Noël Coward: A Biography*. Chicago: University of Chicago Press, 1998.

Horn, Barbara Lee. *Edward Albee: A Research and Production Sourcebook*. Westport, Conn.: Greenwood, 2003.

Hotchner, A. E. *The Day I Fired Alan Ladd and the Other World War II*. Columbia: University of Missouri Press, 2002.

Houseman, John. *Run-Through: A Memoir*. New York: Simon and Schuster, 1972.

Ilson, Carol. *Harold Prince: From "Pajama Game" to "Phantom of the Opera."* Ann Arbor: University of Michigan Research Press, 1989.

Jordan, Richard Tyler. *But Darling, I'm Your Auntie Mame!* New York: Kensington Books, 2004.

Kael, Pauline. "Raising Kane." In *The Citizen Kane Book*. London: Martin Secker and Warburg, 1971.

Kaiser, Charles. *The Gay Metropolis: 1940–1996*. Boston: Houghton Mifflin, 1997.

Kennedy, Harold. *No Pickle No Performance: An Irreverent Theatrical Excursion from Tallulah to Travolta*. Garden City, N.Y.: Doubleday, 1978.

Kirkwood, James. *P.S. Your Cat Is Dead*. New York: Samuel French, 1976.

Kolin, Philip C., ed. *Conversations with Edward Albee*. Jackson: University Press of Mississippi, 1988.

Koppes, Clayton R., and Gregory D. Black. *Hollywood Goes to War: How Politics, Profits, and Propaganda Shaped World War II Movies*. London: Macmillan, 1987.

Lahr, John. *Notes on a Cowardly Lion: The Biography of Bert Lahr*. Berkeley: University of California Press, 2000.

Little, Stuart W. *After the FACT: Conflict and Consensus*. New York: Arno Press, 1975.

———. *Off Broadway: The Prophetic Theatre*. New York: Coward, McCann and Geoghegan, 1972.

LoMonaco, Martha Schmoyer. *Summer Stock! An American Theatrical Phenomenon*. New York: Palgrave Macmillan, 2004.

Londré, Felicia Hardison. *The History of North American Theater: The United States, Canada and Mexico, from Pre-Columbian Times to the Present.* New York: Continuum, 2000.

Lubertozzi, Alex, with Brian Holmsten and John Callaway. *The War of the Worlds: Mars' Invasion of Earth, Inciting Panic and Inspiring Terror from H. G. Wells to Orson Welles and Beyond.* Naperville, Ill.: Sourcebooks, 2003.

Madsen, Axel. *The Sewing Circle: Sappho's Leading Ladies.* Secaucus, N.J.: Carol, 1995.

Mandelbaum, Ken. *Not Since "Carrie": Forty Years of Broadway Musical Flops.* New York: St. Martin's Press, 1991.

Mangan, Richard, ed. *Sir John Gielgud: A Life in Letters.* New York: Arcade, 2004.

Mankiewicz, Herman J., and Orson Welles, "The Shooting Script." In *The Citizen Kane Book.* London: Martin Secker and Warburg, 1971.

McBride, Joseph. *Whatever Happened to Orson Welles?* Louisville: University Press of Kentucky, 2006.

Mellow, James R. *Charmed Circle: Gertrude Stein and Company.* New York: Macmillan, 2003.

Moore, Thomas Gale. *The Economics of the American Theater.* Durham, N.C.: Duke University Press, 1968.

Nathan, George Jean. *The Theatre Book of the Year.* New York: Alfred A. Knopf, 1948.

Nordlinger, Bernard I. "A History of the Washington Hebrew Congregation." In *The Jews of Washington, D.C.*, edited by David Altshuler, 11–65. Jewish Historical Society of Greater Washington. Chappaqua, N.Y.: Rossel Books, 1985.

O'Connor, Carroll. *I Think I'm Outta Here.* New York: Simon and Schuster, 1999.

Parish, James Robert, and Lennard DeCarl. *Hollywood Players: The Forties.* New Rochelle, N.Y.: Arlington House, 1976.

Parone, Edward, ed. *New Theatre in America.* New York: Dell, 1965.

Reagan, Ronald. *An American Life.* New York: Simon and Schuster, 1990.

Schneider, Alan. *Entrances: An American Director's Journey.* New York: Viking, 1986.

Secrest, Meryle. *Stephen Sondheim: A Life.* New York: Alfred A. Knopf, 1998.

Sheratsky, Rodney E. "The Off-Broadway Theatre, 1945–1962." PhD diss., New York University, 1966.

Siegel, Marcia B. *Howling near Heaven: Twyla Tharp and the Reinvention of Modern Dance.* New York: Macmillan, 2006.

Spoto, Donald. *The Kindness of Strangers: The Life of Tennessee Williams.* Jackson, Tenn.: Da Capo Press, 1997.

Sprigge, Elizabeth. *Gertrude Stein: Her Life and Work.* New York: Harper and Brothers, 1957.

Staggs, Sam. *Close-Up on Sunset Boulevard: Billy Wilder, Norma Desmond, and the Dark Hollywood Dream.* New York: Macmillan, 2003.

Stasio, Marilyn. *Broadway's Beautiful Losers.* New York: Delacorte Press, 1972.

Stein, Gertrude. *A Stein Reader.* Edited by Ulla E. Dydo. Evanston, Ill.: Northwestern University Press, 1993.

Taubman, Howard. *The Making of the American Theatre.* New York: Coward-McCann, 1967.

Taylor, Paul. *Private Domain.* New York: Alfred E. Knopf, 1987.

Umstattd, J. G. *B.A.U. in Action: Teaching and Learning at Biarritz American University.* Austin: University of Texas Press, 1947.

Vaughn, Stephen. *Ronald Reagan in Hollywood: Movies and Politics.* Cambridge: Cambridge University Press, 1994.

Vena, Gary, and Andrea Nouryeh, eds. *Drama and Performance, an Anthology.* New York: HarperCollins, 1996.

Waldau, Roy S. *Vintage Years of the Theatre Guild: 1928–1939.* Cleveland: The Press of Case Western Reserve University, 1972.

Warren, Neilla, ed. *The Letters of Ruth Draper, 1920–1956.* New York: Charles Scribner's Sons, 1979.

Welles, Orson. *Orson Welles on Shakespeare: The W.P.A. and Mercury Theatre Playscripts.* New York: Routledge, 2001.

Welles, Orson, and Peter Bogdanovich. *This Is Orson Welles.* Edited by Jonathan Rosenbaum. New York: HarperCollins, 1992.

Woll, Allen. *Dictionary of the Black Theatre: Broadway, Off-Broadway, and Selected Harlem Theatre.* Westport, Conn.: Greenwood Press, 1983.

Young, William C. *Famous American Playhouses, 1900–1971.* Vol. 2 of *Documents of American Theater History.* Chicago: American Library Association, 1973.

Zadan, Craig. *Sondheim & Co.* New York: Harper and Row, 1986.

INDEX

Photographs are indicated with an italicized *g* followed by a number. The gallery of photographs follows page 138.

David A. Crespy is a professor of playwriting, acting, and dramatic literature at the University of Missouri, where he is the founder and co-director of its Writing for Performance program. He is the author of *Off-Off-Broadway Explosion*, and his plays and essays may be found in *Playwriting Master Class*, *Angels in the American Theatre*, and *The Influence of Tennessee Williams.*

Theater in the Americas

The goal of the series is to publish a wide range of scholarship on theater and performance, defining theater in its broadest terms and including subjects that encompass all of the Americas.

The series focuses on the performance and production of theater and theater artists and practitioners but welcomes studies of dramatic literature as well. Meant to be inclusive, the series invites studies of traditional, experimental, and ethnic forms of theater; celebrations, festivals, and rituals that perform culture; and acts of civil disobedience that are performative in nature. We publish studies of theater and performance activities of all cultural groups within the Americas, including biographies of individuals, histories of theater companies, studies of cultural traditions, and collections of plays.

Other Books in the Theater in the Americas Series

Shadowed Cocktails: The Plays of Philip Barry from "Paris Bound" to "The Philadelphia Story"
Donald R. Anderson

A Gambler's Instinct: The Story of Broadway Producer Cheryl Crawford
Milly S. Barranger

Unfriendly Witnesses: Gender, Theater, and Film in the McCarthy Era
Milly S. Barranger

The Theatre of Sabina Berman: "The Agony of Ecstasy" and Other Plays
Translated by Adam Versényi
With an Essay by Jacqueline E. Bixler

Staging Social Justice: Collaborating to Create Activist Theatre
Edited by Norma Bowles and Daniel-Raymond Nadon

Messiah of the New Technique: John Howard Lawson, Communism, and American Theatre, 1923–1937
Jonathan L. Chambers

Composing Ourselves: The Little Theatre Movement and the American Audience
Dorothy Chansky

Ghost Light: An Introductory Handbook for Dramaturgy
Michael Mark Chemers

The Hanlon Brothers: From Daredevil Acrobatics to Spectacle Pantomime, 1833–1931
Mark Cosdon

Women in Turmoil: Six Plays by Mercedes de Acosta
Edited and with an Introduction by Robert A. Schanke

Rediscovering Mordecai Gorelik: Scene Design and the American Theatre
Anne Fletcher

A Spectacle of Suffering: Clara Morris on the American Stage
Barbara Wallace Grossman

American Political Plays after 9/11
Edited by Allan Havis

Performing Loss: Rebuilding Community through Theater and Writing
Jodi Kanter

Unfinished Show Business: Broadway Musicals as Works-in-Process
Bruce Kirle

Staging America: Cornerstone and Community-Based Theater
Sonja Kuftinec

Words at Play: Creative Writing and Dramaturgy
Felicia Hardison Londré

Entertaining the Nation: American Drama in the Eighteenth and Nineteenth Centuries
Tice L. Miller

Documentary Trial Plays in Contemporary American Theater
Jacqueline O'Connor

Stage, Page, Scandals, and Vandals: William E. Burton and Nineteenth-Century American Theatre
David L. Rinear

Contemporary Latina/o Theater: Wrighting Ethnicity
Jon D. Rossini

Angels in the American Theater: Patrons, Patronage, and Philanthropy
Edited and with an Introduction by Robert A. Schanke

"That Furious Lesbian": The Story of Mercedes de Acosta
Robert A. Schanke

Caffe Cino: The Birthplace of Off-Off-Broadway
Wendell C. Stone

Teaching Performance Studies
Edited by Nathan Stucky and Cynthia Wimmer
With a Foreword by Richard Schechner

Broadway's Bravest Woman: Selected Writings of Sophie Treadwell
Edited and with Introductions by Jerry Dickey and Miriam López-Rodríguez

The Humana Festival: The History of New Plays at Actors Theatre of Louisville
Jeffrey Ullom

Our Land Is Made of Courage and Glory: Nationalist Performance of Nicaragua and Guatemala
E. J. Westlake